THEORY AND PRACTICE

NOMOS
XXXVII

NOMOS

Harvard University Press
I   *Authority* 1958, reissued in 1982 by Greenwood
         Press

The Liberal Arts Press
II   *Community* 1959
III   *Responsibility* 1960

Atherton Press
IV   *Liberty* 1962
V   *The Public Interest* 1962
VI   *Justice* 1963, reissued in 1974
VII   *Rational Decision* 1964
VIII   *Revolution* 1966
IX   *Equality* 1967
X   *Representation* 1968
XI   *Voluntary Associations* 1969
XII   *Political and Legal Obligation* 1970
XIII   *Privacy* 1971

Aldine-Atherton Press
XIV   *Coercion* 1972

Lieber-Atherton Press
XV   *The Limits of Law* 1974
XVI   *Participation in Politics* 1975

New York University Press
XVII   *Human Nature in Politics* 1977
XVIII   *Due Process* 1977
XIX   *Anarchism* 1978
XX   *Constitutionalism* 197
XXI   *Compromise in Ethics, Law, and Politics* 1979
XII   *Property* 1980

NOMOS XXXVII

Yearbook of The American Society for Political and Legal Philosophy

THEORY AND PRACTICE

Edited by

Ian Shapiro, *Yale University*

and

Judith Wagner DeCew, *Clark University*

NEW YORK UNIVERSITY PRESS New York and London

NEW YORK UNIVERSITY PRESS
New York and London

Theory and Practice: NOMOS XXXVII
edited by Ian Shapiro & Judith Wagner DeCew
Copyright © 1995 by New York University
Manufactured in the United States of America

Library of Congress Cataloging-in-Publication Data
Theory and practice / edited by Ian Shapiro and Judith Wagner DeCew.
     p. cm.—(Nomos ; 37)
    Papers and commentaries read at the Annual Meeting of the American
Society for Political and Legal Philosophy, held in conjunction with
the Eastern Division of the American Philosophical Association in
Washington, D.C., in Dec. 1992.
    Includes bibliographical references and index.
    ISBN 0-8147-8003-2 (alk. paper)
    1. Theory (Philosophy)—Congresses.   2. Practice (Philosophy)—
Congresses. 3. Law—Philosophy—Congresses. I. Shapiro, Ian.
II. DeCew, Judith Wagner.   III. American Society for Political and
Legal Philosophy. Meeting (1992 : Washington, D.C.)   IV. American
Philosophical Association. Eastern Division. V. Series.
B842.T54   1995   94-23936
                CIP

10   9   8   7   6   5   4   3   2   1

CONTENTS

PART III: ARGUMENTS FOR THE PRIORITY OF PRACTICE

PART IV: THEORY AND PRACTICE IN THE LAW

PART V: THE PUBLIC IMPLICATIONS OF THEORY

PART VI: PRACTITIONERS AS THEORISTS

Contents

PREFACE

This thirty-seventh volume of NOMOS grew out of papers and commentaries read at the Annual Meeting of the American Society for Political and Legal Philosophy, held in conjunction with the Eastern Division of the American Philosophical Association in Washington, D.C., in December 1992. The subject on which we focused our attention, "Theory and Practice," was selected by a vote of the society's members. Judith Wagner DeCew did a superb job as program chair, and I was delighted that she agreed to join me in editing the present volume. As the results in the pages that follow demonstrate, she performed sterling service in that additional role.

Once again our contributors met a demanding production schedule with a maximum of good humor and a minimum of complaint; I would like to thank them all. The production team at New York University Press led by Niko Pfund and Despina Papazoglou Gimbel performed admirably once again, as did our managing editor Kathryn McDermott. The speed of publication and quality of the volume depended critically on these hard-working individuals.

I am pleased to announce that the NOMOS volumes will be appearing in paperback about eighteen months after the cloth edition. This should make it possible for them to reach an audience wider than the Society's membership more easily, and for them to be used in courses. The paperback edition of NOMOS XXIV in *Virtue* was published in 1993, and that of NOMOS XXXV, on *Democratic Community,* in 1994. Authors and readers might also be interested to know that the NOMOS volumes have begun to be indexed in appropriate places in philosophy and the social sciences.

I.S.

CONTRIBUTORS

SUSAN J. BRISON
Philosophy, Dartmouth College

STEPHEN L. CARTER
Law, Yale University

JEAN BETHKE ELSHTAIN
Social and Political Ethics, University of Chicago

KENT GREENAWALT
Law, Columbia University

FRANCES M. KAMM
Philosophy, New York University

JOHN KANE
Politics and Public Policy, Griffith University, Australia

FRANK I. MICHELMAN
Law, Harvard University

JEFFRIE G. MURPHY
Philosophy and Law, Arizona State University

MARTHA C. NUSSBAUM
Philosophy, Brown University

GERALD J. POSTEMA
Philosophy, University of North Carolina, Chapel Hill

HENRY SHUE
Ethics and Public Life, Cornell University

STEVEN B. SMITH
Political Science, Yale University

CASS R. SUNSTEIN
Law and Political Science, University of Chicago

NORMA THOMPSON
Political Science, Yale University

JEREMY WALDRON
Political Theory and Law, University of California, Berkeley

DAVID B. WONG
Philosophy, Brandeis University

INTRODUCTION

JUDITH WAGNER DECEW
AND IAN SHAPIRO

Since time immemorial, students of philosophy, politics, and law have disagreed over the relations between theoretical principles and everyday practice. Some have stressed the value of theory, arguing that it should be pursued for its own merits and that it is difficult, impossible, or misleading to apply its ideals to the real and imperfect world. Others have championed the importance of focus on practical problems in daily life and have urged that theory is not worthwhile unless it sheds light on how to resolve actual conflicts or real-world problems.

Aristotle and Kant made contributions to the discussion that are often taken to be foundational. Whereas Aristotle was interested in practical consequences and the workings of political societies as well as theoretical insights, he elaborated a distinction between *theoria* and *praxis* in a now-famous discussion in *The Politics*. Some commentators have viewed him as defending the priority of theory over practice, but there remains considerable disagreement among interpreters on Aristotle's views on theory and practice. This disagreement is probably due at least in part, as Norma Thompson points out in chapter 1 of the present volume, to several mixed signals Aristotle revealed in his writings. Kant was perhaps clearer than Aristotle in his insistence on the existence of a link between theory and practice. He viewed as incoherent the claim that there must be a

1

definitive distinction or gap between theory and practice. He also sought to vindicate his theory against the charge that it was theoretically interesting but practically useless. He thus hoped to show that his theory could help in the design and critique of just social institutions.

Since Kant wrote, discussions of the relations between theory and practice have been more wide ranging and sometimes obtuse. Often talk of the theory/practice problem is abstract, leaving unclear the exact nature of the debate associated with those notions. How much should we expect of a theory? Must it be comprehensive, and if so in what sense? How do we assess theories? Is it necessary or sufficient to apply theories to practical cases? What if such application cannot be accomplished? What is encompassed by the rather vague term "practice"? Does practice refer to activity within social and political institutions, or any decision making in the real world? Both theoreticians and practitioners have grappled with such questions, and given the many different understandings of the relationship between theory and practice, it is sometimes difficult to compare alternative views.

Despite differences in interpretation between Aristotle and Kant, both are usually taken to be part of a larger group in the history of moral philosophy who defend what is viewed as the traditional approach to the role of ethical theory. On this view, the major goal of a moral theory is to resolve conflicts arising in moral decision making to give clear guidance on how to act. The task of theorists is to systematize moral thought and ultimately provide a principle or set of principles for overcoming or settling what at first appear to be irresolvable moral dilemmas. Teleological theories such as egoism and Mill's and Moore's utilitarianism, as well as deontological views such as Ross's intuitionism and Kant's categorical imperative, all appear to assume this common aim. More recently Kurt Baier has endorsed a similar position, saying, "when there are conflicts of interest, we always look for a 'higher' point of view, one from which such conflicts can be settled. . . . By 'the moral point of view' we *mean* a point of view which furnishes a court of arbitration for conflicts of interest."[1] Advocates of this position have been referred to as systematizers or reductionists. They see theory as fundamental, and useful for providing higher-level resolutions in actual moral decision making.

Over the last twenty years a number of philosophers, including Ruth Barcan Marcus, Bas van Fraassen, Bernard Williams, Thomas Nagel, and Stuart Hampshire, have challenged this standard view about the role of moral theory. These pluralists argue that the inevitability of moral conflicts is moral datum that any theory must accommodate and that it is misleading to believe appeals to universal values or rational principles can always dictate a best moral choice or solution. Traditional abstract and ideal theory is incompatible with the conflicts, disagreements, and divisions that exist in practice. As Hampshire says, "Whether it is Aristotelian, Kantian, Humean, or utilitarian, moral philosophy can do harm when it implies that there ought to be, and that there can be, fundamental agreement on, or even convergence in, moral ideals—the harm is that the reality of conflict, both within individuals and within societies, is disguised by the myth of humanity as a consistent moral unit across time and space. There is a false blandness in the myth, an aversion from reality."[2] For pluralist philosophers, moral theory cannot be expected to provide comprehensive explanations or evaluations. It often cannot generate answers to practical problems in real life, and thus cannot be tested through an evaluation of its implications for actual cases. We would do best either to pursue practical reasoning about actual moral choices independently of theory or to modify ethical theories to account for the reality of the pervasiveness of conflict. Both approaches endorse the priority of practice. A more radical alternative is to reject the need for theory at all. As Jean Bethke Elshtain notes in the last chapter of this volume, if one endorses the elimination of theory suggested by Richard Rorty and others, then the relation between theory and practice ceases to be an issue.

Political theorists have engaged in a similar struggle with respect to understanding the relations between theory and practice. Plato saw theory in all its pristine purity as essential to the discovery of the good life and the nature of the best political order. For Marx, by contrast, there was an intimate link between theory and practice, and in many historical circumstances the imperatives of practice actually determine what can appear theoretically credible. John Rawls tries to divorce theory from practice in a different way. He constructs a conception of justice that is "political, not metaphysical." It "takes deep and unresolvable differences on matters of fundamental significance [religious, philosophical, and moral notions and doctrines] as a permanent condition of human life."[3] For Rawls, like the pluralists in moral philosophy, the political theorist's project of designing just institutions should not rely, any more than necessary, on contestable positions in the great philosophical debates about knowledge, existence, and value.

Arguments about theory and practice in law are perhaps most pronounced in discussions of the nature of law and judicial decision making, particularly in the contrast between legal positivism and natural law theory. For legal positivists such as Bentham, Austin, and H. L. A. Hart, law is basically a system of commands or rules, norms constructed by humans and giving directions concerning how one ought to act. Although such features as formalism and the command theory are often associated with positivism, Hart argued that the separation of law and morals, distinguishing law as it is from law as it ought to be, is the crucial and defining thesis of positivism. He illustrated the distinction with two points also stressed by both Bentham and Austin: (1) "It could not follow from the mere fact that a rule violated standards of morality that it was not a rule of law" and (2) "It could not follow from the mere fact that a rule was morally desirable that it was a rule of law."[4] On this view, actual law may reflect theories of what is right and just only in limited ways. One virtue of this theory of law is that positive law, or law existing by position, is determined by its source. Hence there is a clear way of specifying which norms count as part of law. Hart argued in addition that a major reason for the separation of law and morals is that it allows for an independent set of principles for judging laws as just or unjust.

According to the legal positivists, a judge's task is to determine which rules or legislative enactments are relevant and then apply them to the case at hand. Most cases, on Hart's view, will be determined clearly by statutes and precedents. Others are more difficult cases for which judges must use discretion in interpreting vague words in the legal rules. Although law does not dictate a decision in such cases, a decision is still constrained to some degree. Consequently the practice of applying legal norms to generate actual decisions is largely independent of theoretical assessments about which system of laws would be ideal or which legal outcome would be most fair.

In contrast, natural law theorists such as Aquinas and Blackstone have argued that principles of justice and rightness shape the written law. What is properly viewed as human law is in accordance with the law of nature, dictated by God, and universal, "binding over all the globe, in all countries, and at all times."[5] Human law thus reflects the ideal, and what counts as genuine law is determined by the content, not the source of the law. On Dworkin's modern naturalism as well, morals infuse the law. Dworkin rejects the positivist separation of law and morals, maintaining that other standards, principles, and policies function as law and are part of law and binding on judges as much as rules are.[6] Nevertheless, he acknowledges that there is no master rule, principle, or test for determining the validity of law.

For natural law theorists, a judge must ascertain what the law is and then apply it to the facts of the case. On Dworkin's view, the judge must discover the rights of the parties through an understanding not only of the relevant rules but also of the moral principles embedded in our institutional history that are binding as standards of morality. Theory and practice are deeply interconnected on this approach, for the practice of law requires theorizing, in the sense of articulating and defending the fundamental moral principles that dictate a "right" answer.

Those endorsing the economic analysis of law and those part of the Critical Legal Studies (CLS) movement defend theories of law and judicial decision making radically different from each other and from Dworkin's view, yet both acknowledge a creative role for the practice of judging. On the economic theory, defended by Richard Posner, Richard Epstein, and others, judges do and should base their decisions on what factors will maximize the production of wealth in society. It is thus essential to the enterprise of judging that judges are free to theorize on the consequences of their decisions, and to decide cases in accordance with the dictates of efficiency rather than a set of pre-existing rules or claims. For such CLS scholars as Duncan Kennedy and Mark Tushnet, judicial decisions are never neutral; they implicitly and explicitly endorse social policy arguments and claims. The political content of law and legal decisions may reflect the judge's own predispositions or more often reflects deep (and perhaps unwarranted) assumptions of political theory. Both these accounts, like natural law theory, contrast with positivism insofar as their proponents hold that the practice of judicial decision making is permeated with theoretical reasoning on economics, politics, and morality.

In NOMOS XXXVII, we have gathered sixteen original papers that contribute to this debate about the meaning of the theory/practice problem and the relations between theory and practice in philosophy, political theory, and law. Some of our contributors discuss the history of the theory/practice dichotomy. Others draw out implications of defending either the primacy of pure theory or the importance of practice. Some authors address the impact of practical concerns on moral theory, including psychological possibilities and feminist and critical race perspectives. Others discuss the public dimensions of theorizing and theoretical concerns that arise in approaching practical problems such as global warming. There is considerable focus on the role of theory in the practice of judicial decision making as well as on the theoretical commitments of various political practitioners, both past and present.

We begin in part I with the roots of the debate as articulated by Aristotle and Kant. Norma Thompson focuses on Aristotle's commentary on pre-Socratic philosophers, notably Herodotus. According to Thompson, the dual concepts of theory and practice, which have provided a framework for political thought since ancient times, was in significant measure shaped by Aristotle's largely unrecognized intellectual assault on the "methodology" of Herodotus. The ferocity of this rejection of a pre-Socratic way of thought led Aristotle's successors in political philosophy to construct highly articulated, demarcated, and "objective" structures, categories, and disciplines. Over the centuries, many of the advantages of more comprehensive and less bounded intellectual approaches have been dismissed or ignored. Thompson's examination of the Aristotle-Herodotus "dispute" helps clear up an age-old mystery about the odd reputation of Herodotus and offers new prospects for expanding conventional views of "theory and practice," whether interpreted as in a state of tension or in tandem.

Chapter 2, by Jeffrie G. Murphy, is a commentary on Kant's 1793 essay, "On the Proverb: That May Be True in Theory but Is of No Practical Use." That essay is Kant's attempt to defend his own moral and political theory against the charge that it is simply an idle academic exercise that cannot be brought to bear upon the real world in any useful way. Kant is concerned, in particular, to answer two charges—the charges (leveled by Christian Garve, Moses Mendelssohn, and defenders of Thomas Hobbes) that his theory is (1) motivationally unrealistic, involving an account of moral motivation that is at odds both with scientific psychology and with all plausible philosophical accounts of rational deliberation and (2) not usable in either the design or the critique of actual social institutions. Murphy shows that Kant's essay is interesting because of his argument that a genuine theory/practice gap is impossible in moral and political philosophy, his attempts to refute empiricist theories of motivation and rational deliberation, his defense of the principles of a liberal social and political order, and his attempt to come to terms (in the essay's final section) with the challenge that *evil* poses to the optimistic nature of liberal political thought.

Part II offers contemporary discussions focusing on why pure theory may be of value in its own right. In chapter 3, Frances M. Kamm relates high theory (normative ethical theory) to low theory (applied ethics), then connects both theories to applying applied ethics (the practical). She begins by characterizing different ways of doing high theory, defending the importance of high theory, and dealing with some objections (based on saliency and evolutionary theory) to the significance of high theory. She further describes some problems that arise in applying applied ethics. In the second section of the article, Kamm considers seven possible interpretations of the problem of the relation between theory and practice, including the relation of high theory to low theory, and whether it is reasonable to expect either high theory or its implications to guide actual conduct. She then applies her analysis to the issues of abortion and euthanasia. Kamm concludes by arguing for the importance of doing high and low theory even if there are severe problems for their application in practice.

Chapter 4, by David Wong, is somewhat less optimistic about the value of pure theory, concluding that at best theory can clarify the nature of value conflicts and point to possibilities of resolution. Wong focuses on the debate over the role of the "personal" point of view in morality and the way issues of psychological realism bear on that debate. Much contemporary moral theory presupposes the "impersonal" point of view, which attaches equal weight to the interests of all persons. From that perspective, one's own interests count no more than those of others in decision making. However, some theorists have objected that it is psychologically unrealistic to require human beings to give no disproportionate weight to their own interests and personal relations to particular others. Wong considers the meaning of "realistic possibility" in theory and argues that the notion is more complex than has been supposed. To illustrate this point, he discusses in detail Thomas Nagel's recent argument that we have no realistic conception of how we could require true equality in distributive justice. According to Wong, Nagel's argument neglects crucial complexities of the notion of realistic possibility and does not take into account cross-cultural and historical evidence showing that people have accepted different norms of equality and that they have mediated their commitments to impersonal values such as equality through personal values such as concern for other members of one's community. In the end, Wong argues, we have some notion of how we could make a society truly equal, but that possibility is neither realistic nor unrealistic. In light of this conclusion, moral theory should not compromise on its requirement to promote equality, but it should take into account the most realistic notions of the way that human beings could fulfill that requirement.

In chapter 5, Jeremy Waldron offers a spirited defense of pure theory and the dangers of applying great theoretical works in practice. According to Waldron, students of political philosophy often interpret the classic works of the subject by asking what principles, policies, and practices particular writers favor. Concerning *The Republic,* for example, they might say, "Plato would allow women as guardians but he would not allow them to combine a political career with raising a family." Waldron argues that such an approach to political philosophy is misguided. Certainly it is misguided as a strategy for reading *The Republic:* it is wrong to treat that work as a prescriptive blueprint. In general, what we should seek to glean from classic works are deep insights into the nature of politics and society and the concepts that we use to think about them. We should not treat political philosophers as would-be lawgivers, and we should be alert to the ironical significance of the figure of "the founder" or "the law-giver" when it appears in a philosophical work. Waldron concludes by applying this point to modern political philosophy as well. Despite the success of the "philosophy and public affairs" movement, he believes we should be wary of substituting our own prescriptive moralizing about issues of political importance for the harder and less glamorous tasks of understanding that demand a political philosopher's attention.

Part III changes course to focus on arguments for the priority of practice. In response to Jeremy Waldron's chapter, Martha C. Nussbaum argues in chapter 6 that the Greek and Roman thinkers at the source of the Western philosophical tradition held that there was an urgent and intimate connection between philosophical thought and political and social practice. They understood that connection in many different ways, and the sort of philosophizing pertinent to it. But Plato, Aristotle, and the Epicureans and Stoics would have concurred, in one way or another, with Aristotle's view that in at least some areas of philosophy "the end is not contemplation but action." Nussbaum then argues that they were right: there is an urgent role for good philosophy to play in political life and it does not cease being good philosophy, but actually fulfills its philosophical purpose, when it undertakes this role.

Susan J. Brison continues the assault on pure theory in chapter 7 by defending the theoretical importance of practice. Brison applies a number of insights from feminist theory and critical race theory to help understand the relations between theory and practice. On the basis of these insights, she criticizes Waldron's claim that theory and practice should not be too closely connected in our reading, teaching, and writing. She also argues, contra Waldron, that theorists *should* be concerned with the practical consequences of their theorizing. Brison goes on to discuss the ways in which political theory divorced from practice fails to capture the full range of perspectives needed to yield a theory that is universally applicable. She argues that the engagement with others required by political practice enhances our understanding of the perspectives and concerns of others. Brison calls for an explicit acknowledgment of the positions from which we—and those different from ourselves—theorize. Such acknowledgment can serve as an antidote to the tendency to assume that we are theorizing from a neutral perspective. Brison criticizes Waldron's prescriptions for reading and teaching the canon, and she argues in conclusion that his distinction between what is a proper subject for philosophical inquiry and what is a public policy issue is based on unwarranted assumptions. That Waldron's distinction is untenable becomes apparent, for Brison, once we view historical and contemporary debates in political philosophy from the perspectives of those who have been excluded from them.

Delving even more deeply into practice in chapter 8, Henry Shue utilizes global warming as a problem case with which he can illustrate his theses that the ideal and non-ideal must be intertwined, and that theoretical questions of fairness cannot be divorced from practical considerations and choices. Shue shows that in order to determine what a fair allocation between rich countries and poor countries of emissions of greenhouse gases would be, one must include messy empirical aspects of the role these emissions have been assigned by the political and technological decisions made in the rich countries. He argues, furthermore, that if total global emissions must be reduced in order to slow global warming, the initial reductions in emissions ought to be made, other things equal, by those whose current emissions exceed their fair share of the global total. Empirical judgments about what is in fact avoidable are integral to the argument for a relevant standard of fairness, and judgments about what is politically and ideologically palatable are crucial to the final choice of what specifically to do. Shue defends the view that the relevant standard of fairness—an equal minimum for all—is strongly supported by the fact that the alternative would allow those whose continuing decisions make the use of carbon-emitting fossil fuels an economic necessity, when alternatives could be made feasible, to consume so much of that necessity themselves that powerless others lack the minimum. He concludes that the final choice of what to do—develop alternative sources of energy—is deeply influenced by the fact that voluntary limits on economic growth, which fairness otherwise recommends, seem incompatible with misguided but still pervasive modern ideology.

Part IV is concerned with the respective roles of theory and practice in the law. In chapter 9, Cass R. Sunstein begins by arguing that law and the practice of judicial decision making are inevitably philosophical, in the sense that large-scale theorizing, such as disagreements about the right and the good, typically underlie legal disputes. Even mundane legal claims are often based on contestable philosophical positions. On the other hand, there are serious problems in efforts to transplant philosophical claims to legal contexts, which frequently involve a second-best world. Above all, lawyers might seek to bracket philosophical claims in order to achieve an overlapping consensus on issues for whose resolution philosophical or highly theoretical positions are simply too sectarian. In sum, legal practice is unavoidably theory-laden. But there are advantages to the divorce of legal practice from legal theory, most notably that it enables people to converge on particular outcomes even when they disagree sharply on first principles.

In chapter 10, Stephen L. Carter extends Murphy's discussion of Kant's essay to apply to legal protection for religious resistance. Carter confronts the problem of how a Kantian sovereign, mindful of Kant's disdain for the theory/practice distinction raised by his critics, should respond when a religious community resists its authority. Religious resistance occurs when a community believes that it is required by its faith tradition to follow the commands of a higher sovereign than the secular, Kantian one. Carter outlines an escape from the tyranny that

Kant's essay on theory and practice seems to indicate as a response to religious resistance, then translates this method into constitutional law. If a citizen objects to a command of the sovereign on the ground that with respect to that subject the citizen recognizes a different sovereign, tyranny is avoided only if the sovereign is prepared, if possible, to accommodate that objection.

Part IV concludes with Frank I. Michelman's discussion of the implications of Rawls's theory of justice as fairness for assessing the relation between political ideals and judicial practice. Normative political theories offer accounts of political practices as they ought to be, in their ideal forms. Such theories, Michelman points out, may be employed in critical assessment and in proposed reform of their supposedly correspondent empirical practices. Theories put to such prescriptive uses, he argues, require their own validation. To what extent, Michelman then asks, can we validate a normative theory by showing it to have been drawn—abstracted—from the very practice for which it is meant to prescribe? Insofar as the theory's validation is made to depend on its correspondence with practice, he argues, any significant deviation of the practice from the theory attacks the theory's credentials as a valid theory of *that* practice. Michelman thus discerns the existence of a puzzle about how theory can exert any prescriptive force while simultaneously basing its claim to accreditation on correspondence with practice. For it seems that one cannot criticize a practice without appeal to some regulative notion drawn from beyond the practice and thus not susceptible of correspondence-based accreditation. In trying to resolve this puzzle, we might wonder whether it helps to notice the role *within* empirical practices of ideals that practitioners themselves understand as counterfactual and utopian. Michelman pursues that question, using as a case in point the debatable implications for judicial review of Rawls's *Political Liberalism*.

In part V, contributors assess some provocative public implications of theory. In chapter 12, Gerald J. Postema defends the view that actual public deliberation and discourse can be implemented as a practical exercise to defend the legitimacy (though not necessarily the truth or justice) of political institutions and authority. He first defines and defends an ideal of public justification for politics. On Postema's view, public justification not only concerns matters of public interest but also necessarily involves articulation, deliberation, and argument in a concrete public forum for robustly public reasons. The activity of public justification is governed by the regulative ideal of consensus, Postema argues, which imposes a discipline on all participants in the practice. This discipline defines the necessary structure of justification in public. The discipline is common to moral and political reasoning, but because of the special features of political life, in political practice it takes the specific institutional form of deliberative democracy. Finally, Postema shows that this institutionalized form of public practical reasoning is characterized by a commitment to equality of participation through publicly accountable representatives and radical openness of public deliberation to all issues, opinions, and arguments, subject only to the discipline of public justification.

In chapter 13, Kent Greenawalt addresses a problem of scholarly sincerity, namely, the responsibilities of theorists who believe that stating factual or normative "truths," as they understand them, will probably have harmful effects. For example, if a researcher finds evidence that people of different races differ, on the average, in their intelligence, should she report the results, knowing the information may be used in unjust ways, or remain silent? He reaches the conclusion that people who believe normative judgments have some kind of objective status may in general be more likely than those who do not hold that belief to opt for sincerity at the risk of harmful effects. More generally, whether or not one favors pure theory depends on whether one believes in objective truths.

The contributors to part VI demonstrate the wide variety of approaches that political practitioners take to theoretical claims. John Kane argues in chapter 14 that Marx wished to instill in his fellow revolutionaries a "realistic outlook" that would displace the vain moralizing of bourgeois idealists and "utopian socialists." At the center of this outlook lay the doctrine of the unity of theory and practice. At one level, the realistic outlook was quasi-instrumentalist, with materialist theory advising when conditions were ripe for revolutionary action by a politically organizing proletariat and its "theoreticians," the Communists. However, theory and theorized were intimately connected, for the theory was itself a product of the very processes of development it described and, in describing, helped to further. In a correct understanding of social relations, Kane continues, one discovered the ethical facts of coercion and necessity concealed beneath the ideological appearances of bourgeois freedom and moral rightness, and this discovery was itself a moment of revolutionary *praxis*, a liberating opening of the eyes to one's degraded status in society. Subjective liberation fed naturally into political practice aimed at objective emancipation from class oppression, especially since the theory that liberated also assured the ripeness of the conditions for revolutionary transformation. Morality, itself wholly ideological, could thus arguably be dispensed with as a proletarian instrument. Kane concludes that this implies that Marx was an ethical objectivist but an anti-moralist, a position he never clearly elaborated, with the consequence that his theory could readily be interpreted in crudely instrumentalist terms and his liberationist ethic ignored or perverted with tragic results.

Steven B. Smith turns, in chapter 15, to another philosopher often aligned with tragic consequences in the real world. He argues that Heidegger's Nazi beliefs cannot be explained away as separate from his philosophy, or as beliefs he later abandoned and criticized, but are intrinsically connected to his philosophy. Noting that the relation between Heidegger's philosophical theory and his political practice has recently become a subject of intense controversy, Smith explores his novel thesis that Heidegger's philosophy is intrinsically connected to his support of National Socialism. Smith argues that the basic concepts of Heidegger's Nazism were worked out in his early *Being and Time* (1927) and with some changes of emphasis remained a constant throughout his later "post-metaphysical" writings. He concludes that it was Heidegger's exclusive concern with the question of Being that led to his own peculiar kind of "forgetfulness," the forgetfulness of the primacy of politics.

A contemporary politician and performer of political thought, Vaclav Havel, is the subject of Jean Bethke Elshtain's concluding contribution to the volume. For some political theorists, Elshtain urges, theory names an aspiration yet unattained; hence, practice speaks to a frustrating, even unacceptable way of acting in a world that falls short of what theory makes abstractly possible. Even anti-foundationalists, who eschew totalizing theories, often fall into their own version of a theory/practice divide indebted to utopian or architectonic political schema. Elshtain draws upon Vaclav Havel as an exemplar of a way of *enacting politics* that refuses the pall of inaction, even in dire and difficult political situations, in part by avoiding the seductions of theoretical overreach. He does not offer a *solution* to what is called the "theory/practice problem"; rather, by refusing to engage *that* problem he suggests an alternative way of thinking and acting. Thus, we see how practitioners mirror the range of views on the value and relation of theory and practice that continue to puzzle theorists.[7]

NOTES

1. Kurt Baier, *The Moral Point of View* (New York: Random House, 1965), 96.

2. Stuart Hampshire, *Morality and Conflict* (Cambridge: Harvard University Press, 1983), 155.

3. John Rawls, "Representation of Freedom and Equality," Dewey Lecture no. 2, *Journal of Philosophy* 77 (1980): 515–72 at 542.

4. H. L. A. Hart, "Positivism and the Separation of Law and Morals," *Harvard Law Review* 71 (1958): 593, reprinted in Joel Feinberg and Hyman Gross, eds., *Philosophy of Law* 4th ed. (Belmont, Calif.: Wadsworth Publishing Company, 1991), 65.

5. Sir William Blackstone, *Commentaries on the Laws of England*, 16th ed. (London, 1825), 1:41, cited in Theodore Benditt, *Law As Rule and Principle* (Stanford, Calif.: Stanford University Press, 1978), 1.

6. Ronald Dworkin, *Taking Rights Seriously* (Cambridge: Harvard University Press, 1977); *A Matter of Principle* (Cambridge: Harvard University Press, 1985); and *Law's Empire* (Cambridge: Harvard University Press, 1986).

7. Judith Wagner DeCew gratefully acknowledges support for work on this volume from a 1993–94 Research Fellowship for College Teachers and Independent Scholars, from the National Endowment for the Humanities.

PART I

FOUNDATIONS
OF THE DEBATE
ON THEORY
AND PRACTICE

1

THE DECLINE AND REPUDIATION OF THE WHOLE: NOTES ON ARISTOTLE'S ENCLOSURE OF THE PRE-SOCRATIC WORLD

NORMA THOMPSON

Herodotus' reputation in the ancient world is something exceptional which must be explained.

—Arnaldo Momigliano

Much of political thought as we know it today exists within a universe designed by Aristotle, whose conception of *theoria* and *praxis* is tied up with his notion of the best possible lives for human beings. As is well known, Aristotle found in the theoretical or contemplative life the possibilities for complete human happiness,[1] while for him the practical life of politics offered happiness of a "secondary" sort (*NE* 1178a9). Even so, in his practical writings, Aristotle certainly sought to achieve an integrative conception of theory and practice; in his explication of the *phronimos*, for example, we confront the individual who can, through experience and wisdom, deliberate correctly about what are the best actions and about how to pursue those actions in particular circumstances. Yet Aristotle's work, as variously interpreted over the ages, generally came to be understood as justifying the dominance of theory over practice: practice could not be entirely understood or rightly conducted without close attention to theory.

Reactions to this main stream of interpretation quite naturally appear from time to time,[2] but contemporary critics and thinkers once again are calling for a renewed scrutiny of Aristotelian categories of thought. The concern at present is that out of Aristotle's conception of *theoria* and the *theoretikos* may emerge something fundamentally despotic; thus we find a considerable body of writing "against" theory, produced by those who identify themselves as "anti-foundationalist."[3] The "privileged" role of theory and the theorist is not easily defended in an anti-elitist age: "Theory, in the sense of sustained reflection upon society in order to render one's understanding as comprehensive and as coherent as possible, is for the few; practice is for the many."[4]

However worthy this may be as an intellectual movement, like other reactions to the main current of political thought across the centuries it seems unlikely to provide lasting satisfaction. Indeed, anti-foundationalism could be interpreted itself as a theory, smuggling aboard foundations in disguise under cover of obscurity and setting a course for its own version of despotism by casting off the anchor of admitted theory to leave all to the mercy of raw power politics. Thus, we remain unable to locate satisfactory alternatives to the Aristotelian universe of *theoria* and *praxis*, and remain subject to mood swings between the two, now favoring one, now the other. The theoretically inclined seek comprehensive explanations that ultimately fail to satisfy; the pragmatically inclined eventually come to believe, with cause, that no practice long endures in the absence of its theory. We require more than a mixture of the two positions.

In order to meet this requirement, we might reexamine that Aristotelian moment in which "The Philosopher" establishes his orientation over against a previous pre-Socratic thinking. It has been observed that when Aristotle eschewed Plato's dialogue form in favor of his own "monologue," he was advocating the "replacement of myth by logos."[5] This statement will be explicated in due course; for the moment, I will put a name to it, and claim that the "myth" which Aristotle's "logos" was intended to replace was essentially *Herodotean.*

Momigliano refers to the near-uniform contempt in which Herodotus came to be held in his time, and wonders why. He goes on to note that Herodotus recovered from the attack of Thucydides only after two thousand years.[6] In some form or another, this charge has been repeated throughout the ages, and yet it is incomplete; unmentioned is Herodotus' more unremitting critic, Aristotle. The observations that follow are offered with the suggestion that a close reading of Aristotle's pronouncements on history and historical argumentation indicate that he defined his intellectual system *against* Herodotus and scorned Herodotus' "ancient" ways of thought as chaotically inclusive of virtually all dimensions of human life. In their place, Aristotle constructed the more controlled, dichotomous, demarcated, and abstract structures that have framed and helped to shape Western and world thought ever since.

In this endeavor, Aristotle may be seen as contributing his own version of an apology of the philosophic life. The statement traditionally attributed to Aristotle that Athens was not to be allowed "to sin twice against philosophy" may be apocryphal, but it is certainly true to the spirit and rhetoric of his practical writings; no philosopher has ever moved more cautiously among the "common opinions" of mankind. Tessitore has rightly emphasized "the apologetic dimension" of the *Nicomachean Ethics* in particular: "Aristotle's rhetorical art is calculated to win an at-least-partial acceptance of philosophy on the part of those who are or will be most responsible for directing the affairs of the city."[7] Lobkowicz adds that Aristotle's discussion certainly has an "ideological component": "It serves to justify the way of life of the philosopher who pursues interests which, at first glance, have nothing to do with the problems of society."[8] I intend to demonstrate through an examination of Aristotle's assessment of Herodotus that he considered the (urgent) task of defending the philosophic life as unfinished by his teacher, Plato, or at least in need of reformulation, and that this Aristotelian task would be fulfilled at the expense of the "unsystematic" point of view associated with Herodotus.

For obvious reasons, Plato's apology of the philosophic life

did not have the same effect as Aristotle's in establishing the
primacy of systematic argumentation; the dialogue form itself
seems to counteract any "despotic" tendencies of theory. Indeed, the dramatic action within a Platonic dialogue often serves
to subvert rather than to buttress the claims of theory. Thus,
the extreme character of the "city in speech" as constructed in
The Republic does not eventuate in the sense of *Plato's* own
extremism regarding the role of theory. "Few [works] give such
substance to visions of ideality and longings for perfection,"
observes Euben, "only to suggest the dangers of precisely what
they commend."[9] The dialogue points continuously beyond its
borders, and sabotages its own "closure," as Clay writes: "By
opening new frontiers of argument, and reopening arguments
that had seemed settled . . . the *Republic* is an open dialogue.
. . . [It] seems to challenge its reader to engage it from without,
as do Glaukon, Adeimantus, and Polemarchus within."[10] Something beyond the reach of fixed theoretical propositions propels
the movement of the dialogue, and this is related to something
beyond the reach of theory that propels Socrates himself: "The
power of the daimon leaves Socrates speechless and replaces the
voice of the philosopher with a more primeval one, the voice of
the soul."[11] Thus Plato, who depicts the philosopher's complete
estrangement from society and requires the expulsion of the
poets for the philosopher's proper role in society to be realized,
still seems to limit the claims for philosophical theory by de-
picting its more primal—and more poetic—dependencies.

In contrast, Aristotle describes in his practical works a world
more congenial for philosophers and seemingly more accepting
of poets. It turns out, however, that in the "old quarrel" between philosophy and poetry that Socrates refers to, Aristotle
delivers the harsher blow against poetry.[12] Among the "poetry"
most affected is the poetic history of Herodotus. *The History* is
"poetic" in that Herodotus "made the long and complicated
story both one and *eusunopton*," as Gomme writes, "capable of
being taken in in one view,"[13] though it must be added that his
history still lacks the closure that Aristotle favored. Thus, when
the Herodotean character Croesus asks "who is the happiest of
mankind?" his question will be answered but never settled. The
single image of Croesus serves to connect and illuminate other

instances reported by Herodotus that pertain to the question of human flourishing; the image is repeatedly evoked and further disclosed, yet it never becomes the source for metaphysical propositions. For poetry "drives thinking away from philosophy," as Bruns claims; philosophy "wants to stay in place, not so much residing as presiding, instituting, fixing, determining, clarifying, planning for the future."[14] Aristotle's recasting of the poetic impulse conceals its status as prior to philosophy.

The fact that Aristotle only infrequently names Herodotus as his adversary has masked the character of this defining debate; most commentators have assumed that it was Thucydides to whom Aristotle was referring. A close look at Aristotle's argument reveals that his antagonist was Herodotus. In the following pages, this uncovered aspect of intellectual archaeology will be examined in four steps. First, I will note the striking disagreement among interpreters about how to assess Aristotle on theory and practice; this is a consequence of the mixed signals that Aristotle sends in his thoroughgoing attempt to disparage pre-Socratic thinking as represented by Herodotus. Aristotle intentionally exaggerates his distance from Herodotus and, in the process, exaggerates his claims for the determinative role of theory. Next, I will proceed through three broad categories in which Aristotle identifies himself over against Herodotus. These categories include style, evidence, and the contingent nature of the historian's material.

Aristotle directs toward Herodotus a series of erroneous or misleading criticisms, all in the service of promoting his own philosophical tendencies: to fix definitions, to fix evidence, and to aspire to the theory that holds. The minds of both the philosopher and the historian are revealed to be universal; each seeks to explain all. But Aristotle constantly overestimates his distance from Herodotus and seems oblivious to their common ground. What is remembered is *only* the theory that holds. It is a triumph of rigorous intellectualization over a way of inquiry more willing and able to comprehend uncertainty, contingency, inconsistency, and the varied sources of human constancy and change. It is the beginning of the academic enclosure of the human commons.

ARISTOTLE'S DOUBLE LEGACY

Depending on one's emphasis, Aristotle may be read as either an inspiration for our thinking on theory and practice or a deleterious influence to be overcome. At the root of this dual reading of Aristotle is his basic association of *theoria* with "divine" and *praxis* with "human." This is evident first, in his threefold distinction between ways of knowing and his consequent ranking of the "theoretical" sciences as highest; and second, in his tripartite division of the most choiceworthy lives and his consequent ranking of the theoretical or contemplative life as best. From these formulations, it is easy to construct "settled" theories, even regarding such changeable matters as human conduct.

Aristotle mentions three forms of intellectual activity (theoretical, practical, and productive sciences); of these, he grants superiority to the theoretical sciences of theology, mathematics, and physics on account of the necessity and unchanging principles of their subject matter.[15] *Theoria* involves things that cannot be otherwise, and even the "scanty conceptions to which we can attain of celestial things" give us, Aristotle says, "more pleasure than all our knowledge of the world in which we live."[16] His ranking of the most choiceworthy human lives follows from this estimation of *theoria* and, from the point of view of some readers, is accordingly suspect; it seems to validate the life of the researcher unattached to "mere" human concerns: "For it is absurd to think that Political Science or Prudence is the loftiest kind of knowledge, inasmuch as man is not the highest thing in the world" (*NE* 1141a22).

The theorizing that Aristotle defends seems to be uninvolved with the world around us, and, as Adkins writes, there seems to be no persuading a *theoretikos* "at a time when he is engaged in *theoria* that he should perform some moral or political action instead."[17] That life is deemed highest which is in contact with the "unalterable and unmodified, living the best and most self-sufficient of lives."[18] The life of contemplation is said to be not only superior to any other human life, it is *higher* than human: "Human beings are able to live it in virtue of some divine principle within. ... Accordingly, we should *athanatizein* (play the immortal) so far as in us lies and do our best to live in accordance with the best part of us."[19] In this way, Aristotle encourages us to associate theory with the divine and practice with the human, thus leading some readers to conclude that his separation of theory from practice is so stark as to open the way to extremism: "[There is not] any sustained attempt to bridge the gulf, to show continuity, between the principles of justice which all men must respect and the contemplative activities without which no man can be truly happy."[20]

Nevertheless, because there is a gulf between the realms of theory and practice for Aristotle does not mean that there is an absolutist role for theorizing in human life. Salkever is correct in stating of Aristotle that "the relationship of theory to practice is not direct—not a form of natural law deductivism—but rather an indirect connection that avoids both dogmatism and relativism."[21] Aristotle's appeal today seems to be in line with the search for pluralist thinking with a strong core. Although he recognizes that different political communities define their own versions of the common good, he also subjects them to scrutiny on the question of their "authoritative element": "It is either the multitude, the wealthy, the respectable, the one who is best of all, or the tyrant; but all of these appear to involve difficulties. How could they not?".[22] Aristotle accepts the diversity of political life as given and proceeds to advise us on the means of reforming or maintaining the regime, not on the basis of some transcendent or precisely definable ideal, but based on subjects and premises which "are merely generalities" (*NE* 1094b14f.). As Rorty explains, "What attracts contemporary classical philosophers to [Aristotle] is . . . the investigation of a self-contained, enormously illuminating theory, rich in practical consequences as well as in theoretical insights."[23]

In keeping with our "double reading" of Aristotle, Ackrill has identified a "broken-backed" quality to Aristotle's teaching, and remarked that this puts him "in the company of all philosophers who hold that one element in man is supremely valuable, but are unwilling to embrace the paradoxical and extremist conclusions about life that that view implies."[24] I would like to emphasize the conscious formulation of this position by Aristotle in his dismissive treatment of Herodotus. In the act of contesting Herodotus' pre-Socratic view, Aristotle reveals with the utmost clarity his tendency to seek the comprehensive explanation even as he counsels against such totalizing theory on practical matters.

Herodotus' reputation in the ancient world is exceptional, as Momigliano observed, and consequently the recognition of Herodotus "as our best and most complete document for pre-Socratic philosophy" has not, to say the least, been widespread. This perception, found in Benardete's *Herodotean Inquiries,* is unduly neglected.[25] Herodotus opens his history with the quintessentially pre-Socratic notion that as the basic human condition is one of change and instability, the observer of this condition must take in the whole of it: "Since, then, I know that man's good fortune *(eudaimonia)* never abides in the same place, I will make mention of both [the small and great cities of mankind] alike."[26] For Herodotus, the challenge is to assure "that time may not draw the color from what man has brought into being," that "those great and wonderful deeds . . . [not] fail of their report" (1.1). It is the proposed Herodotean report that seems to distress Aristotle in every way—for its open-ended nature, its implausible embracing of "all" of the stories of mankind, and its resistance to classification. Aristotle opposes this pre-Socratic view with all of his formidable powers. In the process, as Rosen remarks, he *overstates* his case for "the reasonableness of nature," and this has had some dramatic and "un-Aristotelian" consequences. Ultimately, perhaps, "the temptation to master nature by technical devices"[27] is among them; it was an easy step for scientists in the modern age to translate Aristotelian *theoria* as the *highest* form of cognition into *theoria* as the *only* form.

THE FREE-RUNNING STYLE OF HERODOTUS: "SEEING NOTHING IN FRONT OF YOU" AND "GETTING NOWHERE"

Aristotle's disparagement of Herodotus begins with the first line of his history. In *The Rhetoric,* Aristotle remarks that the "free-running" prose style exemplified by Herodotus' opening sentence in *The History* ("Herein is set forth the inquiry of Herodotus . . .") is defined by having "no natural stopping-places, and comes to a stop only because there is no more to say on that subject."[28] Aristotle labels this style the "ancient" one—reminder enough that the writer with the alternative "compact" style represents the way of the future. The impression he conveys is one of utter indifference toward the particular example he has chosen: he has selected Herodotus for his illustration; he might well have chosen others. Upon closer examination, however, Aristotle's choice appears more "studied"; that is, he seeks the appearance of an easy dismissiveness, as if the stylistic advance of "compact" writing were obvious. But if the stylistic differences between Aristotle and Herodotus are genuine enough, it is by no means obvious that the latter represents an unquestioned advance.

Aristotle's distinction between the free-running and the compact prose style gives us a fair sense of the discipline and neatness he expects in any theorizing; this is in marked contrast to Herodotus' practice of inserting "reminders" to his audience of how difficult it is to manage his material in a coherent and effective form. Herodotus' presence in his narrative is conspicuous, and conspicuously unsettling: "I do not know if this is exactly true; I write down just what I am told. Still, anything may happen" (4.195).[29] Aristotle's strong inclination is toward an understanding of the world that controls what is said—and in a way that is readily articulable. Thus, his condemnation of the free-running style is that it lacks discipline: "This style is unsatisfactory just because it goes on indefinitely—one always likes to sight a stopping place in front of one" (1409a31f.). It seems that Herodotus' style may even strain our well-being: "it is only at the goal that men in a race faint and collapse; while they see the end of the course before them, they can keep going."

Aristotle grants no philosophic dignity to the style of *The History,* and for the most part, the Western tradition has followed suit. Behind the alleged lack of control in Herodotus' prose, however, is a subtle and realistic view of the tentative quality of any theorizing. Philosophers and historians alike must begin with the opinions of mankind, and if, as Aristotle himself says, "every man has some contribution to make to the truth," he also knows that opinions conflict, stories change, and story-tellers have ulterior motives; the theorist is on uncertain ground.[30] No one is more successful than Aristotle in smoothing over this shifting, uneven surface, whereas no one is more assiduous than Herodotus in keeping visible its rough edges. Both enterprises, that of the philosopher and the historian, require discipline of the most exacting sort.

Aristotle's criticism of Herodotus may be humorous ("having no more to say" is an "unnatural" place to stop?), but it is fundamentally unfair. Flory rightly observes that *The History* is a tightly woven composition held together by the anecdotes, "both in practical terms by repeating the same themes . . . and in philosophical terms because the repeated themes illuminate the whole historical narrative and the mind of the author."[31] Aristotle encourages the impression that Herodotus somehow does not control what is said, but this is to neglect the ring-composition, analogies, oppositions, and other rhetorical devices that have long impressed readers of Herodotus. And the *single* story of the encounter between Solon and Croesus serves to connect events before, during, and after the Persian War; Croesus is the paradigmatic figure of the prosperous and apparently secure individual (or city, or empire) falling victim to hubris. His example offers us a very clear view of the course before us.

In the Croesus-Solon story, Croesus arranges to have Solon tour his vast stores of treasure, then asks him "whether, of all men, there is one you have seen as the most blessed of all" (1.30). When Solon identifies "Tellus the Athenian," Croesus is provoked. Solon explains that Tellus came from a good city, had a prosperous family, lived well, and had a splendid ending in battle: "the Athenians gave him a public funeral where he fell and so honored him greatly" (1.30). Croesus then asks for Solon's opinion of the second happiest man, expecting that at least this honor would be his own. Solon answers with a description of Cleobis and Biton, Argive brothers who had the following story told about them. When the team of oxen did not arrive to take their mother to the temple for a religious festival, they hitched the wagon to themselves and brought her the distance: "When they had done that and had been seen by all the assembly, there came upon them the best end of a life, and in them the god showed thoroughly how much better it is for a man to be dead than alive" (1.31). After the mother had prayed to the gods that her sons receive whatever it was best for men to win, the two young men "never rose more" and were laid to rest in the temple. Hearing this second account, Croesus objects that Solon has undervalued his own happiness by estimating so highly the lives of private men. Solon responds that the one who consistently possesses the most "good things" and then dies well may earn the title of "happiest," but that this determination cannot be made prematurely: "For to many the god has shown a glimpse of blessedness only to extirpate them in the end" (1.32). And so Croesus sends Solon away, "thinking him assuredly a stupid man who would let by present goods and bid him look to the end of every matter" (1.33).

In Herodotus' portrayal, Croesus' happiness is to be short-lived for all sorts of reasons beyond his control, but there remains an area in which his responsibility for his fate is clearly his own. It is this area that proves so vital to the question of *eudaimonia* as a whole. Croesus' failing is to define "good things" by *measuring* them; he proceeds as if there were nothing in the world that could not be known through instrumental reasoning. Even the gods are subjected to his computations, for he asks the oracles throughout Greece and Libya to report what Croesus, King of Lydia, was doing on a specific day, thereby forcing them to communicate with him in a language he can control. After the Delphic oracle passes this test, Croesus sends massive dedications of gold and silver to the temple, assuming that these quantities matter to the gods. All of this was in preparation for Croesus asking the significant question, should he make war against Cyrus, King of Persia? And the Delphic oracle answered honestly again: If you make war, you will destroy a mighty empire. It turns out, of course, that Croesus did not ask the prior question, which would have led him to discover that the mighty empire that was to be destroyed was his own.

In his drive to accumulate more goods, more land, more subjects, Croesus defines an end for himself that can have no end. His fundamentally irrational behavior is corrected only in total defeat. He is not able to appreciate the wisdom of Solon until all is lost. Thus comes into existence the ineffective "wise advisor"; no ruler in the Croesus paradigm can be affected by good advice, until it is too late. However commonly taught, this lesson somehow always remains counterintuitive: self-determination cannot be achieved in a lasting way without actually *determining* ("weighing" rather than "counting") one's good. The path of least resistance for the rich and powerful ruler, state, or empire is the path toward self-destruction. Hence the Croesus story illuminates the Persian experience, which in turn illuminates the future prospects for the Athenians. But it is a lesson that readers must determine for themselves. Herodotus nowhere states explicitly what we are to learn from his inquiries; understanding comes only with our engagement with the story.

Aristotle himself does not eschew the use of well-known stories to fill out his intended meaning, but he sharply restricts the length of his examples and sets out the conclusions authoritatively. In Book 1 of *The Politics,* he recounts the story of Thales, who bought up all the olive presses in the area during the off-season; eventually he benefitted immensely from his monopoly (1259a5f.). Aristotle concludes that this is a "piece of business expertise" which is "universal." His point (in the context of his contrast between "acquisition" and "use") is less the specific one that philosophers could become wealthy if they only cared to, than the general one: mere accumulation is unnatural ("usury is most reasonably hated") but accumulation in the service of a higher good—say, for the establishment of political rule within a city—is natural and a useful insight for rulers (1259a31). The difference is in the defining principle; enrichment is in the service of some higher aspiration or it is "absurd": "Yet it would be absurd if wealth were something one could have in abundance and die of starvation—like the Midas of the fable, when everything set before him turned into gold on account of the greediness of his prayer" (1257b14–17).

We might conclude that Aristotle's story is compact, Herodotus's is free-running; in the end, this may just be a matter of style. To write compactly is to differentiate one's points, to write in a free-running manner is to seek inclusiveness; the one is not implicitly more satisfying than the other. Aristotle may well strike us as rash to take on Herodotus from this perspective in the first place. Plutarch took exactly the opposite approach in denigrating Herodotus' style; instead of underestimating the historian's grasp of his material, he attributed to him complete and malevolent control: "a style so attractive and effective enables a writer to conceal his moral character as well as the errors in statements."[32] The question Plutarch raises is familiar to readers of Herodotus: in the course of connecting dramatic themes, does he compromise the substantive work of writing history? The recurring pattern of the Croesus figure may be good drama (though Aristotle would not grant so much), but is it history? Here, too, Aristotle enters the debate.

Consider the Source: Herodotus the Mythmaker

Herodotus may stand at the beginning of the Western tradition on the subject of historical evidence, but he is a marginal figure in *forming* it; he is blamed, in Redfield's phrase, for "failing to be Thucydides."[33] Momigliano claims that the only ancient writer "who never said anything unpleasant about Herodotus" was Dionysius, his kinsman.[34] To be blunt, the charge is that Herodotus is a liar. Aristotle, for his part, expresses his exasperation with Herodotus in the *Generation of Animals*, where he describes the fishermen who "join the chorus and repeat the same old stupid tale that we find told by Herodotus, the fableteller [or 'mythmaker,' *ho mythologos*], to the effect that fish conceive by swallowing the milt."[35] Earlier in this same treatise, Aristotle notes that Herodotus was certainly incorrect in his statement that "the semen of Ethiopians is black, as though everything about a person with a black skin is bound to be black—and this too in spite of their teeth being white," (736a10–14). Aristotle completes this statement with uncharacteristic pique: "as [Herodotus] could see for himself."

Factual errors are factual errors, whether they are made by the first historian or the first political scientist. But it is not a matter that should detain us in a discussion of Herodotus. Despite his long-standing double reputation as "father of history" and "father of lies," he is today credited for his serious and consistent attempts at historical accuracy: "He was often misinformed, usually by people who themselves believed what was in fact incorrect. But in the elementary duty of a historian, that is, the discovery of how the events actually took place, Herodotus has a good record."[36] In truth, Aristotle's quarrel with Herodotus is not about whether the historian put a high value on historical accuracy, which surely he did. The real source of Aristotle's ire (and that of Thucydides and others) concerns Herodotus' acceptance of "hearsay"—stories, myths, and opinions of all manner of excess—as valuable historical evidence.

According to Thucydides, it is the responsibility of historians to extract from their retellings of events any traces of myth; he therefore rejects those "prose-writers" who compose their works "more delightfully to the ear than conformably to the truth."[37] The reader for whom Thucydides wrote is instead someone who would "frame a judgment of the things past" after these things past had been "searched out by the most evident signs that can be" (1.21). If the evidence is circumscribed enough, Thucydides argues, then the theorist/historian might dispense with all irrational or simply untrue elements. In this respect, Aristotle would concur and "blame" Herodotus for not being Thucydides. "But into the subtleties of the mythologists," Aristotle concludes, "it is not worth our while to inquire seriously" (*Met* 1000a18).

Herodotus, *ho mythologos*, was not overly interested in circumscribing evidence; he treated what people thought and said about themselves as if they *mattered*, quite apart from their truth content. Indeed, for Herodotus, the accretions of conscious and mythical discourse which build up around the actual moment of action in an event in time past *are* that event insofar as it affects and reveals a community of the present. "History" is not the event but the explanations given the event. And "history" is not found ready-made; the conscious and mythical discourses—the *logoi*—that interest Herodotus first must be mastered by him. Dewald writes, "The *Histories* Herodotus has given us are the record of his heroic encounter: his exploits in capturing the *logoi* and his struggles to pin them down and make them speak to him the truths they contain."[38] Without the subtle shaping hand of the historian, great and wonderful deeds would "fail of their report."

As all-embracing as Herodotus' inquiries are, he did not aim for knowledge of everything that happened in the past. Indeed, in some very basic ways, his aim was patently a *practical* one. Herodotus as author of *The History* shares points of contact with Aristotle as author of the *Ethics*. As historian, Herodotus both shapes and preserves the Greek memory of the Persian war, for the purpose of affecting the identity and resolve of his contemporary audience. As Clark writes, neither the historian nor the *phronimos* merely apply general principles; both must be people of experience and "must be able to guess where the principles do not apply, should not be applied (*NE* 1137b26f.) . . . 'history' is the ground of *phronesis* and impossible without the sense to see the best."[39]

Just as Aristotle is "not investigating the nature of virtue for the sake of *knowing what it is*, but in order that we may become good, without which result our investigation would be *of no use*" (*NE* 1103b30–32; emphasis mine), so Herodotus does not investigate the past for the sake of simply knowing everything that was, but, to adopt Nietzschean terms, to *be useful for life.* "Herodotus did not intend to write a history of all that he knew about the epoch he described," writes Fornara, "He wrote about what was (or should be) 'well known,' 'splendid,' 'worthy of relation.' "[40] This would seem to be his unstated criterion for narrowing down his professed aim to "cover alike" the small and great cities of mankind.

This insight may help us to identify where the Aristotelian and Herodotean uses of evidence coincide. Aristotle suggests in his own writing that an opinion's "persistence in time" may be a more significant claim to our attention than its "theoretical rigor," but he is less than generous in granting the point to Herodotus. (Much would be learned of Socrates' city-in-speech, Aristotle remarks, from its "actually being instituted," *Pol* 1264a5f.; Hippodamus's drive for theoretical purity makes him oblivious to the already existing practices in Athens and elsewhere, *Pol* 1268a9–10). Furthermore, we have seen that Aristotle proceeds in a strikingly Herodotean manner by introducing stories that offer universal lessons, but for Aristotle, too, this may be quite apart from the truth of the particular story. For instance, as he goes through the various beginning points of revolutions in the *Politics*, he lists "contempt" of the ruler as

one such indicator, and says, "as when someone saw Sardanapa-
lus carding wool with the women, if what the retailers of stories
(hoi mythologountes) say is true *(though if not of him, this might well
be true of another)*" *(Pol* 1312a1–2, emphasis mine). Similarly, he
uses stories told by Herodotus (the footbath of Amasis, *Pol*
1259b8; the egg of a crocodile in *Historia Animalium)*[41] to make
his own point; there is no attribution and thus no issue of
historical veracity. This can be illustrated with particular force
on the subject of the Croesus-Solon encounter mentioned
above, for in this instance Aristotle fails to make the accusation
that might easily have been made: that the encounter never
really happened, and certainly never happened in the form of
Herodotus's telling.

In Aristotle's musings on the meaning of *eudaimonia* in the
Nicomachean Ethics, he barely acknowledges the ordinary human
inclination to wish to be "as rich as Croesus," as the saying goes:
"The Life of Money-Making is a constrained kind of life, and
clearly wealth is . . . only good as being useful, a means to
something else" (1096a6–8). His approach in considering the
highest good or happiness begins by formulating his usual question—*what is it? (ti estin).* He does not shirk from the challenges
of defining happiness (if only in outline); to do so, he consults
the opinions of mankind, even though "the many" and "the
wise" disagree about its nature (1095a23). Aristotle considers
the reputable opinions that have come down to him, including
that of Solon. Solon's opinion is *introduced* ("Must we obey Solon's warning, and 'look to the end'?" 1100a13–14), *qualified*
("should we add that [the happy man] must also be destined to
go on living not for any casual period but throughout a complete lifetime in the same manner, and to die accordingly,"
1101a18–20), and *dismissed* ("So much for a discussion of this
question," 1101a25) with never a mention of the author behind
"Solon's opinion." It is as if Aristotle had quoted from the
collected philosophical works of Solon, rather than from *The
History* of Herodotus.[42]

Aristotle's strategy has the effect of transforming the Herodotean, storytelling Solon into a sober Aristotelian philosopher.
The details that Aristotle has left out are apparent; for example,
he does not refer by name to Cleobis and Biton, whose timely

dispatch by the gods is not a subject a "real" philosopher was likely to take up. Aristotle's final comment on Solon in *The Ethics* brings him precisely in line with the moral teaching of Aristotle himself: "Solon also perhaps gave a good description of happiness when he said . . . those men were happy who, being moderately equipped with external goods, had performed noble exploits and had lived temperately" (1179a9f.).[43] Weil comments, "What Aristotle rejoiced to discover in Solon (and was obliged to discover in one of the Seven Sages) is the political embodiment of 'nothing in excess,' of the mean *(mesotes)*."[44]

Herodotus' history-writing and Aristotle's ethical writings are, for all of Aristotle's posturing, comparable in their practical aims. They are less comparable in respect to their aims for theoretical fixity. Herodotus has, in a word, no such aim: "This history of mine has from the beginning sought out the supplementary to the main argument" (4.30). That is, although Herodotus himself reveals a coherent historiographical method (difficult as it is to formulate), he attempts no single theory to "explain" all peoples. The evidence he draws upon to characterize a people is constituted differently in each case, according to the promptings of the people itself. He may stress alternately a people's stories of origin and its rhetorical self-presentations, its embellishments of past events, political forms, heroes, religious beliefs, social customs, or geographical features. He allows the emphasis and animating spirit of his evidence to change with his subjects, keeping him at a far remove from theorists who maintain that a single standard is appropriate and applicable in all places the same. The stories that people tell of themselves— whether they are Persian or Ionian or Greek—are versions or explanations of their own "goodness." Once the story is told and picked up by the community, it is imitated; it is there as an organizing principle to which people repair in moments of crisis. They may break free of it, but they know when they are doing it. As a result, *The History* offers us the prospect of many different peoples who themselves fall within a wide range of positions on theory and practice: from strong theories and despotic practices, to weak theories and undirected practices.

Aristotle, in contrast, closes off and refines common opinions in an effort to attain an enduring theory. This entails cutting off a whole range of expressions of what is said or believed, or even half-believed, among people. With some understatement, he writes, "Now perhaps it would be a somewhat fruitless task to review all the different opinions that are held" (*NE* 1095a29–30; cf. *EE* 1214b29f.). He would like to restrict his attention to those opinions "that seem to have some argument in their favor." The impression he perpetuates in this refining process is that he can explain himself whereas (unnamed) earlier thinkers could not. Aristotle's enterprise comes across as the "higher" one because it is more self-conscious and clearer about first principles. But what is prior to him is not all that he would have us believe.

CONTINGENCY AND NECESSITY

Thus Aristotle has revealed himself as disciplined and principled, next to the free-running and unreliable Herodotus. One final step is required to clinch Aristotle's superior philosophic identity, and this is for him to impugn the historian's subject matter as comprising only singular and contingent events. Aristotle does this in his famous statement about history in *The Poetics*. But here again, all is not as it seems. Aristotle both *overemphasizes* the distinction between history and poetry (thus concealing his more fundamental distinction between theoretical knowledge on the one hand, and practical and productive knowledge on the other), and *underemphasizes* the common ground between practical philosopher, historian, and poet.

Aristotle claims that poetry is "something more philosophic and of graver import than history, since its statements are of the nature rather of universals, whereas those of history are singulars."[45] A universal statement, he explains, is "one as to what such or such a kind of man will probably or necessarily say or do"; whereas a singular statement is "one as to what, say, Alcibiades did or had done to him." This is the passage in which Herodotus is named as the clear representative of the genre of history: "you might put the work of Herodotus into verse, and it would still be a species of history." The true distinction between history and poetry, he states, lies in the fact that the historian "describes what has happened," the poet "what might happen, i.e. what is possible as being probable or necessary." It seems that Aristotle prefers the enterprise of poets to that of historians because historians report not a "single action" (with a coherent beginning, middle, and end) but a "single period," which includes "all that happened in that to one or more persons, however disconnected the several events may have been" (1459a23–24).

In this passage, Aristotle apparently places Herodotus among the ranks of those historians "of lesser import" or seriousness. A number of commentators have argued that Aristotle's disparagement of history is unfair on his own terms,[46] and others have attempted to defend Herodotus against Aristotle's slur, but these exercises remain largely *defensive,* where a more offensive position is in order.[47] Even Glover, sage and diverting reader of Herodotus that he is, answers the philosopher summarily and with understatement ("not in a spirit of revenge, but surely with a certain right").[48] When Gomme supports Herodotus, he remains on the level of "significant hints" about why Aristotle so intently misreads the historian: "[Aristotle's] belief *or his apparent belief* [emphasis mine] that historians can only chronicle *all* events within a period has . . . some truth to it."[49]

Meanwhile, critics have defended *Thucydides* against Aristotle's charge; it has been assumed more than once that Aristotle had Thucydides explicitly in mind as he wrote this passage (largely because of the Alcibiades allusion), and that therefore his argument should be answered from a Thucydidean perspective.[50] This could be, though it is worth recalling that Aristotle nowhere mentions Thucydides either in this particular passage, elsewhere in *The Poetics,* or anywhere in the entire Aristotelian corpus. But the name of Herodotus appears quite prominently, not to say gratuitously ("you might put the work of Herodotus in verse"). Aristotle also uses (without attribution) as his example of "singular" statements events reported in *The History:* the coincidental overlap of the naval battle off Salamis and the battle with the Carthaginians in Sicily. Herodotus' appearance here is no accident; for Aristotle to convince his readers of a decisive break between poetry and history requires him to confront the most poetic of historians. It is not amiss to reconsider that confrontation.

Aristotle's poetry-history distinction lends itself to misreading. That is, Aristotle appears to be distinguishing between poetry and history, and so he is; the basic difference, in Rosenmeyer's words, is that the historian is contrained within a given time unit, whereas the poet "creates his own": "The poet creates words, signifiers, a self-authenticating verbal texture which does not have to be matched with referents in the mass of facts and events we call the past."[51] Yet for Aristotle, the *primary* distinction is between poetry and history on the one hand, and philosophy on the other, between spheres of knowing that treat of changeable matters, and those that treat of the unchanging and the necessary. Hence the questionable aspect of Aristotle's presentation centers on his choice of words in describing poetry as "more philosophic" than history, for it is *not* his argument that poetry has to do with the realm of *theoria*.

Like historians, poets imitate men and women of action; like historians, poets are tied to the practical world. But as Else observes, Aristotle's point is commonly taken to mean that "poetry were actually a branch of philosophy and the representation of universals were the fundamental concept of *poietike*":

> On the contrary, these notions of the "philosophical" content of poetry grow out of the concept that the work of art must be *beautiful*. . . . The structure of events "built" by the poet, in order to be beautiful, must be a unified and complete whole.[52]

The poet's work *(ergon)* for Aristotle is in "making plots," not in "making verses." Thus, putting *anyone's* work into verse would not make of them a poet: "the poet must be more the poet of his stories or Plots than of his verses, inasmuch as he is a poet by virtue of the imitative element in his work, and it is actions that he imitates" (*Poetics* 1451b27). The greater seriousness of poetry is due to the poet's ability to construct a coherent whole of events. And this is quite apart from whether the poet "should come to take a subject from actual history," Aristotle explains, "some historic occurrences may very well be in the probable and possible order of things; and it is in that aspect of them that he is their poet" (1451b29–31).

That "some historic occurrences" may be in "the probable

and possible order of things" might well suggest to us the feasibility of the mixed genre of "poetic history"—on Aristotle's
own terms. For that matter, it is not altogether clear that the
philosopher's activity is unrelated, when directed toward the
practical world. Without denying the essential distinction between the activities of considering "what might happen" and
"what has happened," we could still predict that there will be a
considerable area of overlap between the two. Historians do not
conduct their inquiries without a view of what might happen,
nor do poets (or philosophers, in all cases) compose their works
unattached to what has happened; the "probability" and "necessity" involved in each enterprise is easily blurred.

There are a number of different indicators suggesting that
even as Aristotle makes this sharp distinction between the
realms of the poet and the historian, he consciously qualifies it.
Ste. Croix demonstrates along this line that it is not at all customary in the works of Aristotle for him to limit his terms to the
dichotomy between "universal" and "singular" as he does here.
There is a *third* term ("the as a general rule") which accounts for
the phenomenon of seeing the general in particular events.[53] A
historian who worked on the level of this third term would seem
to be serious, poetic—even, in a sense, philosophic. Ste. Croix
comments, "Aristotle, on his own principles, ought not to have
given 'what Alcibiades did or had done to him' as an illustration
of the essential character of history."[54] Aristotle's illustration
would seem to apply to those who presume to be reporting the
facts and nothing but the facts (the Atthidographers, as Clark
suggests[55]); this is hardly applicable to Herodotus.

There is another, more controversial, indicator that Aristotle
undermines his own sharp distinction between poetry and history. At *Poetics* 1459a21, Aristotle remarks that the "usual" histories fail to base themselves on a single action; as Clark notes,
perhaps the "unusual" histories would not have this failing.[56]
The passage is disputed, both because of the Greek itself, which
is difficult, and because of the implication, which is that Aristotle recognizes something of the nature of a "poetic history"
but will not acknowledge it openly. But if we are to discount this
reading, it should not be because we reject the implication that

Aristotle would recognize the accomplishment of his predecessor only in an underhanded way. Rhetoric, Aristotle teaches us, is an "art."

We are left with the sense that Aristotle is engaged first and foremost with defending philosophy and the theoretical life, and only secondarily with criticizing history over against poetry. His disdain for contingent subject matter, "inasmuch as man is *not* the highest thing in the world" (*NE* 1141a22), is based on the permanent separation between the realms of *theoria* and *praxis,* and on the priority of the former. So historians may connect their material with whatever stories they will; they can do so only up to a point. "[History] does not deal with coherent wholes with a beginning, middle, and end. Such histories are mere aggregates of isolated facts, and fail to reveal the causes, the organic forms involved in the process of time."[57] To some degree or another, this is, for Aristotle, the "unfortunate" attribute of *any* practical or productive science. The result, as Rosen states, is that there is no accounting for the whole as whole; there are "only separate accounts of distinct families of phenomena. Not even the science of first principles provides us with an account . . . of the unity articulated as the tripartition of theory, practice, and production."[58] Aristotle's signals are plain enough: in the end, the disjunction between *theoria* and *praxis*— which was posited at the start—reappears.

From *The Poetics,* it follows that the best kind of history would have a universal character, but Aristotle himself does not engage in a constructive analysis of the relative merits of histories. The very contingency of historical events gives the historian what Aristotle cannot abide: the space to create. When Aristotle defends the philosophic life as the highest, he does so with the apparent intention of leaving behind him the more creative endeavors of poetry and history. Else observes of Aristotle in *The Poetics* that he "stands the creative process on its head," as he goes about defining tragedy and the rules for its construction:

> Aeschylus and Sophocles . . . did not begin with an abstract type or conception ("military conqueror," "king who has unwittingly slain his father," "young-man-about-to-be-slain-by-priestess-sister") and end with Agamemnon, Oedipus, and Orestes. They

began with the concrete individual figures ... and the stories attached to them by tradition.[59]

Steiner considers this phenomenon in which "analysis" apparently displaces "creativity" in priority, and determines that "in the truth-hour of his consciousness," there is not "a commentator, critic, (or) aesthetic theorist ... however masterly, who would not have preferred to be a source of *primary utterance* and shaping."[60] This is to view the quarrel between poetry and philosophy from the point of view of the poet, which is instructive just because it is not Aristotle's view. In the truth-hour of his consciousness, Aristotle would probably have preferred to be—The Philosopher. As such, he is successful in persuading his audience of something remarkable: that the poetic history of Herodotus is inconceivable.

Conclusion

Aristotle's and Herodotus' ordering of the world are related, notwithstanding Aristotle's hints to the contrary. But one aspect of the historian's procedure surely stands alone: he invites infinite additions; his theory will never hold. This is the sense in which Herodotus represents more than a mixture of either the theoretically or pragmatically inclined. He *has* a "theory" that provides an intellectual ordering of the practices and customs of mankind; there is no futile expectation that practices somehow straighten themselves out. But his is a theory that seeks to comprehend rather than differentiate. In being receptive to the stories, myths, and histories of all peoples, Herodotus makes room for "untold" human possibilities, and points the way to a perpetual extension in the range of what might be.

Aristotle, who very nearly did go through all of the cities of the Greek world in his study of constitutions, could not accept Herodotus' claim to cover alike the small and great cities of mankind. And so he "corrects" Herodotus. As we still struggle against the temptation to theorize in a rigid way, it is worth remembering that his correction of Herodotus is itself subject to revision. "Every writer creates his own predecessors," Clark reminds us, "and so does every philosopher."[61] As we come to recognize the vision against which Aristotle defined his system, it appears that a fresh look from a new angle at Herodotus is more than warranted.

NOTES

1. Aristotle, *Nicomachean Ethics*, trans. H. Rackham (Cambridge: Harvard University Press, 1983), 1177625. Hereinafter, references to *NE* will be cited parenthetically in the text.

2. For useful surveys of conceptions of theory and practice, see Nicholas Lobkowicz, *Theory and Practice: History of a Concept from Aristotle to Marx* (Notre Dame: University of Notre Dame Press, 1967); Jürgen Habermas, *Theory and Practice*, trans. John Viertel (Boston: Beacon Press, 1973); and *Political Theory and Praxis: New Perspectives*, ed. Terence Ball (Minneapolis: University of Minnesota Press, 1977). Many excellent studies of Aristotle have appeared recently that attend to his immersion in everyday social and political realities and highlight his methodological openness. See especially: Larry Arnhart, *Aristotle on Political Reasoning: A Commentary on the "Rhetoric"* (DeKalb: Northern Illinois University Press, 1981); Michael Davis, *Aristotle's Poetics: The Poetry of Philosophy* (Lanham, MD: Rowman and Littlefield, 1992); Mary P. Nichols, *Citizens and Statesmen: A Study of Aristotle's Politics* (Savage, MD: Rowman and Littlefield, 1992); Stephen G. Salkever, *Finding the Mean: Theory and Practice in Aristotle's Political Philosophy* (Princeton: Princeton University Press, 1990); Arlene W. Saxonhouse, *Fear of Diversity: The Birth of Political Science in Ancient Greek Thought* (Chicago: University of Chicago Press, 1992); Judith A. Swanson, *The Public and the Private in Aristotle's Political Philosophy* (Ithaca: Cornell University Press, 1992); *Essays on Aristotle's Poetics*, ed. Amelie Oksenberg Rorty (Princeton: Princeton University Press, 1992); and *Essays on the Foundations of Aristotelian Political Science*, ed. Carnes Lord and David K. O'Connor (Berkeley: University of California Press, 1991).

3. Consider the collection of essays *Against Theory*, ed. W. J. T. Mitchell (Chicago: University of Chicago Press, 1985). The titles range from "Against Theory?" (E. D. Hirsch) to "Toward Uncritical Practice" (Jonathan Crewe) to "Philosophy Without Principles" (Richard Rorty).

4. Ronald Beiner, "On the Disunity of Theory and Practice," *Praxis International* 7:1 (April 1987): 30.

5. Stanley Rosen, *The Quarrel Between Philosophy and Poetry* (New York: Routledge, 1993), viii.

6. Arnaldo Momigliano, "The Place of Herodotus in the History of Historiography," *History* 43 (1958): 2, 10.

7. Aristide Tessitore, "Making the City Safe for Philosophy: *Nicomachean Ethics*, Book 10," *American Political Science Review* 84:4 (December 1990): 1260.

8. Nicholas Lobkowicz, "On the History of Theory and Praxis," in *Political Theory and Praxis: New Perspectives*, 15.

9. J. Peter Euben, introduction to *Greek Tragedy and Political Theory*, ed. J. Peter Euben (Berkeley: University of California Press, 1986), 11. I am aware that some readers of Plato see the visions of ideality without any attendant suggestions of danger, and that this reading leads one to conclude with Karl Popper that Plato was the first totalitarian thinker. Such a view has the (implausible) advantage of making it possible to settle one's accounts with Plato.

10. Diskin Clay, "Reading the *Republic*," in *Platonic Writings, Platonic Readings*, ed. Charles L. Griswold, Jr. (New York: Routledge, 1988), 23.

11. Jean-Francois Mattei, "The Theater of Myth in Plato," in *Platonic Writings, Platonic Readings*, 70.

12. Plato, *The Republic*, trans. with notes and interpretive essay by Allan Bloom (New York: Basic Books, 1968), 607b.

13. A. W. Gomme, *The Greek Attitude to Poetry and History* (Berkeley: University of California Press), 101.

14. Gerald L. Bruns, *Heidegger's Estrangements: Language, Truth, and Poetry in the Later Writings* (New Haven: Yale University Press, 1989), xxix.

15. Aristotle, *Metaphysica*, trans. W. D. Ross, in *The Basic Works of Aristotle*, ed. with intro. by Richard McKeon (New York: Random House, 1941), 1025b25f. Hereinafter, references to *Met* will be cited parenthetically in the text.

16. Aristotle, *De Partibus Animalium*, trans. William Ogle, in *The Basic Works of Aristotle*, 644b33–34.

17. A. W. H. Adkins, "*Theoria* Versus *Praxis* in the *Nicomachean Ethics* and the *Republic*," *Classical Philology* 73 (1978): 312.

18. Aristotle, *De Caelo*, trans. J. L. Stocks in *The Basic Works of Aristotle*, 279a22.

19. *NE* 1177b26, summarized by Adkins, 297–98.

20. W. F. R. Hardie, *Aristotle's Ethical Theory* (Oxford: Clarendon Press, 1968), 357.

21. Salkever, 7.

22. Aristotle, *The Politics*, trans. Carnes Lord (Chicago: University of Chicago Press, 1984), 1281a11–15. Hereinafter, references to *Pol* will be cited parenthetically in the text.

23. Amelie Oksenberg Rorty, "Introduction," in *Essays on Aristotle's*

Ethics, ed. A. O. Rorty (Berkeley: University of California Press, 1980), 3.

24. J. L. Ackrill, "Aristotle on *Eudaimonia,*" in *Essays on Aristotle's Ethics,* 33.

25. Seth Benardete, *Herodotean Inquiries* (The Hague: Martinus Nijhoff, 1969). For another compelling treatment of Herodotus' *History* as an embodiment of pre-Socratic wisdom, see Rosen, 27–55.

26. Herodotus, *The History,* trans. David Grene (Chicago: University of Chicago Press, 1987), 1.5. Hereinafter references will appear parenthetically in the text.

27. Rosen, xii.

28. Aristotle, *The Rhetoric,* trans. W. Rhys Roberts, intro. by Edward P. J. Corbett (New York: Random House, 1984), 1409a28f.

29. As Dewald remarks, "we do not experience the narrative as an unmediated mimetic event in which we participate as readers. . . . We read it rather as the achievement of an author acting as a master raconteur, subduing difficult and diverse narrative material to his will." Carolyn Dewald, "Narrative Surface and Authorial Voice in Herodotus' *Histories,*" *Arethusa* 20:1 and 2 (Spring and Fall 1987): 149.

30. Aristotle, *Eudemian Ethics,* trans. J. Solomon, in *The Complete Works of Aristotle,* 2, ed. Jonathan Barnes (Princeton: Princeton University Press, 1984), 1216631. Hereinafter references to *EE* will be cited parenthetically in the text.

31. Stewart Flory, *The Archaic Smile of Herodotus* (Detroit: Wayne State University Press, 1987), 16.

32. Plutarch, *Moralia* 11, trans. Lionel Pearson and F. H. Sandbach (Cambridge: Harvard University Press, 1965), 11.

33. James Redfield, "Commentary on Humphreys and Raaflaub," *Arethusa* 20 (Spring and Fall 1987): 251.

34. Momigliano, 1.

35. Aristotle, *Generation of Animals,* trans. A. L. Peck (Cambridge: Harvard University Press, 1963), 756b4–8. Hereinafter references will appear parenthetically in text.

36. David Grene, "The Historian as Dramatist," *Journal of Philosophy* 58:18 (August 1961): 477. Grene notes, for instance, that although Herodotus was often misinformed by his Egyptian sources, modern Egyptologists are impressed by his diligent efforts to recount "what had happened." W. Kendrick Pritchett elaborates in detail, in both *The Liar School of Herodotus* (Amsterdam: J. C. Gieben, 1993) and "Appendix on some Recent Critiques of the Veracity of Herodotus," *Studies in Ancient Greek Topography: IV* (Berkeley: University of California Publications, 1982), 234–285. These works were written in response to the

latest generation of skeptical readers of *The History,* beginning with
Detlev Fehling, *Die Quellenangaben bei Herodot* (Berlin: De Gruyter,
1971), translated into English by J. G. Howie as *Herodotus and his
'Sources': Citation, Invention, and Narrative Art* (Leeds: Francis Cairns,
1989). This was followed in quick succession by a related series of
articles and a book by O. Kimball Armayor, as well as articles by
Stephanie West. Pritchett's response is easily adequate to the skeptical
challenge, but much more on this topic remains to be said. I will
address the issue of Herodotus' veracity in much more detail in my
forthcoming book *Herodotus and the Origins of the Political Community,*
Yale University Press, 1995.

37. Thucydides, *The Peloponnesian War,* from The Complete
Hobbes Translation, notes and intro. by David Grene (Chicago: University of Chicago Press, 1989), 1.21.

38. Dewald, 147.

39. Stephen R. L. Clark, *Aristotle's Man* (Oxford: Clarendon Press,
1975), 134.

40. Charles W. Fornara, *The Nature of History in Ancient Greece and
Rome* (Berkeley: University of California Press, 1983), 92.

41. Aristotle, *Historia Animalium,* trans. A. L. Peck (Cambridge:
Harvard University Press, 1970), 558a20–24.

42. Solon appears in a number of guises in the works of Aristotle.
Weil notes that in *The Politics,* Aristotle finds it necessary to transform
Solon into a member of the middle class: "on this point as on many
others, he strives to reconcile diverse traditions." Raymond Weil, "Aristotle's View of History," in *Articles on Aristotle: Ethics and Politics,* eds.
Jonathan Barnes, Malcolm Schofield, Richard Sorabji (London: Gerald
Duckworth, 1977), 205.

43. I have corrected Rackham's translation of *isws* from "doubtless"
to "perhaps."

44. Weil, 205.

45. Aristotle, *Poetics,* trans. Ingram Bywater, intro. by Friedrich
Solmsen (New York: Random House, 1954), 1451a36–611. Hereinafter references will appear parenthetically in the text.

46. For example, G. E. M. de Ste. Croix, "Aristotle on History
and Poetry (*Poetics* 9, 1451a36–611)," in *The Ancient Historian and His
Materials,* ed. Barbara Levick (Westmead, England: Gregg International, 1975), 46.

47. See Thomas G. Rosenmeyer, "History or Poetry? The Example
of Herodotus," *Clio* 11, no. 3 (Spring 1982): 239–59. Rosenmeyer
believes that Aristotle, in his "careful manner," is "signalling to us that
these judgments are relative, and that the same text might, with a

moderate shift of emphasis or concern, be moved out of the camp of poetry into the camp of history or vice versa" (240). I am in full agreement with Rosenmeyer on this point; my interest is in why Aristotle has recourse to "signals."

48. Terrot R. Glover, *Herodotus* (Berkeley: University of California Press, 1924), 230.

49. Gomme, 178. See also 100–101.

50. See D. M. Pippidi, "Aristote et Thucydide," in *Melanges a J. Marouzeau* (Paris 1948), 483–90, and Kurt von Fritz, "Aristotle's Contribution to the Practice and Theory of Historiography," *UCPP* 28:3 (September 1958): 132.

51. Rosenmeyer, 247.

52. Gerald F. Else, *Aristotle's Poetics: The Argument* (Cambridge: Harvard University Press, 1967), 302.

53. Ste. Croix, 51.

54. Ibid., 50.

55. Clark, 131.

56. Ibid.

57. Ibid.

58. Rosen, viii.

59. Else, 309.

60. George Steiner, *Real Presences* (Chicago: University of Chicago Press, 1991), 152.

61. Clark, 7.

2

KANT ON THEORY AND PRACTICE

JEFFRIE G. MURPHY

Immanuel Kant's 1793 essay "Theory and Practice" is his attempt to defend his own moral and political theory against the charge that it is simply an idle academic exercise that cannot be brought to bear upon the real world in any useful way.[1] He is concerned, in particular, to answer two charges—the charges that his theory is (1) motivationally unrealistic, involving an account of moral motivation that is at odds both with scientific psychology and with all plausible philosophical accounts of rational deliberation and (2) not usable in either the design or critique of actual social institutions. Following a general discussion of what may be meant by the topic "theory and practice," Kant structures his essay as a response to the challenges to his own theories that are to be found in the writings of three other thinkers: Christian Garve, Thomas Hobbes, and Moses Mendelssohn.

Why is it worth caring about this essay? There are, I think, two reasons. First, it might be instructive to find out what the greatest philosophical mind of the eighteenth century had to say about the topic of the present volume. Second, a return to Kant is timely. There are few things more trendy these days than Kant-bashing, for he is often regarded as the patron saint of individualistic liberalism, Enlightenment rationalism, the idea of the "unsituated self" and a variety of other heresies that

47

communitarians, virtue theorists, and feminists among others enjoy condemning. It might be instructive to see how Kant himself responded to the kind of Kant-bashing that was current in his own day—some of it not all that different from our contemporary forms.

INTRODUCTION: WHAT IS THE PROBLEM OF THEORY AND PRACTICE?

Introductions are not generally Kant's strong point. Though nominally put forth to lay out clearly the topic for discussion and to set the reader up for what is to follow, they are often overly compressed and obscure. The introduction to "Theory and Practice" is, alas, somewhat in this mold. Although it makes (in a reasonably clear way) some important distinctions, it also contains much that is obscure and, as an introduction to what is actually to follow, somewhat misleading.

One thing is reasonably clear: Kant is at some level worried about the moral philistine—the businessman, the politician, the military officer who prides himself on his role as a hard-headed, no-nonsense, realistic *man of affairs (Geschäftsmann)* and who, in pursuing his objective of greed or power or victory, either ridicules morality and moral theory as irrelevant to his practice or who conveniently adopts an account of morality exactly tailored to allow him to do whatever he pleases. (Such notions as "it's just business" or "it's just politics" or "military necessity" might function in this way.) This is the person who, when met with a challenge from the realm of moral principle, tends to respond dismissively with the smug cliché "yes, what you say may be true enough in theory, but it doesn't apply in practice."

What worries Kant the philosopher even more than these moral philistines, however, is the existence of philosophical doctrines that can be used to give a cover of intellectual respectability to the iniquities and deceptions practiced by such persons. There is very little that a philosopher can do directly to combat ordinary human venality and self-deception, but the philosopher can properly assume the task of unmasking the intellectual pretensions of those who would use or misuse philosophical doctrines in support of venality and self-deception. Such is

Kant's objective in "Theory and Practice"—an objective he pursues by attempting to demonstrate how bad theories (or misuses of good theories such as his own) can aid in the corruption of human life and human society.

But what is a "theory" and what is the "practice" to which it is related? Kant writes,

> An aggregation of rules, even of practical rules, is called a *theory*, as long as these rules are thought of as principles possessing a certain generality and, consequently, as being abstracted from a multitude of conditions that nonetheless necessarily influence their application. Conversely, not every undertaking *[Hantierung]* is a *practice [Praxis];* rather, only such ends as are thought of as being brought about in consequence of certain generally conceived *[vorgestellten]* principles of procedure *[Verfahrens]* are designated practices (275,61).

Kant is here making the very clever suggestion that, at least in the domain of morality, the very distinction between theory and practice—and thus the idea that there could be an important gap between them—is incoherent.[2] An activity or institution is properly called a "practice" *(Praxis)*, claims Kant, only if it is viewed as the instantiation of some general principles (i.e., some theory); and a moral theory is adequate only to the degree that it provides a rational reconstruction—in terms of general principles—of those practical judgments that constitute our ordinary moral consciousness. As Dieter Henrich puts the point, "[Kant] speaks of the theory as being inherent in moral consciousness and action itself. As such it *eo ipso* is effective in a practical way."[3] Thus a bad theory, to use Rawlsian language for the method that Kant is here adopting, is a theory that fails to put us in reflective equilibrium with respect to our pretheoretical moral convictions. Such a theory will indeed deviate from practice, but this is because it is a bad theory (bad because of this very deviation) and not because it is somehow inherent in the idea of moral theory itself that it should be practically useless. This account of the necessary connection between moral theory and practical belief recalls, of course, the first two sections of the 1785 *Grundlegung* where Kant speaks of his method as involving the "transition from the common rational knowledge of morals to the philosophical" and of the "transition from the popular moral philosophy to the metaphysics of morals."[4]

If we do conceptualize moral theory as the best rational reconstruction of our shared moral beliefs, then one worry about a theory/practice gap can indeed be met: the possible gap between moral theory and ordinary moral consciousness. (This gap is one that, I would argue, faces the utilitarian much more dramatically than it does the Kantian; and demonstrating the gap is surely the main point of all the well-known scapegoat and other counterexamples to utilitarianism.[5])

As clever as Kant's suggestion is, however, it surely does not address all aspects of the theory/practice challenge to morality. For there are at least two different senses in which a moral theory can be thought to fail in practice. The first sense, one already discussed, involves the charge that a particular theory (e.g., utilitarianism) does not account for our considered moral judgments and thus cannot be the best rational reconstruction of our moral consciousness.

A second sense of the charge, however, involves a possible gap between our moral consciousness itself and the real world—the world of empirical reality. Consider, as an illustration, the retributive theory of punishment. This theory is, it could be argued, the best rational reconstruction of our considered moral judgments about punishment—e.g., the common moral belief that the guilty deserve to suffer. However, it is possible that this judgment itself presupposes a variety of false or self-deceptive views—e.g., about the nature of crime and criminals, about the legal process, about what actually happens to people when they are punished, and about the nature of the societies in which people comfortably make the judgment that the guilty deserve to suffer.[6]

This is a different kind of theory/practice gap than the one already discussed, but one that should not be hastily dismissed. The idea is that a person who lives too much in the world of theory may negligently think that the world in which he actually lives admits of clear application of theory when in fact it does not. Such a person may even come to a distorted view of the world by seeing the world only through the spectacles of his theory—thinking his theory is consistent with the facts because he does not realize that he is unable to accept as a fact anything that is inconsistent with his theory. (Paranoids, seeing all helpful gestures as threats, are masters of this; but the tendency is also present in those who are mentally normal. Think of those who see all welfare recipients as chiselers, all poor people as lazy, all criminals as free and responsible, and—to shift ideologies—all women as really desiring the independent and autonomous status that (supposedly) comes from having a career.[7])

Kant is not indifferent to such problems in "Theory and Practice" and suggests that the existence of such people shows, not a weakness in theory, but a weakness in human nature— the problem that some people simply lack the "natural gift" of *judgment:*

> For to the concept of the understanding that contains the rule must be added an act of judgment by means of which the practitioner decides whether or not something is an instance of the rule. And since further rules cannot always be added to guide judgment in its subsumptions (for that could go on infinitely), there can be theoreticians who, lacking judgment, can never be practical in their lives (275,61).

Kant has part of the story here, but surely there is more that needs to be said. It is true that some people simply lack judgment. It is also true, however, that many people make faulty judgments, not simply because they lack some "natural gift," but because they are caught up in complex webs of false consciousness and self-deception—webs perhaps built and encouraged by certain philosophical theories. Kant clearly saw this in 1793 because the insight plays a profound role in his *Religion,* published in that year.[8] But in "Theory and Practice," published in the same year, the insight is missing.[9]

There is still one additional passage in Kant's introduction that requires comment. Kant writes:

> All is lost when empirical and therefore contingent conditions of the application of law are made conditions of the law itself, and a practice calculated to effect a result made probable by *past* experience is thus allowed to predominate over a self-sufficient theory (277,62).

On one interpretation, Kant is clearly correct in what he says here. If I am really morally required to do X, then the fact that it would now be very difficult for me to do X or the fact that things happened to come out well in the past when I did not do X is irrelevant in determining my duty. Such factors could at most be relevant in excusing me for the nonperformance of my duty.

On another interpretation, however, Kant may well be mistaken. It is not unreasonable to suggest, for example, that the proper specification of the moral duty itself may sometimes quite properly take account of empirical variations in circumstances. Consider, for example, the duties that we have—in both morality and law—to do what is *reasonable* in certain circumstances, where reasonableness is partially understood in terms of what might happen to us (the risks we run) in acting in a certain way.[10] Consider also our concept of a "white lie"—a lie about a minor matter that will do no harm and perhaps great good. Philippa Foot writes instructively on such matters:

> Etiquette, unlike morality, is taught as a rigid set of rules that are on occasion to be broken. We do not, as we might have done, incorporate the exceptions to rules about handshaking and so on into the code of etiquette. . . . But morality we teach differently. Moral rules are not taught as rigid rules that it is sometimes right to ignore; rather we teach that it is sometimes morally permissible to tell lies (social lies), break promises (as e.g. when ill on the day of an appointment) and refuse help (when the cost of giving it would be, as we say, disproportionate). So we tend, in our teaching, to accommodate the exceptions within morality, and with this flexibility it is not surprising that morality can seem "unconditional" and "absolute." In the official code of behavior morality appears as strong because it takes care never to be on the losing side.[11]

Except for the odd—and to me quite unjustified—cynicism of the final sentence, Foot seems to be onto something very important here—something that Kant, with his well-earned reputation for rigidity, often, if not always, misses.[12] If moral theory is indeed a rational reconstruction of our ordinary moral consciousness, and if it is a part of that consciousness that (for example) social lies are sometimes permissible,[13] then Kant can maintain that moral rules never admit of exceptions only if he is willing to accommodate these exceptions into the specification of the rules themselves. And the first formulation of the categorical imperative may often allow this, since the maxim "to pay a false compliment when so doing will build a person's confidence" (for example) is probably universalizable. There are, of course, no exceptions allowed to the categorical imperative itself (morality is indeed rigid in that sense), but it does not follow from this that the categorical imperative (first formulation), when screening specific maxims for their moral permissibility, would never allow us to make exceptions to the rigid rule "never lie." Indeed, the universalization form of the categorical imperative probably would not identify the rule "never lie" as the correct moral rule about lying.[14]

Foot has insight on these matters, and Kant is—in my view— simply mistaken if he does not to some degree incorporate it into his theory. The issue is complicated, however, and the cynicism of Foot's final sentence may suggest that she has a (misplaced?) Kantian scruple or two of her own here.

So much (at last) for Kant's introduction. I shall now proceed to discuss the body of Kant's essay, where Kant will seek to establish that his own theory, properly understood, does pass the test that he himself imposes in the essay—namely, that the theory be motivationally realistic and applicable in the design and critique of actual human institutions:

> Concern over the empty ideality of concepts completely disappears in a theory based on the *concept of duty*. For it would not be a duty to pursue a certain effect of our will (whether it is thought of as completed or as continually approaching completion) if it were not possible to do so in experience, and this is the only kind of theory we are considering in this essay (276–77,62).[15]

Contra Garve

Christian Garve was one of Kant's contemporaries—a writer of popular philosophy (a *philosophe*) whose moral seriousness was respected by Kant. Even though Garve published some criticisms of Kant that Kant regards as in part misinterpretations, Kant treats these criticisms with general courtesy and does not deploy the full polemical force of which he is capable. This courtesy and respect may also be based on Kant's realization that not all of Garve's criticisms are simple misunderstandings and that some of them, indeed, are potentially serious and require a careful response.[16]

Kant's own moral theory stresses that duty is to be *determined* after abstracting from inclination and must (in cases of true moral worth) *motivate* in independence from inclination; he is famous for his claim that an action adds to the moral credit of the agent only if it is motivated by *respect (Achtung) for duty*.[17] Garve (greatly under the influence of British moral philosophy) is the first in a long line of anti-Kantians who argue that this theory is fatally defective because it cannot give proper weight to the role of the *emotions* in morality. Although such later critics as Schopenhauer (in the 1841 *On the Basis of Morality*) will chide Kant for ignoring or downplaying sympathy and other examples of what Barbara Herman calls "motives of connection,"[18] Garve is particularly interested in the emotions of self-regard— particularly the desire for one's own happiness. The selfish desire for one's own happiness is, according to Garve, (1) recognized in common experience as the actual motive for all human action, (2) the only motive that yields a coherent account of rational deliberation, and (3) the only motive that can be "reconciled with the customary principles of psychological explanation (all of which are based on the mechanism of natural necessity)" (285,68).[19] Garve makes points (1) and (2) in the following passages quoted by Kant:

> "States must be perceived and distinguished so that one of them can be given *preference* above the others before a person can proceed to choose among them and, consequently, before one can settle on a certain end. But a state that is *preferred* to other states of being by a creature endowed with consciousness of itself and of its state is, when this state is present and perceived by that creature, a good state; and a series of such good states is the most general concept expressed by the term *happiness*." Further: "A law presupposes motives, and motives in their turn presuppose a previously perceived difference between a worse state and one that is better. This perceived difference is the element of the

concept of happiness, etc." Furthermore: *"The motives behind every effort arise from happiness* in the most general sense of the term, including compliance with the moral law. I must first know in general whether something is good before I can ask whether fulfillment of moral duties falls under the rubric of the good. Man must have an *incentive* to set him in motion before he can establish a goal towards which this motion should be directed" (281–82, 65–66).

Garve is arguing that practical deliberation (including moral deliberation) is instrumental in nature—actions being approved as rational to the degree that they represent efficient steps toward an outcome identified by the agent as "the good." But what does it mean, asks Garve, for an agent to identify some outcome or goal as good *(das Gute)?* Simply this: it is an *object of preference (Vorzug)* (or want, or desire). And what is an object of preference? Simply this: an *object expected to produce happiness* when attained. Thus (oversimplifying a bit) Garve seems to be offering the following equation: good = preference satisfaction = happiness. According to Garve, to say that I regard something as a good is simply to say that I prefer it, and the only intelligible ground for preferring something is the belief that it will ultimately play a role in my overall happiness. Thus respect for duty—Kant's sole candidate for a motive that is truly moral—either does not exist or may be reductively analyzed in terms of the desire for personal happiness. In short, I do my duty either because it pleases me to do so or because I fear that I will feel bad if I do not.[20]

Kant's response to Garve is complex and overlaps, at certain points, with Bishop Butler's well-known response to Hobbes's doctrine of psychological egoism.[21] Kant's response, as I interpret it, can be distilled into three basic arguments: (1) The phenomenological evidence provided by honest introspection reveals that in fact we all recognize a sharp distinction between the motive of respect for duty and all motives concerned with our own welfare or happiness. (2) We do take satisfaction when we do our duty and do indeed fear bad feelings when we do not. Such feelings are not the basis of respect for duty, however, but indeed can themselves be understood only through the realization that we value duty for its own sake. (3) The apparent plausibility of Garve's argument rests upon a variety of conceptual confusions and ambiguities—e.g., with respect to the meanings of such terms as "preference" and "the good." Personal inclination does play a role in determining duty, but not in the way that Garve thinks; the role it does play is not only consistent with Kant's theory but is required to make sense of that theory.

Let me now explore each of these three arguments in more detail.

(1) *The phenomenology of moral experience.* According to Kant, the nature of moral motivation often reveals deep psychological conflicts between what we see as our duty and what we want or desire (in any ordinary sense of "want" or "desire"). Think, for example, of duties owed to strangers (people for whom we have no feelings) or to enemies (people toward whom we have negative feelings and who may even be in a position to harm us). We clearly can have such duties and sometimes at least find ourselves acting because of them in the full consciousness of the fact that, given our feelings, we would prefer to be acting otherwise. The specially conflicted nature of moral motivation (the aspect of it that makes us see duty as a *categorical impera-tive* [22]) simply does not emerge on Garve's account—a flaw that prevents it from being an accurate picture of our shared moral phenomenology. Kant writes,

> Everyone is capable of rigorous self-examination and can perceive himself becoming conscious not just of the absence of such contributing motives [for happiness], but even more of self-denial regarding many motives that conflict with the idea of duty and thus with the maxim of striving toward that purity [in one's concept of duty]. . . . Indeed, if the concept of duty has any validity for him, he will feel disgust at calculating the advantages that could accrue to him through its violation, just as if he still had the choice. . . . [The claim that duty is based on selfishness] contradicts . . . the inward experience that no idea more elevates and inspires enthusiasm in the human mind than that of pure moral conviction, which reveres duty above all else, struggles with life's countless evils, even its most seductive temptations, and nonetheless conquers all. . . . That man is aware that he can

do this because he ought to reveals deep tendencies toward the divine that allow him to feel a sacred awe regarding the greatness and sublimity of his true vocation (285–87,68–70).

We all, of course, experience frequent conflicts between our various desires (should I continue the pleasures of smoking or aim instead for a long if boring life?), but the conflict between duty and any desire seems different in kind—different because it at least appears as a conflict *with* my empirical self (as a bundle of given wants) and not *within* my empirical self (one want against another). The difference in kind is marked, at least in part, in the special pride I feel—the special respect I feel for myself—when I choose duty over inclination.[23]

(2) *The pleasures of being moral.* This last argument by Kant could simply be taken as evidence that the ultimate motivation for moral behavior is indeed selfish. It surely feels good to take pride in one's actions. Thus perhaps the real motive for moral behavior is the desire to get the feeling of pride and sublimity that comes from doing one's duty. (At the very least one may be motivated to avoid the painful guilt feelings that come from not doing one's duty.) Does not moral motivation then boil down to the search for personal happiness after all?

Kant's answer here is clever. He does not deny that we often obtain considerable happiness through acting morally—particularly the pride or self-satisfaction attendant to such behavior. But what is it about such behavior, asks Kant, that gives us the special kind of pleasure involved? Surely it is pleasure—prideful pleasure—that we take in seeing that we are creatures capable of appreciating moral duty and *being motivated by it!* Otherwise what would we have to be proud of? Seeing ourselves as motivated by a desire to get moral pride would necessarily preclude our ever getting moral pride, and thus—if moral pride truly exists—we must actually be motivated by duty (or we must at least deceive ourselves into thinking that we are so motivated). The good feelings generate neither duty nor respect for duty; they are rather generated by duty itself:

> Happiness consists of everything (but nothing more than) nature vouchsafes us; virtue, however, consists of what no one but man can give or take from himself. If one were to demur and say that

by failing to be virtuous a man can at least incur blame and pure
moral self-reproach, thus self-dissatisfaction, and can as a result
make himself unhappy, we might assuredly agree. But only the
virtuous man . . . is capable of suffering this pure moral dissatisfaction (which does not arise from any disadvantageous results
of his actions, but from their very contrariness to law). Consequently, this feeling is not the cause but the effect of his virtu-
ousness, and the motivation to be virtuous cannot be derived
from this unhappiness (if one so chooses to name regret over a
misdeed) (283n, 67n).

Thus, at least in the realm of moral phenomenology, Kant
seems to win the battle with Garve. He is far closer to being
right in his description of the internal life of the normal moral
agent.[24]

Praising Kant for the accuracy of his phenomenological account of morality should not, of course, be confused with an
endorsement of his rich (bloated?) metaphysical account of such
matters.[25] Although Kant has an elaborate and controversial
account of the contra-causal ("noumenal") freedom that he
thinks must be present in the world in order for moral motivation to be distinguishable from typical desire-based motivation,
we do not need to accept all this to grant Kant's phenomenological point. The phenomenological point is simply this: normal
human beings, though often motivated by means/ends rationality, are sometimes motivated in a different way. They understand moral reasons, conduct moral conversations and listen to
moral arguments, and are then moved to act on the basis of
these reasons and arguments. This is at least part of what Kant
means by "moral autonomy," and this part surely requires no
controversial or unscientific assumptions about non-natural causation. (Assume, if you want, that responsiveness to moral reasons is encoded in human nature through some complex inter-
play between biology and conditioning.) Such a minimalist
account of moral autonomy is, for example, totally compatible
with a Freudian theory of the personality—where the "superego" plays the role of respect for duty. Freud's theory of moral
motivation overlaps Kant's to a substantial degree (it was perhaps influenced by it), and anyone who thinks that Freud has

insight on moral phenomenology must agree that Kant has insight here as well.[26]

One additional point, obvious but sometimes missed, is worth stressing. It is easy to misstate the nature of the tension between duty and inclination because the phrase "acting out of respect for duty" is in some cases a misleading way for Kant to put his motivational point. Kant is not suggesting that, against all inclination, one is to go out looking for duties so that one can act with moral worth. This is not how duty arises in the life of the normal person. In the typical case, one wants to do something (e.g., spend a large amount of money on a new wardrobe); and one wants to do it in the perfectly ordinary sense in which "wants" means something like "desires" or "will take pleasure in." (What one wants to do in this subjective sense is, when properly specified, what Kant calls a "maxim.") Before acting on such a subjective maxim, however, the moral person who respects duty will use the categorical imperative to test the maxim for its moral permissibility (i.e., to make sure that the maxim is not *contrary* to duty). If the maxim passes the test, the person is then free to act on it. If the person now acts, is it true to say that he acted from duty? In one sense, the answer is surely *no;* for the best explanation for his new wardrobe is "he wanted it" and a crazy and unbelievable explanation would be "having it was required by duty" or (even stranger) "he bought the wardrobe because buying it was morally permissible." Yet surely the action is properly motivated and surely satisfies the Kantian sense of acting out of respect for duty. The moral: respecting duty should not be interpreted as the shunning of all personal pleasures and desires for happiness in order to respond to the direct call of duty. It should rather be interpreted as the commitment to pass all such desires through a certain kind of *screening* or *filtering* device—the device provided by the categorical imperative and its demand for universalization. When one uses this screening device and accepts its verdict as final, one has—in the important sense—acted out of respect for duty. For the Kantian, the inner voice of morality functions more as a censor than as a drill sergeant.[27]

(3) *The seductive charms of the selfishness theory.* If the kind of

egoism-hedonism taught by Garve fails to capture our ordinary moral consciousness, then why are Garve and others still inclined to reject the Kantian account? The answer, surely, is their belief that the Kantian theory has such deep flaws that it must be rejected even if this requires the rejection of our ordinary moral consciousness as erroneous. What kind of support might they have for such a negative assessment? Such support could be either conceptual (Kant's theory is incoherent) or scientific (Kant's theory is incompatible with the naturalism of scientific psychology). I have already indicated why I think that the latter argument fails, so let me briefly consider the former.

On this issue, we have the familiar Hobbes-Butler dog and pony show with Garve and Kant as stand-ins. Garve argues that it makes no sense to think that a person could ever act unless he prefers to act in that way and that this truth makes any theory other than psychological egoism/hedonism incoherent. Kant responds that this argument plays on two different meanings of "prefer." "I prefer X" may simply mean "I have some reason for choosing X." Kant can happily concede that all actions are in this sense based on preference, for this is just another way of saying that all actions are motivated; the claim that all actions are motivated may be tautological. ("Jones had a preference for his duty" is in this sense harmless and unobjectionable.) A quite different meaning of "I prefer X," however, is "I think it will give me pleasure to do X." Kant cannot, of course, regard "It will give Jones pleasure to do his duty" as a harmless and unobjectionable analysis of moral motivation. He does not really have to confront this possibility, however, since the claim is not self-evident (not even intrinsically plausible) and Garve gives no good argument for it. Although it is true that duty is a matter of preference where preference is simply equivalent to motivation, this does not entail (is not even an argument for) the claim that duty is a matter of preference where preference is equivalent to pleasure.

After arguing that Garve also trades on ambiguity in the phrase "the good" (confusing instrumental good with final good, conditional good with unconditional good, and physical good with moral good), Kant leaves this final assessment of Garve's attack on his theory of moral motivation:

[It] can in no way be said that every state I *prefer* to all others is regarded by me as happiness. For I must first be certain that I do not act contrary to my duty; only then am I allowed to look toward such happiness as I can make compatible with my morally (not physically) good state. ... Therefore, that old litany—namely, that this feeling, consequently a pleasure that we set out as an end, is the first cause of the will's determination and that, as a result, happiness (of which that pleasure is an element) is, indeed, the basis of all objective necessity in action and hence of all obligation—is a trifling sophistry. If one cannot cease asking questions after a cause has been proposed for a particular effect, one will finally make the effect the cause itself (283–84,67).

CONTRA HOBBES

Kant claims that the section on Garve was addressed to the topic of theory and practice as it impacts on the moral *individual*—"in relation to the well-being of each *man*" (277,63). This long second section of the essay is directed to the person as a *political being*—as a being, not now simply worrying about the possibility of moral motivation, but seeking to enjoy the benefits of a basic social structure that guarantees fundamental rights at a constitutional level. If Kant's theory cannot help in this political task, it will have failed in one important way to apply in practice. Thus Kant needs to show that it can help, and this is the primary task of the section.

Kant sees this task as having two main aspects—aspects that do not sit comfortably together. He wishes (1) to demonstrate that his theory can help in the design of just (i.e., rights-respecting) civic institutions and (2) to demonstrate that his theory shows why citizens have no right to revolt against legal authority even when that authority violates their rights and ignores or perverts the justice of their institutions.

Although I think that most of Kant's arguments against revolution are confused (e.g., involving simplistic positivistic doctrines of sovereignty), I plan to ignore this issue in the present essay and concentrate solely on his account of justice—drawing on the material on revolution only when it is useful to the other project. I do this for the following reason: since even before the publication of "Theory and Practice," the material on revolution has received essentially all of the attention. (It is indeed the only aspect of this essay that has not been generally neglected.) Kant's contemporaries eagerly awaited the work because they wanted to see if Kant, the world's leading philosophical liberal, would support the French revolution. Later commentators, generally uncomfortable with Kant's apparent refusal in the essay to support revolution under any circumstances, have generally probed the consistency of this refusal with his general moral and political doctrines. Anyone now writing on this topic would need to survey this enormous body of literature—a task not possible in the present context.[28]

Although the second section of the essay is said by Kant to be "against Hobbes," Hobbes's thought receives no detailed commentary. The negative reference to Hobbes essentially serves one main purpose: Kant wants to put his reader on notice that, in spite of his agreement with Hobbes that citizens have no *coercive* rights against political authorities, he does *not* agree with Hobbes that citizens have no important rights of any kind against the state. (Recall the United States Constitution here. It grants citizens many fundamental rights against the state, but among these is not the right of revolution.) Thus, the primary point of this section of Kant's essay is to identify the basic rights of citizens and to place those rights within a general scheme of justification—i.e., within a theory of justice.

Kant's primary purpose in this section is to defend the principles of a liberal social and political order—i.e., a basic social structure that will be just in the sense that it will protect the fundamental natural rights of all citizens—particularly the inalienable right of freedom.[29] If such a liberal theory is to survive the challenge that it works in theory but not in practice, it must provide a test or criterion for such a social order—i.e., some device that will allow us to recognize when a social order does respect rights in the proper way. For Kant, a model of universal agreement (adapted from social contract theory) is such a device. He writes,

> [The original contract] is a *mere idea* of reason, one, however, that has indubitable (practical) reality. Specifically, it obligates every legislator to formulate laws in such a way that they *could* have sprung from the unified will of the entire people and to regard

every subject, insofar as he desires to be a citizen, as if he had joined in voting for such a will. For that is the criterion of every public law's conformity with right. If a public law is so formulated that an entire people *could not possibly* agree to it (as, e.g., that a particular class of *subjects* has the hereditary privilege of being a *ruling class*), it is not just; however, if *only* it is *possible* that a people could agree to it, it is a duty to regard that law as just, even if the people are presently in such a position or disposition of mind *[Denkungsart]* that if asked it would probably withhold its consent (297,77–78).

Kant is, I think, outlining some very important ideas here—setting the groundwork for the constructivist methodology of Rawls and the related conversational methodologies of Habermas and others.

If a just society is essentially (as Kant says) a society that treats the natural right of freedom as sacred, this freedom cannot be interpreted simply to mean the freedom to do what you want or the freedom to be bound only by rules to which you actually consent. This account of freedom would allow no punishment of criminals (who wants to be punished?), no taxation (who wants to be taxed?), and no duties imposed on those citizens of a democracy who did not vote with the majority (where is their actual consent?) Such an account would, in short, allow no *coercion;* and even just states, as states, are necessarily coercive. Coercion (forcing people to do what they do not want to do) is thus a political necessity. However, certain forms of coercion are clearly inconsistent with respect for human freedom. For Kant, a clear example is *paternalism:*

> No one can compel me (in accordance with his beliefs about the welfare of others) to be happy after his fashion; instead, every person may seek happiness in the way that seems best to him, if only he does not violate the freedom of others to strive toward such similar ends as are compatible with everyone's freedom under a possible universal law (i.e., this right of others) (290,72).

For the state to compel as a parent (treating subjects like "immature children," 290–91,73) is necessarily to fail to respect the freedom of citizens. For the state to thwart the actual desires of citizens and to compel them even when they do not actually consent, however, is not necessarily to fail in such duties of respect. The difference? In the former case, it is impossible to imagine all citizens capable of moral reasoning consenting, after extended argument and conversation, to a strong principle of paternalism.[30] (It is also impossible to imagine all such citizens consenting to permanent humiliation and powerlessness based on hereditary class or racial status.) It is, however, not difficult to imagine them all consenting to some legal principles that require punishment, some principles of taxation, and the general principle of majority rule. This, then, is Kant's test for justice: a principle of coercion is just if it is *possible* that every citizen could consent to it in an environment of mutually respectful moral conversation.

Is this a good test? When it seems to work well, it is tacitly operating on one very important assumption—an assumption that perhaps keeps the test from being as foundational as Kant thinks. The assumption is that the imagined grounds for consent or dissent be *reasonable*. The powerful idea, I take it, is this: To respect all persons as moral equals, we must consider (anticipate if necessary) the kind of objections that any thoughtful and morally sensitive person might make against our proposed coercion and regard the coercion as unjust if we see such objections as possible grounds for a reasonable refusal of consent. Mere imagined refusal or assent—regardless of its reasonableness—would surely not do, however. I can, for example, *imagine* persons failing to see the importance of free political speech for the preservation of just institutions and thus I can imagine them agreeing to coercive curtailment of political speech. I would not want to conclude from this, however, that such coercion is just. Like Kant, who defends the "freedom of the pen" as the most basic political right (304,82), I would want to maintain that free political speech is a requirement of justice even in the face of my thought experiment (wherein I can imagine all citizens agreeing to its unreasonable curtailment). Thus surely the operative test must really be this: a coercive rule is just if it is possible that all citizens could agree to it *on grounds that are informed and reasonable.*

If reasonableness is accepted as a constraint on possible consent, however, then consent itself perhaps cannot play quite the foundational role that Kant envisions. It will at least share the foundational role with an account of reasonableness. Although Kant speaks generally of the natural right of freedom, he clearly does not regard all freedoms as equally fundamental. (This is revealed in his own insistence on the priority of freedom of the pen.) It is impossible, however, to sort freedoms into categories of differential importance in terms of freedom itself. Some other value is required. My own view is that the best candidate is a concept of the *human good*—a concept allowing us to rank as most important those freedoms that are intrinsically bound up with a reasonable account of the human good. Political freedom is more important than (for example) the freedom to collect string, because the former is closely tied to the human good in a way that the latter is not. And what about sexual freedom—e.g., for homosexuals? We surely cannot even begin to make a case for such freedom as fundamental without developing an account of love, sexuality, intimacy, and the role they play in a full and good human life. If we see sexual freedom purely as freedom of recreational pleasure, we will trivialize it and make it a very poor candidate indeed for a fundamental liberty. Could we imagine all citizens reasonably consenting to repressive rules with respect to homosexuality? If sex is just recreation, I think the answer is yes. If sex is more deeply tied to the good life, however, I think the answer is no. In short, if liberal societies must rank liberties (some more fundamental than others), then strong forms of the neutrality principle advocated by Ronald Dworkin and others must be rejected.[31]

Kant seems officially committed to a neutrality principle (290,72), in part because he finds it difficult to articulate a complex account of the human good. Either he sees it simply in terms of our moral powers (much too narrow—too moralistic—an account) or he thinks that it cannot be distinguished merely from the desire to be happy—a value on which he pours (as usual) a large dose of contempt:

> The concept of external right in general derives entirely from the concept of freedom in the external relations among men and has nothing whatsoever to do with the ends that men have from nature (the objective of obtaining happiness), or with setting out

the means for achieving them; and, thus, these latter ends must never be intermixed as determining grounds with those laws. (289,72)

[W]hen one looks to the *people's welfare,* everything depends not in the least on theory but only on practice that derives from experience. . . . [The concept of right] is grounded in *a priori* principles (for what is right can never be taught by experience) (306,84).[32]

Even if one agrees with Kant that the concept of external right should not depend upon happiness (as mere pleasure), one does not have to conclude from this that the concept of external right should not depend on any account of the human good. (Indeed, in my view, no plausible account of the human good will attempt to interpret it merely as pleasure.) At one point in "Theory and Practice" Kant seems to recognize this. The issue is religious freedom and Kant's desire to defend it as a fundamental right:

Whatever a people cannot decree for itself cannot be decreed for it by the legislator. . . . If, for example, the question is whether one can view a certain previously instituted ecclesiastical constitution as expressing the permanently enduring actual will . . . of the legislator, one would have first to ask whether a people *may* enact for itself a law [specifying] that, once adopted, certain articles of faith and religious practices should endure forever, and thus whether it may prevent itself in the person of its descendants from further advancement in religious insight or from eventually correcting old errors? It will now be clear that an original contract among the people that made this a law would be null and void, for it would conflict with humanity's vocation and end (304–5,83).

Here Kant seems to impose a constraint on his consent test— a constraint involving the value of "humanity's vocation and end." It is unclear just what this means, but it strikes me that it must in part be some notion of the human good that is not a mere matter of personal preference. What seems crucial to Kant here is not a general failure of possible consent to such a law, but rather a failure of consent on the part of persons who *understand the nature and value of religion in human life.* There are, then, perhaps some beginnings here of the kind of account that Kant needs and that he develops in more detail in other writings.[33] In "Theory and Practice," however, it is nothing more than a mere hint.

Contra Mendelssohn

This final section of Kant's essay is not, in my view, really about what Kant says it is about: right and justice in international law. It is directed against Moses Mendelssohn, but not against anything Mendelssohn said about international law or "the cosmopolitan point of view." Most commentators take Kant's own gloss to heart, however, and note this final section of "Theory and Practice" merely as a brief anticipation of the doctrines that will be developed in detail in the 1795 *Perpetual Peace*.

What, then, is the real point of this section? It is, in my view, a *counsel against moral despair*. Note the question with which Kant begins the section—a question having little to do with international justice but a great deal to do with the temptations of moral pessimism:

> Is the human race as a whole to be loved; or is it something that one is to view with distaste, wishing it all the best (so as not to become misanthropic), but not really expecting it, so that we turn our attention away from it, though with feelings of regret? . . . We cannot avoid hating in human nature . . . what is and will remain evil, especially the deliberate and mutual violation of man's most sacred rights. We may not actually want to do men harm because of this evil, yet we do want as little to do with them as possible (307,85).

Mendelssohn had defended the pessimistic view,[34] and this is the sense in which Kant's final section—an attempt to meet the pessimism—is truly *contra* Mendelssohn. There is nothing more basic to Kant's moral and political outlook than his view of human beings as sacred or precious—beings having the unique value of *dignity* (*Würde*) that is the foundation of their basic rights. If human beings do not deserve such respect, however, then Kant's theory—which assumes that they do—will fail in practice. The view that human beings are sacred is, of course, basic to the Christian worldview in which Kant was raised, but Kant the philosopher will not allow himself, through mere faith, to avail himself of its theological defense, that people are sacred because they are created in God's image. If people are genuinely sacred, it must be because of something about them that can be understood in a secular, empirical way.

But is this possible? Some philosophers, such as Robert Nozick, have argued that the demonstrated human capacity for unspeakable evil (e.g., the Holocaust) shows that human beings are dramatically unworthy of the kind of deference paid to them by Kant.[35] Though Mendelssohn's view was not as bleak as Nozick's, neither is it terribly upbeat: "The human race as a whole swings slowly back and forth, and it never takes a few steps forward without soon afterwards relapsing twice as fast into its previous state" (307,85).[36]

It is in responding to Mendelssohn's pessimism that Kant makes reference to emerging international law—only as an *example* of a general point he wants to make about humanity as a progressive species: "Human nature never seems less lovable than in the relations among entire peoples" (312,89). Yet Kant sees signs that moral tendencies in (at least some) people are gradually moving the world toward an international legal order, an order that will end the wars that have brought out the worst in humanity. If human history does indeed continue to move in this way, it will be easier (according to Kant) to see humanity as a moral and progressive species that is perhaps deserving of some special respect. But who really knows? Kant, rejecting (in philosophy) all appeals to religious faith, can do no better than close "Theory and Practice" with a statement of secular faith:

> If seeing a virtuous man struggling with tribulations and temptations towards evil and yet holding his own against them is a sight fit for a divinity, so is it a most unfit sight for even the commonest but well intentioned man, not to mention a divinity, to see the human race advancing from period to period towards virtue and then soon afterwards to see it again falling as deeply back into vice and misery as it was before. . . . I will thus permit myself to assume that since the human race's natural end is to make steady cultural progress, its moral end is to be conceived as progressing toward the better. . . . For I rest my case on my innate duty . . . to affect posterity that it will become continually better. . . . In this latter I also take into account human nature, which, since

respect for right and duty remains alive in it, I cannot regard as so immersed in evil that after many unsuccessful attempts, morally practical reason will finally triumph and show it to be lovable. Thus, even on the cosmopolitan level I stand by my assertion: What on rational grounds is true in theory is also useful in practice (311–13,86–89).[37]

Kant had not, of course, seen evil on the scale that we have known in the twentieth century. Suppose he had known of the Holocaust. Would he have joined Nozick in seeing it as evidence of total human worthlessness? I think not; I think his moral faith would have survived even this. After all, unless human beings are precious, what is so bad about murdering six million of them? Properly to condemn the Holocaust—as a crime against humanity—requires a view of humanity as having a value at least very like Kant's value of dignity.[38] Thus Nozick's moral pessimism is probably premature—probably even inconsistent with his own activities as a concerned philosopher. Kant says this of Mendelssohn:

> The hope for better times, without which an earnest desire to do something that benefits the general good would never have warmed the human heart, has always influenced the work of the well-intentioned; and good Mendelssohn must have counted on it when he so eagerly strove for the enlightenment and welfare of the nation to which he belonged. Because unless others after him continued further down the same path, he could not by himself, alone, rationally hope to bring them about (309,86–87).

Thus here we find Kant, the great secular rationalist, adopting as an article of faith the view of humanity and its possibilities necessary to avoid moral despair and to leave the door open for whatever good may be realizable. (We must think and act *as if* what is true in theory is also possible in practice, since life is bearable and meaningful on no other assumption.) Here also we find Kant, one of the supposed founders of the philosophy of "possessive individualism," adopting a communitarianism of the most ambitious sort: hopeful and sympathetic fellowship with the entire human community in its present and future generations and admiration for those who (like Mendelssohn with respect to Judaism) seek to preserve the special values of their own subcommunities within such an ongoing scheme of human progress. Perhaps rationalistic libertarians are not Kant's only natural bedfellows after all.

NOTES

1. The full title of Kant's essay is "Über den Gemeinspruch: Das mag in der Theorie richtig sein, taugt aber nicht für die Praxis" ("On the Proverb: That May Be True in Theory but Is of No Practical Use"). The standard citation source for this essay is Band VIII (volume 8) of *Kant's gesammelte Schriften*, hrsg. Konigliche Preussische Akademie der Wissenschaften (Berlin and Leipzig: Walter de Gruyter, 1904–). In the present essay I am mainly relying on the translation by my colleague Ted Humphrey in his *Perpetual Peace and Other Essays* (Indianapolis: Hackett, 1983), 61–92. All page references to Kant's essay will be given in the following form in the body of the text: the page number from the Academy edition will be given first, followed by the page number from the Humphrey translation—e.g., (275, 61).

2. Kant says that morality is quite different from speculative metaphysics in this regard. The claims of speculative metaphysics (e.g., claims to detailed knowledge about the nature and will of God) tend to involve "mere empty ideas that have either no practical use whatsoever or even one that would be disadvantageous. In such cases, therefore, that proverbial saying could be perfectly correct" (276, 62).

3. Dieter Henrich, ed. *Kant, Gentz, Rehberg: Über Theorie und Praxis, Einleitung von Dieter Henrich* (Frankfurt am Main: Suhrkamp Verlag, 1967), 10. ("Er spricht von der Theorie, welche dem sittlichen Bewusstsein und Handeln selbst innewohnt. Als solche ist sie eo ipso in praktischer Wirkung.") This very useful volume contains Kant's essay, the passages from Christian Garve to which Kant responds, and essays written in response to Kant by Friedrich Gentz and August Wilhelm Rehberg. Henrich's introduction is very useful.

4. *Grundlegung zur Metaphysik der Sitten* (*Foundations of the Metaphysics of Morals*, trans. Lewis White Beck, Indianapolis: Bobbs-Merrill Library of Liberal Arts, 1959, First Section and Second Section).

5. Kant is perhaps more confident than he should be that it will be easy to identify shared moral beliefs—a confidence perhaps generated by his generally addressing too narrow a sample even of his own culture. But, unless we propose to treat other persons with contempt and not attempt to engage them in moral conversation at all, what

alternative do we have except to search for some points of shared agreement? Idealized models of conversation and agreement (in Kant, Rawls, and Habermas) can perhaps be of assistance here.

6. I expand on this idea in my essay "Marxism and Retribution," *Philosophy and Public Affairs* 2:3 (Spring 1973), reprinted in my *Retribution, Justice and Therapy: Essays in the Philosophy of Law* (Dordrecht: Reidel, 1979). See also *Life Sentences, Rage and Survival Behind Bars,* ed. Wilbert Rideau and Ron Wikberg (New York: Times Books, 1992). I wonder how many people, after reading this book and seeing what life in an American prison is really like, will continue to feel comfortable saying "they deserve it"? There is, of course, this very important point still to be said in defense of the retributive theory: only by regarding deserved suffering as the norm for legitimate punishment can we see the terrible injustice of what we are actually doing. For more on this point see my "Three Mistakes About Retributivism," *Analysis* (April 1971), reprinted in *Retribution, Justice and Therapy.*

7. Stephen Carter has noted that the way in which minority academics are perceived is to a large degree a function of the current debates over the justice and wisdom of affirmative action in university hiring. See his *Reflections of an Affirmative Action Baby* (New York: Basic Books, 1991).

8. "[People] may ... picture themselves as meritorious, feeling themselves guilty of no such offenses as they see others burdened with; nor do they ever inquire whether good luck should not have the credit, or whether by reason of the cast of mind which they could discover, if they only would, in their own inmost nature, they would not have practiced similar vices, had not inability, temperament, training, and circumstances of time and place which serve to tempt one (matters which are not imputable), kept them out of the way of those vices. This dishonesty, by which we humbug ourselves and which thwarts the establishing of a true moral disposition in us, extends itself outwardly also to falsehood and deception of others. If this is not to be termed wickedness, it at least deserves the name of worthlessness, and is an element in the radical evil of human nature, which (inasmuch as it puts out of tune the moral capacity to judge what a man is to be taken for, and renders wholly uncertain both internal and external attribution of responsibility) constitutes the foul taint in our race," *Religion innerhalb Grenzen der blossen Vernunft (Religion Within the Limits of Reason Alone,)* trans. T. Greene and H. Hudson (New York: Harper and Row, 1960), 33–34.

9. Except, perhaps, in passing. In discussing the defects in Christian Garve's account of moral consciousness (284–85,68), Kant specu-

lates that Garve knows in his heart that Kant's account is correct but is mislead by his head—i.e., by some faulty theoretical assumptions in speculative metaphysics.

10. So-called "Good Samaritan Statutes" often impose duties of this nature: "A person who knows that another is exposed to grave physical harm shall, to the extent that the same can be rendered without danger or peril to himself or without interference with important duties owed to others, give reasonable assistance to the exposed person unless that assistance or care is being provided by others" (Vt. Stat. Ann. tit 12, Section 519).

11. Philippa Foot, "Are Moral Considerations Overriding?" in her *Virtues and Vices* (Berkeley: University of California Press, 1978), 186–87. A very rich discussion of the issues raised by Foot is to be found in Samuel Scheffler, *Human Morality* (Oxford: Oxford University Press, 1992), esp. chapter 4.

12. Kant does not always miss this point, of course. Indeed, he characterizes an *imperfect duty* as one that "permits exceptions in the interest of inclination" (*Foundations*, 39, note 10). What he means by this is that an imperfect duty such as charity allows each person to exercise some choice over the persons or causes which will be the beneficiaries of his charity (e.g., cancer research or food for the hungry) and the nature and quantity of the sacrifices that will be made (e.g., volunteer work or financial contributions). "Exception" (*Ausnahme*) is a poor word choice here, since Kant does not really mean to say that one may make exceptions to the duty out of inclination but rather that some inclinations with respect to person, time, place, and manner may enter into the specification of the duty itself—the duty being understood informally as a duty to do something for somebody sometime. So specified, the duty allows us some choice—based on inclination—of how to fill in the variables. The issue of the limits that might be placed on such choices raises interesting questions, but they must be left for another paper. For a rich discussion of Kant on the duty never to lie, see Christine M. Korsgaard, "The Right to Lie: Kant on Dealing with Evil," *Philosophy and Public Affairs* 15:4 (Fall 1986), 325–49. For more on the perfect/imperfect duty distinction see my *Kant: The Philosophy of Right* (London: Macmillan, 1970), 51–53, and especially Lewis White Beck, *A Commentary on Kant's Critique of Practical Reason* (Chicago: University of Chicago Press, 1960), 147ff.

13. I think that at best you look all right but I lie and say "you look great" to build your confidence immediately before you give a public speech. Do we not all consider this permissible?

14. As I long ago argued in my *Kant: The Philosophy of Right* (*supra*

note 12), I think that Kantian universalizability is best understood not as what Seyla Benhabib has called "a silent thought experiment" but rather in terms of models of conversation and agreement of the kind that one finds in the writings of John Rawls. (Kant's own best statement of such a model is to be found in the second section of "Theory and Practice.") Perhaps the question "Is lying under these circumstances universalizable?" is best interpreted as "Would lying in these circumstances be permitted by the best account of the rules of truth telling?"—where "best account" is interpreted as "the account that would emerge from a certain model of conversation and agreement." Even if social lies are universalizable, however, it is less clear that they are consistent with the duty to treat all persons with the respect owed to them as ends in themselves. For the claim that lying runs into particular problems from the respect for persons (second) formulation of the categorical imperative, see Korsgaard, "The Right to Lie." In Kant's 1797 essay "On a Supposed Right to Lie from Altruistic Motives" (*Über ein vermeintes Recht aus Menschenliebe zu lügen*) he argues, unpersuasively in my judgment, that all lies fail the universalizability test. See also his argument in the *Doctrine of Virtue (Tugendlehre)* (chapter 2, section 1) that lying, involving a misuse of our faculty of communication, violates a duty we have to ourselves. (The best translation of the essay may be found in Immanuel Kant, *Critique of Practical Reason and Other Writings in Moral Philosophy*, trans. Lewis W. Beck [Chicago: University of Chicago Press, 1949], 346–50. The best translation of the passage from the *Tugendlehre* is to be found in Mary Gregor's translation of the entire *Metaphysics of Morals (Metaphysik der Sitten)* [Cambridge: Cambridge University Press, 1991], 225–27. A revised Beck translation of the *Critique of Practical Reason* alone was published by Macmillan in 1992.) For more on the conversation-agreement model of universalizability, see Seyla Benhabib, "Afterword: Communicative Ethics and Contemporary Controversies in Practical Philosophy" in *The Communicative Ethics Controversy*, ed. Seyla Benhabib and Fred Dallmayr (Cambridge: MIT Press, 1990).

15. Kant is here, of course, doing nothing more than stating his famous principle that "ought" implies "can"—a principle he never actually stated in the exact form in which it is often quoted: "One of Kant's most famous 'statements'—"Thou canst because thou shouldst"—does not exist in his writings in this neat form (see David Baumgardt, 'Legendary Quotations and the Lack of References,' *Journal of the History of Ideas* 7 [1947]: 116). But statements that express this inference less succinctly abound, e.g., *Critique of Practical Reason* 30:118–19; *Critique of Pure Reason*, A807-B835; *Über den Gemeinspruch*

8:287; *Metaphysik der Sitten* 6:380; *Streit der Fakultäten* 7:43–44; *Vorlesungen über Metaphysik,* ed. Kowalewski, 600; *Opus postumum 21:16."* (Beck, *Commentary,* 200n.)

16. Kant's response is directed primarily to some explicit criticisms of his views made by Garve in the 1792 *Versuche über verschiedene Gegenstände aus der Moral, der Litteratur und dem gesellschaftlichen Leben (Essays on Various Topics from Morals, Literature, and Social Life).* The most relevant portions will be found in Henrich, *Kant, Gentz, Rehberg.*

17. See, for example, *Foundations,* 16ff. Kant's actual claim is that *acts* have moral worth only if performed from a motive of respect for duty, but *agent* assessment is (at least in my judgment) his real concern in such passages. As he makes clear in his distinction between *pflichtmässig* actions (right actions or actions in accord with duty) and actions performed *aus Pflicht* (actions motivated by duty), he does not think that motives must enter into all relevant moral assessments of actions. See my "Kant's Concept of a Right Action," *Monist* 51:4 (1967), 574–98.

18. The depth of the conflict between such motives and Kantian duty is often overstated. The Kantian can surely grant, for example, the value of these motives and actions based on them so long as they are pursued with the constraints of a basic structure that is just. By far the richest discussion of such matters is to be found in the essays of Barbara Herman—who argues not merely that Kant can allow a place for such motivational considerations but that he must acknowledge them as "principles of moral salience" in order to apply the categorical imperative. See her "The Practice of Moral Judgment," *Journal of Philosophy* 82 (1985), 414–36, and "Agency, Attachment, and Difference," *Ethics* 101:4 (1991), 775–97.

19. Some of Garve's other claims really are just simple misunderstandings of Kant, and I will not bother to discuss them in detail. Contrary to Garve, Kant is not a sour killjoy who counsels that human beings should renounce their desires for happiness; he simply argues that they must forget about such motives when determining their moral duties. Neither does Kant's belief that a moral world (e.g., a world governed by a just God) would distribute human happiness in proportion to human virtue commit him to the belief that either human beings or God is motivated by a desire for happiness in seeking this outcome. They are motivated, surely, by the perceived *justice* of such a pattern of distribution.

20. The challenge posed by Garve is essentially the same challenge addressed by Kant in the long second footnote on pages 17–18 of *Foundations.* The footnote begins this way: "It might be objected that I

seek to take refuge in an obscure feeling behind the world 'respect.' "
Several of Kant's arguments in the note appear again in the response
to Garve.

21. Those not familiar with Butler's attempted refutation of the
doctrine of psychological egoism that he imputes to Hobbes will find a
good general discussion of the matter in the chapter on Butler in C. D.
Broad, *Five Types of Ethical Theory* (Patterson, N.J.: Littlefield, Adams,
1959).

22. Any rational demand—even a prudential one—can conflict
with some powerful desires, and this is why (according to Kant) all
demands of reason often appear as imperatives. Moral imperatives
appear as *categorical,* however—by which Kant means they appear to
bind regardless of *any* of our desires and continue to bind even when
they are in conflict with *all* of our desires. See Lewis White Beck,
"Apodictic Imperatives," in his *Studies in the Philosophy of Kant* (Indianapolis: Bobbs-Merrill, 1965).

23. Someone might well argue that Kant is making more out of this
than he should. Might one not also feel considerable pride in being
able to give up smoking? It is difficult to be moral, but it is also difficult
to be prudent. Thus overcoming difficulties in either realm could be
an occasion of enhanced self-esteem. Kant may still be on to something,
however. Perhaps his adjectives "divine," "sublime," and "greatness"
have a special phenomenological fit with duty that is not present for
mere prudential rationality. The claims of prudence allow one aspect
of the empirical self to dominate another. Perhaps the motive of duty
allows one to transcend the given empirical self entirely. This at least
seems to be Kant's thought.

24. This is not to say that there are no important problems remaining for Kant's account. Kant has, I think, successfully established
that there is a distinct moral motive of respect for duty—a motive that
is not reducible to a mere selfish desire for personal happiness. Another argument would be required, however, to show that this is the
sole moral motive—e.g., that sympathy and other "motives of connection" lack moral standing. Kant tends to confuse these motives with
selfishness, and thus perhaps he wrongly believes that in giving reasons
to discard selfishness as a moral motive he has also given reasons to
discard these other motives as well. He is wrong about this, however. A
separate argument would be required, and he gives no such argument
in "Theory and Practice."

25. In "Theory and Practice," Kant makes only one explicit reference to his metaphysical views about freedom of will and to his belief
that these metaphysical views are necessarily presupposed to render

morality as he understands it possible. This reference is in the brief footnote on freedom at 285,68–69.

26. For an interesting and persuasive attempt to harness Freud to the Kantian project, see Scheffler, *supra* note 11, chapter 5.

27. There are, of course, numerous positive duties on the Kantian theory; for, with respect to any maxim that is *not* universalizable, the agent has a duty not to perform it—feeling at that point the direct conflict between duty and inclination that Kant often describes. (For example, since, according to Kant, the maxim of neglecting others in distress is not universalizable, agents have positive duties of beneficence.) The point is that, for Kant, the starting point in developing duties is always some contemplated action that the agent seeks to perform for subjective reasons (e.g., personal happiness). Thus the subjective dimension is always present in moral calculation (in the form of maxims) from the outset. In this way, Kant's deontology differs from, for example, that found in divine command theory—a theory that starts, not with subjectively generated maxims, but with a list of duties imposed at the outset from "outside."

28. For a recent discussion of Kant on revolution (and a generous listing of other studies on the topic) see 341ff. of Leslie A. Mulholland's splendid *Kant's System of Rights* (New York: Columbia University Press, 1990).

29. According to Kant, the basic rights are *freedom* (freedom to be limited only to guarantee like freedom to others), *equality* (formal equality before the law—the right of each citizen to have others coerced to protect his freedom and to have his own prospects in life limited solely by his own talents, industry and fortune), and *independence* (the right to function in a legislative—i.e., voting-capacity with respect to the laws that bind him). Although, when abstractly stated, these are good candidates for basic rights, Kant's own interpretation of them is occasionally shallow and shows that to a considerable degree he simply adopted the prejudices of his age. For example: He sees differentials in wealth resulting from inheritance as merely a matter of "fortune," and he sees no problem in limiting the right to vote to adult males (children and women being called "naturally" unsuited at 295,76). Even among adult males the right is to be limited to those who are their "own masters"—i.e., *property owners* (not laborers). This latter constraint is the occasion for one of the most bizarre (and unintentionally humorous) passages in Kant—a passage (295–96,76) in which Kant takes pains to attempt to show why barbers and woodchoppers may not vote even though tailors and wig-makers may. It has something to do with the relation in which they stand to the commodities

with which they work, but the whole discussion defies intelligibility. Even Kant concludes his discussion by saying: "It is, I admit, somewhat difficult to determine what requirements a person must meet so that he can be his own master."

30. Think of strong paternalism as coercing someone on the basis of your own (or the community's) conception of the good. A weaker form of paternalism would involve coercing someone to help him realize his own conception of the good. The stronger the form of paternalism, of course, the more difficult it will be to justify within a Kantian framework. See Gerald Dworkin's "Paternalism" in *Morality and the Law* ed. Richard A. Wasserstrom (Belmont: Wadsworth, 1971).

31. See Ronald Dworkin's "Liberalism" in his *A Matter of Principle* (Cambridge: Harvard University Press, 1985), 181–204.

32. Kant's desire to keep all considerations of happiness or welfare out of moral and political theory may result from a confusion on his part over the concept of "determining ground." His theory of motivation requires that a desire for happiness may not motivate (and in that sense be a determining ground for) the moral will. It does not follow from this, however, that happiness cannot be a right-making characteristic and in that sense be a determining ground for moral duty. (Even a utilitarian could act out of a motive of respect for duty—something not ruled out merely because the utilitarian defines duty partially in terms of happiness.) A full theory of the human good would, of course, involve much more than happiness. It would not, however, involve only elements that "could never be taught by experience."

33. Browse, for example, through the *Doctrine of Virtue, supra* note 14. A rich and complex (even if not totally satisfying) conception of the human good is developed there.

34. Kant is responding to views expressed by Moses Mendelssohn in his 1783 *Jerusalem, oder über religiöse Macht und Judentum (Jerusalem, or on Religious Power and Judaism)*. Kant's own views on radical evil in his *Religion* show that he was by no means blind to humanity's dark side.

35. Robert Nozick, *The Examined Life* (New York: Simon and Schuster, 1989), 236–42.

36. As I read this passage I cannot help thinking of Eastern Europe—particularly the "ethnic cleansing" currently taking place in the former Yugoslavia. We did not get to celebrate the lifting of totalitarianism for more than a few days before human bestiality raised its ugly head in a different form. It is hard not to become discouraged.

37. As Philip Quinn pointed out to me in correspondence, having faith in the moral progress of the species does not alone provide

reasons for respecting each individual member of that species. This individualized respect may require something very like the kind of religious faith that Kant wants to reject as foundational in his moral theory. Perhaps human dignity itself can only be defended as a "postulate of practical reason." I have started a very superficial exploration of the possible religious basis for Kantian dignity in my "Constitutionalism, Moral Skepticism, and Religious Belief" in *Constitutionalism: The Philosophical Dimension,* ed. Alan S. Rosenbaum (New York: Greenwood Press, 1988), 239–49, and in my forthcoming "Human Decency and the Limitations of Kantianism" (as yet untitled proceedings of the Sixteenth World Congress of the International Association for Philosophy of Law and Social Philosophy).

38. But Kantian dignity does not quite, at least to my mind, capture it all. I have never felt more deeply the moral horror of the Holocaust than when I read of the murder (at Babi Yar) of the central character in D. M. Thomas's novel *The White Hotel.* So much that was wonderful and precious was lost in the death of this woman (a fictional representative of all the victims of that atrocity), and not all of it is (in my view) to be captured in some ideal of moral autonomy (the core idea in Kant's concept of dignity). Kant is perhaps inclined to overmoralize the value incarnate in the human person.

PART II

THE VALUE OF
PURE THEORY

3

HIGH THEORY, LOW THEORY,
AND THE DEMANDS
OF MORALITY

FRANCES M. KAMM

My basic concern in this article is with the relation between theory and practice. More particularly I am concerned with high theory, with what I call "low" theory (sometimes the derivative of high theory), and with the actual (acted out) application of these in the real world. By high theory I mean ethical theories such as utilitarianism, Kantianism, Ross's theory of prima facie duties, contractarianism. By low theory I mean the theory of particular moral problems, such as whether affirmative action should be prohibited and what sort of rules of war there should be. (This is what some refer to as "applied ethics." In using "low" I do not mean to imply inferior. Low theory in ethics need be no more inferior to high theory than Bauhaus utensils or art nouveau architecture are inferior to painting in the same styles. It is only lower to the ground or bottom line.) The application to the world is the problem of "applying applied ethics." I will consider various ways of doing ethical theory and also what might be meant by the "theory/practice distinction," dealing with the role of moral theory in political argument and the construction of theory specifically for practical problems. I will focus finally on the obstacles that inhibit the application of morality, including partiality, and the importance of doing high and low theory even if we have little success in applying our results to the world.[1]

When people discuss the relation between theory and practice, there are several different things they may have in mind. I will consider seven. First, people may ask about the relation between theory and practice when they really mean to speak about the relation between doing high theory and doing low theory, the theory of particular moral problems. For the purpose of situating ourselves, let us consider five major ways of doing high ethical theory, moving from top-down theories to bottom-up ones, as follows: (1) A theory might have one major principle (or a few) that seems intuitively plausible and from which recommendations in particular cases can be derived in conjunction with empirical data. (Utilitarianism functions in this way.) (2) A theory might be based on a core concept (or concepts) with a less ambitious range of derivations than the principles in (1) (e.g., contractarianism). (3) A theory (an example is that of W. D. Ross) might list intuitively plausible principles concerned with many factors that must be balanced. (4) A theory similarly based on many factors might yield more instructive specific principles that would be helpful. (For instance, instead of just saying that, in general, not harming others is to take precedence over aiding others, one might, based on an examination of intuitive responses to cases, describe in principled fashion when not harming should take precedence over aiding and when it should not.[2] (5) Relevant factors might be teased out of a direct examination of cases, so that new factors not noted by any previously held theory might arise, leading to principles or the other types of theories described in (1) through (4).

One relation between high and low theory I have noticed in my own work is the straightforward application of high theory principles to cases. I emphasize this because some have said that this straightforward application never occurs. For example, in theoretical discussion (closest to type (4)) of the possible moral distinction between killing and letting die, I emphasized that the two could differ morally per se, in virtue of their different definitional properties, and yet not lead to moral differences in certain cases. This was because we could export some of the definitional properties of one behavior (properties that made it morally different from the other behavior) into cases involving the other behavior, thereby compensating for the per se difference. I focused on one exportable definitional property of letting die: that the person we let die loses only a life he would have had via our aid, not a life he would have had independently of us. I argued that cases in which we kill someone who was already receiving life support from us are morally more like letting-die cases than are other cases of killing, because they share this definitional property of letting die. This principle finds a direct application in low theory on abortion, where we focus on killing a fetus, which is clearly dependent for life support.

A second example: in theoretical work on the distribution of scarce resources, I argued for a principle of irrelevant utility, according to which small differences in utility achievable by saving one person's life rather than another's did not constitute a reason for depriving either party of the equal chance to survive which a random decision procedure would give him. This principle was (almost) directly applicable to decision making about who should get an organ transplant when the outcome of one patient differed only slightly from that of another. (I say "almost" since a new wrinkle arose because the extra utility involved in a better outcome in an organ transplant was located in the same person in whom the major utility [having his life saved] was located, rather than added on in a different person. Applying the principle of irrelevant utility therefore required us to reflect on the distinction between a concentrated and a dispersed extra utility.)[3]

These two examples indicate that a case may offer the opportunity for a straightforward application of a theory or principle, where the case is merely an instance of a more generally formulated rule. The second example shows that variations in cases may lead to recharacterization of a theoretical principle (e.g., about concentration versus dispersal of benefits) as approaches (4) and (5) to doing theory suggested.

But sometimes, in order to do low theory, I found that one had actually to do *new* theory at the lower case level. Furthermore, this was not the sort of new theory that merely led one to recharacterize one's theoretical principles as in approach (4) to theorizing. For example, in the case of abortion one couldn't get a result on the question of the permissibility of abortion from applying the principle about killing to terminate life support without considering whether the fetus is worse off for having lived a short life in the womb and then dying than it would be if it had never lived at all. This is because, in its general formulation, the principle that defines the significance of killing in cases that have the definitional property of letting die implies that it is permissible to kill only if the person killed is no worse off for having been supported and killed than he would have been if he had never been supported. So we cannot tell whether abortion is, in a morally important sense, even an instance of the general principle until we deal with whether being created and dying at an early age is worse than never being created. Doing this requires the consideration of the specifics of creation and abortion. I believe that this involves doing nonderivative low theory.

It may be useful to employ the words "thick" and "thin" in discussing some relations of high and low theory.[4] Straightforward direct application, as instance of a general principle, is *thin* in that nothing "thickly" particular and distinguishing about the case at hand need be brought in. By contrast, theorizing directly at the low level (perhaps to see whether the case presents an instance of a general principle) is *thick,* heavily involved with the significance of particular factors of the case. (Of course, these notions of thick and thin are relative, yet still useful, I think.) Another way of describing this distinction is to contrast topic-neutral theory with topic-specific theory. Low theory that is thick rather than thin and topic-specific rather than topic-neutral can be just as deep as high theory, only it arises from, and is designed to deal with, a particular problem. Hence it is not as likely as thin, topic-neutral theory to have implications that are more than analogies for other problems.[5] The distinction is one of breadth not depth. Of course, new advances in thin higher theory can arise in the course of working on a particular low theoretical problem. Then the danger is that the advances in high theory will be buried in the low theory literature, when they could be of more general use. The philosopher may have a responsibility to re-present her general results in a more general context.

To some people, it seems disappointing if we can solve problems using thin theory; it seems much more exciting to require thick theory, for then, in a sense, every problem is a new problem. But it is also exciting to find that a problem yields to perfectly general concepts without thick theorizing being necessary. A good example of this is Philippa Foot's discussion of euthanasia, in which the distinction between negative and positive rights is applied to anything that is one's own (and only as an instance to one's own life in particular).[6] Furthermore, the general distinction between injustice, in taking away what belongs to someone without his or her consent, and uncharitableness, in showing no concern for what happens to what belongs to another, goes far toward solving problems. An analysis peculiar to euthanasia itself is called for only near the end of Foot's discussion, in order to deal with a slippery slope problem that may be serious because life, rather than something else, is at stake.

A second idea that people may have in mind when they discuss the relation between theory and practice is the view that the correctness of a theory can be tested, and a theory be changed, by seeing its implications for hypothetical cases and also for real cases. I believe that theories *should* be tested, at least in part, in this way. (But notice that insofar as discussion of cases is supposed to change one's view of high theory, it may be through thick, low theorizing that it has this effect). It is possible to test a theory in this way because judgments about cases are often not theory driven; i.e., people who hold different theories may have the same judgments about cases. For example, Shelly Kagan, who is an act utilitarian, claims that he shares many of the intuitions that deontologists have about cases. He just thinks these intuitions are wrong, and he accepts the need to find an error theory to explain our belief in them. If an error theory is less plausible than the correctness of those intuitions, they will provide support for a nonutilitarian theory.

The idea that change may also go in the other direction, that is, from high theory to a change in judgment about cases, is one reason to think theory is related to practice in a third sense; namely, it can lead us to change our minds about what to do in practical cases. One danger in thinking, as Stephen Toulmin does, that so long as we all agree on cases we need not worry about theoretical justification, is that we may all agree on the wrong answer to a case.[7] Doing theory can help us discover our mistakes and make us change our minds about cases. Furthermore, depending upon what identity conditions we have for decisions, we may classify many more decisions as "different from what they would otherwise have been" in virtue of philosophizing. For example, suppose someone would have voted for a bomber before philosophical reflection, and will vote for it after philosophical reflection. But before reflection he was in favor of it as a way of starting a war, after reflection he is in favor of it as a way of avoiding a war. To say that philosophical reflection made no difference to what act he performed conceals a lot.

But there are dangers in emphasizing the way in which theory can lead to change in case judgments. For often we are interested in theory even though we are quite certain of the correctness of our case judgments. Indeed we are more certain of these judgments than we could be of the correctness of any theory. In such instances, we are interested in a theory because it gives us hope of understanding our case judgments in a deeper and more penetrating way, not because it will change our minds or because we are more certain of the theory than of the cases.

One particular view on the way in which theories are to be tested by cases and case judgments revised by theory is distinctively constructivist. There are no necessary truths either at the level of high theory or intuitive judgments about cases, and because it is up to us to decide how much complexity we want in our moral system, we can simply decide to give no moral significance to certain fine points in theory or in intuitive judgments about cases. I do not believe such voluntarism in theory construction is either possible or appropriate, and the testing of high theory by cases, and the revision of case judgments by theory, does not commit one to such voluntarism. For, as Ronald Dworkin notes, there is a difference between changing one's judgment about a case and ignoring a judgment that refuses to change.

A fourth notion of the theory/practice distinction is invoked sometimes when people say that things are true in theory but not in practice, when what they really mean is that a theoretical difference does not show up in cases; it makes no difference in practice. For example, it is possible that killing and letting die differ morally per se, i.e., in virtue of differing conceptual properties, and yet, in many *cases,* killing is no worse than letting die, because, as described above, in our descriptions we have equalized the cases so that the killing case has a property not usually true of killing cases but definitionally true of letting die. Some will describe this as illustrating the fact that killing and letting die differ morally in theory but not in practice; but really it should be described as their exhibiting a per se difference that may not show up even in hypothetical cases.

A fifth interpretation of the theory/practice question is suggested by Rawls's view (as described, for example, in *Political Liberalism*) on the relation between theory and public reason.[8] His is a complex position, and here I will comment on it only briefly. He claims that in justifying public policy on constitutional issues and the basics of justice, we may not need theoretically correct or true positions but rather politically acceptable reasons. Now, one understanding of politically acceptable reason, or public reason as Rawls calls it, is that it is reason for certain important practical purposes rather than for theoretical purposes. On Rawls's view the theoretical arguments are given by comprehensive views (such as philosophical or religious systems), many of which are reasonable and reasonably held by members of a democratic society. These arguments are not usually used in public justification of a position, except insofar as their terms overlap with those of public reason. (He does, however, adopt an "inclusive" sense of public reason that allows the terms of a comprehensive doctrine to figure in public discussion of constitutional essentials if on occasion this is necessary to ultimately gain support for the values of public reason.[9]) Rawls's position is different from such an anti-theorist as Toulmin, since public reason provides some justification that all can share; we are not asked merely to accept agreement on cases without justification at all. (Notice that defenses in terms of public reason are shallow relative to the deeper justifications of comprehensive views, even if the former includes in its explanatory arsenal such devices as the original position and the veil of ignorance. By contrast, I have allowed that low theory may be as deep as high theory, only topic specific rather than topic neutral. Reason for public purposes does not then overlap with low theory.)

Nevertheless, Rawls's view may give rise, correctly or incorrectly, to the same sort of discomfort that we can feel with Toulmin's view. That is, we may feel uncomfortable, as holders of comprehensive views, if we are restrained in any context from offering what are conceived of as the most complete, deep and true justifications for a position, and also uncomfortable if we find that comprehensive views with which we disagree reach the same conclusions on cases. From a practical (political) point of view we should be happy that there is an overlapping consensus on a position as well as a justification in the language of public reason. We may also be pleased that we cannot be forced to discuss and justify our deepest beliefs for public purposes, nor have to force these views on unwilling others. We also recall that moral and political theory, unlike scientific theory, demands some application of its results, and anything that threatens to hinder right action, including disputes about theory, raises worries. Yet as theoreticians, we want to know how it is that very different theories lead to the same conclusion and we want to judge between the comprehensive views. One can feel uncomfortable in the company of those who support the same actions one does, actions one does not think them wrong to support, but for what one considers bad reasons. Certainly, that different theories lead to the same answer in some cases does not imply they are equally good if they diverge on other cases, and some theories may give the wrong *reasons* for the right answer to certain problems.

Ronald Dworkin does not share Rawls's views on the bracketing of comprehensive philosophical doctrines in public political debate of constitutional fundamentals. Nevertheless, in his recent work on abortion and euthanasia, he follows a different route—one less plausible, I think, than Rawls's—which has the same effect of limiting discussion of certain issues in legal contexts. In short, he classifies much of what many would argue is (or could be) philosophical argumentation as religious, and so not to be part of legal justification on grounds of separation of Church and State. I would like to examine in some detail the problem with Dworkin's route of classifying theoretical reasoning so that it has limited impact on practical decision making.[10]

According to Dworkin, because the early fetus has never been conscious it clearly has no interests or rights to protect those interests, and no one could coherently believe it has. Therefore, the objection to abortion, that we are killing a person with interests and rights, cannot be correct or even prevalent. The rhetoric people use when they speak of the fetus as a person does not represent their real beliefs, according to Dworkin. But there is another possible objection to abortion, namely that it is an inappropriate response to the sacredness of each individual life. Dworkin believes that this is what really lies at the heart of the abortion debate.

Dworkin's idea of the sacred is complex. For our present purposes it is enough to note that it is a form of intrinsic value and that the term "sacred" suggests something *religious*. Indeed, Dworkin says that the view that life has intrinsic value is religious (157, 163, 174–5). He says that moral and political philosophy are about rights and interests; discussion of the sacred goes beyond their provenance. Nevertheless, he says that there is a secular term that conveys what he means by sacred. It is "inviolability." What makes something be sacred and inviolable? Although this is supposed to be a notion of *intrinsic* value, i.e., the value the thing has in itself, Dworkin says that the nerve of the sacred is the *history* of the entity. God, nature, and human action as creative forces give sacredness to many (but not all) of their products; the more investment of these creative forces in the entities, the more value.

The problem that is crucial for abortion, Dworkin thinks, is that there are at least two different types of investment—biological (or God-driven) and human—and both the woman and the fetus will embody both types of creative investments to lesser and greater degrees. For some people, God's or nature's investment is of paramount importance, and a payoff that is the continued existence of that natural or God-given component is a big payoff. For other people, it is the human creative investment and the payoff in terms of human achievement that is of importance. The balancing of these sources of sacredness in the fetus and in the woman, Dworkin thinks, is not a matter of philosophical argumentation. It comes closer to a matter of religious belief, where this does not necessarily imply belief in God. A view is religious on Dworkin's reading if it tries to answer those questions which, he thinks, have been dealt with in the past by religion. These questions concern the place of an individual life in an impersonal and infinite universe, the ultimate point and meaning of human life (163, 171); they are at stake when we try to balance the values of natural, God-given, and human creative efforts and their payoffs. Since various views on the sacredness of fetal and adult life are religious, views on abortion will be to an important extent a question of religious belief, and the secular State may not support one side over the other.

There is a final important consideration in the conflict between fetus and woman. Not only do fetus and woman represent two different instances of sacredness which can conflict, but the woman also has interests and rights, being a person in a philosophical, moral, and constitutional sense. When preserving, rather than destroying, a sacred entity (just how sacred it is being a matter of dispute, and a religious dispute at that) would result in a serious imposition on the rights and interests of a full-fledged person, then the sacred value is overridden. I believe that the idea of the "sanctity of life" that Dworkin is talking about, and the idea that the frustration of energy invested in a project compromises the inviolability of life has little to do with the ordinary notion of inviolability (89). Inviolability, as commonly understood, implies a high degree of protection for individuals from destructive attacks upon them, even for the sake of minimizing destructive attacks on the inviolability of others. Dworkin does not believe in such a high degree of protection for the things he calls sacred.

One problem that arises for Dworkin, then, is that he would need to emphasize in some other way than by using "inviolability" his idea that the sacred is not merely religious, but also secular. But emphasizing any secular equivalent of the sacred introduces a different kind of trouble; for Dworkin wants to argue that views about the intrinsic value of life and debates about the weighing and balancing of sacredness are fundamentally religious rather than philosophical, since they give an answer to the question he thinks only religion has dealt with in the past, i.e., what is the ultimate value and meaning of human life? At this point, it is worth noting some unclarity in his position. At least two possibilities are available.

(1) Any position that says life *does* have some intrinsic value, separate from its value to the person who lives it, is religious. Different views will vary on how much value it has and how to balance intrinsic value in different loci. But positions that say life itself has no intrinsic value, or only persons have intrinsic value, or even that persons lack it, are nonreligious. Then even if someone who thinks that fetal life is only minimally sacred, outweighed by other values or rights, and does not seek an abortion as a matter of positive religious requirement, should not be prevented from acting on her own religious view by someone else's view on greater fetal sacredness.

(2) Any position on the issue of whether or not life has intrinsic value is a religious position. Then even if one's negative belief, such as that Jesus is not the Lord, or there is no God, or life is not sacred at all, does not have a strong motivational role in one's life, that belief is to be respected as religious. (On this analysis atheists have religious views, versus just having views about religion.) Certainly, the Supreme Court refuses to allow one person's strong positive religious views to rule the life of another person who has merely negative religious views.

However, we can ask in what sense is taking a positive or negative position on the sacredness of life a religious view, if, as noted above, there is an admittedly secular interpretation of sacredness (whether correctly thought of as inviolability or not)? My sense is that ultimately Dworkin wants to use "religious" to connote an area of discourse that is not subject to rational proof. This keeps it outside the area of political debate. For Dworkin, as noted, unlike Rawls, believes that (what Rawls refers to as) comprehensive philosophical doctrines do have a place in public discussion of constitutional issues. For example, Dworkin thinks that the issue of personhood is a philosophical, not a religious, issue, subject to philosophical argumentation and rational proof.

But two problems arise if the sacred is regarded as not subject to rigorous argument, safely within the religion clause and outside the business of the enforcement agencies of the State. First, weighing natural and human creative inputs may be capable of more rigor and conclusiveness than Dworkin thinks. In that case, it might enter the category of secular philosophy. Second, by Dworkin's own test of the religious, i.e., what has traditionally been discussed under that title, many of the issues that Dworkin says are within the realm of the sacred *have* traditionally been discussed by secular philosophy as well as by religion. For example, what is the meaning and point of human life? Does a person's life matter independent of its use to him? Dworkin places these questions under the topic of the sanctity of life but, clearly, moral philosophers have discussed them. After all, Kant—a philosopher—said that rational humanity was an end in itself, a categorical end; whether people cared about their lives or not, they had a duty to make something of their lives. Even Dworkin often refers to the decision to have an abortion as a matter of *moral* gravity (e.g., 174). But when philosophers have discussed the meaning and point of human life, they have usually argued for the value of characteristics or functions of personhood, whether in humans or in other animals, such as consciousness and rationality. They have concluded that mere life, the pulse in the mud so to speak, is worthwhile primarily as a *means* to such functions as sentience or self-consciousness. This, of course, implies that they have concluded that *life itself* does not have much value, a position Dworkin might think is only one possible (religious) position on this question or even a nonreligious view, depending on which of the two interpretations I have presented are true. (But then other more positive answers on the value of life may also be argued as a matter of philosophy.)

So, historically, secular philosophy has dealt with the issues Dworkin says are religious (despite his own claim that there are secular analogies to his terminology) and it has often reached conclusions that give low rank to biological life. When Dworkin discusses euthanasia, he seems to allow more overlap between the realm of interests (dealt with by moral philosophy) and the realm of the sacred. *Critical* interests are concerns that one's life has amounted to something, independent of how it merely felt as one was living it (one's experiential interests). And although it is in one's critical interest to live a truly worthwhile life, there is also another question beyond the scope of one's interests: whether one's life is ultimately worthwhile. Indeed, Dworkin says that believing in critical interests, i.e., that it is possible for one's life to be worth something, is a species of believing in the sacredness of life (215). But if one's critical interests are a matter of moral philosophical reflection, why cannot the same issues of the worth of one's life, looked at aside from one's interests, also be a matter of philosophical reflection?

So many may think that discussion of the meaning of life is philosophical rather than religious and any view (positive or negative on this issue) is philosophical rather than religious. Then it could not be argued that we should not enforce some view of intrinsic value because it is a religious issue and we believe in separation of Church and State. This is one objection to Dworkin's view. But there is a different significant problem internal to his view, because, after all, he does not think the State must be or should be totally uninvolved in regulating abortion. He thinks, for example, that the State should encourage women to decide in a responsible way, because fetal intrinsic value is at stake.

If only some form of a *positive* answer on the question of whether life has intrinsic value is religious, then Dworkin's view that the State has a "legitimate interest in maintaining a moral environment in which decisions about life and death are taken seriously and treated as matters of moral gravity" (168), because life has intrinsic value, involves the State in taking sides with a religious versus a nonreligious view (that mere life has no intrinsic value). But separation of Church and State has usually been taken to mean that the government cannot side with religion against atheism.

On the other hand, if taking any negative or positive view on the issue of whether life has intrinsic value is to have a religious view, the State, in intervening to see to it that women took abortion as a grave matter, would be siding with one religious view over another, and this is also impermissible. Even if the State intervened just to have people think in some way about what might possibly be an important religious matter, it would still be in a position analogous to one in which it encouraged people to think about the possibility that there is a God. This too is something the State may not do if there is separation of Church and State.[11]

I have argued that it is a mistake to limit the role of the moral theory in legal argumentation when discussing the intrinsic value of life on grounds that such theory is merely religious. I have also argued that it is a mistake to give it some limited role while claiming that it is religious. This has been part of my examination of the claim that philosophical theory is not relevant to certain political discussions in a liberal state. But this is still consistent with saying that no philosophical view on intrinsic value should determine public policy. For it remains open for Dworkin to modify his position in the following way, called D*: There is *philosophical* (vs. religious) disagreement on the value of the early fetus, except that it is agreed that it is not a philosophical person with rights and interests since it has never been conscious. The State should not interfere with a person's own decision on abortion (1) when there is philosophical disagreement on the value of the early fetus that has no rights and interests and (2) when the State's taking one side would impose significantly on the rights and interests of a person. We can afford to enforce a philosophically contested position (e.g., on taxation) only when there is no physical impact comparable to pregnancy on any given person and others rights and interests are at stake (e.g., beneficiaries of taxes). No doubt Dworkin would find D* unappealing. First, it does not make use of the nonestablishment clause of the Constitution in an argument permitting abortion. Second, it does not aim to bring together all those who take a wide range of views on abortion as common believers in a religious notion of life, as varied as their religious interpretations may be. But this is not necessarily a defect, for just as many object to the creationists' view that secular humanism is just another religion, so many in the abortion debate may object to characterizing their views on the value of life as religious.

Let us return now to the sixth and seventh notion of the relation of theory and practice. It seems to me that two meaningful questions about the relation between theory and practice are whether people will or can reasonably be expected to use a theory in deliberation, and whether they can reasonably be expected even to act as if they were deliberating by a theory. The first question raises the possiblity that a theory is *self-effacing*, that is, even though the theory is true, the results it demands would be better achieved if no one believed it or used it in deliberation. Utilitarianism may be such a theory. Sidgwick thought that nonconsequentialist theories should be used in deliberation but that consequentialism was the ultimate truth about morality; one simply achieved the best consequences more often if one forgot about the truth. But not all theories are self-effacing. This characteristic may tell against one theory or another, but not against theory in general.

Stuart Hampshire raises a more general objection to the relevance of theory to moral decision making. He says that, for evolutionary reasons, it would not be surprising if most people could unconsciously and rapidly weigh factors correctly and yet not be able explicitly to give their reasons for deciding as they do. There are good evolutionary (survival) reasons for our being creatures who can make right decisions quickly and, he says, no good survival reasons for being able to give reasons.

In rebuttal of Hampshire, but arguing within his own framework, one might suggest that the ability to justify one's judgments to others might well have survival value. Certainly the innate capacity for moral judgment may well be at a disadvantage in trying to deal with complex problems that arise as a result of technology and social changes, changes that proceed more rapidly than biological evolution either alone or combined with early acculturation. Theorizing could help here. Furthermore, the thesis that any moral judging per se programmed into us should be left untouched conflicts with the idea that morality goes beyond any biologically/culturally given dispositions and is subject to rational evaluation which may lead to changes in intuitive decisions.

Hampshire's thesis might seem to imply that everyone (uncorrupted by theory) would make equally good moral judgments (since our capacity to make moral judgments is a matter of evolution and early acculturation), just as we all speak a language pretty much the same way. But it seems clearly false that all (theory-innocent) persons make equally good moral judgments, let alone act equally well. However, variation in performance need not necessarily hold against an evolutionary account, such as Hampshire's, since variations in perceptual abilities (e.g., measurement of distance) is compatible with an evolutionary origin.[12] Nevertheless, variation in ability will still imply that while some people judge well without explicit reasoning as an aid, others, if they are to judge well, may need to have their attention directed to principles and general factors. It is also worth noting that, if *evolution* were responsible for implanting ethical judgments, one would expect such good judgments to lead, more uniformly than they in fact do, to good behavior. For would it be evolutionarily sound for nature to attend to judgments but not to acts?

The sort of rapid judgment Hampshire admires may have been made possible, at least sometimes, by prior explicit acquaintance with concepts and principles which then seep back to form the unconscious background of a person's thought. Ideally, all instruction in general theories, concepts, and principles should come to be internalized, allowing for the rapid perception of the moral character of a situation. So there is no necessary conflict between improvement in judgment through acquaintance with general conceptions first consciously brought to mind and quick "intuitive reasoning."[13]

The seventh concern with the theory/practice question might arise if we merely had the morally right answer to a problem, regardless of how we came to it, but obstacles stood in the way of our acting on the right answer. This is the sense of "theory" Kant uses when he argues against the "old saw: that it may be true in theory but it won't work in practice." It is the ideal/real split.[14]

To summarize, I have discussed seven types of issues and concerns people may be referring to when they talk about the theory/practice relation: (1) the relation between doing high theory and doing low theory; (2) testing a high theory by its implications for cases; (3) modifying judgments about cases because of theoretical reflection; (4) a difference true per se but not always significant in cases; (5) the relation of philosophical or religious views to public reason; (6) the relation of both high and low theory to how people can be expected to deliberate; and (7) the relation of both high and low theory to what is actually done. I will focus on (7) in the rest of this discussion, dealing with potential obstacles to applying high and low theory.

Partiality in one's own behalf is often thought of as an obstacle to acting correctly. In *Equality and Partiality*, Thomas Nagel argues that high moral theory about right and wrong conduct does not require complete impartiality, but itself endorses a certain range of decision making and behavior stemming from a partial point of view.[15] This is because morality must, he thinks, take into account the sort of creature it is for, and humans value many things out of proportion to their value from an impartial perspective. They are creatures with both an impartial and a partial perspective. One way of looking at this is that we are tailoring the demands of morality, justifying the claims of morality, to some according to motivational capacities. This is a form of internalism in ethics, to be contrasted with the externalist view that says we may have reason to do what we are not capable of being motivated to do.

Nagel takes the partial perspective into account in deciding what the demands of morality are, not merely because morality would not be a practical success if we didn't do this, but because he thinks there are other good reasons to do so; i.e., the creatures with the partial point of view have good reason to reject totally impartial morality. However, Nagel also says that as rational beings we are capable of developing new motives, besides desires or commitments we already have, if we are convinced by argument that there is reason for us to do so.

If there were reason to take a partial perspective into account in framing moral demands, this would mean that within a certain range, preferences for the self or partialist values are not really an obstacle to acting as morality requires. That is, the parital view would be less of an obstacle to applying ethics.

Nagel may accept this view too easily. For example, one may wonder why we cannot be required to suffer great personal economic loss for the sake of others, as Nagel claims, even though morality *does require* that we be prepared even to lose our lives rather than kill another to save ourselves. In criminal law, we do not believe someone is justified in killing an innocent bystander just because a third party threatened to kill him if he didn't, though we may excuse his conduct if he does kill. We distinguish between justification and excuse. That is, the fact that large sacrifices are required is not always a sufficient reason for modifying the demands of morality; why then is it a sufficient reason sometimes?

Nagel argues that unless we can find a proposal which is such that *no* one who is interested in reaching unforced general agreement with others can reasonably reject it, we cannot speak of any proposal as having binding moral force. He further argues that within a certain range of sacrifice required from the better off to help the worse off, there is no proposal that rich and poor could not each reasonably reject. That is, sometimes the rich will not be obliged to give up a great deal and sometimes the poor will not be obliged to accept the condition in which this would leave them. How does this happen? Specifically he says the well off from their impartial perspective see that the needs of the worse off count equally with their own (50). However from their *partial perspective* they see they have their own lives to lead. On the other hand, the worse off from their partial perspective see that they have their lives to lead, and from their impartial perspective, Nagel says, they see that the well off also have their own lives to lead. The impression Nagel gives here is that there is a balance between factors favoring the well off making sacrifices and factors favoring their not making such sacrifices—that is, one group's impartial perspective favors the poor, one group's impartial perspective favors the rich, and each group's partial perspective favors itself. But Nagel seems to forget that from the poor person's impartial perspective he sees that the satisfaction of his personal needs (but not those of the rich) would move us toward the equality favored by impartiality. Leading his own life is endorsed both by his partial perspective and by the impartial perspective. This means that there is more to be said for the rich making the large sacrifice than for the poor going without.

Nevertheless it is true that the partial point of view of the well off and a certain aspect of the impartial point of view of the poor recognize the need of the well off to live their own lives. These are components that hold out to a harmonious solution. Should they have veto power over a result rather than vector power to modify a result, even when the balance of factors is against them? Are they side constraints on the asymmetrical weighting of factors in favor of the poor, to which I have pointed? Nagel and contractarians in general believe in pairwise comparison of individual claims rather than aggregation of those claims. This means we check to see if anyone has more of an objection to a proposal than anyone else, and we do not aggregate lesser objections of many to weigh against a more significant objection of one. This potentially gives each individual person a veto. But in seeking perfect harmony of all perspectives *internal* to persons, Nagel moves beyond this idea of pairwise comparison, to giving parts of persons, e.g., their partial perspective, a veto power.

Note a further asymmetry in our attitude to the rich and poor when they each do what they are *not* obliged to do. If the rich do more than they are required, this is seen as morally good, supererogatory. But if the poor do not keep pressing their needs, we may think them lacking in self-respect. This indicates a moral asymmetry in their positions, even if not one that can be directly used to prove that there is an obligation to help the poor at great cost. All of this suggests, I believe, that the partial perspective is more a hindrance to morality than Nagel believes. It often serves as an excuse rather than a justification.

On the other hand, sometimes people do behave more altruistically than Nagel believes people are in general capable of behaving. Perhaps this nonobligatory ability to act well in practice should have an impact on theory; for suppose there are enough people who *in fact* perform charitable acts beyond what

is ordinarily thought to be required. Would it then not be necessary *in practice* to worry about constructing a theory that requires as many sacrifices of *everyone* as Nagel thinks necessary in
order to produce a good society? If some are very good, the
partiality of others will not be a hindrance to an overall satisfactory result, but it will still affect the degree to which each person
in the society behaves as an equal member of the society, by
doing their fair share to produce the result.

The role of the partial perspective in altering the demands
of high and low theories or in inhibiting the actual application
of what theory demands must, then, be considered if we are
interested in the relation and gap between theory and practice.

When the partial point of view is being accommodated, either
by changing a theory to reflect its weight or by giving in to it as
an obstacle to implementing a true theory in practice, at least
someone's good is being pursued. But arguably the worst obstacles to a theory or to its results being applied in practice are
such greater vices as envy, avarice, meanness, and competitiveness. With these often no one's good is being served, and there
may be reason to believe that these are very widespread motives.
Indeed, it is worth entertaining the hypothesis that things are
even worse than commonly thought. Consider the following
hypothetical suppositions, of relevance to areas often dealt with
by low theory.[16]

(1) Low theory on hiring for jobs, when it does not endorse
something like quotas for affirmative action, at least speaks of
hiring according to merit directly related to job performance,
assuming that the candidate behaves in other ways in a minimally civilized way. Imagine the following hypothetical, however. Suppose that in reality an important consideration in hiring were how someone fit into a pseudo "family structure" in
place in a work environment. In particular, getting or retaining
a job would be a function of someone's willingness to "couple"
in something like a real or celibate marriage with someone of
the opposite sex, who would have to be designated on the basis
of having accomplishments similar to that of the person to be
hired or retained. Suppose, further, that this state of affairs
were in place as a function of psycho- or sociobiological tenden-

cies of a good portion of the population. Then theoretical principles for hiring would be a sham. Furthermore, there would be much less of a distinction between the public and private realms than liberal political theory recommends because the public realm would be modeled on the family/coupling structure of the private realm, and such things as attitudes of partiality could play a role in both. For example, if only the chief male in an organization is permitted to "couple," and monogamy rather than polygamy is the social norm, two women could not be hired in an institution, only one. Enforcing impartial strictures on merit in this Public Family might even have bad effects in practice: pressure might have to be brought on candidates to make them look bad in job performance so as to have "legitimate" grounds for dismissal or non-advancement.

(2) Theoretical positions typically support the idea and implications of sex equality. But suppose, as a hypothetical case, that no one in fact believed in sex equality. Indeed suppose most people—even those who professed to be feminists—believed that women could not be agents independent of male energy; those who were in favor of female presence in the professions would then at most be looking for people who could express and share the energy of male consorts. In this hypothetical world, true sex equality might be an ideal of reason but not part of practice.

(3) Most moral theories support some important degree of individualism, with rights theory especially emphasizing the individual as the important moral unit. But suppose, as a hypothetical case, that a good part of the population operated to succeed by bonding together into groups in which individuals quite literally functioned as members of that group rather than as individuals; for example, they could speak or be silenced at the direction of others, silence signifying domination. Then the idea of individual performance and entitlement would be stamped out in practice.

(4) Most moral theories laud friendship and the formation of close relationships. But suppose, hypothetically, that our true support came from strangers, while friends and colleagues were primary sources of envy, competitiveness, and destructive attitudes toward the individual.

If these hypotheticals were true, our ideals of friendship, individualism, merit, and female agency could still remain crucial parts of moral truth, telling us how people ought to be in a sense that comes close to having duties to be like this, though impractical given the nature of persons in the hypothetical worlds. The people in the hypotheticals would be shown to be living far from the requirements of moral truth.

If the world in which morality had to be practiced were actually as these hypotheticals described, what would have to be done? One way of dealing with the gap between the theoretically right answer and practice in this hypothetical world would be to do what some have recommended we do in dealing with the business activities in our world; i.e., the practice is likened to a game and exempted from having to be judged by most of the standards of morality.[17] I assume this would be the wrong way to handle matters. Second, it might be suggested that we should alter the conception of moral duties in the hypothetical world so that they come closer to the reality of people's conduct. The cases I describe, I believe, involve both intrinsically evil and inherently ridiculous patterns of behavior (however prevalent or hard-wired they are). These are not merely the pursuit of personal goods that conflict with the achievement of more impartial goods. Revising theory is therefore not a reasonable recommendation. Notice that we use the ideal standards of our high and low theories to judge the worthiness of whatever we uncover about the nature of people in the hypotheticals, deciding that a characteristic which science uncovers is something we would prefer they be rid of if only they could be. We certainly do not revise our theory of right and wrong, and good and bad in the light of everything we find. It does not seem incorrect to say that this means that conceptions of right and wrong, good and bad are heavily *a priori* rather than *a posteriori*.

This view seems to contrast with one recently presented by Samuel Scheffler. He says, "morality is addressed from the outset to human beings as they are. It affords them the prospect of integrating two different motivational tendencies [by which he means the partial and impartial], and it has no 'prior' content that must be 'reduced' or 'modified' when it is brought into contact with human nature."[18] He argues that morality is best presented as offering an Ideal (with a capital "I") of Humanity, which is about the integration of partial and impartial points of view. It is important to understand what "Ideal" (with a capital "I")—which I shall refer to as capital-Ideal—means. I take it that Scheffler's meaning of capital-Ideal is that it is the highest goal for which we should aim. This is a different sense from that attached to ideal (with a lower case "i") when it is used to speak of ideal duty or ideal theory of right and wrong. Here ideal is being used to convey the notion of what we are truly required to do, independent of consideration of the many characteristics natural to our species which may be obstacles to what we should do. It is used to express the distinction between a strongly *a priori* versus *a posteriori* morality. (But note that a capital-Ideal can be *a priori* rather than *a posteriori*.) Insofar as Scheffler thinks morality is molded in part to people as they are, and that this is the capital-Ideal of morality, then he should, I believe, think that if there are other deep characteristics of human beings besides the partial and impartial points of view, then morality should of its nature give some weight to these deep characteristics, and make them part of a theory of duty as well as part of an Ideal with a capital "I." This suggests morality will be heavily *a posteriori*, unless there is some principled way of distinguishing between the partial/impartial factors of which it should take account and any other deep characteristics of humans which it should ignore. It also suggests, contrary to what Scheffler says, that the Ideal of Humanity cannot accept a life of self-sacrifice as morally laudable but supererogatory, since it (as much as egoism) is not part of the Ideal of integration of partial and impartial views.

Let us return to what I have called the *a priori* view of morality. If morality is heavily *a priori*, we shall have to develop a theory of how to overcome the obstacles to it. Developing a theory to deal with partial compliance is extremely difficult. It cannot merely be a matter of arranging things so that we come out as close as possible to the end state we would have been in with perfect compliance, since arranging things in this manner, e.g., checking up on hypocrisy or harassment, may itself involve us in doing something wrong. Further it can seem artificial to distinguish between applied ethics and applying applied ethics, since if we should take into account real life obstacles to applying a theory, we will merely be theorizing again about what we should do in imperfect situations and situations of partial compliance. This is a new part of applied theory, making it more complete, rather than anything separate from it. While this is true, I still believe it pays to distinguish ideal high and low theory from theory that includes all real-world factors. For we want to be sure we recognize the real-world factors as obstacles which we might prefer to change, rather than deal with, if we could. It is by the standards of ideal high and low theory that we can see their removal as desirable even if not possible.

What both high and low theory would continue to do—even if not applied and not heeded in action—is show people what the truth is. For example, they might teach persons what their true status is, what they continue to be and are entitled to, even if this status were not respected. For example, being entitled to inviolability is compatible with actually being violated by people's acts. It can in this sense be true in theory even if not in practice, and it may be more important that it is true in theory than that many lives can be saved in practice because it is not true. For example, if it is morally impermissible to kill one person in order to save more persons from being killed, then, even if people are killed impermissibly, they die with the status of persons who should not be killed; in contrast, if morality endorsed the permissibility of killing one person to save others (i.e., said that it was true in theory that people could be killed morally in these cases), each person's status would be diminished.[19]

Doing theory and inculcating it in others can also habituate people to high standards that make them dissatisfied with the inadequacies they and others exhibit in practice, unless, of course, there is so much false consciousness that they cannot notice true practice. This dissatisfaction is worthwhile in its own right, I believe, even if it has no further consequences, for at least we then evaluate ourselves and our failings correctly. But this dissatisfaction may also lead to a desire for improvement, and may at least lead to tolerance and perhaps some admiration, for the few "rationalists" whose behavior is not governed by, for example, the laws governing a Public Family. These are indirect practical effects which the theory could still have even if it didn't motivate much action directly.

The consideration of these hypotheticals helps us to see that theory is worth doing for its own sake. But it also helps us to see that the easier it is to bridge the theory/practice gap, the greater one's obligation to do so, and the more terrible the consequence of not bridging the gap, the more one's obligation increases as well.

NOTES

1. I am grateful to the editors of this NOMOS volume, to Leigh Cauman, Sigrun Svavarsdottir, Julia Driver, and to the faculty and students at the University of Rochester Philosophy Department and at the Harvard Program in Ethics and the Professions for help with this article. It is a successor to my "Ethics, Applied Ethics, and Applying Applied Ethics," in *Applied Ethics and Ethical Theory*, ed. D. Rosenthol and F. Shehadi (Salt Lake City: University of Utah Press, 1988).

2. Making either general principles, as in (1), or a mass of factors, as in (3), into more specific principles, as in (4), has been discussed (since my earlier article) by Henry Richardson in "Specifying Norms as a Way to Resolve Concrete Ethical Problems," *Philosophy and Public Affairs* 19:4 (Fall 1990): 279–310. Richardson refers to the process described in (4) as "specification" and uses it to do what I refer to as "low theory." In my view, by contrast, the specification process is actually part of doing high theory itself. What is brought out very nicely in Richardson's article is the way that the new, specified principles are continuations of the more general principles (or a bag of factors), so that in using the specific principles one can really be seen to be making use of the more general principles (or factors) even though one is not using them strictly speaking to *deduce* a result for a case.

3. For my views on killing and letting die, see *Morality, Mortality II* (New York: Oxford University Press, 1995), and "Killing and Letting Die: Methodological and Substantive Issues," *Pacific Philosophical Quarterly* 64 (1983): 297–312. For the application to abortion, see *Creation and Abortion* (New York: Oxford University Press, 1992). For the discussion of scarce resources and organ transplants, see *Morality, Mortal-*

ity I (New York: Oxford University Press, 1993), and "The Report of the U.S. Task Force on Organ Transplantation: Criticisms and Alternatives," *Mt. Sinai Journal of Medicine* (May 1989): 207–20.

4. Bernard Williams has spoken of "thick" and "thin" moral terms in *Ethics and the Limits of Philosophy* (London: Fontana, 1985). His use of these designations is different from the use to which I would put them.

5. Since writing this essay, I have read Ronald Dworkin's endorsement in *Life's Dominion* (New York: Knopf, 1993) of creating theory explicitly for a practical problem. He writes: "When we reason from the outside in, a practical issue must shop from among ready-made theories on the racks to see which theory asks and tries to answer questions that best fit its own dimensions. When we reason from the inside out, theories are bespoke, made for the occasion, Savile Row not Seventh Avenue. Theories homemade in that way, rather than wholesaled or imported, may be more likely to succeed in the political forum. They may be better suited to the academy, too" (29). Hereinafter references to Dworkin will appear parenthetically in the text of this essay.

6. Philippa Foot, "Euthanasia," *Philosophy & Public Affairs* 6:2 (Winter 1977): 85–112.

7. Stephen Toulmin, "The Tyranny of Principles," *Hastings Center Report* 11:6 (December 1981): 31–39.

8. John Rawls, *Political Liberalism* (New York: Columbia University Press, 1993).

9. See Lecture VI in Rawls, *Political Liberalism*.

10. These remarks are drawn from my "Abortion, Euthanasia, and the Value of Life: A Discussion of *Life's Dominion*," a longer study of Dworkin's *Life's Dominion* (New York: Knopf, 1993), to appear in *Columbia Law Review* (January 1995), and in *Dworkin and his Critics*, ed. Justine Burley (Oxford: Blackwell, forthcoming).

11. Thomas Scanlon makes this last point in his "Partisan for Life" in *New York Review of Books* (July 15, 1993), 45.

12. I owe this point to Sigrun Svavarsdottir.

13. These suggestions for how theorizing can be helpful do not depend on the psychological hypothesis that those who do theory are smarter than those who do not, and because they are smarter it is more likely that they will reach correct answers about particular problem cases. Here a common underlying cause of doing theory and of solving practical moral problems is posited, but the solution to the practical problems does not come through theorizing itself.

14. See, for example, "Theory and Practice," in *Kant's Political Writings*, ed. Hans Reiss (Cambridge: Cambridge University Press, 1970).

15. Thomas Nagel, *Equality and Partiality* (New York: Oxford University Press, 1991). Hereinafter references will appear parenthetically in the body of this essay.

16. Those who find the hypotheticals reminiscent of reality will find this description of them as hypotheticals merely ironic.

17. See, for example, Albert Carr "Is Business Bluffing Ethical?" reprinted in *Ethical Issues in Professional Life,* ed. Joan C. Callahan (New York: Oxford University Press, 1988) 69–72.

18. Samuel Scheffler, *Human Morality,* (New York: Oxford University Press, 1992) 125.

19. On this issue, see my "Non-consequentialism, the Person as an End-in-Itself and the Significance of Status," *Philosophy and Public Affairs* (Fall 1992): 354–89, and *Morality, Mortality II* (1994).

4

PSYCHOLOGICAL REALISM
AND MORAL THEORY

DAVID B. WONG

SETTING THE STAGE

Much contemporary moral theorizing revolves around a distinction between the personal and impersonal points of view. From the impersonal point of view one attaches equal weight to the interests of all persons, and when one takes that point of view, one acts on reasons that do not depend on one's particular identity as an agent. For example, when one acts to relieve someone's pain because any person in a position to relieve such a bad thing should do so, one is acting from the impersonal point of view. From the personal point of view one attaches greater weight to one's own interests and to personal relations to particular people, and one acts in ways that are justified and motivated by one's particular identity as an agent. For example, when I write this essay because it answers to *my* interests as a philosopher and not because I think that anyone who can do so ought to do so, I am acting from the personal point of view.

Modern moral theory is associated with the impersonal point of view, but some have argued that theory should take into account the personal point of view and attempt to achieve some sort of balance between the two. One reason for thinking that it should do so is the difficulty of conceiving human beings as giving *no* disproportionate weight whatsoever to their own interests and personal relations. Realism about the psychology of human beings suggests that moral theory should take into account the content and strength of personal motives. But the difficult question is *how* theory should take this content and strength into account. There are at least two general ways for theory to incorporate the content and strength of personal motives: there may be limits on the *manner* in which people ought to be required to give impersonal consideration to the interests of others; and there may be limits on the *extent* to which people ought to give such impersonal consideration. I shall argue that there are limits on the manner of requirement. But whether there are limits on the extent of requirement is more inconclusive and is related in complicated ways to the limits on manner of requirement. To unfold my argument, I will discuss some recent attempts to relate issues of psychological realism to moral theory.

STRONG AND MINIMAL FORMS OF PSYCHOLOGICAL REALISM

Bernard Williams provides the clearest example of criticism of moral theory on the grounds that it does not give enough weight to personal motives. Williams includes within the personal those "ground" projects of the individual that make life meaningful for her. Such projects include long-term personal goals and personal relations with particular people. Given their role in making life meaningful and coherent, Williams argues that it is unreasonable to require that the individual always set aside her ground projects if they conflict with impersonal principles. Modern moral theory in either utilitarian or Kantian forms, he believes, is committed to such an unreasonable requirement.[1] He calls for a rejection of modern theory for an ethics (exemplified in ancient Greece) that embraces the importance of personal ends to the individual as well as the values of freedom and of social justice that are the genuinely valuable elements of modern moral theory.[2]

Owen Flanagan has characterized Williams as a "strong psychological realist" who "given a life form which lies above some minimal standard of decency" sets his "standards of moral decency closer to, rather than farther from, the personalities of the agents to whom the theory is already addressed."[3] In response to his arguments, Flanagan points out that it is possible for agents, e.g., in following Buddhism, to be committed to a highly impersonal moral perspective and that there is nothing necessarily unreasonable about such a commitment. To the argument that it is neither normal nor natural to be as alienated from one's personal relations and projects as impersonal morality requires, Flanagan points out that what is natural or normal deserves sometimes to be suppressed, modified, or transcended. Further, it is difficult to say what *is* a normal or natural way to be attached to the personal, given actual variations in attachment to it across individuals, cultures, and historical periods. Finally, Flanagan argues that it sometimes is possible and desirable to teach succeeding generations what one cannot oneself learn. For example, if one's upbringing places a limit on the extent to which one can care for distant persons, that may be a reason to raise one's children differently, not a reason to place a limit on what impersonal morality can demand of us.[4]

In place of strong realism, Flanagan offers his Principle of Minimal Psychological Realism: "Make sure when constructing a moral theory or projecting a moral ideal that the character, decision processing, and behavior prescribed are possible, or are perceived to be possible, for creatures like us."[5] Flanagan rules out on the basis of this principle theories that require an individual to set aside all defensible aims whenever the nonessential desires of many others would be met by so doing.[6] In effect, this would rule out extreme consequentialist theories that require raw quantitative optimizing of agglomerated satisfactions with no deontological constraints whatsoever.

I think Flanagan's principle, as a minimal constraint on theory, is more plausible than strong psychological realism. But the issue merits further exploration. A person worried about the psychological realism of many mainstream moral theories may accept Flanagan's warning not to take our local, socially formed traits as universal, natural traits. She further may accept Flanagan's point that a good moral theory should provide a critical perspective on the most entrenched of our socially formed traits. She may grant that it is "possible" in some rather extended sense that human beings can be motivated to conform to impersonal moral theory as minimally qualified by deontological constraints. But she may insist that Flanagan is missing some important issues about psychological realism.

In particular, she may insist that we descend from talk about what is abstractly possible to what is "realistically" or "practically" possible. She may point out, in reply to Flanagan's use of Buddhism, that the religion in its most popular forms imposes on its lay people rather modest requirements for action. To claim that Buddhism in some forms may require a far stronger and pervasive expression of concern for life is not to show that most people could actually live that way. She further may point out that teaching succeeding generations to be very different from us may be merely an abstract possibility, if we cannot specify how our teaching would actually make people different. For example, we can stress to our children our obligations to distant persons more forcefully and more consistently than our parents did for us, but that does not mean that our children have a realistic possibility *of being* more concerned for distant persons and of acting on that concern.

THE COMPLEXITY OF REALISTIC POSSIBILITY

We should note at the outset that talk about realistic possibility is dangerous. Being "realistic" about the possibilities for change may wed us to the cultural, political, social, and economic institutions that have shaped our current motivations. Those institutions shape not only our motivations but our vision of what is possible. To some extent, we can mitigate this danger by taking the widest possible range of information—e.g., from anthropology, sociology, psychology, and from history—as our base for estimating the extent of realistic possibility. We reflect from this base on the question of whether we can reasonably expect to realize new institutions and practices that would effect the change in our actual motivations required by the impersonal point of view.

Notice that there are two dimensions to the notion of realistic possibility. To say that something is such a possibility is, first, to say that we have a conception of the *process* by which the possibility could be realized; and, secondly, that there is *evidence* for our ability to initiate and complete that process. By contrast, an unrealistic possibility may be one for which we have no conception of a process of realization or one for which there is no evidence (indeed, in the strongest case of unrealism there would be strong counterevidence) that we could initiate and complete any purported path to realization. Pretty clearly, we must allow for *degrees* of realism and unrealism. Conceptions of processes of realization will vary in the degree of their specificity. If we have only a vague and sketchy conception of a process of realization, we have a weaker case for the realism of the relevant possibility. Or our evidence for ability to initiate and implement may be sketchy, sparse, and even contradictory. Some possibilities will fall midway on the spectrum from the most unrealistic to the most realistic and hence will be neither realistic nor unrealistic.

What is a realistic possibility for human beings under certain circumstances, furthermore, is not necessarily a realistic possibility for *us* under our circumstances. Some of the circumstances that constrain our possibilities for change are unalterable, at least by us. Other constraining circumstances could be changed but should not be. For example, some alterable features of our institutions may render more difficult a desired change in our motivations, but they are so morally valuable or required that we should give them up. Further, what is a realistic possibility for us may depend on which of "us" are in question. For example, there may be a relevant distinction between what is realistic to expect of most people and what is realistic to expect of a few, perhaps exceptional, individuals. The existence of a Gandhi or a Mother Theresa may show that exemplary commitment to an impersonal moral ideal is within the range of human possibility, but their existence does not show that such commitment is possible for most people.

REALISTIC POSSIBILITY AND EQUALITY

An argument by Thomas Nagel provides good material for discussing the complexities of realistic possibility and its relation to the personal and impersonal in moral theory, so I shall summarize it in some detail. His argument is that we do not yet have an acceptable political ideal because we do not yet have an acceptable integration of the impersonal and personal viewpoints.[7] From the impersonal viewpoint, where no one is more important than anyone else, the alleviation of urgent needs and serious deprivation has particularly strong importance in the resolution of conflicts of interest. Also, argues Nagel, preferential weight is given to improvements in the lives of those who are worse off as against adding to the advantages of those better off. The personal viewpoint, on the other hand, gives rise to individualistic motives and requirements which present obstacles to the pursuit and realization of impersonal ideals. To be sure, it is not egoistic. It involves strong personal allegiance to particular communities of interest or conviction or emotional identification, larger than those defined by family or friendship, but it still is far less than universal.

The problem is to design institutions that do justice to the equal importance of all persons, without making unacceptable demands on individuals. "The ideal, then, is a set of institutions within which persons can live a collective life that meets the impartial requirements of the impersonal standpoint while at the same time having to conduct themselves only in ways that it is reasonable to require of individuals with strong personal motives."[8] Nagel wants to avoid utopianism, which he defines as describing "a collective form of life that humans, or most humans, could not lead and could not come to be able to lead through any feasible process of social and mental development."[9] He argues, "if real people find it psychologically very difficult or even impossible to live as the theory requires, or to adopt the relevant institutions, that should carry some weight against the ideal."[10] On the other hand, he cautions against an undue pessimism that would legitimate current apathy and wickedness.

What makes the task of finding realistic solutions especially difficult is that our ultimate aim in political theory should "be to approach as nearly as possible to unanimity, at some level, in support of those political institutions which are maintained by force and into which we are born."[11] Nagel suspects there are no general principles governing both agent-relative,[12] personal reasons and agent-neutral, impartial reasons, and their combination, which are acceptable from all points of view in light of their consequences under all realistically possible conditions. Under some conditions—including, I think, those of the actual world—any standards of individual conduct which try to accommodate both sorts of reasons will be either too demanding in terms of the first or not demanding enough in terms of the second.[13]

It is unacceptable to fall below a modest overall level of aid to others, but as we move above that level we enter a region where we "cannot will as a universal principle *either* that one *must* or that one *need not* help the needy at that level of sacrifice to one's personal aims."[14] We cannot will that one must help because of the strength of personal motives and certain intuitions we have about the reasonableness of letting people live their lives within wide boundaries. But we cannot will that one need not help beyond that modest level because reflection from the impersonal viewpoint compels recognition of our duty to correct for the advantages or disadvantages that are out of people's control:

> What seems bad is not that people should be unequal in advantages or disadvantages generally, but that they should be unequal in the advantages or disadvantages for which they are not responsible . . . whatever remotely plausible positive condition of responsibility one takes as correct, many of the important things in life—especially the advantages and disadvantages with which people are born or which form the basic framework within which they must lead their lives—cannot be regarded as goods or evils for which they are responsible, and so fall under the egalitarian principle.[15]

Nagel admits that a significant step towards equality might be embodied in constitutional guarantees for everyone of medical care, education, decent housing, unemployment insurance, child care allowances, retirement benefits, and even a minimum income. But a strongly egalitarian system is beyond the reach of constitutionalization, and the prospects of realizing it through legislation are remote: "As things are, democracy is the enemy of comprehensive equality once the poor cease to be a majority."[16] In large, ethnically diverse societies such as our own, "a politically secure combination of equality with liberty and democracy would require a far greater transformation of human nature than there is reason either to expect or to require."[17]

Clearly, Nagel believes that the power of personal motives puts some abstractly possible solutions beyond the boundaries of realistic possibility. An example he gives is the failure of attempts to create a classless society. If the personal element of most people's motivation cannot be shrunk enough or the impersonal element expanded enough, states Nagel, "a system of comprehensive public ownership seems doomed to degenerate under a combination of stagnation, nepotism, and a parallel black market, not to mention the political oppression and cruelty which may be required to keep it in place."[18] Here Nagel seems to have in mind what is realistically possible for *most* people and given certain desirable features of Western capitalist democracies: relatively efficient and productive economies and individual civil liberties:

> Going by contemporary evidence, the advantages of a significant private sector in the economy of a modern society are enormous, as measured by productivity, innovation, variety, and growth. The productive advantages of competitive market economies are due to the familiar acquisitive motives of individuals, which lead them to exert themselves most energetically to produce or supply what others need or want not from benevolence, but from the hope of reward and the fear of failure.[19]

Since "it does not belong to the socialized nature of modern man in general to be motivated by a concern for the good of all in most of his working, let alone private, life,"[20] a debilitating conflict of motives emerges:

> As acquisitive individuals they must force their socially conscientious selves to permit talent-dependent rewards as the unavoidable price of productivity, efficiency, and growth. As participants in the system they are expected, indeed encouraged, to pursue those advantages, but as citizens they are expected to allow them only reluctantly. They must regard it as legitimate and natural to want them, but in another light not legitimate to have them.[21]

"So long as private motives remain significantly acquisitive and strongly partial," he concludes, "it is impossible to create a strongly egalitarian system without unacceptable invasions of personal freedom and disastrous economic consequences."[22] On the possibility of substituting other personal motives for acquisitiveness, Nagel grants that "people can of course be motivated to work hard at something they are interested in for its own sake, and sometimes this will yield a product which others also want. But it is a romantic fantasy to imagine the world run on such a basis. We cannot all be creative artists, research scientists, or professional athletes."[23] He further argues that even if everyone were motivated to do his job well, design and manufacture must be motivated by economically expressed demand. Such decisions will not be motivated as a form of self-expression, and neither will benevolence provide a basis for them. And the most effective motive for responding to market information is "a strong investment of personal ambition and desire for success in productive activities that pay off. It is hard to do without people who work hard and exercise their ingenuity for gain and competitive success; yet in a stable egalitarian society they would have to combine this with a desire to live under a system which made as difficult as possible for them to achieve these goals." While such a combination of attitudes is not contradictory, grants Nagel, it is "not strictly intelligible."

I find compelling Nagel's case from the impersonal perspective for a strong form of equality. He is right in pointing out that many of the advantages and disadvantages with which people are born, and the basic framework within which they must live their lives, are not under their control. One could, of course, take the libertarian perspective and assert that it is freedom that matters and economic freedom without pervasive interference from government that matters especially. That is a coherent view, but a view that the vast majority of people have rejected in practice, however many times some of them bring it up when it is in their interest. The fact is that it is a core belief of our moral traditions that we do have collective responsibility for the harms and absence of significant goods that befall people no matter what they do. Much of the political argument in the United States at present is over the question of how much control people do have over the harms and benefits that befall them. But much of the division on this matter, as I will note below, rests on myth. Nagel cannot be more right when he considers the serious effects of class advantage and disadvantage.

Nagel, I think, is certainly right to bring considerations of realistic possibility into the evaluation and construction of moral theory. And he is right to be impressed by the need for incentives in the form of differential rewards for one's contributions in an economic system. In support of this point he briefly mentions the failures of communism in Europe. But whether the failures that precipitated change were political or economic or both is arguable. A clearer and more impressive example is China.[24] What impresses there is that it is the Communist government effecting the transition to a "socialist market economy"[25] and that the burst of entrepreneurial energy released is astonishing in its magnitude, resulting in double-digit growth and the third-largest economy in the world.[26] Furthermore, Nagel is right in trying to find the fine line between a sensible realism and an undue pessimism that ends up legitimating the institutions and motivations already in place.

But while he acknowledges the need to locate that line, he too frequently falls onto the side of undue pessimism. He does not take the widest range of evidence on what is realistic for human beings or even for human beings in modern, industrialized economies with democratic political structures. Nor does he distinguish the question of what is realistic given the "socialized nature" of modern human beings and what is realistic for people in the United States given their culture, current institutions, and dominant motivations.

THE DANGERS OF UNDERESTIMATING THE COMPLEXITIES OF REALISTIC POSSIBILITY

Consider Nagel's worry about the intelligibility of combining impersonal motives with personal motives of acquisitiveness and competitiveness. I do not find this worry persuasive. People are sufficiently complicated to be able on the one hand to try to get the most out of an economic system given its present rules but on the other hand to think that the system ought to have different rules. They are highly capable of contextualizing different attitudes. For example, studies have shown that people in modernizing societies are able to retain traditional attitudes and beliefs that have been thought to have been incompatible with their being able to function in developed economies. The trick is precisely the ability to contextualize one's attitudes, so that one set is appropriate for work and another for life in the family and the community.[27] The same contextualizing strategy applies to one's role in the economic system and one's role as a citizen.

Perhaps Nagel thinks that the desire for as much gain as possible would undermine the desire to live under a more egalitarian system. But even his version of strong equality would presumably not eliminate all rewards for ability or effort. It is just that the rewards would be smaller. Perhaps the worry is that someone who exercises her ingenuity and works hard for gain and competitive success would not want to live under a system that provides her with smaller rewards. But then I am surprised that an academic would not be struck by the extent to which people can be motivated to work hard for the sake of small rewards. Sometimes Nagel treats such fields as exceptions to the rule, along with the arts, entertainment, and sports, where intrinsic satisfaction of the work itself or recognition and honor of some kind is sufficient to motivate great effort. But to hold these fields so much apart from all others is to neglect the evident fact that people in many of these other fields *do* get satisfaction from doing their jobs well and in having their accomplishments recognized by a very small number of peers, subordinates, and superiors.

More generally, Nagel's estimate of the realistic possibilities for strong egalitarianism seems too much influenced by his perceptions of the present situation in the United States. His emphasis on acquisitiveness as the primary personal motive in productive economies seems very much culture-bound. It ignores, for example, the impressive successes of the Japanese economy, together with studies done on the configuration of personal motives that help to fuel that economy. The powerful achievement motivations displayed by many Japanese seems anchored not in acquisitiveness but partly in their identifications with family and the desire to reflect well on them and partly in the feeling of a debt owed to them for their care.[28] The desire to reflect well on one's family and community also seems a primary motive for high achievement in modernizing sectors of the economy in India.[29] Such work on other cultures suggests that modernization and economic competitiveness do not necessarily require the psychology of competitive individualism that is much more dominant in the United States at present and that seems to inspire Nagel's pessimism.

Consider also his pessimism about the prospects of reasonable agreement on a strong form of equality. Behind that pessimism lies the thought that the more advantaged can reasonably reject strong egalitarian principles requiring substantial sacrifice of their personal ends for the sake of the less advantaged, while the less advantaged can reasonably reject principles that require less sacrifice by the more advantaged. Now I am in fact more pessimistic than Nagel is about the prospects for universal rational consensus on principles of distributive justice. My reason, however, is not so much the difficulties of balancing the personal and the impersonal in theory but a view about the scope of principles of reason, if such principles are conceived (as Nagel conceives them) as universally valid across all cultures, societies, and historical periods.

I simply do not believe that disputes over the proper balance between personal and impersonal values can be settled by such principles of reason even when combined with all the psychological, political, economic, sociological, and anthropological evidence we desire. This particular disagreement I have with Nagel is too large to address here.[30] What I am concerned to show here is that the problem of balancing the personal and impersonal can be more or less difficult to resolve, more or less subject to radical disagreement among people in a society, depending on the particular content and strength of personal motives that are dominant in a society. Ultimately, I shall be recommending that we seek consensus (or as much of it as we can achieve) on principles of distributive justice by examining the configuration of personal motives in our particular society, and not by seeking a universal consensus that applies across all sorts of societies.

Recall that Nagel's pessimism on the prospects for reaching

consensus involves the thought that what is reasonable for the more advantaged to reject conflicts with what is reasonable for the less advantaged to reject. We may ask, however, what justifies that thought, and whether it is anything more than our intuitions of what degree of personal sacrifice is reasonable to demand of people. And if it is nothing more than our intuitions, we must ask whether they are not greatly shaped by the norms of our particular culture here in the United States. Here again, in estimating the realistic possibilities for the "socialized nature of modern man," we must look to the broadest range of information about the actual range of attitudes. Relevant to this question is a study by Sidney Verba and his colleagues on the attitudes about equality held by leadership elites in the United States, Japan, and Sweden.[31]

Leaders (from business and labor groups, feminists, advocates for ethnic minorities, political parties, the media, and intellectual elites) were asked to choose between two definitions of a fair economic system—one in which all people would earn about the same and one in which earnings would be commensurate with ability. In the United States, all groups among the elites surveyed were on the conservative side of the scale, rejecting to a greater or lesser degree rough equality of earnings. In Sweden, by contrast, the issue is more open. Two groups take positions on the equal-shares side. Japan fell at about the midpoint between the other two nations. Interestingly, almost all groups in the United States and Japan want to see some reduction in the income gap between the top earner and the skilled or unskilled worker (this was less true in Sweden, but the cause was significantly greater equality of income than in Japan and especially in the United States).

No leadership group would reduce the income disparity completely, primarily for the familiar reasons of efficiency and productivity. In the United States, even the most radical groups would accept as fair a ratio of executive to unskilled worker earnings of between 8:1 to 10:1. In Japan there is a tendency to favor a somewhat narrower income gap. Business and labor leaders favor ratios slightly more than half as large as those favored by their counterparts in the United States. Views of the Swedish elite are of a different order of magnitude. Each group in the United States and Japan favor ratios that are many times as large as those that their counterparts in Sweden consider to be fair. Further, there is no overlap between the preferred ratios among the Swedish groups and those of the groups in the other two nations. The *left* party leaders in Japan and the United States favor an earnings ratio about three times as large as that favored by the *conservative* leaders in Sweden. The *least* egalitarian group in Sweden, business leaders, consider as fair a ratio of their income to that of the unskilled worker that is very close in magnitude to that of the *most* egalitarian groups in Japan and the United States. Views of Japanese leaders lie between those of other two, though they are if anything closer to those in Sweden than in the United States.[32]

There is, of course, the much-observed phenomenon of "backing away" from the welfare state and equality in Sweden. Verba and his colleagues, however, remind us that this backing away must be understood within the context of an already well-developed egalitarian commitment. If some Swedish leaders would move back from that direction, the level of commitment to welfare and redistribution would still be greater than that to which the most radical of leadership groups in Japan and the United States aspire.[33] In Sweden, and other parts of the democratic West, the authors observe, economic crisis seems to have strengthened the hand of the conservatives.

Consider the findings that in Sweden a radical equality more stringent than Nagel's strong equality is still an open question and that the entire left-right range of attitudes is considerably to the left of those in the United States. Even a backing away from equality in Sweden on the matter of preferred ratio of income would leave the conservatives still to the left of the most radical groups in the United States. Consider that the study was conducted at a time of economic downturn, which seems to push people toward the conservative end of the spectrum. The broad range of *actual* attitudes (never mind possible ones) about equality even among the democratic developed nations, and the significant influence of particular economic conditions on these attitudes, should make us wary about accepting any particular set of intuitions as to what the more advantaged could reasonably be required to sacrifice. In particular, Nagel's intuitions about reasonableness on this matter seem to have been overly influenced by the psychology of competitive individualism as found in the United States.

Even with respect to the United States, Nagel seems excessively pessimistic about the dominance of this psychology. It was not that long ago that the "organization man" was said to be the dominant middle-class character type, for whom making money was fine but only a by-product of belonging to an organization where one could make a contribution, where one could be proud of the work one was doing.[34] Perhaps this way of being motivated appeared quite natural to people who had lived through New Deal cooperation to combat the Great Depression and the mobilization of the nation to fight the Second World War. On the other hand, it does seem that the time for dominance of such a character type is over, and Nagel's pessimism has a basis in the present situation. Even now, however, the children of the organization men may be motivated not primarily by acquisitiveness but by a search for self-fulfillment and self-expression.[35] This is not to deny the place of acquisitiveness as a powerful motivation. But if it is not the primary one or simply one among several primary ones, the case for pessimism about the prospects of strong equality weakens.

Furthermore, a closer look at the way that Sweden and Japan have achieved greater equality than the United States will lead us to question Nagel's rather simple contrast between commitment to personal values versus commitment to impersonal values. As Verba and his colleagues tell the story, Sweden's course to making the strongest effort toward equality of any industrialized nation was set by a long tradition of acceptance of hierarchy (ironically enough) and of deference to governmental authority, a process of industrialization that promoted compromise and accommodation between established groups and the working class, the dominant political role of the Social Democratic Party, and a strong Socialist party allied with strong unions. Compared to Sweden, the Japanese government has undertaken relatively few measures to promote equality (it does not, for example, use the tax and transfer system for redistribution as in Sweden). Rather, greater equality seems to have resulted partly from a group-oriented ethic and from the weakening (though certainly not disappearance) of the tendency to accept hierarchical statuses. These factors have contributed to a shrinkage in the disparity of top and bottom wage-earners within private firms.[36]

Shall we say that Swedish and Japanese commitments to equality are commitments to an impersonal value? The impersonal element is certainly there. But just as present in the Swedish case is the tendency to defer to governmental authority, and it is not clear which side such a tendency falls in Nagel's contrast. If it belongs anywhere it belongs in the personal. In the Japanese case there is something that Nagel would classify as a personal commitment—personal allegiance to a "community of interest . . . larger than those defined by family or friendship" but still "far less than universal." However, there is also the absorption of values of equality from the time of American occupation. In both cases the personal and impersonal elements seem inseparable from the actual commitment that promoted equality.[37]

To return to the issue of whether the project of promoting the impersonal value of strong equality is a psychologically realistic one: this issue now becomes partly one about the realistically possible *ways* to link the impersonal value with sufficiently strong "personal" values, i.e., ways to mediate the commitment to the impersonal through sufficiently strong personal commitments. In other words, the question of whether it is realistic to require a robust commitment to strong equality may depend on the *manner* in which that requirement is to be fulfilled. Nagel, I suspect, did not explore this aspect of the issue because of his implicit identification of the impersonal realm of values with public morality. Another reason, I also suspect, is his implicit assumption about the power of the acquisitive motive for most people given the kind of work they do. At crucial places, where Nagel argues for his pessimism, the acquisitive motive stands in for personal motives. But an important lesson of this essay's examination of the Verba study is not only that commitments to impersonal values are typically mediated by commitments to personal values, but that significant distinctions must be made within the class of personal motives.

A Communitarian Commitment to Equality?

To some extent, the argument thus far has provided some support for communitarian criticisms of liberal political theory. Especially relevant is a criticism made by Michael Sandel of the liberal inability to provide persuasive justifications for principles of strong equality such as Rawls's Difference Principle. In the end, he argues, the better off will be able to accept the sacrifices required by such principles only if they see their individual good as intertwined with the common good. Sandel argues, for example, that when such a mode of self-understanding becomes widespread within a group, its members regard each other less as others and more as participants in a common identity, "be it family or community or class or people or nation." A consequence of such a self-understanding is that

> when "my" assets or life prospects are enlisted in the service of a common endeavor, I am likely to experience this less as a case of being used for others' ends and more as a way of contributing to the purposes of a community I regard as my own. The justification of my sacrifice, if it can be called a sacrifice, is not the abstract assurance that unknown others will gain more than I will lose, but the rather more compelling notion that by my efforts I contribute to the realization of a way of life in which I take pride and with which my identity is bound.[38]

Sandel's point about sacrifice becoming a contribution to a community with which one identifies, instead of an "abstract assurance that unknown others will gain," is close to the conclusion here that the most realistic possibility of realizing strong equality is by mediating commitment to it through certain kinds of personal values.[39] The present conclusion also supports the type of ethic that attempts to connect the good or the flourishing of the individual with that individual's duties toward others. Consider Aristotle's attempt to link the flourishing of the individual with his participation in the political community, via the claim that human beings are political animals. Or consider the Confucian notion that human beings find their fulfillment in community with others, where the notion of community is less political in nature than in Aristotle's theory.[40] But the conclusion reached here, we should note, does not confirm certain other themes sometimes found in communitarian philosophy: the categorical rejection of impersonal values, the claim (mistaken, in my view) that liberalism presupposes some queer metaphysical notion of the self as existing independently of relationship to others and to communities. Nor, of course, does the conclusion reached here reveal how we are to promote a mediation of impersonal equality through personal values.

It does not seem realistic to think that most people in the U.S. would come to a stronger commitment to equality via a Swedish-style deference to governmental authority. Nor would most of us regard such a route as desirable. It would require a change in the political culture that most of us value highly. Yet, as Verba and his colleagues note, the American antipathy toward established authority limits the state's ability to lead its citizens toward a stronger commitment to equality.[41] If there are realistic prospects for a greater commitment to equality in the United States, they would seem to depend on a stronger and more pervasive commitment to community-oriented values. But is that a realistic prospect?

IS A COMMUNITARIAN COMMITMENT TO EQUALITY REALISTIC?

As noted above, strengthened commitment to equality emerged in certain historical periods. After the Second World War, minorities "who had long perceived themselves as having unfulfilled claims on the moral sense of the whole nation" were able to "exert an unusual degree of purchase on that moral sense and make it bear on the processes of law and law-making." This new ability was tied partly to the general recognition that members of these minorities had contributed, often at very great cost, to the collective war effort. It also was tied, observes J. R. Pole, to the clarification of American social and political values that resulted in fighting enemies representing "racial and religious hatred, tyranny over the spiritual, intellectual, and physical liberties of all individuals and associations that failed to conform to the state's prescriptions . . . fairly clear opposites to anything that Americans were willing to claim as their own inheritance."[42] The changed attitude toward minorities exemplifies the kind of mix of personal and impersonal values present in the Swedish and Japanese efforts toward equality: a recognition of minorities as contributing members to a collective effort of the greatest importance on the one hand, and a clarification and intensified commitment to impersonal values of liberty and equality that were seen to be at the core of the national community's moral tradition.

Noting the effect of the Second World War, however, brings out a new issue about the realism of mediating a commitment to strong equality through a commitment to a national community. It is of course absurd and perverse to propose that we start a war in order to promote a greater spirit of community in the nation. But do we have alternative means of comparable efficacy? It is notable that political leaders often use the metaphor of war when they call on their people to make some sacrifice for a collective end. The question is whether such calls are ineffective in the context of a strong cultural current of individualism, in which people are looking inward and increasingly reluctant to acknowledge that they have obligations to address the situation of the less advantaged.

Furthermore, don't Sweden and Japan differ from the United States in a way that is crucially relevant to the question of whether it is realistic to try to promote equality through strengthening a community-oriented ethic? The former two societies are relatively homogeneous in ethnic and cultural terms, while the United States is heterogeneous in just these terms (remember Nagel's reference to the difficulties of establishing a "politically secure" combination of liberty and equality in "large, ethnically diverse" societies). Doesn't that make a strong community-oriented ethic (with the nation as community) an unlikely prospect?

These are the most frequently expressed criticisms of the call to strengthen the communitarian strains in the American moral and political tradition. There is a fair amount of tension between the different criticisms. On the one hand, our society is too heterogeneous to be a genuine community, and on the other hand, it is too homogeneous to become a community. The rising tide of individualism, after all, consists in more and more people adopting the *same* set of values. Whether or not these two sorts of criticism are compatible, I am more concerned about the conflicts generated by increasing homogeneity rather than by the potential conflicts generated by heterogeneity.

Those who associate harmonious community with shared values (both communitarians and their liberal critics make this association) should realize that it all depends on what values are shared. Groups that are otherwise heterogeneous can live together and even join in common projects if they share some values, including those of tolerance and accommodation with each other.[43] And groups that share many values can conflict severely. The values associated with individualism, after all, can and do generate conflicts of claims—competing claims for rights, opportunities and material resources. The older and more established ethnic groups in the United States have learned this language of claims very well. The new groups may bring a different language, corresponding to a different political culture, but to the extent that they do, they seem less inclined or less able to even enter the political process of competing claims.

Nevertheless there is a serious issue about the realistic prospects for implementing the ideal of a communitarian commitment to strong equality. The reasons for this differ importantly. One reason why the prospects are in doubt is a deeply entrenched *moral* belief held by Americans: a preference for the ideal of equality of *opportunity* rather than equality of *result*. Lawrence Blum has pointed out that what equality of opportunity has come to mean is equality of *competitive* opportunity—in the great majority of cases, opportunity to compete with a great many others for a few desirable positions. Blum has pointed out how deeply problematic this notion is (for one thing, competition results in winners and losers, and competitive advantages or disadvantages accrue, both to the winners and losers and those closely connected to them, such that equality of competition is undermined.[44]) He also points out how far this current notion of equal opportunity differs from the original mythic notion when Americans had a genuine frontier, where something closer to equal life prospects seemed available.[45] But so far such arguments have not undermined the strength of belief in competitive opportunity and its equation with the original mythic opportunity.

At this point, however, we have reached another level of realistic possibility. We have descended from talk about realistic possibility for human beings per se to people in modern, industrialized democracies to people in the United States and now finally to people in the United States given certain entrenched moral beliefs. At this point we must ask whether moral theory should be evaluated while holding constant certain entrenched though problematic moral beliefs. We must preserve the difference between moral theories that should be adjusted to the realistic possibilities of what people can do and be, on the one hand, and moral theories that simply demand too little of people because of entrenched unreasonableness and the acceptance of myth. When realistic possibility is estimated on the basis of entrenched moral belief independently of its reasonableness, it cannot be used to evaluate moral *theory*.

This is not to deny this kind of realistic possibility a proper place in influencing our pragmatic and strategic decisions concerning what to do now in addressing the situation of the less advantaged. The resistance of Americans to the idea of equal results, for example, can move us to press for universal entitlement programs instead of ones specially targeted at the less advantaged. It can move us to press for a more extensive and higher minimal floor of welfare in the short term. As Nagel says, perhaps it is too difficult to see our way to a distant goal such as strong equality until we have taken more intermediate steps. But it should be obvious by now that we are not evaluating the requirement of strong equality in *theory*. Instead of bringing realistic possibility to bear on moral theory from the *outside*, so to speak, we are now bringing it to bear from the inside, where it influences our considerations as to how best strategically to attempt to realize the values of the theory.

There is, however, another reason why the prospects for a communitarian commitment to strong equality are in doubt, and this reason may bear on the adequacy of moral theories that require such a commitment. The reason is the progressive weakening of the apparent base for strengthening that communitarian commitment. Traditional forms of community (extended and nuclear families, neighborhoods, work organizations to which one can expect to be attached for the long term, labor unions, and organized religion)[46] seem to be weakening, and it is unclear what other forms of community, if any, will evolve. Yet smaller forms of community seem necessary to mediate the relation between individuals and the enormous nation. Individuals by themselves will not have enough voice and influence to have the sort of membership necessary for genuine community. And, of course, we never can remind ourselves too frequently of the dangers of atomized individuals whose only bonds are to a huge national community.

Individuals need to learn within the smaller forms of community the habits, skills, and values that would enable them to be genuine members of a national community. Edward Shils has discussed those smallest forms of community that are crucial in shaping the identities and values of their members. Calling them "primary groups," after Charles Horton Cooley,[47] Shils draws some conclusions from studies of their importance for morale within the military. He was struck by

> the relative unimportance of direct identification with the total symbols of the military organization as a whole, of the state, or of the political cause in the name of which a war is fought, as contrasted with the feelings of strength and security in the military primary group and of loyalty to one's immediate comrades. The soldier's motivation to fight is not derived from his perceiving and striving toward any strategic or political goals; it is a function of his need to protect his primary group and to conform with its expectations. The military machine thus obtains its inner cohesion . . . through a system of overlapping primary groups. The effective transmission and execution of commands along the formal line of authority can be successful only when it coincides with this system of informal groups.[48]

More generally, Shils maintains that

> individuals who are members of larger social structures make their decisions and concert their actions within those structures, not by the direct focus of attention on the central authority and the agents who bear the symbols of that authority, but rather by identification with some individual with whom they have primary-group relationships and who serves to transmit to them ideas from and concerning the larger structure.[49]

In recognizing how it is that the moral concerns and commitments fostered in primary groups could give rise to larger concerns and commitments, we must also inquire into the possible role of associations that are intermediate between primary groups and large-scale societies. They would be intermediate in terms of size and intimacy of interaction. Such associations may serve as channels of communication from the smallest primary groups to the largest structures containing them. William de Bary has recently identified two reasons for the failure of Confucianism to be more influential than it has been in its native country: (1) an inability to realize its ideal of education for all people that would infuse a unified national consciousness, and (2) a failure to mobilize the people as a politically active body, capable of supporting its initiatives and proposed reforms. The second failure, suggests de Bary, was linked to the lack of an infrastructure of politically effective associations that could serve as channels of communication and influence between the family and local forms of community on the one hand, and the ruling elite on the other.[50] Strikingly, a major and justifiable concern of many political theorists in this country is the disappearance or eroding authority of precisely such an intermediate infrastructure.

Some see hope in the relationally-oriented ethics attributed to women by Gilligan and others and in the more community-oriented ethics of some ethnic minorities.[51] The extent to which the ethics of these groups are significantly different and whether the greater participation of these groups in the political and economic life of the nation would affect the values of the other groups is unclear. That greater participation by these groups would weaken and dilute any distinctive ethic they possess is also a distinct possibility. Moreover, it is unclear that a relationally-oriented ethic would make a significant difference because, in part, such an ethic can be extremely circumscribed in its boundaries of concern. To care about relationships may merely be to care about one's own relationships to particular others, or about others like oneself.[52]

Do these points weigh against the realism of a greater communitarian commitment to equality? Recall that the realism or unrealism of a possibility may fall somewhere on a spectrum between the most realistic to the most unrealistic, depending on the specificity of our conception of the process by which the given possibility could be realized and on the evidence for or against our ability to initiate and complete that process. In this case, we certainly cannot deem a sufficiently strengthened communitarian commitment a clearly realistic possibility for *us here and now*, but neither can we deem it a clearly unrealistic possibility. There are pockets where such a strengthened commitment exists. Such a commitment, after all, does not require the moral level of a Mother Theresa or a Gandhi. Some fair number of people, far less than the majority but far greater than the number of exceptional moral exemplars, have demonstrated this kind of commitment. Thus we know it is possible under some circumstances. But whether it can take place under something like our circumstances on a sufficiently large scale is a question we simply do not know how to answer. What is the proper conclusion, then? In light of our inability to say that strong equality is a realistic possibility, shall we moderate the requirement to have impersonal concern for all? Or shall we retain that requirement simply because we are unable to say that it is an *un*realistic possibility?

MORAL CONFLICT IN THEORY AND IN PRACTICE

To pose the question this way is reminiscent of Nagel's claim that we neither can will as a universal principle that one must help the needy (at a level of sacrifice that goes far beyond modest aid) nor that one need not do so. Unlike Nagel, however, I think we can will as a universal principle that one must help. We must do that because we cannot take as a given the strength of acquisitive and competitive motives as found here in the United States. The fact that we do not know whether a communitarian commitment to strong equality is an *un*realistic possibility weighs in favor of retaining the requirement of impersonal concern. If nothing else, we need to retain that requirement as a spur to keep looking for genuine possibilities of change and to keep striving to make our local forms of community more consistent with the aspiration to strong equality. And if we do not know now the path to implementing strong equality on a large scale, we can join and create local forms of community that have among their aims aid to the less advantaged. The possibilities for actually aiding some number of people are real enough. Further, nothing at all justifies the level of creature comforts that the more advantaged in the United States have come to regard as their just entitlement.

On the other hand, Nagel is right in recognizing that acting on other sorts of personal motives has some ethical justification even when doing so exacts some cost (though it cannot be an unlimited cost) to one's efforts for strong equality. If we cannot envision anywhere near a realistic possibility for realizing strong equality other than by its mediation through personal values, we must recognize the essential place of the personal in realizing *impersonal* values.[53] We further must recognize that in any healthy moral life there are commitments to communities and personal relationships other than the commitment to one's society as a community. These other commitments involve special duties to particular persons and particular local communities. The smaller forms of community have a moral life of their own. It is not just that, from a certain point of view, people should be permitted to act on their ties to these persons and communities. It is that they often are *required* to do so.

Beyond the level of modest aid to the less advantaged, then, the more advantaged will always be facing a potential conflict. On the one hand there is that which they reasonably need to live a personally meaningful life and their obligations to those people and communities with whom they have a personal relationship. On the other hand, there are the pressing claims on them posed by needs of those far worse off than they. Yet realizing those pressing claims depends on cultivating and strengthening the smaller forms of community. I believe there is no consistent theory that can absolve most of us from wrong doing when faced with such conflicts. But unlike Nagel, I do not regard this as a defect of theory. It is a reflection on our moral condition.

It is both true that we can reasonably devote many of our efforts to particular people and to smaller communities than the nation (not to speak, even, of the world) to whom we have special duties *and* that since these communities have a moral life of their own many of those efforts cannot be justified on the level of impersonal value. Whatever is required to maintain an effective commitment to strong equality, for instance, may amount to far less than always performing our special duties to particular persons and communities. The upshot is that we may do wrong either in giving priority to those people or communities with whom we have some personal relationship or in giving priority to the less advantaged in general.

In moral practice, we often leave such irresolvable conflicts of values in place. We acknowledge the conflict and do not attempt to provide some resolution at a level of abstraction higher than the values in conflict (as is attempted under utilitarian theories, for example). In practice, we sometimes acknowledge that we cannot avoid some wrongdoing, given the way we are and the way the world is. The discussion in this essay weighs in favor of the conclusion that we (in the United States, not all human beings, not all in the modern industrialized democracies) simply do not have a solution at a higher level of abstraction. At present and at best, theory can clarify the nature of our present value conflicts and point to the possibilities of resolution — possibilities that are neither realistic nor unrealistic.

To individuals who face conflicts between their commitments to strong equality and to more local forms of community and who must do something wrong no matter what they do, theory can offer a partial excuse: some wrongdoing is unavoidable and in that sense partially excusing. Theory can also offer the consolation that without local forms of community, we would not have a base for realizing strong equality. But theory should not lower the requirement to seek larger forms of community that would truly realize that equality.

NOTES

1. See Bernard Williams, "Persons, Character, and Morality," in *Moral Luck* (Cambridge: Cambridge University Press, 1981), 1–19.
2. Bernard Williams, *Ethics and the Limits of Philosophy* (Cambridge: Harvard University Press, 1985), 198.
3. Owen Flanagan, *Varieties of Moral Personality* (Cambridge: Harvard University Press, 1991), 56.

4. Flanagan, 97–98.
5. Flanagan, 32.
6. Flanagan, 73.
7. Thomas Nagel, *Equality and Partiality* (New York: Oxford University Press, 1991).
8. Nagel, 18.
9. Nagel, 6.
10. Nagel, 21.
11. Nagel, 8.
12. Agent-relative reasons are "reasons specified by universal principles which nevertheless refer ineliminably to features or circumstances of the agent for whom they are reasons. The contrast is with *agent-neutral* reasons, which depend on what everyone ought to value, independently of its relation to himself" (Nagel, 40).
13. Nagel, 49.
14. Nagel, 50.
15. Nagel, 71.
16. Nagel, 89–90.
17. Nagel, 90.
18. Nagel, 27–28.
19. Nagel, 91.
20. Nagel, 91.
21. Nagel, 115.
22. Nagel, 116.
23. Nagel, 121.
24. A national liquor and confectionery fair staged in Chengdu recently is symbolic of the radical changes in that country: Huge balloons and giant inflatable liquor bottles and soft-drink cans surround a titanic statue of Mao (Bruce W. Nelan, "Watch Out for China," *Time*, November 29, 1993, 38.
25. Indicative was the pronouncement on May Day by the Communist Party that workers must adapt to market economics and never return to centralized socialist planning (*Agence France Presse*, May 1, 1993).
26. What is sobering, however, is the fact that the rural population is falling further and further behind the standard of living that is rising in the urban areas. The government has done little to mitigate this severe inequality, along with the severe forms of dislocation and social instability created by rapid industrialization. This reminds, unfortunately, of the costs imposed by the Industrial Revolution in Europe and the United States. Given these problems, it is an open question whether the People's Republic will survive in its present form for very long.
27. For a description of this work on India, see Alan Roland, *In*

Search of Self in India and Japan: Toward a Cross-Cultural Psychology (Princeton: Princeton University Press, 1988).

28. See George DeVos, *Socialization and Achievement* (Berkeley: University of California Press, 1973), and "Dimensions of the Self in Japanese Culture," in *Culture and Self: Asian and Western Perspectives*, ed. A. J. Marsella, G. DeVos, and F. L. K. Hsu (London: Tavistock, 1985), 141–84. See also Roland, especially 130–37.

29. See Roland, 90–104.

30. This matter I address in *Moral Relativity* (Berkeley: University of California Press, 1984).

31. Sidney Verba and Steven Kelman, Gary R. Orren, Ichiro Miyake, Joji Watanuki, Ikuo Kabashima, and G. Donald Ferree, Jr., *Elites and the Idea of Equality: A Comparison of Japan, Sweden, and the United States* (Cambridge: Harvard University Press, 1987).

32. Verba, 146.

33. Verba, 146.

34. See William H. Whyte, Jr., *The Organization Man* (New York: Simon & Schuster, 1956).

35. See Paul Leinberger and Bruce Tucker, *The New Individualists: The Generation After the Organization Man* (New York: HarperCollins, 1991). See also Robert N. Bellah, Richard Madsen, William N. Sullivan, Ann Swidler, and Steven M. Tipton, *Habits of the Heart* (Berkeley: University of California Press, 1985) and Charles Taylor, *The Ethics of Authenticity* (Cambridge: Harvard University Press, 1992).

36. See Verba, 20–57.

37. Or consider Norman Sheehan, an Irishman currently living in Boston, who served as a relief worker helping the victims of famine and war in the Sudan, Liberia, Iraq, and Somalia. One might assume that such a person would exemplify the purest of commitments to impersonal values, yet he explained his initial decision to be a relief worker in a way that intermingles the impersonal, his individual ends, and his identification with a community: "I'm not religious. I'm the greatest rogue you ever met. It's just a calling. You feel as though you can do something, make a difference. We Irish, we love the underdog." (Kevin Cullen, "Haunted by Death in Somalia," *Boston Globe* (July 15, 1993): 19.

38. Michael Sandel, *Liberalism and the Limits of Justice* (Cambridge: Cambridge University Press, 1982), 143.

39. It seems to me that Jonathan Kozol appeals to this very kind of commitment when he asserts in *Savage Inequalities* (New York: Crown, 1991) that "the advocates of fiscal equity seem to be more confident about American potentials than their adversaries are. 'America,' they

say, 'is wealthy, wise, ingenious. We can give terrific schools to *all* our children'. . . . Conservatives are generally the ones who speak more passionately of patriotic values. They are often the first to rise up to protest an insult to the flag. But, in this instance, they reduce America to something rather tight and mean and sour, and they make the flag less beautiful than it should be. They soil the flag in telling us to fly it over ruined children's heads in ugly segregated schools. . . . Children in a dirty school are asked to pledge a dirtied flag. What they learn of patriotism is not clear" (173).

40. On this topic in Confucianism, and on the matter of whether issues related to psychological realism support a Confucian type of ethic, see my "Universalism versus Love with Distinctions: An Ancient Debate Revived," *Journal of Chinese Philosophy* 16 (1989): 252–72.

41. Verba, 55.

42. J. R. Pole, *The Pursuit of Equality in American History* (Berkeley: University of California Press, 1978), 256.

43. I discuss strategies of accommodating to serious disagreement with others in "Coping with Moral Conflict and Ambiguity," *Ethics* 102 (1992): 763–84.

44. Consider Jonathan Kozol's statement in *Savage Inequalities*, 83: "Denial of the 'means of competition' is perhaps the single most consistent outcome of the education offered to poor children in the schools of our large cities." He notes that average expenditures per pupil in the city of New York in 1987 were some fifty-five hundred dollars. In the highest spending suburbs of New York, funding levels rose above eleven thousand dollars with the highest districts at fifteen thousand dollars. Even within the city, there is gross inequity: the poor income schools need to use funds earmarked for computers to buy such supplies as pen and paper. They have the worst teachers when outstanding ones are needed to address diverse needs in overcrowded classrooms (84–85).

45. Lawrence Blum, "Opportunity and Equality of Opportunity," *Public Affairs Quarterly* 2 (1988): 1–18.

46. For example, Leinberger and Tucker cite a number of statistics to argue for the increasingly marginal importance that churches have for Americans: a steep increase in the proportions of those born Protestant who leave their churches, a big drop in the percentage of Catholics who attend mass, a decrease in religious giving relative to inflation, and the increasing numbers willing to call themselves "unaffiliated" to pollsters (147–48).

47. Charles Cooley, Robert C. Angell, and Lowell J. Carr, *Introductory Sociology* (New York: C. Scribner's Sons, 1933), 55–56.

48. Edward Shils, "The Study of the Primary Group," in *The Policy Sciences: Recent Developments in Scope and Method,* ed. Daniel Lerner and Harold D. Lasswell (Stanford: Stanford University Press, 1951), 64.

49. Shils, 67.

50. William Theodore de Bary, *The Trouble with Confucianism* (Cambridge: Harvard University Press, 1992).

51. For example, Leinberger and Tucker in *The New Individualists,* 358–62. They refer to Gilligan's work and to African-Americans as having a more inclusive sense of self in relation to the group.

52. See Elizabeth Spelman, *The Inessential Woman: Problems of Exclusion in Feminist Thought* (Boston: Beacon Press, 1988), for a perceptive discussion of the way that nineteenth-century white, middle-class suffragists exhibited the "caring" virtues while mistreating the black women who were their slaves or servants and using racist arguments to advance "women's interests."

53. Elsewhere, I have argued that effective moral agency—the ability to act on one's moral values—must be formed and nurtured within a set of personal relationships. See "On Flourishing and Finding One's Identity in Community," *Midwest Studies in Philosophy* 13 (1988): 324–41.

5

WHAT PLATO WOULD ALLOW

JEREMY WALDRON

How do we teach political philosophy? What do we encourage our students to think a writer is doing when she (or more usually he) is laying out a theory of politics? What are we asking them to do as they read the *Republic, Leviathan,* the *Social Contract* or the other books that constitute the canon of Western political thought? How do we teach them to respond to writings by their contemporaries—particularly works which, like John Rawls's *A Theory of Justice* and Robert Nozick's *Anarchy, State, and Utopia,* can be classified as normative theory, as attempts to articulate principles of justice, liberty, and rights?

I do not know the answers to these questions, but over the years I have collected an unscientific sample of the things my students write when I attempt to test the understandings I have cultivated:

Plato would allow women as guardians but he would not allow them to combine a political career with raising a family.

Hobbes would prohibit the public expression of dissident political views.

Even where an individual was the only one affected by an oppressive governmental act, Locke would still allow resistance.

Jean-Jacques Rousseau would require citizens to devote the larger part of their energies to public life, and he would restrict the amount of energy spent in private or commercial pursuits.

The first thing to say about these claims is that they are all true, at least if you construe them generously; they are more or less accurate representations of the views of the thinkers cited on the issues mentioned.[1] Or so I shall assume; it is not the point of this chapter to discuss whether they are true or false, sound or unsound as interpretations. I want to reflect on the way they are presented.

For me the striking thing about these statements is their wording: what Plato and Locke would *allow,* what Rousseau would *require,* and what Hobbes would *prohibit.* The language is odd. Who are Plato, Hobbes, Locke, and Rousseau to allow, require, or prohibit things? They are not the holders of public office, nor the framers of a constitution. Plato was disillusioned with politics. Rousseau was a social outcast. Hobbes and Locke may have rubbed shoulders with powerful men, but they were always on the margins of contemporary political life; they never had the authority to propose laws or a constitution for the government of England. All four of these writers were regarded with indifference and suspicion—as idle and impractical word-spinners or as dangerous and unreliable radicals—by those who actually took on the responsibility of making laws for the societies in which they lived. Why then do we insist on describing their writings as though we were issuing Amnesty International or State Department reports on the human rights record of some dubious regime?

It is important perhaps to note that the statements I am considering do not talk directly about these philosophers' requirements or prohibitions. They talk about what Plato *would* allow, what Hobbes *would* prohibit, what Rousseau *would* require. What is the significance of that?

The auxiliary "would" is an interesting one. The term is used in the apodosis of a conditional sentence: if *P were* to happen, then *Q would* occur. Sometimes the connection between *P* and *Q* is purely naturalistic: if the temperature were to rise suddenly, there would be an avalanche. But in human affairs, "would" straddles the distinction between prognostication and promise, between reporting an expression of will and predicting what some person or organization is actually likely to do. Its most common use in politics is to characterize what one might expect from an individual or party in the event of its accession to office: if C were elected, he would lift the ban on gays in the military. While it is still partly a matter of forecast—if B were elected, the Chinese leadership would breathe a sigh of relief— its main function, particularly in democratic politics, is to report campaign promises. Statements about what B or C *would* do are renderings in *oratio obliqua* of the familiar proclamations we hear all the time on the hustings: "If elected, I will do X" or "If you vote for me, I will do Y."

That is the impression I get from these statements by my students. We all know—and many of us are grateful—that philosophers do not rule the world. Still, on the basis of what has been said in their assigned texts—in Plato's or Hobbes's election manifestos—my students are telling me what these theorists *would* do *if* they were appointed to public office, or what they *would* enact in the unlikely event of being given some other opportunity to reform society as they pleased. The event is improbable, but they seem to think it worth finding out anyway exactly what the thinkers are promising.

More importantly, they *judge* the classic theorists by these promises: Aristotle would allow slavery; Locke would allow a husband "as the abler and the stronger" to speak for his wife in a matter of family concern.[2] Who could hope to be elected on these platforms? Why, they ask, should they be required to study the views of such obviously unsound candidates? A manifesto containing such promises as these is discredited; like the thirteenth chime of a crazy clock, the policies call not only themselves, but everything that went before into question. Thus Aristotle's theory of citizenship is deemed not worth studying because Athens was a slave state and Locke's theory of natural rights, like most liberal theories, is discredited by the unsoundness of his policy towards women. I am sure readers are familiar with this way of approaching the canon.

The statements I quoted are from students, and probably I am putting more weight on their precise wording than it can bear. But they are not altogether different from the attitudes many colleagues take both towards the canon of classic texts and towards the writings of their contemporaries. Susan Okin's commentary, *Women in Western Political Thought,* is a good example. She talks about "Plato's abolition of the family" in the *Republic* and his "reinstatement" of that institution in the *Laws*.[3] She says that "Rousseau allows that a man can be either an individual or a citizen. He does not allow a woman to be either."[4] John Stuart Mill, by contrast, "made a determined effort to emancipate [women] into citizenship."[5] I am sure these are mere *façons de parler*. All the same, we do well to remember that Plato in fact abolished nothing and reinstated nothing; all he did was write. Mill did not emancipate women; the most he did was call for the emancipation of women. And Rousseau was rarely in a position to allow or disallow anything, even in his own household, let alone in any of the countries in which from time to time he resided.

Or consider the reaction of the philosophical community to the publication of Robert Nozick's book, *Anarchy, State, and Utopia* in 1974. Brian Barry's review was typical and a now-famous passage of it ran as follows:

> [T]he intellectual texture is of a sort of cuteness that would be wearing in a graduate student and seems to me quite indecent in someone who, from the lofty heights of a professorial chair, is proposing to starve or humiliate ten percent of his fellow citizens (if he recognizes the word) by eliminating all transfer payments through the state, leaving the sick, the old, the disabled, the mothers with young children and no breadwinner, and so on, to the tender mercies of private charity, given at the whim and pleasure of the donors and on any terms they choose to impose.[6]

If Nozick were standing for office and these were his policies, I guess there would be reason to vote for some other candidate. In fact, however, he was not in a position to starve or humiliate anyone or to eliminate any transfer payments through the state, nor was he was aspiring to any office where his "proposals" to this effect would be a matter of political concern. He was, as Barry reminds us, sitting on a professorial chair in a philosophy department. He was not in fact *proposing* anything, or *calling for* anything, or indeed *urging* anything, except this—that we might try thinking about justice in a slightly different way:

> My emphasis upon the conclusions which diverge from what most readers believe may mislead one into thinking this book is

some sort of political tract. It is not; it is a philosophical exploration of issues, many fascinating in their own right, which arise
and interconnect when we consider individual rights and the
state.[7]

Some have criticized Nozick's book for an insufficient elaboration of the policies and principles he was proposing: he was
shameless, for example, about not formulating the content of
his favored principle governing the original acquisition of property. But Nozick was right, I think, to anticipate such criticisms
by stressing the philosophical rather than the policy implications
of what he was doing. The idea was to consider whether such
theories as John Rawls's determined an adequate way of *thinking*
about justice: "we do not need any *particular* developed historical entitlement theory as a basis from which to criticize Rawls's
construction. If *any* such fundamental historical-entitlement
view is correct, then Rawls's theory is not."[8] He was even prepared to concede that something like the Rawlsian Difference
Principle might converge, in its practical implications, with the
principles of rectification that an entitlement theory would have
to deploy in order to cope with a history of admitted injustice
like that of the United States: "One *cannot* use the analysis and
theory presented here to condemn any particular scheme of
transfer payments, unless it is clear that no considerations of
rectification of injustice could apply to justify it."[9] But again,
practical implications were not the point; the aim of *Anarchy,
State, and Utopia* was to alter the perspective brought to bear in
our thinking and reflection on issues of justice, not to argue for
or against any particular scheme of policy.

Oddly enough, something exactly similar seems true of Plato
as well. It is common to view the *Republic* as one man's prescription for a perfect society, a set of proposals for the construction
of utopia. A distinguished recent commentator, for example,
begins his discussion of Plato's political philosophy as follows:
"Let us look first at the political institutions which Plato actually
recommends and then see what justifications he can find for
their adoption. The *Republic* contains his first full-scale design
for an ideal state."[10] In fact, that is not at all how Plato presented it: he recommends *nothing* in the dialogue unless it be
that one should live honestly and avoid the temptations of bad

philosophy. The construction of an ideal society is imagined by Socrates and his friends not as the articulation of a political proposal but as a way of answering an ethical challenge. Thrasymachus, Glaucon, and Adeimantus require Socrates to show that an individual is better off being just than being unjust, no matter what sort of society he lives in.[11] Socrates suggests that we imagine designing an ideal community as a heuristic to answer this challenge. His hunch is that the precise effects of justice and injustice may initially be easier to discern in the case of whole communities than in the case of individuals. So we begin by comparing what we know about unjust societies with some imagined model of what would be a perfectly just community. We do this, not for the purposes of political prescription, but with a view to extrapolating some conclusions about what would be the benefits and the costs of cultivating justice and honesty rather than injustice and opportunism in one's own individual soul. Thus, the positing of ideal laws and optimal social principles—"What Plato proposes," "What Plato would allow"—is but one step in an intellectual strategy to deepen our understanding of what it is for a person to have these virtues and to deploy standards of justice in his dealings with others.

That, at any rate, is the reading of the *Republic* that I want to urge.[12] The point of doing so is not to pursue any particular agenda in classical philosophy, but to broaden and complicate our view of what political theorizing is and the purposes for which it can be undertaken. In our reading of the canon, and in the development and criticism of our own current theories and models, we run a great danger if we think of theory—even *evaluative* theory—as primarily political advocacy or as primarily the laying out of a social or a constitutional "wish-list." We should think of it instead, I want to say, literally as political *philosophy*—a deepening of our insight into the realm of the political and of our understanding of what is involved in making judgments and decisions in that realm.

Historians of ideas will be irritated by the "Plato would allow" approach for a somewhat different reason. They will think that there is something ludicrously anachronistic about comparing Plato's views on women, for example, with Locke's views, Nozick's views, or our own, as though we were all fellow symposiasts in the most recent issue of *Philosophy and Public Affairs*. Consider the formulation of the first of the students' statements that I cited:

> Plato would allow women as guardians but he would not allow them to combine a political career with raising a family.

The reference to "combining a political career with raising a family" is a late-twentieth-century phrase: it connotes images of Margaret Thatcher or Hillary Clinton. Our understanding of the term "raising a family" is embedded in a whole array of cultural practices, connoting the intimacy of a nuclear or perhaps even single-parent household, and raising issues about latch-keys, parental leave, school districts and shared arrangements for child care that would have been barely intelligible in John Locke's day, let alone twenty-three hundred years ago in Athens. The same is true of "political career." The fact that the student uses this term in the same breath as "guardian"—a concept combining social insight and warrior status in a way that simply cannot be rendered by any modern equivalent [13]—shows how fatuous it is to evaluate Plato's "proposals" by reference to what we think now on we take to be equivalent issues. Certainly Plato held very striking views about women; they startled and provoked many of his contemporaries. But we would be making a philosophical mistake—according to the historians that I have in mind [14]—if we were to assimilate his claim that "there is no social function peculiar to women" [15] with any thesis that a modern feminist might formulate in those terms.

On the most extreme version of this critique, every work of political theory is locked into the context of the culture and situation that produced it, and its meaning is irrecoverable except by one who has immersed himself in the study and understanding of that context. Plato was a traveling teacher in a caste society, whose philosophical method had barely succeeded in extricating itself from superstition and numerology. [16] His critique of democracy (an institution that in Athens bore little resemblance to the systems we operate under that name) was profoundly influenced by the political crisis that followed Athens's humiliation in the Peloponnesian War. John Locke was an amateur scientist and physician who wrote the *Two Treatises of Government* as a way of advancing the cause of the Shaftesbury faction during the Exclusion Crisis in England around 1680. It is impossible to grasp why he wrote what he did about resistance and revolution without understanding the intense political positioning that was going on at that time; and it is impossible to understand the premises that he brought to bear on those crises without immersing oneself in a fairly literal subscription to the seventeenth-century doctrine that we are "all the Workmanship of one Omnipotent, and infinitely wise Maker . . . sent into the World by his order and about his business . . . made to last during his, not one anothers Pleasure." [17] Robert Nozick is a professional scholar, tenured at a great American university at the end of the twentieth century, in circumstances where he is free to write or teach anything he pleases, without political repercussions. He published his book at the beginning of the modern crisis of Keynesian economics and the welfare state, and, as he himself notes in the preface to *Anarchy, State, and Utopia,* he uses the "flashy" tools of "contemporary philosophical work in epistemology or metaphysics" [18]—the *cute* "intellectual texture" that so offended Brian Barry.[19] Given the immense differences of culture, practice, history, and understanding that separate these works, why on earth should an intelligent scholar think that it is worth comparing their respective policy "proposals" on some modern matrix of political correctness?

The historians' worry is an important one, but I want to dissociate my critique from theirs. For one thing, these concerns about historical anachronism give us no guidance about how *we* should do political philosophy. They tell us nothing about how we should read the work of theorists who are undoubtedly our contemporaries and with whom we do share a culture, a language and an array of political understandings. In my view it is a mistake *for us* to comb *Anarchy, State, and Utopia,* or any modern work of political theory, for the bottom line: "Well, *is* Nozick in favor of free child care, or isn't he?" But nothing in the historians' critique explains why that is a mistake. Indeed if, on their view, it is right to see Plato's work as a response to the Peloponnesian War and Locke's as a response to the Exclusion

Crisis, rather than both of them as contributions to some transcendent abstraction called "political philosophy," then presumably we should read Nozick, too, in exactly the same spirit. On
that approach, it is perfectly in order to respond to *Anarchy,
State, and Utopia* as Brian Barry did[20]—that is, in just the way
that Athenian democrats would have responded to the *Republic*,
or in just the way that Anglican divines in the late Stuart era
would have responded to Locke's *Second Treatise*.

For another thing, the historians' critique neglects the fact
that the practice of political philosophy that we have developed
in our culture is a practice of attempting, against all hermeneutical odds, to compare different understandings of society with
one another, even though they were formulated in different
contexts as responses to historically quite specific situations. We
cannot understand what Aristotle was doing in the *Politics*, for
example, unless we notice that among other things he thought
it worth criticizing Plato's conceptions in the *Republic* and the
Laws.[21] We cannot understand the arguments in *Leviathan* some
eighteen hundred years later except in part as Hobbes's attempt
to repudiate Aristotle: he criticized Aristotle's theory of slavery
and natural inequality,[22] his doctrine of man as *zoon politikon*,[23]
and his rejection of monarchy.[24] G. W. F. Hegel, who was more
concerned about context than most of these writers, was happy
to remark that "the Idea of Plato's republic contains as a universal principle a wrong against the person, inasmuch as the person is forbidden to own private property,"[25] and to make fun
of Plato for including prescriptions about rocking children in
the arms of their nurses in the *Laws*.[26] In this age of exquisite
hermeneutic sensitivity, *we* may be anxious to avoid the anachronism of reading the traditional texts in the light of our own
concerns. But the authors whose works we are handling with
this sensitivity had no such scruples themselves, and I think it is
fair to say that our sensitivity to their context seriously distorts
our understanding of their philosophical intentions. They took
it for granted that political theory was a dialogue across the
ages. They wrote in response to books that were written centuries, even millennia ago; and it is impossible to read such works
as *Leviathan*, for example, without getting the impression that
the authors also intended their works to survive the historical

vicissitudes that elicited them.[27] The idea that Thomas Hobbes would have been outraged either by our deployment of *Leviathan* to understand modern conundrums about sovereignty and the rule of law, or for that matter by our attempt to reconstruct his argument using the techniques of modern rational choice and game theory[28]—the idea that he would have insisted indignantly that we confine his work to its "context" strikes me as absurd, and absurd as a matter of historical understanding not just absurd as political theory.

I do not mean by this that the "Plato would allow" approach is endemic to our tradition. It is a further question what Hobbes was doing in attacking Aristotle's theory, or what Hegel was doing in arguing against "the Idea of Plato's republic." On my view, Hobbes and Hegel were taking issue with the understanding of political life evinced in the works they were discussing; they were not normative policy advocates taking issue with Aristotle's or Plato's "bottom line." But whatever is wrong with the "bottom line" approach, it is not a hermeneutical error. Political theory in the West has thrived on anachronism; and modern historians of ideas have given us no compelling reason to deviate from tradition in this regard.

It would be wrong for me to suggest that there is no place for a philosophically informed and rigorous contribution to the civic discussion of legal and constitutional reform. Sometimes citizens' contributions to such discussions acquire the stature of philosophical classics—*The Federalist* is perhaps the best clearest example. And sometimes civic discussants look to those who have already distinguished themselves as philosophers for a distinctive and valuable contribution to an on going political debate: people solicit the views of Jurgen Habermas on German politics, or the views of Michael Sandel on the enforcement of community standards.

One way of understanding these contributions is to insist on a basic continuity between political theory and civic discourse. Both citizens and theorists argue about politics, economy, rights, and justice: we do it in our seminars and journals; they do it in town halls and on the streets; and many of us wear both hats. The idea is that when citizens and politicians disagree with

one another—about abortion, or pornography, or taxes, or
welfare, or constitutional reform—they are in their disagreements just like us in our journals and symposia, with this proviso: we have the luxury of not actually having to make a decision; they have to engage not only in hard thinking about
justice, but also in what we in the academy may too easily dismiss as the sordid and distasteful business of actually having to
make a collective decision in the absence of moral consensus. Of
course, we pride ourselves that our thinking in books, articles,
and seminars is more reasoned and more profound than the
thinking engaged in by working politicians and their constituents. And so it should be: in the social division of labor, it is
our task to take time and energy to think these things through
as carefully as it is possible to think them, free from the exigen-
cies of log-rolling and compromise. But, on this approach, it is
a mistake to regard our thinking and arguing in political philosophy as qualitatively different from that of a citizen-participant
in politics. Political theory is simply conscientious civic discussion without a deadline.[29]

There is a lot to be said for this approach. At least since the
seventeenth century, our conception of *argument* in political
philosophy has been guided by the idea that social, political, and
legal institutions are to be explicable and justifiable to all who
have to live under them. We have abandoned the esoteric in the
theory of politics; we have rejected the idea of *arcana imperii*.[30]
The model-theoretic ideas of consent and social contract, and
the corresponding constraints of publicity and transparency,
commit us to producing arguments that purport to be intelligible to anyone whose interests they affect, and that—in spirit, if
not in idiom—are consonant with the arguments that they
would find persuasive in their conversations with one another.
There is, as I have argued elsewhere, an important connection
between liberal argumentation and the Enlightenment conviction that everything real can in principle be explained, and
everything right can in principle be justified, to everyone.[31]
Liberalism is committed to the idea that theoretical argument
aims not merely to justify laws or political proposals, but to
justify them to the ordinary men and women whom they will
affect. It follows that *if* our philosophical arguments have pre-

scriptive implications, then their character and grounds must be such that ordinary citizens can make sense of them. It must not be the case that the philosophers' recommendations involve forms of insight that are in principle inaccessible to those whose interests they affect.[32]

Even so, it is a mistake to think that a body of political understanding is valuable only to the extent that it is phrased, oriented and presented as a legislative or civic contribution. Claude-Adrien Helvetius insisted that "if philosophers would be of use to the world, they should survey objects from the same point of view as the legislator." Morality, he said, "is evidently no more than a frivolous science, unless blended with policy and legislation."[33] In fact it is remarkable how little useful to mankind philosophical schemes have been when they have been presented in this spirit. Who now reads John Locke's constitution for the Carolinas? Who reads Jean-Jacques Rousseau's *Considerations on the Government of Poland?* Who, apart from antiquarians, spends any time at all with the detail of Jeremy Bentham's curious legal and constitutional schemes? We know that none of these documents played an important part in the governance of any of the societies to which they were addressed. Who now derives from them anything like the insight that they get from the *Two Treatises,* from the *Social Contract* and the *Discourses,* from *Of Laws in General* or *An Introduction to the Principles of Morals and Legislation?*

Some philosophers, taking Helvetius's position to heart, write as though they were constitution-framers, legislators, or policy advisers. Sometimes, however, they write *about* those roles, and include that discussion in their theories. It is worth pausing to reflect on the significance for our argument of such figures as Plato's philosopher/statesman and the superior intelligence of Rousseau's "law-giver" in book 2 of the *Social Contract.* Each of these thinkers, in his musing on the possibility of a well-ordered republic, invoked the image of a leader of surpassing wisdom and understanding who would be able to cut through the morass of popular politics—"How can a blind multitude, which often does not know what is good for it, undertake by itself an enterprise as vast and difficult as a scheme of legislation?"[34]—

and guide a people to the adoption of a set of well-founded laws and principles for political life. It is the image of Lycurgus of Sparta, Solon of Athens, Moses of Israel, Romulus for Rome, Calvin for Rousseau's Geneva, and for us, the Founding Fathers of the American constitution.

There are two and possibly three ways of misunderstanding such imagery. The first is to understand it as necessarily the advocacy of dictatorship. The most vehement critics of Rousseau's political theory have taken his discussion of the lawgiver in the *Social Contract* to indicate his commitment, by historical anticipation, to the idea of fascist or communist totalitarianism.[35] Though he uses the language of liberty and democracy, Rousseau's ideal state is one in which people would be "forced to be free"; [36] indeed it is a state where (in a chilling anticipation of Dachau) "the word *Libertas* may be seen on the doors of all the prisons and on the fetters of the galleys." [37] Though the ideology of such a state would be that of subjection only to oneself through the general will, the latter concept is distinguished insistently from its majoritarian counterpart, "the will of all," [38] and it is assumed that the people themselves are incapable of making that discrimination, and need a superior intelligence to do it for them: "the public must be taught to recognize what it desires." [39] As the working class needs its vanguard movement—the Party—to achieve its inherent ends, so Rousseau is said to have believed that ordinary men and women needed the guidance of a great leader to subordinate their will and their desires to their reason.

Fortunately, even as an account of what Rousseau would allow, this view of the law giver is misleading. There is an evident distinction between the extraordinary function of the framer of the laws, on his account, and, for example, the continuing rule of the philosopher-kings in Plato's imagined ideal. In the latter account, the rule of philosophical reason is associated with a clear and sustained critique of democracy. By contrast, in the former there is an insistence that the lawgiver is only the proponent of laws, and that he is to have no legislative or other political authority. Maurice Cranston says that the role of the ordinary people in Rousseau's ideal is limited to mere *assent* to laws devised by somebody else; [40] but Rousseau himself insists again and again in this passage on the importance of "the free suffrage of the people."[41]

The contrast between Rousseau's ostensible rejection of autocracy and Plato's explicit embrace of it may seem naive to those who (for reasons that escape me) are interested in finding out what Rousseau would *really* have favored if he had ever been elected to office. As with any political candidate, they say, you have to read between the lines. Thus some commentators have argued that the law giver fulfills the same role for Rousseau's republic as the Tutor fulfills in *Emile,* and they cite the plea of the pupil in that work who, now married and about to have a child himself, begs his tutor to stay with him: "Advise and control us," he implores the tutor, "as long as I live I shall need you. I need you more than ever now that I am taking on the duties of manhood."[42] The talk of democracy is a front and a sham, they say, as is the talk of autonomous maturity in the theory of education.

But once one abandons this mysterious interest in what Rousseau would allow, the dark significance of such hints evaporates. His book is a philosophical exploration of the possibility of reconciling the ideas of government and freedom. It pursues this possibility by connecting the notion (later taken up by Kant) of autonomous self-discipline with the idea of a contractarian arrangement which both depends upon and guarantees the well-being of each member. Rousseau's aim is to construct something like a Kantian deduction of that possibility, "taking men as they are and laws as they might be." The passage dealing with the law giver is one of a number of places in the book where the contrast between those modalities—men as they *are,* laws as they *might be*—comes to the surface. For example, Rousseau suspects that some communities may have become too large, and may have forged bonds of nationality that are now simply too strong to enable them to be broken down into units of optimal size for the kind of polity he envisages. Also, like Machiavelli, Rousseau speculates that certain peoples may have become too corrupt for legitimate politics. In both these cases, the possibilities that he explores in the *Social Contract* turn out to be, lamentably, irrelevant from a political point of view. But even if one finds a people apt for Rousseauian politics, a people satisfying the conditions that he sketches at the end of chapter 10 of book 2, there are yet other reasons to worry that they will be unable to reconcile freedom and self-government in the way that Rousseau's theory suggests they can be combined. The reconciliation is a complicated one: it will not work unless it is understood by those whose lives it affects; but it may be impossible to understand and trust until one has experienced its transformative effects. This conundrum raises severe problems about the practicability of Rousseau's reconciliation. The traditional role that great law givers such as Moses or Lycurgus have played in setting up other types of ordered polity is therefore mentioned as a way of rebutting that imputation of hopeless impracticability. For one way in which a people could come to know and trust political arrangements reconciling order and freedom would be to have had them prescribed by a leader of great insight and to have experienced them on his initiative long enough to take the life of such institutions into their own hands.

Seen in this light, the image of the law giver is not Rousseau's covert advocacy of totalitarian dictatorship, but his invocation of an aspect of our historical experience—the experience of great Founders—to rebut what might otherwise seen radical and insurmountable objections about the place of his reconciliation of freedom and order in the realm of *practical* philosophy.[43]

The second way of misunderstanding the imagery of the Founder is to read it as the philosopher's own self-image, as though Plato were positing himself as philosopher-statesman or as though Rousseau dreamt wishfully of himself as the law giver for whatever people—the Corsicans, for example—that he thought worthy of his schemes. The latter interpretation at least is easily rebutted. Says Rousseau at the outset in a passage that could be taken as a motto for this paper:

> I may be asked whether I am a prince or a legislator that I should be writing about politics. I answer no: and indeed that is my reason for doing so. If I were a prince or a legislator I should not waste my time saying what ought to be done; I should do it or keep silent.[44]

The matter is less clear in Plato's case, for he seems to insist both that the true statesman would be distinguished by his[45] insight into the political, and also that that insight is exactly what Socrates and his friends are eliciting in the course of the dialogue itself. Though they develop a complex theory of upbringing and education for "the conversion of the mind from a kind of twilight to the true day, that climb up into reality which we shall say is true philosophy,"[46] we are left in no doubt that their own conversations are also a way of leaving the cave and acquainting themselves with the shining reality of truth and justice. It would seem to follow that in the dialogue Socrates and his friends think of themselves as in the business of acquiring the very insight that is the mark of the philosopher-ruler, and *a fortiori* that Plato, who constructs the dialogue, should think of it as a way of exhibiting also *his* title to that role. There appears something unashamedly self-referential about the claim that

> [t]he society we have described can never grow into a reality or see the light of day, and there will be no end to the troubles of states, or indeed, my dear Glaucon, of humanity itself, till philosophers become kings in this world, or till those we now call kings and rulers really and truly become philosophers, and political power and philosophy thus come into the same hands, while the many natures now content to follow either to the exclusion of the other are forcibly debarred from doing so.[47]

It is easy to infer from this passage that Plato is defining a job for himself, and accordingly, that the business of doing philosophy is simply the business of preparing oneself for that vocation.

This is an easy inference, but it would be a mistake, at least on the internal logic of the *Republic*. The inference ignores an aspect of Plato's account of the character of the true philosopher-statesman, and it ignores his theory of the social determination of such character. The philosopher-statesman is not only a person of insight and wisdom, a lover of truth and one who can gaze unblinkingly at the eternal. He must also be one who combines these characteristics with a clear-headed disposition to rule and to participate in the governance of a society. That combination, moreover, must be more than merely accidental: his wisdom and his political vocation must deeply inform one another. Plato is adamant that this combination is not to be

expected in any of the societies in which he has lived, or in the
Athens in which Socrates and Glaucon are placed in the dialogue. Given the prejudice that exists against the idea of political insight, he says, the prudent philosopher will keep his head
down and say nothing, like the true navigator in book 6's ship
of state.[48] He will not develop any taste or vocation for the
political, and so his understanding of justice will never mature
by combining itself with any practical disposition to realize it in
the lives of others as well as his own.[49] Moreover, the conditions
that make it imprudent to combine insight with political vocation, will also conspire to corrupt such philosophical natures as
there are: "There's no existing form of society good enough for
the philosophical nature, with the result that it gets warped and
altered, like a foreign seed sown in alien soil under whose
influence it commonly degenerates into the local growth."[50]
The best one can hope for, Plato concludes, is a handful of
uncorrupted natures, whose commitment to philosophy has not
been tainted by social circumstances:

> This small company . . . when they have tasted the happiness of
> philosophy and seen the frenzy of the masses, understand that
> political life has virtually nothing sound about it, and that they'll
> find no ally to save them in the fight for justice; and if they're
> not prepared to join others in their wickedness, and yet are
> unable to fight the general savagery single-handed, they are
> likely to perish like a man thrown among wild beasts, without
> profit to themselves or others, before they can do any good to
> their friends or society. When they reckon all this up, they live
> quietly and keep to themselves, like a man who stands under the
> shelter of a wall during a driving storm of dust and hail; they see
> the rest of the world full of wrongdoing, and are content to keep
> themselves unspotted from wickedness and wrong in this life,
> and finally leave it with cheerful composure and good hope.[51]

This, not the philosopher-statesman, is the self-image of Socrates; and this is the figure whose blessed happiness is ultimately
established to rebut Thrasymachus's complaint.[52]

To establish its status as an individually just nature, we do
need to show, as Plato recognizes, that in a suitable social environment, such a nature would develop more fully, to its own

salvation and that of the community.[53] Like Rousseau, we need to show that such an environment, no matter how unlikely, is not in principle impossible.[54] It is important to emphasize, however, that in such an environment, natures of this kind would not be educated as Socrates was educated, nor behave as Socrates behaved, nor preach and converse as Socrates preached and conversed. Socrates has followed philosophy to the exclusion of politics, and we have already heard him say that in an ideal state, people would be prevented from doing just that.[55]

I mentioned a third possible way of misunderstanding the imagery of the Founder in the *Republic* and the *Social Contract*. We misunderstand it if we fail to discern the irony in the entanglement of the philosopher's own voice and that of his founder-hero.[56]

Thus, we find Socrates and his friends sometimes referring to *themselves* as the law givers, since they are the ones designing in imagination an ideal society, and to the philosopher-statesman as their employee: "Then *our* job as law-givers is to compel the best minds to attain what we have called the highest form of knowledge." It is, they say, for *us* to tell potential philosopher-statesmen that they must not spurn public service when the social conditions are right.[57] Indeed sometimes the philosopher-statesman seems to be their dupe: we are told, on the one hand, about the latter's defining love of truth, and on the other, about the Noble Lie, which is to be cultivated presumably among all the classes—guardians included—of the ideal republic that is being imagined.[58]

Turning now to Rousseau, we find that in the very passages for which he is accused by Talmon and others of advocating totalitarianism as a human institution, he says the following about the potential dictator:

> To discover the rules of society that are best suited to nations, there would need to exist a superior intelligence, who could understand the passions of men without feeling any of them, who had no affinity with our nature but knew it to the full, whose happiness was independent of ours, but who would nevertheless make our happiness his concern, who would be content to wait

in the fullness of time for a distant glory, and to labour in one
age to enjoy the fruits in another. Gods would be needed to give
men laws.[59]

There is irony here in the conscious impossibility of the job
description, irony that amounts to a good indication that something other than literal political prescription is going on. I hear
in this passage more than a hint of Adam Smith's conception of
the "impartial spectator"—by which I don't mean to associate
Rousseau with Smith's utilitarianism, but to suggest that it may
well be worth thinking about the law giver as (in Rawls's terms)
a model-conception,[60] or to at least consider the possibility that
Rousseau's thought is as complex and philosophically sophisticated on these matters as Adam Smith's discussion in *The Theory
of Moral Sentiments*.[61] Offhand, once we grant that Rousseau is
writing as a political philosopher rather than simply telling us
what he would do if he ruled the world, there is no more reason
to impute to him the advocacy of authoritarian government by
a single law giver than there is to impute to John Rawls advocacy of an actual constitutional convention conducted behind a
veil of ignorance.

Some of the most alarming passages in the *Social Contract* have
to do with the scale of the task that the legislator is required to
attempt. He must be ready, Rousseau says, "to change human
nature, to transform each individual . . . into a part of a much
greater whole. . . . The founder of nations must weaken the
structure of man in order to fortify it."[62] And Plato writes in a
vein similarly reminiscent of Pol Pot and the "Year Zero" mentality:

> "The first thing our artists must do," I replied, "—and it's not
> easy—is to wipe the slate of human society and human habits
> clean. For our philosophic artists differ at once from all others in
> being unwilling to start work on an individual or a city, until they
> are given or have made themselves, a clean canvas."[63]

The world is not short of critiques of this sort of "utopianism."[64] Desmond Lee's comment in the introduction to his edition of the *Republic* is typical:

Plato was a . . . Utopian and thought, as his critics charge, that politics could be a much more exact study than it is. He wanted a plan, he wanted power to order society according to it, and he had, perhaps, a touch of the ruthlessness which this kind of approach often engenders. You only have to be determined enough to realize heaven on earth to be sure of raising hell.[65]

The point is not lost on a number of the theorists we are studying. One finds it acknowledged, with considerable irony, by Machiavelli. The founder of a well-ordered kingdom or republic, says Machiavelli, is deserving of the highest praise, and he deserves that praise notwithstanding the fact that he must sometimes use great violence to establish his regime:

> Nor will any reasonable man blame him for taking any action, however extraordinary, which may be of service in the organizing of a kingdom or the constituting of a republic. It is a sound maxim that reprehensible actions may be justified by their effects, and that when the effect is good, as it was in the case of Romulus, it always justifies the action. For it is the man who uses violence to spoil things, not the man who uses it to mend them, that is blameworthy.[66]

Yet Machiavelli says also that in certain circumstances the founding of a new republic requires a law giver "to organize everything in the state afresh; . . . to make the rich poor and the poor rich . . . ; as well as to build new cities, to destroy those already existing, and to move the inhabitants from one place to another far distant from it . . . as shepherds move their sheep." And he adds this comment:

> Such methods are exceedingly cruel, and are repugnant to any community, not only to a Christian one, but to any composed of men. It behooves, therefore, every man to shun them, and to prefer rather to live as a private citizen than as a king with such ruination of men to his score.[67]

Confronted with passages like this, my students say to me, "Well, is he in favor of founding a republic in these circumstances or isn't he?" They are confused too by his suggestion that in a republic that has degenerated, one must seize power and use force as a prince in order to rehabilitate the political life of the society:

[T]o reconstitute political life in a state presupposes a good man, whereas to have recourse to violence in order to make oneself prince in a republic supposes a bad man. Hence very rarely will there be found a good man ready to use bad methods in order to make himself prince, though with a good end in view, nor yet a bad man who, having become a prince, is ready to do the right thing and to whose mind it will occur to use well that authority which he has acquired by bad means.[68]

Again, they ask, "Well, is he saying that a potential savior of the republic should seize power or that he shouldn't seize power? Is he saying that it's a good thing to do, or a bad thing to do? What's the bottom line?"

The truth is: there is no bottom line. Machiavelli is not telling us what to do. He is attempting to convey complex insights into the relation between politics, violence, personal ethics and political morality—insights that enrich our understanding of the political without necessarily laying out any course of conduct as normative for his readers. This is not to say that the discussion is purely descriptive or concerned only with the dry analysis of concepts. It is an attempt to elicit an understanding of values and ethics in political life, weaving subtly back and forth between the perspective of an insider who can say, in his own voice, "such methods are exceedingly cruel," and that of an outsider who can complain, in almost Nietzschean fashion, that "our religion has glorified humble and contemplative men, rather than men of action."[69]

Machiavelli aside, I hope it is clear that my critique of the "Plato would allow" approach is not a critique of utopianism. Much of the twentieth-century attack on utopian political thought was predicated on assumptions that have long since been discredited. It was assumed that piecemeal political reform is always to be preferred to revolutionary or large-scale transformation. But now that theorists on the Right have discovered (what theorists on the Left knew all along) how resilient and resourceful are the specific programs and institutions that they want to change, they too are finding it necessary to talk about changing the whole political culture and mounting an attack on what they see as the evils of public spending and entitlement programs on a wide rather than on a narrow front. In any case, the idea that incremental tinkering with the system was always to be preferred to large-scale transformation simply collapsed in 1989 in the wake of the quiet, brave resolution of ordinary men and women who stood on the streets of Berlin, Leipzig, Prague, and Bucharest and did there what the anti-utopians of the Cold War were adamant could never be done: they faced down the police and the soldiers and swiftly consigned an entire social and institutional system, a whole political world, to oblivion. For the process of reconstruction that these people are facing, nothing is more important than the articulation of wholesale visions of a new and better society.

The mistake on both sides, however, would be to assume that it is always the intention of a "utopian" theorist to lay out a blueprint for immediate implementation. The Cold War attack on utopianism was predicated on the claim made famous by Karl Popper that such thinkers as Plato intended ruthlessly to *impose* their ideal plan on the rest of us. We have already seen why this is a misinterpretation of the *Republic*. Socrates got involved in detailed speculation about a just society because the challenge was to produce not only a philosophical "demonstration that justice is superior to injustice, but a *description* of the essential effects, harmful or otherwise, which each produces on its possessor." [70] The idea was that we would be able to discern or "read" those effects more easily by comparing first in our imaginations just and unjust communities, and then extrapolating that reading to the less easily legible case of just versus unjust individuals: "I accordingly propose that we start our inquiry with the community, and then proceed to the individual, and see if we can find in the conformation of the smaller entity anything similar to what we have found in the larger." [71] In the dialogue Socrates himself doubted whether "the society which we have been describing and which we have theoretically founded . . . will ever exist on earth," [72] and there is no reason to suppose that those doubts were not also Plato's. [73]

If we were to view the *Republic* as a normative proposal, it would seem a forlorn and hopeless enterprise: the constitution of a utopia whose founder spends pages acknowledging its impossibility. But if we view it as an attempt to understand the worth of justice, its futility as utopia and the ruthlessness of the methods that would have to be used in any (ill-advised, on Plato's view) attempt to impose it, become irrelevant. It is a thought-experiment and, like all thought-experiments in philosophy, it points beyond itself. It is not conducted for the purpose of rehearsing the imposition of the very idea that is being entertained. It was, says Socrates, "an ideal pattern we were looking for when we tried to say what justice and injustice are in themselves, and to describe what the perfectly just or perfectly unjust man would be like if he ever existed. By turning our eyes to *them* and seeing what measure of happiness or its opposite they enjoyed, we would be forced to admit that the nearer we approximate to them the more nearly we share their lot. That was our purpose, rather than to show that the ideal could be realized in practice, was it not?" [74]

The contention that social and political philosophy should not be thought of as primarily prescriptive is of course not unfamiliar in the works of the philosophers. Karl Marx's famous refusal to write "recipes . . . for the cookshops of the future" [75] and his contempt for "utopian socialism, playing with fantastic pictures of the future structure of society" [76] is an echo of Hegel's fury at philosophers "issuing instructions on how the world ought to be." [77] Both believed, though for somewhat different reasons, that the idiosyncratic thought-processes of particular theorists bore little reliable relation to future prospects for social change. Neither of them had a conception of social and historical development which called for an intellectualized blueprint from such a person as himself. As Marx put it,

> The working class . . . have no ready-made Utopias to introduce *par decret du peuple*. They know that in order to work out their own emancipation, and along with it that higher form to which present society is irresistibly tending by its own economical agencies, they will have to pass through long struggles, through a series of historic processes transforming circumstances and men. They have no ideals to realize but to set free the elements of the new society with which the old collapsing bourgeois society itself is pregnant. [78]

According to Hegel, philosophers inevitably come on the scene too late to mold reality with their intellectual prescriptions. Things do change, and social institutions do grow and develop on the basis of implicit rational principles. But the principles become explicitly representable in thought only when they have already had their effect. "[I]t is only when actuality has reached maturity that the ideal appears opposite the real and reconstructs this real world . . . in the shape of an intellectual realm."[79]

> To comprehend *what is* is the task of philosophy, for *what is* is reason. As far as the individual is concerned, each individual is in any case a *child of his time;* thus philosophy, too, is *its own time comprehended in thoughts.* It is just as foolish to imagine that any philosophy can transcend its contemporary world as that an individual can overleap his own time. . . . If his theory does indeed transcend his own time, if it builds itself a world *as it ought to be,* then it certainly has an existence, but only within his opinions—a pliant medium in which the imagination can construct anything it pleases.[80]

This conception of Hegel's puts one in mind of Wittgenstein's dictum about philosophy: "It leaves everything as it is. . . . Philosophy simply puts everything before us, and neither explains nor deduces anything. —Since everything lies open to view there is nothing to explain. For what is hidden, for example, is of no interest to us."[81] In fact, Hegel's approach did require some degree of probing beneath the surface of things, some degree of critical discernment. For him, the point of the philosophical comprehension of political institutions was a sense that our institutions must answer at the tribunal of individual reason, as part of the modern triumph of consciousness: "Since thought has set itself up as the essential form, we must attempt to grasp right, too, in terms of thought."[82] Such an exercise would have to be in some sense evaluative, if only to distinguish the essential from the inessential in legal and political forms.[83] The task of philosophy is to penetrate the "infinite wealth of forms, appearances and shapes" in which spirit inheres in contemporary institutions, "in order to find the inner pulse, and detect its continued beat."[84] But evaluative is not the same as prescriptive, and discerning the reason inherent in what already exists is not the same as setting out, in imagination, a plan for social construction.

It is easy to dismiss all this as part of a metaphysical package which we no longer accept when we entertain ourselves with books like the *Philosophy of Right.* Hegel says that the political philosopher's task has always been "to recognize reason as the rose in the cross of the present."[85] That seems an agenda quite at odds with the prescriptive, critical, even oppositional stance which more metaphysically sober theorists in our tradition have taken in regard to their political surroundings. Surely—it will be said—in the heyday of the liberal tradition at least, philosophers saw themselves as critics of the existing order, and as activists in the forefront of those who were calling for political and constitutional reform.

I find it intriguing that this simple model does not always withstand strict scrutiny, not even in the liberal heartland. Take the case of John Locke, for example. Recent scholarship has certainly established his oppositional political stance: he was part of a dissident circle that plotted incessantly against the later Stuarts, and, as we have seen, he drafted the *Two Treatises* as ammunition with which to intervene in a pamphlet war concerning his country's chronic constitutional crisis.[86] Locke was certainly neither a scholarly recluse nor an apologist for the legitimacy of conventional rules and rights. Yet even when he is at his most critical, Locke presents a conception of political and constitutional theory that is far from the sort of prescriptive "wish-list" which characterizes modern philosophical interventions in the world of public affairs.

The problem addressed in the *Second Treatise* is that people have misconceived political power and confused it with the power of a parent and with the despotic power of a conqueror in a just war: "great mistakes of late about Government," says Locke, "have arisen from confounding these distinct Powers one with another."[87] He acknowledges that the failure to distinguish different kinds of authority is understandable and usually benign. Political authority, he speculates, grew naturally out of enlarged family structures, and was often vested in one person on conditions of trust that were more or less entirely implicit.[88] Nobody found it necessary in prelapsarian circumstances to inquire too closely into the precise character, purpose, and limitations of this power. It is only lately that political theory has become necessary:

> Yet, when Ambition and Luxury, in future Ages would retain and increase the Power, without doing the Business, for which it was given, and aided by Flattery, taught Princes to have distinct and separate Interests from their People, Men found it necessary to examine more carefully the Original and Rights of Government.[89]

What was called for in the practical crisis of the English constitution was not so much a list of practical prescriptions, but a closer examination of the nature of political life, as proof against the distortions of contemporary "Learning and Religion."[90] That is what political theory should comprise, and that is the background against which the *Second* and then the *First* of Locke's *Treatises of Government* were written.

It may be said, in response, that a call for a better understanding of government is in fact equivalent to a set of constitutional prescriptions, if the understanding in question is purely *functionalist* in character. After all, to specify the proper functions of government is to prescribe that those tasks and those tasks only be carried out by agents of the state. But Locke breaks free of this equivalence by insisting at the outset that the aim is "to understand Political Power right, *and derive it from its Original.*"[91] For him, it is not enough to posit a new form of power or a new social and political structure in the normative intellect or imagination—a form that he thinks would better serve the liberal values that he favors than the structures that he sees around him. Instead, the aim is to recover a sense of what we have, and what we have had, in the way of political organization, and to tease out an understanding of it which may be of some use in the resolution of our intensely practical present disputes.

I am sure there is more to be said on this matter. Certainly, many instances could be cited of liberal (and for that matter non-liberal) theorists simply *taking a position* on some principle, and elaborating and defending it, rather than seeking what I have referred to as a philosophical understanding of politics.

And certainly it is possible that what is presented as pure philosophy may turn out in fact to be the prescription of some normative proposal. But the cases that we have been considering show that the opposite is possible too. What looks like nothing more thoughtful than the presentation of a normative blueprint—a utopia, an ideal society, a new dispensation—can often be a cover for much deeper speculation in philosophy. We will miss this, I contend, if we think that there is nothing more to political philosophy than "normative theory," and that one must really be doing something of a quite different character—sociological theory, perhaps—if all one is doing is seeking an understanding of social and political structures.

Enough of the canon. What becomes of *our* normative work in this subject, if we take these observations to heart?

It has been for many a matter of pride that normative political philosophy has revived in Britain and America over the last twenty years, out of what was generally regarded as an analytic wasteland of disputes about conceptual definition. In 1956, Peter Laslett made his famous pronouncement, "For the moment, anyway, political philosophy is dead." There was, he said, no longer a tradition among us of bringing sustained philosophical thought to bear on the great issues of government, law, and policy.[92] By 1979, he was able to report enthusiastically a contrary verdict: political philosophy "obviously flourishes, all over the English-speaking world."[93] The debates initiated by John Rawls's work in 1971, and compounded in 1974 by Robert Nozick's critique, nourished an intense and lasting interest among philosophers and political theorists in issues of distributive justice, private property, and individual rights. The involvement of students and professors in the Vietnam protest movement in the 1960s and 1970s evoked a crop of new work on civil disobedience, just war theory, political obligation, and the proper use of violence. The women's movement engendered a new specialty of feminist philosophy, as well as opening traditional discussions up to a radical and disconcerting array of feminist perspectives. Such journals as *Philosophy and Public Affairs* now display, as a matter of course, titles like "A Defense of Abortion," "Is Inheritance Justified?", "Residential Rent Con-

trol," and "Morality and Nuclear Weapons Policy." Their articles flaunt such bottom lines as "Drunk drivers who kill must no
longer be allowed to hide behind excuses,"[94] and "All parents
should be licenced by the state."[95] In their capacity as writers,
political philosophers, it seems, are issuing policy prescriptions
like never before.

Is it the suggestion of this chapter—in the light of my reading of Plato, Machiavelli, Locke, Rousseau, and Hegel—that we
abandon this concern with principles, rights, and values, and
their implications for law and public policy, and that we return
to the closeted and sterile analysis of the past?

Before answering this question, there are a couple of preliminary comments to make. First, it is worth noting that the sterile
analysis of concepts can sometimes be the result of, not an
alternative to, treating philosophy as policy prescription. Consider, for example, the endless discussion of how to understand
the terms of John Stuart Mill's famous "Harm Principle" in *On
Liberty:* "That the only purpose for which power can be right-
fully exercised over any member of a civilized community,
against his will, is to prevent harm to others."[96] The Mill literature is full of discussions about what is to count as "harm,"
whether the incidence of mere distress and outrage is harmful
to those who experience it, whether harm is confined to physical
injury, and the connection between the concepts *harm, interests,*
and *preferences.*[97] The debates are roughly comparable in character to those endless discussions of what is to count as "speech"
for the purposes of the First Amendment—Is flag-burning
speech? Is topless dancing speech?—just as though the Harm
Principle were a statutory clause or a constitutional provision
which we were required to interpret, or as though it were something being proposed for acceptance in one or other of these
capacities and we wanted to explore the interpretive possibilities
in advance. Never mind that the principle was being put forward specifically *not* as a legal proposal, but as part of a campaign to enable "the intelligent part of the public" to apprehend
the value of individuality and to raise "a strong barrier of moral
conviction" against philanthropic paternalism.[98] Never mind
that it is put forward solely as the conclusion of *an argument*
(which is to be developed in the second and third chapters) so

that its meaning can have no interest for us apart from that argument.[99] If we treat such a proposition as a policy proposal, we are going to have get involved in the same legalistic dissection of its meaning as we do with the proposals we make for one another in faculty meetings or on academic senates. The better course, it seems to me, is to treat the conclusion of a philosopher's argument no differently from the rest of it—from the premises and the reasoning. It is the argument itself that is interesting, for the way it weaves certain values and principles together. If a particular form of words doesn't quite capture what the argument shows, that matters little and can be easily adjusted as our understanding evolves, for—unlike a policy proposal—nothing of *political* or *legal* moment hangs on our having formulated it one way or the other.

The second preliminary point is that we should not be so sure that we have had (from the thirties through the early sixties) all the conceptual analysis that we need, and that we now perfectly well understand the concepts of politics—like *power, the state, politics, civil society, community, morality, violence, justice, democracy, order, freedom* and *law*—and that the only issue remaining is the normative question, "What is to be done?" It seems to me that we still need to complement whatever else we are doing in political philosophy with a healthy dose of conceptual understanding, including an understanding of the nature of conceptual understanding itself. What are the distinctive characteristics of the *political* realm? What makes a social entity a *community*? Is there a difference between the concepts *government* and *state*? What if anything do we learn from our unwillingness to describe the regime of a Somali warlord as a *legal system*? What other concepts are put in play when we talk of *power,* or when we talk of *liberty*? What is it for people who seem to share a language to disagree about the answers to questions like these? What is it to share a concept?

Maybe what we should avoid are *sterile* conceptual discussions—those with no normative ramifications. (Or maybe Thomas Hobbes is right and there is no such thing as a sterile dispute: people argue only about the things that affect their interests.)[100] Maybe, as the pragmatists suggest, we should do *all* our thinking about politics, philosophical as well as moral and empirical, to help us sort out the things that really matter to us. Even so, it is not necessary to have a particular bottom line of policy in mind when one discusses the meaning of a concept. There is a division of labor in these matters, and we (that is, philosophers) are depended upon to play a *particular,* not an all-purpose, role in the evolution of the understandings that are requisite for intelligent political decision-making.

My main point, however, is that there are a large number of issues that ought to be on the agenda for political philosophy which are not purely conceptual—concerned with meanings— but not purely oriented to the prescription of policies either. They have to do with an understanding of the relation between individual and group deliberation and decision which we call politics. The issues I have in mind can be read as purely conceptual, or they can be read as purely normative, if the reader is determined enough to squeeze them under one or another rubric. But they are issues about what (on earth) is going on, what we think we are doing, when we engage in political life and activity, and when we make judgments about the manner in which we or others engage in it.

Consider, for example, the account of the distinctive features of the political realm offered by Hannah Arendt. Arendt believes that there is an immense gulf between the pleasures and concerns of the private household and the joys and vicissitudes that are properly associated with politics. She argued that men have often embarked on political action to achieve some limited material end and found to their surprise that there is a happiness associated with public life—"the speech-making and decision-taking, the oratory and the business, the thinking and the persuading, and the actual doing"—that private well-being could never offer.[101] It is a form of happiness that has to do with the ability to act and initiate things in the presence and memory of others, in a realm where what matters is what one appears to be, not what one might or might not be, as it were, in one's hidden essence. She has argued, too, that "the joys of public happiness and the responsibilities for public business . . . become the share of those few from all walks of life who have a taste for public freedom and cannot be 'happy' without it."[102] And she has maintained, notoriously, that these opportunities and this distinctive joy of the political world will tend to evaporate the more public life takes on the functions of the household at a society-wide level. She has called "the politically most pernicious doctrine of the modern age" the idea that "life is the highest good, and that the life process of society is the very centre of human endeavour." [103]

From all of which my students infer: "Hannah Arendt was in favor of participatory democracy. She would allow anyone who wanted to participate, and she would not be concerned if that desire was confined to an elite. She was, however, opposed to welfare institutions, and she would restrict political discussion to non-economic and non-social matters." And they judge her candidacy accordingly. The more intelligent of them do note that her normative tone is that of a lamentation, rather than a direct prescription, and that it is tinged with nostalgia for the imagined past of Periclean Athens. But that barely gives them pause in their anxiety to find out what she was in favor of.

In fact Arendt's work is precisely an attempt to understand the political sphere, and what its distinctive possibilities are and have been, even if it has never appeared on earth in unalloyed form. It is not exactly a definitional analysis of the *word* "politics"—but an attempt to tease out and recover a sense of what a certain practice could have been, and to illuminate the connections of this possibility with some other themes—natality, oblivion, nature, free will—in our striving and self-understanding. Compared with that task of recovery and explication, finding out what Arendt would allow, at the level of policy or constitutional politics, seems trite and irrelevant.

Arendt's is not the only understanding of politics. Others see it as the arena of collective action, where the tasks are understood primarily in game theoretic terms. We come together to act politically when a series of unilateral initiatives by a mass of individual agents for some reason will not do. There are questions about whether the logic and structure of collective action is amenable to the same sort of moral governance as that of individual action: "When what happens depends on strategic interactions, what *I* do is inherently less important than what we do; indeed, what I should do may depend on what you have done or will do. . . . It would therefore be odd if a strictly action-based theory could yield morally compelling results for these interactions."[104] So how are we to relate collective action with individual responsibility, collective neglect with the failure of individual initiatives, and our own pessimism about "making a difference" with a collective failure of nerve? These are questions about values and responsibility; they are in a very real sense questions within moral theory; but they are only remotely and indirectly questions about what we should do, here and now, on the issues of policy that we face.

Other questions relate to the issues raised originally by Machiavelli (and revisited at the end of the First World War by Max Weber).[105] What is the place of value judgment in the realm of the political? What are we to make of the feelings of inevitable unpleasantness, the indispensable moral uneasiness, the sense of "dirty hands," that even (especially) the most able and scrupulous politician will experience if he spends any time successfully in office? Does that indicate, as Weber thought, a radical discontinuity between the ethics of the political and the ethics of the personal ideal? Or do we need to bring deeper resources from moral philosophy—the idea of moral tragedy, for example—to bear in our understanding of political values?[106]

Again, politics arises, as Hannah Arendt noted, because not man but *men* live in the world.[107] There are many of us with different views, hopes, and aspirations. We disagree with one another about what is important, about priorities and about what ought to be done. A political system which is not paralyzed must develop processes for determining social decisions as some sort of resultant of these opinions even in the face of trenchant disagreement.[108] But how are we to think about the relation between a citizen's allegiance to his own principles and his allegiance to the system which merges his principled opinion with that of others?[109] When members of a minority faction yield to the majority view, is that a case of the moral principle for which they stand being *overridden* by the principle of majority rule (in the way that, say, the rule that one should keep a promise might be overridden in an emergency)? Or should we conceive the relation between the two principles in some more complex way? What sort of compromises or resultants are we to envisage in politics? Can a view emerge even though it is nobody's view, or even though it is not a view that anyone could coherently hold? How are we to think about the plurality and diversity of voters and legislators in our society in relation to what is alleged to be the unequivocal content of our laws? [110]

The issues raised in this and the preceding paragraph are issues of and about values—they are not "merely" conceptual— but they are not themselves issues of policy or prescription. They have no direct ramifications for what we should do, and the arguments that address them would be, in themselves, of little use to a judge and his clerks, or a legislator and his aides. Still, they are issues of political philosophy—a branch of philosophy that emerges as a distinct intellectual endeavor once the underlying sense of what it is to have political processes and institutions, and of what it is to speak, act, and judge in and around the political realm, is thrown in question in some way.

The answer, then, to the query with which I began this final section is that the normative does not disappear when we abandon our modern preoccupation with the prescriptive bottom line. We might produce fewer articles on drunk driving or residential rent control, figuring there is only a limited amount that we, in our professional capacity, can say over and above what any informed citizen could say on issues of such moment. More likely, the articles will appear as before, but we will be inclined to read them a little differently. We may ask: what can I learn about the nature of responsibility, or what can I learn about the idea of identifying with one's property, from this or that article even when I disagree with the author's concluding prescriptions? What connections can I draw, what contributions can this make, to a deeper understanding of what is involved in legal, social, and political processes?

We call ourselves political *philosophers,* we write in journals with names like *"Philosophy* and Public Affairs," but we treat our subject sometimes as though we were just political animals and the journals were just "Public Affairs." An area of inquiry cannot become *philosophy* until people have seen reason to throw its fundamental presuppositions into doubt. We engage in the philosophy of mathematics only when it seems a mystery that Fermat's Last Theorem might be true or might be false and we do not know which. We engage in the philosophy of science only when the amenability of nature to our mathematical talents seems too much of a coincidence. We engage in moral philosophy, when there starts to be something odd or hollow about talk of duty, when for an atheist duty starts to seem like the grin of the Cheshire cat left after the cat has vanished. We respond to these mysteries and engage with them, and it is our vocation to persevere in doing so long after the point when a man of good sense would have put down his *Logic* and gone home to play backgammon. Unless our speculations appear, by ordinary standards, "cold, and strain'd and ridiculous," we are not doing philosophy.[111]

In what passes for political philosophy, in recent times, too much of our work is done in the light of precisely those assumptions we should have to extinguish, or at least call in question, to earn that name for our discipline. We write as though there were no question about what a state was, or a legal system, as though the only question is what we should get it to do. We write as though there were no issue about the meaning of "ought," or the sense of ethical judgments, as though it were the easiest thing in the world to find them, to take one and apply it to a decision of a whole people. We write as though there were no mystery about what a "bottom line" amounts to in politics, as though the only question were: "What *is* the bottom line?" It seems to me—and I have tried to show it in this chapter—that in fact much of the most interesting work in the subject has been done by people who were prepared to call in question the very things that underpin our ability to write glibly on matters of policy.

I guess most of us—authors, readers, fellow-symposiasts—are from time to time asked the following question by those not cursed with philosophical pretensions: "What's the point of your work? What difference is it going to make? How is it going to help the fight against poverty, racism, and sexism?" My bottom line is that we are not really doing political philosophy, and thus paradoxically that we are probably not really being of much use, unless we are largely at a loss as to how to answer that question.

NOTES

1. Plato, *The Republic*, trans. Desmond Lee (Harmondsworth: Penguin Books, 1974), book 5:230–43 (453a–61e); Thomas Hobbes, *Leviathan*, ed. Richard Tuck (Cambridge: Cambridge University Press, 1991), chap. 18:123–25; John Locke, *Two Treatises of Government*, ed. Peter Laslett (Cambridge: Cambridge University Press, 1988), book 2, chap. 19:400–401 (sect. 202); and Jean-Jacques Rousseau, *The Social Contract*, trans. Maurice Cranston (Harmondsworth: Penguin Books, 1968), book 3, chap. 15:140–43.

2. Aristotle, *The Politics*, ed. Stephen Everson (Cambridge: Cambridge University Press, 1988), book 1, chaps.: 4–7, 5–9 (1253b23–1255b40); and Locke, *Two Treatises of Government*, book 2, chap. 7:321 (sect. 82).

3. Susan Moller Okin, *Women in Western Political Thought* (Princeton: Princeton University Press, 1979), 36 and 44.

4. Ibid., 194.

5. Ibid., 279.

6. Brian Barry, "Review of *Anarchy, State, and Utopia*," in *Political Theory* 3 (1975), 331–32.

7. Robert Nozick, *Anarchy, State, and Utopia* (Oxford: Basil Blackwell, 1974), xii.

8. Ibid., 202.

9. Ibid., 230–31.

10. R. M. Hare, *Plato*, collected with Jonathan Barnes, *Aristotle*, and Henry Chadwick, *Augustine*, as *Founders of Thought* (Oxford: Oxford University Press, 1991), 64–65.

11. "You have agreed that justice falls into the highest category of goods, of goods, that is, which are worth choosing not only for their consequences but also, and far more, for themselves such things as sight, hearing, intelligence, health, and all other qualities which bring us a real and not merely apparent benefit. Let us therefore hear you commending justice for the real benefits it brings its possessor, compared with the damage injustice does him. . . . Prove to us therefore, not only that justice is superior to injustice, but that, irrespective of whether gods or men know it or not, one is good and the other evil because of its inherent effects on its possessor." (Plato, *Republic*, book 2:114 [367c–e]).

12. The challenge from Thrasymachus and Glaucon should not be viewed as merely a way of setting up a discussion that is *really* devoted to the elaboration of a normative blueprint. If there is a set-up, it is rather the discussion with Cephalus about the joys of old age at the

beginning of book 1. That yields quickly to an analytic discussion about the nature of justice as an individual virtue, which is followed by an expostulation and development of the Thrasymachean challenge we have already noted, a challenge which lasts well into book 2, some thirty or so pages (in the traditional pagination). What is more, Socrates returns to the theme again and again throughout the dialogue, and he certainly speaks as though answering that challenge, rather than normative political prescription for its own sake, were the general point of the enterprise: "Well, we seem to have got your city founded for you, Adeimantus," I said. "Now you must look at it and get your brother and Polemachus and the rest of them to see if they can help you throw enough light on it for us to see where justice and injustice are to be found, how they differ from each other, and which of them anyone who is to be happy needs, irrespective of whether gods or men think he has it or not." (Plato, *Republic,* book 4:196 [427d]. See also ibid., book 4:185–186 [422b–c], book 5:261 [472c–d], and the whole second half of book 9:398–420 [576c–92b].)

13. What, after all, does "guardians" mean to us except that it is the English term we use to translate Plato's *"phylakes"?*

14. See particularly the work of Quentin Skinner in, for example, "Meaning and Understanding in the History of Ideas," *History and Theory* 8 (1969).

15. Plato, *Republic,* book 5:233 (455b).

16. Cf. "Conversely, you will find, if you work out the cube, that the measure of difference between the two in terms of true pleasure is that the philosopher king lives seven hundred and twenty-nine times more pleasantly than the tyrant." Plato, *Republic,* book 9:415 [587e].

17. Locke, *Two Treatises,* book 2, chap. 2:271 (sect. 6).

18. Nozick, *Anarchy, State, and Utopia,* x.

19. See note 8, above, and accompanying text.

20. See note 8, above, and accompanying text.

21. Aristotle, *Politics,* book 2, chaps. 1–7:20–36 (1260b27–1267b21).

22. Hobbes, *Leviathan,* chap. 15:107.

23. Ibid., chap. 17:119.

24. Ibid., chap. 21:150.

25. G. W. F. Hegel, *Elements of the Philosophy of Right,* ed. Allen Wood (Cambridge: Cambridge University Press, 1991), 77 (para. 46, Remark).

26. Ibid., 21.

27. See also Jeremy Waldron, *The Right to Private Property* (Oxford: Clarendon Press, 1988), 134–35.

28. See especially the excellent reconstruction and critique in Jean Hampton, *Hobbes and the Social Contract Tradition* (Cambridge: Cambridge University Press, 1986).

29. I have defended this view of political theory in Jeremy Waldron, "A Right-Based Critique of Constitutional Rights," *Oxford Journal of Legal Studies* 13 (1993): esp. 34–38.

30. Cf. Peter Donaldson, *Machiavelli and Mystery of State* (Cambridge: Cambridge University Press, 1988).

31. See Jeremy Waldron, "Theoretical Foundations of Liberalism," *Philosophical Quarterly* 37 (1987), esp. 134ff., reprinted in Waldron, *Liberal Rights: Collected Papers, 1981–91* (Cambridge: Cambridge University Press, 1993), 43ff.

32. It does not, however, follow that any time a citizen, an official, or a judge is asked to make a moral judgment, she is being asked to do moral philosophy. For this misunderstanding (e.g., that constitutional theories that require judges to make moral judgments are in effect requiring them to become philosophers), see Mark Tushnet, *Red, White, and Blue: A Critical Analysis of Constitutional Law* (Cambridge: Harvard University Press, 1988), chap. 3:108–46.

33. C. Helvetius, *De l'esprit: or Essay on the Mind and its Several Faculties,* quoted in Gerald Postema, *Bentham and the Common Law Tradition* (Oxford: Clarendon Press, 1986), 263.

34. Rousseau, *Social Contract,* book 2, chap. 6:83.

35. See, e.g., J. L. Talmon, *The Origins of Totalitarian Democracy* (London: Sphere Books, 1970).

36. Rousseau, *Social Contract,* book 1, chap. 7, 64: "whoever refuses to obey the general will shall be constrained to do so by the whole body, which means nothing other than that he shall be forced to be free."

37. Ibid., book 4, chap. 2:153n.

38. Ibid., book 2, chap. 3:72.

39. Ibid., book 2, chap. 6:83.

40. Maurice Cranston, "Introduction" to Rousseau, *Social Contract,* 42.

41. Ibid., book 2, chap. 7:86. "I have said this already," he continues, "But it is worth repeating."

42. See Cranston, "Introduction" to Rousseau, *Social Contract,* 42, citing Judith Shklar, "Rousseau's Images of Authority," *American Political Science Review* (1964).

43. Rousseau did not share Machiavelli's confidence that well-ordered republics might on occasion emerge *without* a founder, in an invisible-hand sort of way: see Machiavelli, *Discourses,* book 1, chaps. 1–

2. See also J. G. A. Pocock, *The Machiavellian Moment: Florentine Political Thought and the Atlantic Republican Tradition* (Princeton: Princeton University Press, 1975), 187ff.

44. Rousseau, *Social Contract,* book 1:49.

45. Everything I say about Plato's image of the states*man* should be read in the light of comments like this: "And some of them will be women. . . . All I have said about men applies equally to women, if they have the requisite natural capacities." Plato, *Republic,* book 7:354 [540c].

46. Ibid., book 7:326 (521c).

47. Ibid., book 5:263 (473c–e).

48. Ibid., book 6:282–184 (488b–89d).

49. Ibid., book 6:297 (500d).

50. Ibid., book 6:293 (497b).

51. Ibid., book 6:292 (496c–e).

52. See ibid., book 9:420 (592a–b).

53. Ibid., book 6:292 (497a).

54. See ibid., book 6:295–96 (499b–d).

55. See above, the final few lines in the text accompanying note 45.

56. There is an excellent discussion of this in Norman Jacobson, *Pride and Solace: The Functions and Limits of Political Theory* (Berkeley: University of California Press, 1978).

57. Plato, *Republic,* book 7:323–25 (519c–20e).

58. Compare ibid., book 6:278 (485c–d) and book 3:180–82 (414–15d).

59. Rousseau, *Social Contract,* book 2, chap. 7:84.

60. See John Rawls, "Kantian Constructivism in Moral Theory: The John Dewey Lectures," *Journal of Philosophy* 77 (1980): 520.

61. See Adam Smith, *The Theory of Moral Sentiments,* ed. D. D. Raphael and A. L. Macfie (Indianapolis: Liberty Classics, 1976), esp. the long footnote on 128–30.

62. Rousseau, *Social Contract,* book 2, chap. 7:84.

63. Plato, *Republic,* book 6:297 (501a).

64. Karl Popper, *The Open Society and Its Enemies* (London: Routledge and Kegan Paul, 1962).

65. Desmond Lee, "Introduction" to Plato, *Republic,* 55.

66. Niccolo Machiavelli, *The Discourses,* ed. Bernard Crick (Harmondsworth: Penguin Books, 1974), book 1, chap. 9:132.

67. Ibid., book 1, chap. 26:176–77.

68. Ibid., book 1, chap. 18:163–64.

69. Ibid., book 2, chap. 2:278.

70. Plato, *Republic,* book 2:114 (367b). My emphasis.

71. Ibid., book 2:117 (369a).

72. Ibid., book 9:420 (592a–b).

73. The passage continues: "Perhaps . . . it [i.e., the ideal state] is laid up as a pattern in heaven, where he who wishes can see it and found it in his own heart. But it doesn't matter whether it exists or ever will exist; in it alone, and in no other society, could he [the just man] take part in public affairs." Ibid., book 9:420 [592b].

74. Ibid., book 5:261, 472c–d.

75. Karl Marx, "Postface to Second Edition," in *Capital*, trans. Ben Fowkes (Harmondsworth: Penguin Books, 1976), 1:99. I am grateful to Paul Thomas for this reference.

76. Letter from Marx to Friedrich Adolph Sorge, 19 October 1877, in *Karl Marx: Selected Writings*, ed. David McLellan (Oxford: Oxford University Press, 1977), 589.

77. Hegel, *Philosophy of Right*, 23.

78. Karl Marx, excerpt from *The Civil War in France* in *Karl Marx: Selected Writings*, 545.

79. Hegel, *Philosophy of Right*, 23.

80. Ibid., 21–22.

81. Ludwig Wittgenstein, *Philosophical Investigations*, trans. G. E. M. Anscombe (Oxford: Basil Blackwell, 1974), 49e–50e (paras. 124 and 126).

82. Hegel, *Philosophy of Right*, 14n. (Hotho's Addition).

83. See the discussion in Waldron, *The Right to Private Property*, 344–47.

84. Hegel, *Philosophy of Right*, 21.

85. Ibid., 22.

86. See Peter Laslett, Introduction to Locke, *Two Treatises*, 16–92, and Richard Ashcraft, *Revolutionary Politics and Locke's "Two Treatises of Government"* (Princeton: Princeton University Press, 1986).

87. Locke, *Two Treatises*, book 2, chap. 15:380 (sect. 169).

88. Ibid., book 2, chap. 6:316–18 (sects. 74–6) and chap. 8:336–44 (sects. 105–12). See also Jeremy Waldron, "John Locke: Social Contract versus Political Anthropology," *Review of Politics* (1989): 3–28.

89. Locke, *Two Treatises*, book 2, chap. 8:343 (sect. 111).

90. Ibid., book 2, chap. 7:327 (sect. 92).

91. Locke, *Two Treatises*, book 2, chap. 2:269 (sect. 4). My emphasis.

92. Peter Laslett, ed., "Introduction," *Philosophy, Politics, and Society* (Oxford: Basil Blackwell, 1956), vii.

93. Peter Laslett and James Fishkin, eds., "Introduction," *Philosophy, Politics, and Society*, Fifth Series (Oxford: Basil Blackwell, 1979), 2.

94. Bonnie Steinbock, "Drunk Driving," *Philosophy and Public Affairs* 14 (1985): 295.

95. Hugh La Follette, "Licencing Parents," *Philosophy and Public Affairs* 9 (1980): 195.

96. John Stuart Mill, *On Liberty*, ed. C. V. Shields (Indianapolis: Bobbs-Merrill, 1956), chap. 1:13.

97. There is a good summary of the recent literature in C. L. Ten, *Mill on Liberty* (Oxford: Clarendon Press, 1980). See also Joel Feinberg, *The Moral Limits of the Criminal Law: Harm to Others* (New York: Oxford University Press, 1984).

98. See Mill, *On Liberty*, chap. 1:18, and chap. 3:90.

99. See Jeremy Waldron, "Mill and the Value of Moral Distress," *Political Studies* 35 (1987): 410–23 (reprinted in Waldron, *Liberal Rights*, 115–33).

100. Hobbes, *Leviathan*, chap. 11:73–74: "This is the cause, that the doctrine of Right and Wrong, is perpetually disputed, both by the Pen and the Sword: Whereas the doctrine of Lines, and Figures, is not so; because men care not, in that subject what be truth, as a thing that crosses no mans ambition, profit, or lust. For I doubt not, but if it had been a thing contrary to any mans right of dominion, or to the interest of men that have dominion, *That the three Angles of a Triangle should be equall to two angles of a Square;* that doctrine should have been, if not disputed, yet by the burning of all books of Geometry, suppressed, as farre as he whom it concerned was able."

101. See Hannah Arendt, *On Revolution* (Harmondsworth: Penguin Books, 1977), 28–35 and 115–40. The passage quoted is from ibid., 34.

102. Ibid., 279.

103. Ibid., 64.

104. Russell Hardin, *Morality within the Limits of Reason* (Chicago: University of Chicago Press, 1988), 68–69. See also Derek Parfit, *Reasons and Persons* (Oxford: Clarendon Press, 1984), and Donald H. Regan, *Utilitarianism and Co-operation* (Oxford: Clarendon Press, 1980).

105. Machiavelli, *The Prince*, ed. Quentin Skinner and Russell Price (Cambridge: Cambridge University Press, 1988) esp. chaps. 15–18; Max Weber, "Politics as a Vocation," in W. Gerth and C. Wright Mills, eds., *From Max Weber: Essays in Sociology* (London: Routledge and Kegan Paul, 1948).

106. See the excellent essays by Bernard Williams, "Politics and Moral Character," and Thomas Nagel, "Ruthlesness in Public Life," in Stuart Hampshire (ed.) *Public and Private Morality* (Cambridge: Cambridge University Press, 1978).

107. Arendt, *The Human Condition*, 234.

108. See Waldron, "A Right-Based Critique of Constitutional Rights," 28–31.

109. See Richard Wollheim, "A Paradox in the Theory of Democracy," in Laslett and Runciman, *Philosophy, Politics, and Society,* Second Series.

110. See Ronald Dworkin, *Law's Empire* (Cambridge: Harvard University Press, 1986), 176–86.

111. The reference is to David Hume, *A Treatise of Human Nature,* ed. L. A. Selby-Bigge (Oxford: Clarendon Press, 1888), book 1, part 4, sect. 7:269.

PART III

ARGUMENTS
FOR THE PRIORITY
OF PRACTICE

6

"LAWYER FOR HUMANITY:" THEORY AND PRACTICE IN ANCIENT POLITICAL THOUGHT

MARTHA C. NUSSBAUM

I begin with the death of Socrates—for this is the moment in relation to which, above all, the Greco-Roman philosophical tradition defines itself.[1] Here we see a philosophical teacher who was so far from being thought irrelevant to political life that the city judged it urgent to put him to death. Here we see a philosophical thinker who was so far from being indifferent to the conduct of affairs in the city that he put his life on the line to awaken it to self-examination.[2] At his trial he did not say, "Sorry boys, you have made a big mistake about me. I don't aim to change things; I aim to make you think fine and clever thoughts." He said that if he were discharged with an injunction not to do it again he would do it again—biting the city every day of his life, like a gadfly on the back of a noble but sluggish horse (*Apology* 30E).

Five centuries later, Seneca, political philosopher and primary advisor to the emperor Nero, also lost his life for his political and philosophical beliefs, which eventually led him to support a Stoic anti-imperial conspiracy. He imitated Socrates in the manner of his state-ordered suicide.[3] Before his death,[4]

he wrote the following words to his friend Lucilius, whose letters to Seneca showed the influence of the fashionable view that
philosophy is a detached business, without practical involvements:

> Do you want to know what philosophy offers humanity? Practical
> guidance. One man is on the verge of death. Another is rubbed
> down by poverty. Another is tormented by riches—either some-
> one else's or his own. This one dreads bad luck; that one longs to
> escape from his good luck. These are ill treated by men, those by
> the gods. Why, then, do you write me these frivolities? There is
> no time for playing around: you have been retained as lawyer[5]
> for unhappy humanity. You have promised to bring help to the
> shipwrecked, the imprisoned, the sick, the poor, to those whose
> heads are under the poised axe. Where are you deflecting your
> attention? What are you doing? (*Epistulae Morales* 48, 8)

In his final hours, Seneca affirmed the deep connection between
philosophy and committed political action. First, he wrote a
letter to his imperial pupil, trying to persuade him by argument
to change his mind. Like Socrates' courtroom speech, this letter
doomed the writer by its refusal to flatter or to back off from
the argument. Then, in his final hours, he got on with his work.
His veins opened, "he called in scribes and dictated a good deal,
which"—comments the historian Tacitus—"since it is published
in his collected works, I shall not bother to repeat" (*Annals*
XV.63).

Philosophers sometimes sit on professorial chairs in philosophy departments.[6] Sometimes, however, they are inclined to
follow a peripatetic tradition. Sometimes, like Socrates, these
ambulatory philosophers democratically buttonhole every citizen they meet, looking into the health of their souls. Sometimes,
like Plato,[7] Aristotle, and Seneca, they adopt the equally risky
strategy of teaching young rulers, in the hope of realizing their
philosophical ideals in a more direct way than democracy will
generally permit. Sometimes, like Marcus Aurelius, they have
the good or bad fortune to be rulers themselves, and do their
best in that capacity to realize their philosophical ideals. He
constructed for himself the following poignant modal syllogism:

"Wherever it is possible to live, it is possible to live a reflective virtuous life. It is possible to live in a palace. Therefore it is possible to live a reflective virtuous life in a palace" (V.16). And sometimes they have no political weapons but their words, no way of realizing ideals but through the power of writing. Does this mean that they do not seek to realize those ideals? Does this mean that they do not sometimes succeed? Sometimes, the chairs on which they sit are in the British Library.[8]

I shall argue here that Jeremy Waldron is wrong about the Western philosophical tradition. I shall argue, against him, that the Greek and Roman thinkers at the tradition's source held that there was an urgent and intimate connection between philosophical thought and political and social practice. They understood that connection in many different ways, and the sort of philosophizing pertinent to it. Yet they would all have concurred, in one way or another, with Aristotle's view that in at least some areas of philosophy "the end is not contemplation but action" Nicomachean Ethics (*EN* 1095a5).[9] And I shall then argue that they were right: that there is an urgent role for good philosophy to play in political life, and that it does not necessarily cease being good philosophy, but actually fulfills its philosophical purpose, when it undertakes this role.

The scope of my analysis will be different from that of Waldron's paper in two ways. I shall confine my historical remarks to the Greek and Roman traditions, and shall not attempt to deal with Locke or Rousseau.[10] Within those traditions I shall cast my net somewhat wider than he does, speaking not only of Plato and Aristotle but also of their Hellenistic successors, the Epicureans and Stoics. This seems to me important: for the Hellenistic thinkers actually had at least as great an influence on the tradition as their predecessors, and, in the case of the Stoics, a greater influence. So if our aim is to understand the tradition, we should not omit them.[11]

The core of Waldron's analysis, where the ancient Greek and Roman traditions are concerned, lies in his remarks about Plato's *Republic*. Though it seems to me quite difficult to reply to such a brief position-statement, given the complexity of the texts and the centuries of discussion they have engendered, I shall make an attempt. Waldron's position seems to be the following. Since the political conception in the *Republic* is introduced as a heuristic device in which to see the justice of an individual more clearly, we should not suppose that Plato is really advocating its realization. Moreover, he gives us reasons to suppose that he believes its realization to be impossible. The conclusion of the work, then, is simply that being a certain sort of just individual is a good thing to be. In addition, Waldron suggests that Plato was not in a position to make political proposals, since he was not the holder of public office, nor the framer of a constitution, but was instead a "social outcast."

I reply first to the biographical point. Plato was no social outcast. He belonged to an extremely wealthy and influential Athenian family.[12] Two of his close relatives were Critias and Charmides, members of the Thirty Tyrants, the small group of oligarchs who briefly seized control of the city in 404, displacing the democracy and putting many of its prominent citizens to death. His entire family was prominently linked with the oligarchic cause. Throughout his life, then, Plato was an influential well-to-do citizen of the Athenian democracy (except when the oligarchs, his relatives, were briefly in power), and in that sense both the holder of a public role (in the Athenian democracy all offices but that of general were filled by lot), and also the potential framer of a constitution.

Moreover, in the autobiographical *Letter VII*, Plato describes himself as passionately concerned with politics throughout his life. Early in his life, he reports, his concern took the form of backing his family's efforts and having high hopes that they would indeed succeed in realizing justice, as their propaganda claimed (324CD). When they showed their true colors by their attempt to manipulate Socrates into taking part in illegal activities (*Letter* VII 324E–325A, parallel to *Apology* 32B–E), he was disillusioned, and looked for other approaches, becoming in time increasingly critical of the restored democracy itself (325D). He stresses that his concern to realize his conceptions in practice never abated; but he became more and more convinced of the value of a philosophical perspective for the guidance of public life:

> while I did not stop considering how to improve the situation at hand, and indeed how to reform the whole constitution, nonetheless I waited, looking for a suitable time to act. Finally I saw clearly that all cities now existing are badly governed ... and I was forced to say, praising the truths of philosophy, that it was from that vantage point that one could truly see what is just in public and private life. Therefore, the human race would not cease from its ills, until either those who philosophize well and truly should take political office, or the class who hold power in the cities should by some lucky chance start to think philosophically. It was with this thought in my mind that I made my first trip to Sicily. (326AB)

Notice that Plato closely paraphrases the words of the *Republic* in order to explicate the motives for his own very real political activity in Syracuse. He continues, describing the many years he spent in various doomed efforts to get the young ruler Dionysius to govern in a philosophically guided way, and in backing the intelligent political program of Dion, with whom he apparently had an erotic involvement.[13] Plato's account of himself draws attention throughout to the seamless unity of theory and practice in his life, and to the risks he ran to make his commitments practical.

Moreover, the *Republic* situates itself in the drama of this life by its very choice of characters and dramatic date. As has been remarked before, Plato chooses as interlocutors personae who figured prominently in the traumatic events of the Thirty-Tyrant takeover: his two half-brothers, Glaucon and Adeimantus, who seem to have shared the family's oligarchic sympathies, and, on the other side, Polemarchus and Niceratus, both prominent and wealthy democrats who were killed by the Thirty. As the murder of Polemarchus is described later by his brother the orator Lysias, who managed to escape, the pretext of the Thirty was "cleansing the city of the unjust"[14]—but really, he plausibly claims, the motive was to get hold of their wealth. The Thirty were so greedy, he adds, that they dragged Polemarchus' wife out into the courtyard and ripped the gold earrings out of her ear lobes. By putting such characters on the stage, in a peaceful time years before this event, and by orchestrating a calm discussion of justice among them, the *Republic* makes vivid, from its very opening words (in which the banter about compulsion and persuasion takes on an ominous resonance) the problem of political justice and its practical urgency.

While it is perfectly correct to say that Socrates originally introduces the political scheme as a device to "read" the structure of the soul more clearly, he soon makes it clear that things are more complicated, insisting that the two structures will actually illuminate one another mutually (435A). To this end he establishes the internal structure of the person (the parts of the person's soul) using an argument that, as he tells us, at no point presupposes the correctness of the political divisions that have preceded (434Dff., 436Aff.). A great deal of the political design has no relevant parallel at the psychic level. As the argument proceeds, there also unfolds a different relationship between the political and the psychic: a causal relationship. For it emerges that a fully just and fully knowledgeable person can be produced only by the sort of upbringing and education that the city described makes possible. It is for this reason that the rule of philosophers is said, here as in *Letter* VII, to be a necessary condition for "any human happiness, public or private" (473DE).

The necessary conditions for human happiness prominently include the abolition of the traditional nuclear family and the equal education of women: so in that sense, the students who wrote of what "Plato would allow" here are perfectly correct.[15] What that "would allow" means is, "If there is to be a state in which human beings truly flourish, this is how it must be—and I, Plato, am not only writing this book about it but am also trying to take my opportunities where I find them, to make this come into being in real life." I would not think well of a student paper that simply listed these conclusions, without the arguments about the soul and political order that lead to them. But this (as I shall say at greater length below) is not because I think that the arguments have more importance than their conclusions or somehow stand apart from their conclusions; it is because one could not do good practical thinking in Plato's way without this deeper understanding.[16] I also would not think well of a student paper that failed to investigate the arguments seriously because the student repudiated many of Plato's conclusions—as few of his readers do not. But again: this is not because I think the conclusions unimportant; it is because the arguments leading to the apparently unpalatable conclusions follow from premises that have intuitive power—and so it is an important part of understanding one's own relation to political action to understand whether in fact the conclusions do follow by a valid argument from the premises.

I have argued against a merely heuristic reading of the political design in the *Republic*. When we arrive at the *Laws*, no such reading is even possible, since the dramatic "plot" is that the characters are in fact legislating for a new colony—a not implausible scenario at this time. Yet the concerns of the *Laws* in most respects are parallel to those of the *Republic*. So one further deficit in Waldron's approach is that it would prevent us from considering the two works together. Indeed, it would force us to say, most implausibly, that they are engaged in entirely different sorts of tasks.

As for the claim that Plato repeatedly indicates that the scheme is impossible—this is a more delicate matter. Certainly throughout the work his characters are at pains to insist on its possibility, not impossibility. Yet Waldron is correct in stating that at the end of the ninth book Socrates does express (1) a conviction that it is currently not in existence anywhere, and (2) a doubt as to whether it can be realized. In the light of this doubt he does hold it forth as a "paradigm in the heavens" for a person in a deficient regime, who may "enroll himself as its citizen" while inhabiting a defective regime. But of course this is perfectly consistent with attempting to bring it into real existence at the same time, as Plato spent years doing in Sicily. One may imagine that it could not in fact come into existence unless by the agency of some people who had already "enrolled themselves in it" before that time, and one may well imagine, too, that one who was so enrolled would be eager to see things done better in reality. Socrates concludes, "It makes no difference whether it exists now or will ever come into being. For his actions will be those of that city and no other" (592B). But this does not mean, "It makes no difference to humanity whether this city exists or doesn't, and he will not try for that." It means, "Whether or not there is such a city in real life, he will act according to its laws." That no more means that he won't be interested in political change than the fact that the Kingdom of Ends imposes obligations on us all here and now means that Kant cannot or should not have been interested in world peace and political reform. "Acting according to the laws" of the ideal city might well mean doing the sort of thing Plato did in fact, trying to bring about political change in the direction of the good whenever and however one can. Indeed, the next sentence of the work, at the start of Book X, goes right back to institutional design, concerning the education of the young citizens through poetry. This is an aspect of the political program that has no parallel at the level of the soul, that indeed to some extent requires the breakup of the parallel—for the characters have to read the things they censor. But they do not repudiate this institutional concern as irrelevant; they pursue it.

Aristotle is not an unerring interpreter of his predecessors. Yet, he lived and worked in close association with Plato for about twenty years. He might then be expected not to err wildly about the general point and direction of Plato's political thought. He takes the *Republic* and the *Laws* absolutely seriously as practical political proposals. He does find impossibilities in them—but at a deep level, having to do with the psychology of political motivation. (If one removes the family, one won't get the happy result Plato predicts.) Aristotle reviews these proposals with the greatest practical earnestness, alongside other theoretical proposals and the real-life constitutions of Sparta and Crete, eventually producing his own ideal plan out of this critical scrutiny.[17] He begins with an observation and a question: "Citizens might conceivably have wives and children and property in common, as Socrates proposes in the *Republic* of Plato. Which is better, our present condition, or one conforming to the law laid down in the *Republic*?" (1261a5–7)

But what is the goal of his own normative inquiry? He himself tells us again and again: "not contemplation, but action"; or, to translate differently, "not theory, but practice."[18] Aristotle, unlike Plato, had no political influence at Athens, indeed no political rights at all, not even the right to own property.[19] As a resident alien, all he could do there was teach those who would be in a position to make a difference. But this he proposed to do, insisting that his pupils in ethics and politics should be well brought up young adults who would be on the verge of a political life. He urged them to understand that any genuine concern for the well-being of humans should issue in a commitment to political law-making (*EN* 1180b24–28). He then set them to study the history and structure of many different regimes and their laws,[20] with this normative project in view.

I point out that for good measure, though not with conspicuous success, he also followed Plato's lead in becoming the tutor to rulers. For a time, during his long exile from Athens, he resided at the court of Hermeias, the one-man ruler of Atarneus, whose daughter he married, and whose aptitude for political philosophy he seems to have praised in a poem on the topic of *arete*. But his most famous pupil was Alexander the Great, not exactly a powerless social outcast—though also not, it seems, a great lover of philosophy.[21] Teaching a future one-man ruler is not a bad way to have influence if the person is receptive to influence; and in the developing world one still may encounter this sort of role for philosophy, for better or for worse.[22]

I turn now to the Hellenistic thinkers, who, as I have said, had a more profound influence than did Plato and Aristotle on later conceptions of the theory-practice connection. I begin with Epicurus, who used the connection to define what good philosophy is: "Empty is that philosopher's argument by which no human suffering is therapeutically treated. For just as there is no use in a medical art that does not cast out the sicknesses of bodies, so too there is no use in philosophy, if it does not cast out suffering from the soul."[23] Epicurus here picks up the analogy between philosophy and medicine that had been on the scene for many years, and develops it in a bold way, making practical benefit a criterion of worth for a philosophical argument.

The core of Epicurus' conception is a conception of emotion and desire that he shares (in its broad outlines at least) with his rivals, the Stoics. His idea is that emotions, for example fear, anger, passionate love, and desires, for example those for particular foods and for particular sorts of sexual activities and relationships,[24] are all not innate, but socially shaped, formed along with the shaping of belief and evaluation in a child's familial and social upbringing. I believe that this conception, both in its large outlines and in its detail, is a powerful one. My main philosophical project at present is to articulate it in a contemporary philosophical way, modifying it so as to make it fully defensible. I shall therefore not try to articulate it fully here. Let it suffice to say that in addition to a general argument linking emotion to belief and teaching, Epicurus also has a normative argument to the conclusion that many of the beliefs that ground the most common emotions are false. To give just one famous example, he argues that the fear of death, as most people experience it, is based on false beliefs about the survival of the person and about whether something can be either good or bad for a person who does not survive. It is his view that getting rid of the passions that cause upheaval and misery in human life is the central business of philosophy. And it is the business centrally of philosophy, given the nature of the passions' reliance on a cognitive structure that only good argument can dismantle.

Epicurus plainly holds that quite a lot of systematic and elaborate philosophical argument is necessary to free the pupil from fear and anger and greed and other false concerns. For only a systematic picture of the entire universe, with elaborate physical and cosmological arguments, will suffice to dislodge the world view of popular religion, on which so much of our misery is based. Thus Epicureans will learn a great deal of metaphysics and theory of knowledge; they will learn about the nonteleological structure of natural processes; they will learn about the relationship between mind and body; and only then will they approach ethical and political topics. But he makes it very plain that they do not do this for love of learning alone: "If we had never been burdened by suspicious fears about things in the heavens, and about death, lest it might be something to us, and by not apprehending the limits of pain and desire, we would not have had any need of the philosophical study of nature"

(*Kuriai Doxai* 11). And this means that they will not devote any time at all to parts of philosophy that seem irrelevant for good choice, such as aesthetics and logic—with the result that Epicureans are often caricatured as boorish and ill-educated.[25] From their point of view, however, they are people with transformed lives, and Epicurus is their hero and savior.

Epicurus' primary rivals, the Greek and Roman Stoics, were equally firm in their commitment to a transformation of human life through argument. Like Epicurus, they frequently compared the philosopher to the doctor—and also, as we have seen, to a lawyer who pleads the cause of humanity. They share Epicurus' conviction that philosophy can cure the diseased soul, producing surprising benefits in both personal and public life. The greatest Greek Stoic philosopher, Chrysippus, announced that philosophy is the medical art of the soul; and he plainly believed that all the many branches of philosophy were pertinent to the soul's health. Chrysippus was the founder of propositional logic and the first great philosopher of language, as well as having a remarkable record of achievement in ethics, the philosophy of mind, ethics, and political philosophy. It appears that he saw practical benefit in all these studies.

Like the Epicureans, the Stoics rely for their conception of philosophy's practical role on a conception of emotion and desire. They seem to have developed this conception in greater detail than did the Epicureans, and I would say that they are the most profound thinkers about emotion in the entire history of Western philosophy, with the most subtle, cogent, and rigorous arguments. What is equally striking about these arguments is their commitment to practice. Chrysippus apparently wrote three books analyzing the passions, and a fourth putting the analysis to work in the construction of therapeutic techniques. Similarly, Seneca and Epictetus, following his lead, combine analysis with treatment, argument about the passions with argument designed to remove the beliefs that ground the (destructive) passions. They represent their practical commitment in the very structure of their writings: Epictetus by delivering oral public speeches addressed to Romans whose lives he wishes to change, Seneca by writing always in either epistolary or dialogue form, illustrating the therapeutic interaction between philosophical teacher and addressee. In the treatise *On Mercy,* his addressee is none other than his imperial pupil Nero, at the start of his reign; in the earlier *On Anger,* addressed to his politically influential brother Novatus, he reflects on the goals and prospects of the Claudian principate. The remaking of public life is the theme of both of these works; when Seneca ends the *On Anger* with the famous injunction, "Let us cultivate *humanitas,*" he is summarizing the whole course of an argument in favor of replacing Roman norms of honor and manly aggression with new norms of patience and gentleness. It is this, apparently, that being a "lawyer for humanity" requires. *On Anger* gives many illustrations of the public results to be expected from this normative shift, particularly in the conduct of military affairs, but also in the structure of the legal system and imperial administration. *On Mercy* shows us that the shift can be expected to have large-scale consequences for the character of political, and especially judicial, institutions. As for the letters to Lucilius, they represent a highly concrete practical interaction, in which Seneca teaches and advises an influential Roman *eques* who is at the time of writing imperial procurator in Sicily. But the correspondence is also, plainly, a work for public consumption in which both self and other are philosophical *exempla:* in that sense it is practical in a broader and longer-lasting way, giving advice to politically involved people similar to Lucilius.

In the time after the assassination of Nero, philosophy and politics had a happier collaboration. The Flavian emperors encouraged others to view them as ideal rulers in the Stoic sense, and made a decent effort at enacting some of those norms. And of course in Marcus Aurelius we have the thing that Plato and Aristotle tried so hard to produce, albeit with recalcitrant material: a real philosopher-ruler. Much of Marcus's *Meditations* is intimately personal, directed toward the management of bad passions in himself. But we have seen that for a Stoic the personal is political. Emotion and desire lie, in fact, at the heart of politics. Making a just public act requires making oneself anew; and if one succeed in that effort, one need not fear that greed and anger will obscure one's view of the good for all humans, as that good is within one's power to promote.

Stoics differ from Epicureans in ascribing intrinsic value to the mind's philosophical activity, as it understands nature and the structure of being. Thus metaphysics and philosophy of nature have a somewhat larger scope in their scheme of things than they do for Epicurus. But I would not characterize this as a de-emphasis on the practical role of philosophy, for three reasons. First of all, they hold that all this contemplative activity *is* practical: it is their conception of what practical wisdom and virtue involve. Second, they hold that it does really have a decisive influence on choice and action, and they are prepared to show how logic, the philosophy of language, and teleological understandings of nature all make us choose more wisely. Epictetus, for example, argues in favor of logic and epistemology by saying that one cannot use a measuring stick to examine other things unless one has first examined the measuring stick itself (*Discourses,* I.17.4–12).[26] "You see," he concludes, "you have to become a pupil of the schools, that animal at whom everyone laughs, if in fact you want to make a critical examination of your own beliefs" (I.11.39–40). Finally, Stoics, like Epicureans, are still quick to repudiate the idea of studying philosophical niceties for the sake of playing around. To a pupil who announces that his main purpose in studying philosophy is to master the liar paradox, Epictetus replies, "If that is your plan, go hang" (2.17.34). To a Roman husband who objects that if his wife studies philosophy she will sit around arguing instead of managing the household, Musonius Rufus replies that the husband should worry about the same tendency in himself: no human being should fail to learn philosophy, and none should learn it in a way divorced from practical goals. "Whatever arguments they undertake, I say that these should be undertaken for the sake of deeds" (*That Women Too Should Do Philosophy,* 2).

What does it mean to become a "lawyer for humanity"? The Greek and Roman philosophers seem to have had two distinct conceptions of that action-guiding role. These conceptions at first appear sharply opposed, but I believe that matters are more complicated.

The first approach I shall call the Aristotelian approach. It focuses on the design of political institutions and on the philosopher's role as advisor to statesmen who will themselves be in a position to effect institutional change. The Aristotelian approach emphasizes the fact that human beings need "external goods"—food, possessions, political participation, friendship, education—in order to flourish, and that government is frequently crucial in getting them the things they need. No one can "do fine things without resources" (*EN* 1099a31–33), and a good political arrangement is one in which people will have the resources they need—one, in short, "in accordance with which anyone whatsoever might do well and live a flourishing life" (*Pol.* 1324a22–24). The Aristotelian, accordingly, is concerned with such apparently unphilosophical matters as the class structure of society,[27] the distribution of wealth, arrangements for holding property, the financial structure of civic festivals and "common meals," the location and management of the water supply, population control, and above all the structure of the educational system.

These aspects of Aristotle's work are not always taught in philosophy courses, but, to judge from the way he arranged his writings, he did not consider them separate from his contribution to political philosophy. He argues that his normative concern with human functioning generates concrete conclusions in these practical domains—showing, for example, that a scheme in which poor citizens are debarred by their poverty from participation in essential civic functions is an unjust system; showing, for example, that institutions promoting the unlimited accumulation of wealth are barriers to human flourishing for both rich and poor.[28] And he explicitly states that the whole point of his ethical inquiry is given by its political goal: to provide the account of good human functioning without which no sensible political planning can take place (*EN* X.9, cf. *Pol.* VII.I).

In the Aristotelian conception, then, being a "lawyer for humanity" means intervening on behalf of basic human needs, interests, and capacities with those privileged ones who will have a chance to design and manage institutions.[29]

The Hellenistic philosophers have a somewhat different conception of the philosopher's practical goal. Their "therapy" seems to be addressed to all individuals rather than to designers of social institutions; and its goal seems to be to relieve suffering and improve practice through changes of belief and desire.

Rather than bringing the world to people, then, they teach people to be more independent of the world. Rather than arranging for a world in which nobody is too poor to participate in the affairs of the city, they arrange for a world in which people do not care whether or not they participate in the affairs of the city, because they believe that the only thing of true importance is the activity of their souls.

This difference is seen at its starkest if we compare Aristotle with Epicurus: for while Aristotle argues that political participation is an essential component of human flourishing, and works to arrange things with that end in view, Epicurus teaches that political participation puts one at the mercy of chance, and is therefore of no true worth. Stoics have a richer conception of the good person's social involvements; yet they, too, teach their pupil to despise the things of chance; they, too, seek to cultivate inner freedom and capability more than to realize in the outer world the conditions for its expression in action. Instead of working for a political arrangement in which their ideal of the equal dignity of all rational beings is realized, they teach that the distinctions between slave and free, rich and poor, are of no moral salience, since the only truly free person is the one who is free within.

This might seem to confirm a part of Waldron's claim: that the philosophers are not legislating for the "bottom line," but are more concerned with the inner world. But I believe that matters are not so simple, for the picture I have just painted is far too crude. First of all, the entire approach of the Hellenistic philosophers is of political importance and has political implications. Their view that preferences and desires are not given in nature, but are socially formed and deformed, has, if we take it seriously, many striking consequences for the way we will conduct affairs in a democracy, the role we will give to utilitarian economics in the formation of public policy, the way we will shape our dealings with people whose lives are distant from our own. The modern slogan that "the personal is political" is exactly what the Epicureans and Stoics were after: that we should never assume that our fears, our angers, our concern with money and status, our sexual desires, are just natural and immutable: we should always ask, in what social conditions were they formed and how conducive are they to human dignity and flourishing? That, I think, is a practical political conclusion of enormous importance.

Second, these thinkers were concerned above all with moral education. And moral education is certainly part of the social fabric. Here, in fact, they are in a close alliance with Aristotle, who reproves legislators for thinking of institutional design without thinking of the education—both familial and private— that will be necessary to support the institutions. Furthermore, their arguments were not just arguments that showed how we might effect moral transformation—the claim was that they produced moral transformation, by transforming the beliefs that were the grounds of the passions. Although Waldron to some extent grants that the improvement of character was a concern of the philosophers, he does not seem to grant that their arguments were themselves directly improving.

Third, the Hellenistic thinkers did not ignore the design of political institutions. The original Greek Stoics Zeno and Chrysippus famously designed an Ideal City along Platonic lines, shocking their contemporaries by proposing equal citizenship for men and women, the abolition of all local and national boundaries, a central role for erotic relationships in political life, and things more startling still.[30] Roman Stoics were involved in politics when and insofar as politics allowed. Seneca and Marcus clearly believed that there was a natural connection between doing philosophy and playing a political role. And the period of eight or so years during which Seneca and his associate Burrus ran the empire on behalf of the young Nero was famous as a brief period of good government in the midst of imperial excess and craziness.[31] Epictetus and Musonius Rufus seem not to have had social positions conducive to direct political influence, but instead gave speeches in public that were said to have been highly influential. Stoic philosophy frequently inspired and guided dissident political movements—most famously in the conspiracy of Piso, for which Seneca and his nephew the Stoic poet Lucan lost their lives,[32] and in the republicanism of Thrasea Paetus, put to death in 66.[33]

Fourth, even when Stoic thinkers were not directly involved in government, they were always concerned with the status of institutions whose shape has a direct effect on government—such as customs associated with honor and revenge, the conduct of erotic relations, marriage, and the family. Epicureans believe that philosophical management of the passions will have a large effect on marriage, on child-rearing, on economic activity, on the conduct of politics, even on the frequency and the conduct of war. So too, Stoicism holds that being a Stoic penetrates into every corner of one's life, altering all one's dealings with others, including those mediated by institutions. They have detailed accounts of how certain institutions will be shaped. It is in Roman Stoicism that we find our most vivid portrait, in the ancient Greco-Roman world, of a public life without the cultivation of revenge, and of the impact of this change on both daily affairs and juridical institutions. It is in Roman Stoicism that we find the first concrete practical proposals for the equal education of girls and boys, and for the equal sharing of practical duties between husband and wife; it is here, too, that we find the first proposals for an end to the sexual double standard, and for an end to infanticide, which of course disproportionately affected girls, then as now.[34] So we should not say that the Hellenistic emphasis on the inner world led to a philosophy that had no interest in details of practice. Waldron might not like Musonius' "On the Goal of Marriage" and "That One Should Raise All the Children Who Are Born" any more than he likes "Residential Rent-Control." But the fact is that this is the sort of treatise leading Stoic thinkers did in fact produce, again and again.

Finally, one reason why the Hellenistic thinkers prefer to begin from within is that they hold that politics needs wise individuals: we cannot get everything by good institutional design alone. Like Aristotle, the Stoics have much to say about the limitations of laws and rules, the need, especially, for judges who can render equitable judgments in particular cases. I shall be discussing this point further in the following section. It has the consequence that good institutions require good people: and by producing people capable of independent judgment, philosophy can be claiming to be performing its practical role as "lawyer for humanity" in the best possible way.

In short, the contrast between the Hellenistic thinkers and

Aristotle is not stark, but complex and subtle. Both agree that politics needs philosophically trained people in at least some capacities; both agree that one of the main things wrong with political life is that people desire the wrong things, or in the wrong amount, and both believe that education is the best way to remedy those deficiencies. Both are concerned with the structure of political institutions, especially those, such as marriage and the family, that intimately shape people's daily lives and education. Aristotle's normative view, which makes a certain degree of reliance on "external goods" appropriate for a rational life, naturally leads him to take a somewhat more intense interest in the institutions through which those goods are secured to persons; we find less talk in the Hellenistic thinkers about water and air, about food and land. But the difference is one of degree not of kind, I believe. Above all, both agree in seeing the inner world as political and a scene for the formation of a rational politics. It is on this basis that they hold that philosophy is the art of life.

The dangers about which Waldron is concerned are real enough. They were topics of much anxious reflection in the ancient Greek and Roman thinkers, who identified at least five distinct issues that should concern the working practical philosopher. First is the question of the role to be played by the parts of philosophy that do not have obvious practical importance. Here there was much disagreement. At one end of the spectrum we find Epicurus,[35] for whom (as Marx correctly argued[36]) no part of philosophy was worth cultivating unless it had a rather direct bearing on achieving a practical goal. This meant, it appears, casting aspersions on the study of logic, aesthetics, much of metaphysics and the philosophy of language, and on whatever in the philosophy of nature did not make a difference to our views about our own life and death. Much of traditional epistemology and philosophy of mind and nature is, however, still admitted for its role in helping people live and choose well; but the result is, I would say, a certain impoverishment in the range of studies. At the other end of the spectrum is Plato, who favors contemplative activity over any practical pursuit. Not too far away are the Stoics and Aristotelians, both of whom hold the study of nature and metaphysics to be intrinsically worthwhile alongside ethical and political study— and, the Stoics add, agreeing with Plato, essential as well for good personal and political practice. Stoic thinkers still attack an interest in logical puzzles for the sake of dazzling others or playing around; but they are convinced, too, that a good deal of logical refinement is important if one is to avoid being led astray by the fallacious arguments of others on issues of importance to the conduct of life. I believe that they are right: philosophical work that bears on the conduct of life subverts its own practical goals if it confines itself too narrowly to what is of immediate and obvious relevance to the "bottom line."

Second, there is the issue Waldron rightly emphasizes, about the importance of conceptual inquiry. Again, the Greek and Roman schools vary here, the Epicureans sometimes showing disdain for the practice of defining terms and for detailed conceptual analysis, Stoics and Aristotelians (along, again, with earlier Platonists) defending this activity as of the most central importance, practical as well as theoretical. Again, I would side with the latter group[37] in feeling that Epicureans frequently do too little conceptual analysis for their own goals to be adequately understood and realized. Here, then, the demand for the "bottom line" may well have eclipsed some good philosophy— though we should not forget that it was the insistent demand for the "bottom line" that led to the analyses of fear and love and anger for which the school is so justly praised.

Third, we sometimes find a shortchanging of argument itself, and an insistent emphasis on dogma and orthodoxy, that make the Hellenistic schools sound at times very unphilosophical indeed. Again, it is Epicurus who makes the most disturbing moves, insisting on much memorization of epitomes and summaries of doctrine, and frequently shortchanging the dialectical side of the enterprise.[38] Stoics insist, against Epicurus, on the mind's autonomy and dignity, making it clear that getting the conclusion without the argument would be of no worth at all, even for practice. In so holding they are following an older tradition that begins at least with Socrates, one that is prominently exemplified in both Plato and Aristotle.

Finally, there is the issue of learning from the arguments of those with whom you disagree. Waldron is right to inquire about this, and right again to think that this virtue is sometimes absent in people who comb the canon for "the bottom line." But when we look at our practical tradition, we find that only the Epicureans, if they, give their adversaries this treatment. "Hoist sail young man," wrote Epicurus to a pupil, "and keep yourself pure of all education." His image of the pupil's whole being as suffused with "the sayings of the correct philosophy" is one that Waldron would be right to view with alarm. (On the other hand, a pupil who already knew a lot of technical philosophy would clearly receive a different treatment, and Epicurus is concerned to answer his rivals on matters of much sophistication.[39]) In the middle on this issue are the Stoics, who have a special reverence for the traditions of their own school, but are still interested in studying opponents, especially Epicurus, for the insights his work contains.[40] Aristotle, at the other end of the spectrum, makes learning from the opposing positions on a topic a constitutive feature of his method in ethics: for, as he nicely puts it, "Some of these things have been said by many people over a long period of time, others by a few distinguished people. It is reasonable to suppose that none of them has missed the mark totally, but that each has gotten something, or even a lot of things, right" (*EN* 1098a28–30). Studying one's opponents is, then, important for practice as well as theory: for what practice wants is, of course, to get it right.

The view of the philosopher as doctor or lawyer for humanity carries with it, then, certain dangers. The nature of the danger was well expressed by Marx, commenting, in his doctoral dissertation, on the difference between the early Greek Atomists, who investigated nature without much practical concern, and the Hellenistic thinkers, for whom philosophy of nature was itself practical:

> When philosophy turns itself as will against the world of appearance, then . . . it has become one aspect of the world which opposes another one. Its relationship to the world is that of reflection. Inspired by the urge to realize itself, it enters into tension against the other. The inner self-contentment and completeness has been broken. What was inner light has become

consuming flame turning outwards. The result is that as the world becomes philosophical, philosophy also becomes worldly, that its realisation is also its loss, that what it struggles against on the outside is its own inner deficiency.

Marx is right to this extent: it takes a lot of work, in this tradition, to keep pupils engaged with philosophical activity at a sufficiently deep level. But the Stoics and Epicureans would have had cogent replies to make. First, they would have cast doubt on the idea that there was a necessary tension between philosophical compassion and philosophical rigor: for they would have insisted that it is only by good rigorous argument that one really achieves a practical benefit.[41] They would also have objected to the "consuming flame" imagery, which suggests that emotion is being substituted for reason. For this image seems to presuppose an opposition between emotion and cognition that it has been the business of their entire philosophical enterprise to question. To undo bad passions requires not mindless passion but good argument. Finally, they would have insisted that danger is found in both directions: for just as pupils can slack off before doing enough logic, so too, they know well, pupils can get hooked on logical game-playing and forget about the ills of humanity. Both errors are diagnosed and reproved in the tradition.

One point emerges unambiguously: even the tradition's rationale for doing philosophy broadly, deeply, and systematically is in part a practical rationale. The more conceptual and less immediately practical parts of philosophy are important in part on account of their intrinsic value and beauty—but also on account of their relevance to personal and political choice. Stoics study more logic than Epicureans because they know that a logical paradox might catch them out where important choices are at stake, and they want to be well prepared. Aristotelians study Platonism because they feel that it will teach them something of practical worth, pertinent to good legislating. In fact, even the schools' reason for avoiding the "bottom line," insofar as they do avoid it, is itself a practical reason: namely, that if one goes too quickly to the "bottom line" in advance of the particular case, and fixes one's verdict in a text of some generality, one will not be so likely to get the "bottom line" right for the particular case when it does turn up. It is the same way, they all insist, in the art of medicine: if you set concrete prescriptions down too much in advance, you will be less likely to have the flexibility and the responsiveness to prescribe for what you see before you.[42] It is the same way, they insist, in the law: for if a judge construes his activity as simply that of applying prescriptions set down in advance, he will lack the flexibility a good judge should exercise, when confronted with a case in which the prescriptions offer unclear or defective guidance.[43]

Here we come upon a remarkable alliance between deep philosophical theory and "the bottom line." The general point— whether in medicine or in the law or in political life generally— is that if you give a lot of prescriptions at an intermediate level of generality, you won't necessarily understand the rationale behind these prescriptions and thus will be at a loss to prescribe for a new case of some complexity. You will tend to be rigid, and afraid to depart from the rule. If, on the other hand, you have a deeper and more general theoretical understanding of what generates the prescriptions—if you really understand the concepts involved and can connect them in a systematic way— you will be in a far better position to face the new case, especially where the existing prescriptions are ambiguous or incomplete. This idea lies behind Socrates' defense of "the examined life"; it is central to Plato's argument in favor of philosophers as rulers[44]; it is at work in Aristotle's distinction between knowledge of "the why" and mere knowledge of "the that"[45]; it is given an extended and remarkable treatment in Seneca.[46] Through Aristotle and Seneca, it has entered into our traditions of thought about the good political agent, and especially the good judge—who cannot act well as "lawyer for humanity" without the kind of comprehensive understanding that reveals the properties of the particular.

There are many places in the contemporary world where we may look for this kind of link between theory and practice. As Waldron's paper insists, our philosophical culture has seen a remarkable revival of the connection—to focus only on the United States, in journals such as *Philosophy and Public Affairs* and in the burgeoning fields of medical, legal, and business ethics. Philosophers are in hospitals, advising doctors on decisions involving life and death; they are in law schools, offering guidance on conceptions of legal rationality, interpretation, and justice; they are even in the government, participating in legislative debate on matters ranging from AIDS to evolution, from sexuality to the conduct of war, participating even in the setting of the national agenda for health care and family policy.[47]

Have these people, as Waldron alleges, forgotten to do philosophy? There is, of course, no simple answer to this question. As in the ancient world, so here. There are people who think about immediate practical results without doing profound conceptual or philosophical inquiry. There are people who enjoy logical game-playing without thinking at all of the good of human beings. And then there are people who reach a practical conclusion through profound and conceptually precise philosophical arguments.

Waldron alleges that any philosopher who can answer the question, "What's the point of your work? What difference is it going to make?" is not really doing political philosophy any more. I have argued against him throughout this paper, but at this point I want to offer just one contemporary case that follows my picture of the ancient traditions. There are, as I said, many such cases; but I select an area in which I am familiar with the work and some of its practical results. It is the general area of quality of life measurement in development economics and public policy, where philosophers have been involved for some time in pressing conceptual and foundational questions about the whole idea of measuring "the quality of life" in developing countries—in a way that has had an influence on the ways in which international agencies now gather information and assess the performance of nations.

In development economics, when the quality of life is measured, the usual measure until recently has been simply to look at GNP per capita. This measure does not even inform us about the distribution of wealth and income, and thus can give high marks to a country with large inequalities. Nor is it well-correlated with other items that might be thought to be important for life quality, such as life expectancy, education, and infant mortality. To give just one very graphic example, the 1993 *Human Development Report* published by the United Nations Development Program (UNDP)[48] informs us that the United Arab Emirates has a Real GNP of $16,753, tenth highest in the world (higher, for example, than Norway or Australia). Its adult literacy rate, however, is only 55%, which puts it down around one hundredth in the world. (Both Norway and Australia have adult literacy of 99%.) The maternal mortality rate is 130 per 100,000 live births. Only 76% of pregnant women receive prenatal care, far worse than the 100% in the Bahamas, 95% in Singapore, 86% in Sri Lanka—though, on the other hand, far better than 56% in Uruguay, 53% in Thailand, 25% in Iran,[49] 9% in Nepal. The proportion of women progressing beyond secondary education is very low, and only 6% of the labor force is female—as opposed, for example, to 42% in the Seychelles, 35% in Brazil, 43% in China, 47% in Vietnam, 26% in India, 20% in Nigeria. In fact, in all the world only Algeria (4%) has a lower proportion of females in the labor force, only Iraq (6%) ties it, and only Qatar (7%), Saudi Arabia (7%), Libya (9%), Jordan (10%), Pakistan (11%), Bangladesh (7%) and Afganistan (8%) come even close.[50] Evidence strongly links female economic activity to female nutrition, health care, and life expectancy.[51] In fact, one finds that the ratio of females to males in the United Arab Emirates is an amazing 48 to 100, lowest in all the world.[52] If this figure is discounted as employment-related, we may examine the other countries in our low out-of-home employment group. The sex ratio in Qatar is 60 to 100, in Saudi Arabia 84, Libya 91, Jordan 95, Pakistan 92, Bangladesh 94, and Afganistan 94. For the millions of women who are thus "missing," that is indeed the bottom line.

The structure of the Report draws attention to these figures as salient indicators of life quality. In so doing, it is implicitly taking a stand against the GNP approach to measurement. This is no accident, since philosophers and philosophically trained economists such as Amartya Sen, who are critics of the approach, were involved in its design.[53] The Report is also, it turns out, taking a stand against approaches that measure life quality in terms of utility, construed as the satisfaction of preferences. For Sen's philosophical work on this issue shares with the ancient Greek and Roman traditions the belief that many preferences are deformed by oppression and bad education. It is generally women who put insufficient food on the plates of little girls. It is generally women who (however pushed) seek sex-selective abortions.[54] And finally, in offering its cross-cultural comparisons, the Report is taking a stand against those who hold that the quality of life in each region must be assessed using local measures relative to a nation's traditions: for Sen's approach insists on using measures that are, at least at a general level, international and universal.

Sen, and others, including Onora O'Neill, David Crocker, and Xiaorong Li, who have recently done philosophical work on this issue[55] do not simply take a stand, however—they attempt to justify their approach. To do so they need to engage in philosophical argument on a broad range of issues at a level of considerable generality and sophistication. The reasons they offer for holding their practical view are philosophical reasons, closely related to some of the arguments about human flourishing that were central in the ancient Greek traditions. Sen's approach owes a particular debt to some Aristotelian views about the centrality of a notion of full human functioning in the definition of human flourishing. There are interesting arguments backing these views against their liberal and utilitarian alternatives. Unlike Aristotle, however, any modern defender of this kind of universalism must also offer convincing arguments against cultural relativists. And this means that, in addition to engaging in the type of conceptual analysis and philosophical argumentation familiar in moral and political philosophy, the development philosopher will need to call upon the philosophy of science, where those debates are worked out, today, in an especially powerful form. (This is all the more true since cultural relativism, in the development debate, has become intertwined with neoclassical economists' views about the subjectivity of value judgments, and economists will be most likely to be swayed by criticisms of the fact-value distinction if they come from the side of science.) An important contribution to the current development debate has recently been made by Hilary Putnam, on precisely this issue. Putnam writes at a very high level of philosophical abstraction, criticizing the fact-value and science-ethics distinctions; but his writing shows that he is always be prepared to answer the question, "What difference does your work make? How is it going to help?"[56] Putnam's work is not only strategically important, in the debate with economists; it is essential to the completion of the argument in favor of Sen's approach to development issues. Reaching the bottom line does not preclude but actually requires a systematic theoretical understanding.

Waldron's question throughout the paper is, what are these philosophical writers actually doing? He typically suggests that they cannot be making practical policy proposals if they are not holders of political positions. So I shall answer him on behalf of this quality-of-life work: the people involved in it are trying to convince economists and policy makers to do things differently in many countries all around the world. And they know that they do not hold positions of influence in any of them. Therefore, they write. Writing has the political disadvantage that it can easily be dismissed or disregarded. It has the advantage that it can speak in all countries of the world, to both the powerful and the excluded, and can survive the vicissitudes of political fortune. Sen has of course done much more than write, for he worked closely with the UNDP in developing the techniques of measurement that are used in the current *Human Development Report.* But it was on account of his writings that he had the influence he has had on that report, and on development policy generally.

In short: philosophers who work in this area do not hold political power and yet their aim is indeed to influence political life. There is no contradiction in that, because many of the most far-reaching influences on political life do not come from holders of political office. If a student of mine were to write a paper on what Aristotle—or what one of those philosophers— let's say what Sen, or Putnam, or Susan Okin—"would require" of the UNDP, or the development agency of a nation, I would applaud the exercise, so long as the paper showed evidence of the level of argument and analysis and historical understanding that I think essential to carry forward philosophy's practical aims. For I think that there is nothing more exciting than to teach students—who are going to become not philosophers for the most part, but parents and lawyers and journalists and politicians and economists and activists—how philosophy can illuminate the world they know, and generate proposals for a world that is better.

The truth in Waldron's paper is that those who focus very closely on immediate practical choices frequently lose (or fail to acquire) a larger vision and a deeper, more precise understanding. This is all too easy to notice, if one works a lot of the time with policy makers and activists. That is indeed what philosophy can supply, so that it would indeed be a tragedy were philosophy to lose itself in these other more immediate activities. What is wrong with Waldron's paper is that the larger vision is itself practical, and a commitment to the practical drives one deeper and deeper into the philosophical vision. Seneca's point is not just that the philosopher should recall his or her commitments to the human species. It is, too, that the human being who signs on as "lawyer for humanity" will be led by the compassion inherent in that very role into doing, or at least caring about, philosophy. For, as Epicurus put it, defining our discipline, "Philosophy is the activity that promotes human flourishing by means of reasonings and arguments."[57]

NOTES

1. Much of the material in this article is further discussed in my *The Therapy of Desire: Theory and Practice in Hellenistic Ethics* (Princeton: Princeton University Press, 1994).

2. I find very odd Jeremy Waldron's claim, in his essay in this volume, that Socrates "has followed philosophy to the exclusion of politics" (155). Surely the *Apology*, in addition to establishing Socrates' courageous performance of conventional political roles (32B–E, and see Alcibiades' account of his military service at *Symposium* 219E–220D) shows, as well, his conception of the political urgency of his whole philosophical enterprise. His proposal that he really deserves to be rewarded for his benefits by free maintenance at the public expense (36Cff.) is bound to fall on deaf ears, but it is nonetheless perfectly serious. On all of this see Thomas Brickhouse and Nicholas Smith, *Socrates on Trial* (Princeton: Princeton University Press, 1990).

3. On Seneca's suicide, see Miriam Griffin, *Seneca: A Philosopher in Politics* (Oxford: Clarendon Press, 1976), a masterful study of the connections between philosophy and political life in Seneca's career as a whole. For a more general study of these interactions in the period, see her "Philosophy, Politics, and Politicians at Rome," in *Philosophia Togata*, ed. M. Griffin and J. Barnes (Oxford: Clarendon Press, 1989). And on the role of Stoic philosophy in inspiring political suicides, see her definitive account of Roman suicide, "Philosophy, Cato, and Roman Suicide: I and II," *Greece and Rome* 33 (1986): 64–77, 192–202.

4. I don't mean to suggest that *Letter* 48 stands in any especially close relation to the suicide; but the *Letters to Lucilius* were all written during the final years of Seneca's life, and the topic of preparation for death is a central theme of his Socratism.

5. The obvious fact that Roman *advocati* performed somewhat different functions from those of modern American lawyers does not show that it is a naive error to think that in many ways the two can fruitfully be compared—especially here, where the idea of being duty-bound to act on behalf of those too weak to help themselves has clear modern parallels. So too, Waldron's hasty assertion that "raising a family" is a concept inapplicable to the ancient world fails to convince. Waldron introduces no historical material about the ancient Greek family in support of his claim; but I would say that a close look at what women (both mothers and nurses) did in ancient Athenian families would suggest that "raise a family" might not be so bad a rendering of terms such as *trephein* and *paideuein*. By using such a phrase one does not at all assume that the concept "family" means the same thing in the two cultures; the multi-facetedness of the concept "family" is obvious and well known. The idea that we would evaluate Plato's ideas on the family by comparing them with our own and asking what policies each would generate is no more "fatuous" (Waldron, 144) than the United Nations' current exercise (in connection with the International Year of the Family) of comparing family structures around the world and asking what can be learned from this about practical equality and justice.

6. See Waldron's paper on Nozick.

7. But note that Waldron's characterization of Plato as a "travelling teacher" is extremely misleading. Plato was an extremely wealthy and influential member of the Athenian citizenry, as I shall discuss below. He owned his own school, as well as much other property, and he taught and traveled as he did out of his own philosophical commitments. Itinerant teachers in the Greek world, by contrast, were usually non-citizens, and were not always terribly respectable. Nor does

it seem precise or illuminating to call the Athenian democracy a "caste society." Almost all societies in world history have excluded women and slaves from full political participation, and within that number the Indian caste system is a distinctive formation that would have been incompatible with the type of democracy that emerged at Athens. True, these characterizations are in a paragraph in which Waldron summarizes a historicist position with which he does not fully agree; but he nowhere says that one of the things wrong with it is historical inaccuracy.

8. Waldron is right when he says (160) that Marx sometimes made disparaging remarks about the role of philosophical ideas in political change. But matters are actually far more complex than Waldron allows. First of all, the young Marx of the Doctoral Dissertation (an eloquent and convincing account of the practical goal of Epicurean philosophizing) and other related works, derives from the ancient Greek tradition, especially the Hellenistic tradition, the idea that the primary goal of philosophy is indeed to change political life by changing thought. Later on, he comes to doubt this—but because he becomes persuaded that the right role for philosophy in politics is not the Hellenistic but the Aristotelian role, namely, to reflect about the role of material conditions in human flourishing. The disparaging remarks reject his earlier blend of Epicurus and Hegel; they do not show a rejection of the conception he derived from Aristotle, and continued to enact in his own work. On these two roles, see further below.

9. See also *EN* 1103b26ff., 1143b18ff., 1179b35ff; *EE* 1214b12ff., 1215a8ff., discussed in *Therapy*, ch. 2.

10. I note in passing Waldron's complete silence about Bentham, who could not easily have been accommodated to his analysis, and his very odd treatment of Mill, when he says that it is a mere "façon de parler" to say, as Susan Okin says, that Mill "made a determined effort to emancipate women into citizenship." But isn't to produce an excellent piece of public writing to make a particular sort of "determined effort" to change the ways people think and act, and one that a trained philosopher is especially well equipped to make?

11. See *Therapy*, preface; see also my "Comments" in *Symposium on Classical Philosophy and the American Constitutional Order*, *Chicago-Kent Law Review* 66 (1990): 213–42. Descartes, Spinoza, Kant, Adam Smith, and the American Founders were all deeply influenced by Stoicism, more so than by Platonic or Aristotelian thought.

12. On this issue, see J. K. Davies, *Athenian Propertied Families* (Oxford: Clarendon Press, 1971).

13. The authenticity of *Letter* VII is now accepted by more or less

all major scholars, though some would continue to have doubts about the "metaphysical digression" in which Plato presents an account of the Theory of Forms that appears incompatible with the dialogues. It seems important to remember that, like Seneca's Letters, the Platonic Epistles are intended as philosophical *exempla:* hence we would not expect factual accuracy as judged by modern historical standards. But we may rely on the fact that the letter presents the account of his philosophical motivations, and the link between theory and practice in his life, that Plato wished his public to have as they read his philosophical work. For my argument here, this is more important than their literal truth.

14. For a vivid account of the period, and the murder of Polemarchus, see Lysias, *Oration* 12; on the opening of the *Republic,* see F. E. Sparshott, "Plato and Thrasymachus," *University of Toronto Quarterly* (1957): 54–61.

15. The best account of Plato's position and its historical and cultural background is now in Stephen Halliwell, *Plato: Republic V* (Warminster: Aris and Phillips, 1993), Introduction and commentary. With painstaking historical detail, Halliwell shows how close Plato's proposals are to some aspects of real life in Sparta, and how thoroughly enmeshed all his arguments are in the real political argument of his day. He provides a conclusive refutation of the position of those who, like Allan Bloom, hold that the material on women is meant to indicate that the entire political proposal is "ironic." He thus confirms Susan Okin's account of Plato (in *Women in Western Political Thought*), criticized here by Waldron: Plato is best read as making serious, if radical proposals for the reform of women's education and the family along lines suggested by the real situation in Sparta.

16. Of course one often finds when one investigates these connections that the arguments of a thinker do not suffice to generate his or her conclusions, or actually generate opposing conclusions. So much, I think, is true for some of Aristotle's notorious conclusions about women: he has good arguments that the Stoics later use to generate the conclusion that women should be given equal treatment, but he himself fails to apply them to the case of women because he accepts several false premises about them that he does not even investigate.

17. Cf. *Politics* II.I: "We must therefore examine . . . other constitutions, both such as actually exist in well-governed states, and any theoretical forms which are held in esteem, so that what is good and useful may be brought to light" (1260a26ff.).

18. For references, see above note 9. All this is discussed at greater length in *Therapy,* ch. 2.

19. See David Whitehead, "Aristotle the Metic," *Proceedings of the Cambridge Philological Society* 21 (1975): 94–99.

20. Famously, he and his pupils are said to have written up accounts of one hundred fifty-three different constitutions, though of these only the *Athenian Constitution* survives.

21. On the reasons for Aristotle's exile, and the connection with Alexander, see I. Düring, *Aristoteles* (Heidelberg, 1966).

22. I am thinking above all of the strange case of Singapore; but one can find philosophically trained rulers in many parts of Africa and Asia; much of South Asian Marxism was produced in Paris.

23. Epicurus, Usener fragment 221, Porphyry *Ad Marc.* 31, p. 209, 23n.

24. Epicurus does grant that some desire for food, drink, and sex is part of the pre-social equipment of the human being; but without the intervention of society these desires would have been easily satisfied with what is ready to hand. In the case of sex, he holds that non-satisfaction would not be painful, if it were not for the intensity supplied by erotic love.

25. See Cicero's *De Finibus* I.17.

26. One vivid example of Epictetus' value as practical guide is in former Vice-Presidential candidate Stockdale's account of his experience in a North Vietnamese prisoner-of-war camp, in his book *A Vietnam Experience: Ten Years of Reflection* (Stanford, CA: Hoover Institute Press, 1984).

27. The best account of Aristotle's views on the rich and the poor, and their great influence on Marx, is in G. E. M. de Ste. Croix, *The Class Struggle in the Ancient Greek World* (London: Duckworth, 1981).

28. I have discussed these arguments in "Nature, Function, and Capability: Aristotle on Political Distribution," *Oxford Studies in Ancient Philosophy,* Supplementary Volume I (1988); in "Aristotelian Social Democracy," in *Liberalism and the Good,* ed. R. B. Douglass, G. Mara, and H. Richardson (New York: Routledge, 1990); and in "Aristotle on Human Nature and the Foundations of Ethics," forthcoming in *World, Mind, and Action: Essays on the Philosophy of Bernard Williams,* ed. J. Altham and R. Harrison (Cambridge: Cambridge University Press, 1994).

29. I mean to include, here, the role that a philosopher might play in adjudicating between the claims of rival theories that offer guidance to public life—giving reasons, for example, why "creation science" is not really science and Darwinian theory is, or offering defenses or critiques of economic theorizing.

30. Chrysippus, for example, is said to have urged people to eat the corpses of their parents—as a graphic way of bringing home the fact that the person ends at death. On the evidence for these views, see M. Schofield, *The Stoic Idea of the City* (Cambridge: Cambridge University Press, 1992).

31. See Tacitus, *Annals* XIII.2: the two regents prevent various illegal murders and encourage restraint in the "slippery youth," Burrus by military exercises, Seneca by moral instruction and example. The regency came to be called the *quinquennium Neronis,* and was looked back on with nostalgia.

32. The conspiracy of Piso was a large mixed affair, but it included Stoics as prominent participants, and Lucan had dramatized Stoic ideals of government in his portrait of Cato in the *Pharsalia.*

33. Thrasea, like Seneca, is renowned for his *libertas,* a kind of dignified non-subservient political outspokenness associated with Stoic conceptions of virtue. The manner of his political suicide invokes Stoic norms. See Tacitus, *Annals* XIV.49, XVI.35.

34. For these views, see the fragments of Seneca's *On Marriage,* preserved in the Teubner edition of Haase; and, above all, the writings of Musonius Rufus, the teacher of Epictetus (collected in a single Teubner volume, ed. Hense, Leipzig 1903, and translated by Cora Lutz in *Yale Classical Studies* (1966). The most important treatises include "On the Goal of Marriage" (arguing in favor of monogamy for both sexes, and against viewing servants as sexually available, proposing "living together" and "breathing together" as a conception of the goal of the institution); "That One Should Raise all the Children Who are Born"; "Should Daughters Receive the Same Education as Sons?"; and "That Women Too Should Do Philosophy." Musonius does not propose ending the conventional division of spheres of activity—and, since he is giving actual practical advice for the imperial Rome of his day, he is in no position to do so. So his wives are imagined running the house, the husbands doing politics in the city. But for Musonius these are occupations of equal dignity, spheres in which practical wisdom can be exercised. He emphasizes that both should have the "higher education" offered by philosophy, so that these practical duties will be informed by the discrimination and judgment that philosophy teaches. He gives many examples of the way in which philosophical education makes a difference to "the bottom line" in such matters as rearing of children, dealing with immoral requests from the emperor, and other matters of real immediacy in the first century AD.

35. I leave the ancient skeptics to one side in this section, as in this paper generally, since their views about the removal of all belief are so

radical as to be irrelevant to deciding the issue between me and Waldron.

36. Marx, "On the Difference between the Democritean and the Epicurean Philosophies of Nature," doctoral dissertation, in Marx and Engels, *Collected Works,* vol. I.

37. And with Cicero, who makes this criticism central to his otherwise somewhat strident attack on Epicureanism in *De Finibus* II.

38. Our evidence is very imperfect, consisting, as it does, above all of three letters written to be summaries of longer works; and Lucretius' poem makes it clear that Epicureanism had much wonderful argument. I discuss all this in *Therapy,* chaps. 4 and 13.

39. An example is his defense of atomism against Aristotelian attacks using the theory of "minimal parts"—see, on this, David Furley, *Two Studies in the Greek Atomists* (Princeton: Princeton University Press, 1967).

40. See, for example, Seneca, *Moral Epistle* 33.

41. I am not suggesting that Marx ultimately disagrees with this: the passage I cite is from the opening of the dissertation, and the evaluation of Epicurus in the body of the argument is overwhelmingly positive.

42. This is a motif that runs right through the tradition, and I forbear giving examples here, though *Therapy* contains dozens. See also my "Equity and Mercy," *Philosophy and Public Affairs* (Spring 1993).

43. For an analysis of Aristotelian and Stoic views of the "equitable" judge, see "Equity and Mercy."

44. See esp. *Republic* 520C: because the philosophers have a systematic general understanding of political concepts, they will be able to recognize exactly where these properties are instantiated in the world, with an accuracy unavailable to the untrained. They will "know each of the resembling things [i.e. things in the city that have the properties of justice, etc.], what they are and what they resemble, in virtue of the fact that they have seen the truth concerning the fine and the just and the good. And in this way our city will be managed in a wide-awake manner, and not as in a dream."

45. *EN* 1095b1–10.

46. *Moral Epistles* 94 and 95. Seneca also points out that prescriptions at the intermediate level of generality may be very useful for people who do not have time to seek agreement about first principles. For a convincing contemporary development of a similar argument, see Cass Sunstein's paper in this volume.

47. A group of medical ethicists participated in the Health Care

Commission; and political philosopher William Galston is second-in-command on the Domestic Policy Council, in charge of policy on such matters as youth services, children's well-being, and the family. Nor are such connections confined to Democratic administrations: political philosophers William Kristol and Carnes Lord served as Chief of Staff and Issues Advisor, respectively, to former Vice President Dan Quayle.

48. *Human Development Report 1993* (Oxford and New York: Clarendon Press, 1993).

49. A complicating factor in this case is the government's position opposing gynecological examinations of women by male doctors. Although there are training programs for female doctors, the supply is vastly less than the demand, and current policy is that even if the woman's health is at risk such an examination is morally inappropriate. I owe this information—based on official statements in a recent official conference on Islamic medical ethics—to Jonathan Glover.

50. The Report defines labor-force participation in such a way as to include unpaid agricultural activity on the family farm and related outside-of-home labor, though not domestic labor. Thus the situation of women in many of the countries cited, where actual wage-earning labor is concerned, is actually quite a lot worse than the numbers indicate. But women who work on the farm are at any rate obvious contributors to the family's well-being and, as such, have a claim to be fed that "idle" women who only do domestic labor do not, since such labor does not count, either in official statistics or in unofficial views of value. On the connection between the style of agricultural production and women's relatively high status in sub-Saharan Africa, see Ester Boserup's classic study, *Women's Role in Economic Development* (New York: St. Martin's Press, 1970); for more recent studies along these lines, see *Women, Employment, and the Family in the International Division of Labour*, ed. Sharon Stichter and Jane L. Parpart (New York: Macmillan, 1990).

51. See Amartya Sen, "More that a Million Women are Missing," *New York Review of Books*, and Jean Drèze and Amartya Sen, *Hunger and Public Action* (Oxford: Clarendon Press, 1989).

52. Data indicate that where nutrition and health care are equal, women live on the average slightly longer than men. The sex ratio of Europe and North America has varied in recent years between 104 (women) to 100 (men) and 106 to 100. The ratio in sub-Saharan Africa is 102 to 100. Sen's number of "missing women" for a country is reached by asking how many women that are not around in that country would be around, were its sex ratio the same as that in sub-Saharan Africa. This region is chosen as a part of the developing world

in which women and girls do not appear to suffer discrimination in basic nutrition and health care.

53. Both Amartya Sen and Sudir Anand were consultants to the report. For Sen's general approach to welfare and quality of life measurement, see *Choice, Welfare, and Measurement* (Oxford: Blackwell, 1982) and *Resources, Values, and Development* (Oxford: Blackwell, 1984). Anand has been Sen's collaborator at the World Institute for Development Economics Research in Helsinki. For that Institute's work on quality of life definition, see Nussbaum and Sen, eds., *The Quality of Life* (Oxford: Clarendon Press, 1993). Others whose work has been influential in the development of this approach include Hilary Putnam, Susan Moller Okin, Onora O'Neill, G. A. Cohen, and Charles Taylor— see below.

54. For this reason, some Indian feminists seek criminal penalties against women who seek such abortions. The debate raises fascinating philosophical issues, not just about liberty and consequences, but also about what it is to promote someone's agency and personhood. (For that is the rationale of the proposal: that only such penalties will make women view themselves as agents.)

55. See the related papers by Gerald Cohen, Onora O'Neill, John Roemer, and Charles Taylor in *The Quality of Life;* and, on women's life quality, the papers by Sen, Susan Moller Okin, Margarita Valdes, Xiaorong Li, Marty Chen, David Crocker, and Roop Rekha Verma in *Women, Culture, and Development*, ed. M. Nussbaum and J. Glover (Oxford: Clarendon Press, 1995). See also David Crocker, "Functioning and Capability: The Foundation of Sen's and Nussbaum's Development Ethic," *Political Theory* (Fall 1992), and Xiaorong Li, Ph.D. diss., Stanford University, 1993.

56. See Putnam's "Objectivity and the Science-Ethics Distinction" in *The Quality of Life,* and "Pragmatism and Moral Objectivity" in *Women, Culture, and Development.*

57. I wish to thank Victor Caston, Richard Posner, and Cass Sunstein for very helpful comments that contributed to the revision of this paper.

7

THE THEORETICAL
IMPORTANCE OF PRACTICE

SUSAN J. BRISON

I. INTRODUCTION

In "What Plato Would Allow," Jeremy Waldron argues that (1) we should not be doing political philosophy in a way that links it so closely to public policy pronouncements and (2) we should not be reading (and teaching) the canon as though it could speak to current policy debates.[1] I think he is wrong about both points. In this chapter, I argue that political theory is still not linked closely enough to practice. We need to examine the practical import of theoretical work and to acknowledge the dependence of theory on practice—not just in the testing and evaluating of public policies issuing from the theory, but also in the formulation of the theory itself. And, although Waldron is right to warn of anachronistic readings of the classics, he is wrong in thinking that the racism and sexism in these writings ought to be overlooked as irrelevant to the understanding of political life that we can gain from such works.

Despite Waldron's claims, it is now commonplace to acknowledge that practice requires a theoretical foundation. Whether one is engaged in formulating public policy, legislating it, interpreting it, or adjudicating conflicts concerning it, one needs theory to carry out the practice in question. Not only is a theoretical framework required to justify the practice, but also it is needed to accurately construe the nature of the practice itself.[2]

Less obvious, though, are the ways that theory is, or should be, dependent on practice. This dependency emerges, in part, because it is through political practice that we come to know the needs and perspectives of those different from ourselves. It is the arena in which we not only effect change, but are ourselves changed. Even if the goal of theorizing is not to transform the political realm, but rather, as Waldron claims, to deepen our understanding of it, we need to be involved in practice—in the sense of political engagement that leads to a recognition of others' perspectives—to get there.

It is not surprising that legal and political theorists emphasize that practice is dependent on theory, even if the nature of the dependence is hard to articulate. Academics attracted to the philosophy of law or political philosophy tend to have more than a merely academic interest in their subject. Some even harbor hopes of influencing political movements (especially now that other countries in transition are inviting American scholars to advise them on constitutions and political policies) or of writing articles that will be cited in Supreme Court opinions.

There is, however, less of a personal motivation to see the ways in which theory is dependent on practice. Although it is not unusual for law professors to also be practicing lawyers, political philosophers rarely run for office or in some other way devote themselves to politics. Moreover, the professional disincentives for ignoring practice are great. Academic research, teaching, and administrative responsibilities leave little time for involvement in politics, and those who manage to make time find that such engagement can be taken as a sign that they are not serious about their scholarship. Practice—whether it takes the form of lobbying for legislation, supporting candidates, running for office, forming coalitions, participating in grassroots movements, or some other activity—is generally viewed by academics as a luxury, something one should do, if at all, only in one's spare time, perhaps instead of taking that long-awaited vacation.

Such personal and professional pressures make it difficult for many academics to acknowledge the importance of practice to theory. For some scholars, however—members of groups whose political power is minimal and whose presence in the academy is still marginal and precarious—engaging in practice is often a personal and professional necessity. Practice is, for those who have historically been excluded from academic discourse and continue to feel alienated from traditional theoretical concerns, an essential element in the reevaluation of the canon and the reconstruction of contemporary theory.

In the last two decades, feminist legal theory and critical race theory have emerged from, and have in turn informed, ongoing struggles for greater political enfranchisement for women and for people of color. Members of both these movements have viewed their theoretical work as a force for social change and their political activism as shaping their theories. Self-described theorist-activists, they have rejected the theory/practice distinction along with other arguably false, yet academically still *de rigueur,* dichotomies that privilege the universal over the particular, the public over the private, the political over the personal, argument over narrative, reason over imagination, rule-following over empathy, and abstract generalizations over context-dependent truths.

It is not a coincidence that both of these theoretical movements have departed from more traditional approaches to politics and the law in undermining these time-honored dichotomies and devaluing their traditionally privileged terms. Both movements have brought practice closer to theory by paying greater attention to the contexts in which theories are formulated and their practical consequences are played out, to the particular lives of theorists and those theorized about, and to first person narratives as a way of contextualizing law and politics. Both have also undermined the alleged distinction between the private and the public and have shown how the personal is political. As Charles Lawrence, Mari Matsuda, Richard Delgado, and Kimberlè Crenshaw write in their introduction to *Words That Wound: Critical Race Theory, Assaultive Speech, and the First Amendment* "Critical race theory is grounded in the particulars of a social reality that is defined by our experiences and the collective historical experience of our communities of origin. Critical race theorists embrace subjectivity of perspective and are avowedly political. . . . Critical race theory cannot be understood as an abstract set of ideas or principles. Among its basic theoretical themes is that of privileging contextual and historical descriptions over transhistorical or purely abstract ones."[3] And in the introduction to the anthology she coedited, *At the Boundaries of Law: Feminism and Legal Theory,* Martha Fineman writes that "the real distinction between feminist approaches to theory (legal and otherwise) and the more traditional varieties of legal theory is a belief in the desirability of the concrete." She is a proponent of "middle range theory" that mediates between "stories" and "grand theory," between "the material circumstances of women's lives and the grand realizations that law is gendered, that law is a manifestation of power, that law is detrimental to women."[4]

One form practice takes for feminist philosophers and critical race theorists is to make political and legal theory more inclusive of "outsiders' " voices and more responsive to their concerns. It is this sense of "practice"—engaging with others, especially those who have been marginalized, and acknowledging their perspectives—that I will emphasize in this paper. Political activism, consciousness-raising, and empathizing with those different from oneself, are among the ways theorists can engage in this kind of practice. The concerns and perspectives of those who have not traditionally been the ones doing the theorizing, however, are still not commonly addressed by mainstream theorists. In his most recent book, for example, John Rawls expresses confidence that his theory can withstand the feminist critique, while neglecting to discuss the substance of the critique or even to mention those who have made it.[5]

In this chapter, I apply a number of insights from feminist theory and critical race theory to the question of the interrelation of theory and practice. I use these insights to criticize Waldron's claim that theory and practice should not be too closely connected in our reading, teaching, and writing in political philosophy. In Section II, I argue, contra Waldron, that theorists *should* be concerned with the practical consequences of their theorizing. In Section III, I discuss the ways in which political theory divorced from practice fails to capture the full range of perspectives needed to yield a theory that is universally

applicable. Section IV calls for an explicit acknowledgement of
the positions from which we—and those different from ourselves—theorize. Such acknowledgement should serve as an
antidote to the tendency to assume that we are theorizing from
a neutral perspective. In the final section, I criticize Waldron's
prescriptions for reading and teaching the canon, and I argue
that his distinction between what is a proper subject for philosophical inquiry and what is a public policy issue is based on
unwarranted assumptions.

II. On the Usefulness of Legal
and Political Theory

Waldron laments that political philosophers these days seem to
think they're in the business of changing the world; the point,
however, is to interpret it, or, as Waldron would say, *understand*
it. But what is this understanding? And what is it good for?

Most legal and political theorists would probably assert that
the point of theorizing *is* to change the world, but to do it
through changing our understanding of it. I doubt that there
are many such theorists who would, but for inertia and the need
to make a living, choose to continue in the profession if they
became convinced that nothing they said or wrote or taught
would ever contribute, in the slightest way, to making the world
a better—more just or in some other way more bearable—
place.

Waldron is right to point out that the pressure to articulate
and defend "the bottom line" on questions of public policy can
lead to anachronistic readings of the canon and to some most
unhelpful debates in contemporary political philosophy. In academic debates about freedom of expression, for example, public policy considerations—about whether or not to restrict hate
speech or pornography—typically get launched in a preemp-
tive strike that silences philosophical discourse about such important conceptual matters as the distinction between speech
and conduct, the difference between harm and offense, even
the value of having a principle of free speech. People—including philosophers who should know better—allow themselves to
be bullied into choosing sides before they have reached an

understanding of what is at stake in the debate. And they adopt a "which side are you on?" attitude toward those attempting to reach a deeper theoretical understanding of a subject. Philosophers, unlike legislators and other policy makers, are, and should be, able to think about such issues at greater leisure, without the pressure of clamoring constituents.

It is intriguing that in an earlier article, Waldron characterized political philosophy as "simply conscientious civic discussion without a deadline."[6] He argued there that theoretical discussions should not be viewed as different in kind from public policy debates and he urged theorists to pay attention to others' perspectives, stressing that "[m]odern philosophy evinces a commitment to the idea that theoretical argument aims not merely to justify laws or political proposals, but to justify them *to* the ordinary men and women whom whey will affect."[7] In his contribution to this volume, Waldron still seems to think political philosophy can and should be a useful enterprise. He argues, however, that those engaging in political philosophy should not concern themselves with its practical implications. Such concern, in fact, is construed as a sign that theory has taken a wrong turn somewhere. At the end of his article Waldron alludes to a paradox concerning the usefulness of political philosophy: if we are able to say just what the point of our work is—what difference it will make in the real world—then "we are not really doing political philosophy" and thus "are probably not really being of much use."[8] Apparently, his view is that even if, in doing political philosophy, our ultimate goal is to change the world, we can best do that by refraining from pursuing that goal in our philosophizing. There is a parallel here to the paradox of the pursuit of happiness: If one wants to be happy, one had better not set that up as one's primary goal, because happiness can be achieved only by pursuing other goals—or, rather, by pursuing the means to happiness as if they were themselves ends.

In a recent article, "On the Usefulness of Final Ends," Harry Frankfurt argues that final ends have instrumental value in virtue of having intrinsic value.[9] A similar claim is, I think, hinted at in Waldron's discussion of the relation between political philosophy and public policy. Philosophy *can* have instru-

mental value in influencing public policy, but it has this in virtue
of having intrinsic value. But just what is this intrinsic value?

Waldron suggests that this value is to be found in something
other than political advocacy, on the one hand, and "sterile
conceptual analysis," on the other. Political philosophy should
be carried out with the goal of increasing what he calls "understanding." It is hard to imagine anyone disagreeing with that.
But much more needs to be said about the nature of this understanding. Why should we suppose that this understanding can
be reached in the absence of engagement in political practice?
And how are we to explicate or evaluate the understanding
imparted by a political philosophy without making reference to
the policies that would issue from it?

Waldron's assumption that the "understanding" to be gained
from political philosophy is necessarily to be found in areas of
the field not directly connected to public policy questions has
been undermined by much recent work in feminist theory and
critical race theory. Issues such as domestic violence, child care,
sexist language, and the household division of labor were once
considered too trivial for philosophical discussion.[10] Now that
feminists have brought these issues to the fore, it is no longer
socially acceptable to say they are not important. Instead, what
one hears is that these issues are not properly "philosophical,"
or, as Waldron would put it, not part of the project of *understanding* the nature of political life. But as philosophy becomes
more inclusive as a discipline, it becomes clearer that what was
traditionally viewed as a properly philosophical subject was a
function of who was doing the philosophizing. The distinction
between public policy issues and philosophical issues which Waldron assumes is itself in need of examination.

III. The Pitfalls of Ignoring Practice

Political philosophers who theorize without paying sufficient
attention to practice are subject to a range of hazards, including
the overvaluing of traditionally privileged terms in distinctions
such as those between universal and particular, public and private, and abstraction and contextualization. They are also apt to
neglect important differences between themselves and others,

leading to a misguided confidence in the impartiality and universal justifiability of their theories. In contrast, those engaged in practice, especially of the sort involved in trying to bring about political change, have to engage with others, forming coalitions and agreeing on compromises. This activity makes it imperative that those in the position of making—and lobbying for—public policy decisions listen responsively to others' opinions. Although philosophers theorizing about such matters have to take into account the reactions of potential journal referees and critical colleagues, they do not have to concern themselves with the responses of the actual people who would be affected by the policies they advocate. Consider, for example, Ronald Dworkin's blithe disregard for the ways actual women are affected by the pornography he argues "we" have a right to.[11] It is especially interesting to then compare this approach to pornography with Dworkin's approach to abortion in his most recent book.[12] In the latter case, he is doing political philosophy, as he puts it, "from within" a public policy issue. Whereas in the former, he began with his theory of liberalism, which posited a right to moral autonomy, from which, he argued, flows a right to pornography. In his writings about pornography (and other forms of hate speech), his theoretical starting point precluded even the acknowledgement of the injurious effects of such speech or of a competing right (to be free of discriminatory harassment, for example) that might prove to be overriding. For if you have, a priori, a *right* to engage in some activity, it cannot be the case that people are being unjustly harmed by it.[13]

Political philosophers have, at least since the Enlightenment, strived to develop theories that are comprehensive and universally justifiable. As Waldron points out, there is "an important connection between liberal argumentation and the Enlightenment conviction that . . . everything right can in principle be justified, to everyone."[14] But here, too, theory needs to be informed by practice. We cannot know, a priori, what everyone is going to consider reasonable or justifiable. The assumption that we can know this without rigorous self-examination to uncover our own biases and extensive engagement with others to learn about different viewpoints is misguided.[15] As Martha Minow has argued in her work on difference, if we are to see more clearly the perspectives of others we need first "to explore our own stereotypes, our own attitudes toward people we treat as different—and, indeed, our own categories for organizing the world. Audre Lorde put it powerfully: 'I urge each one of us here to reach down into that deep place of knowledge inside herself and touch that terror and loathing of any difference that lives there. See whose face it wears. Then the personal as the political can begin to illuminate all our choices.' "[16]

Engaging in political practice forces us to confront our own stereotypes and to take seriously the standpoints of others. As I pointed out earlier, political theorizing done in the absence of practice can lead to a false sense of neutrality and of the universal applicability of the theory. Feminist legal theorists such as Catharine MacKinnon, Martha Minow, Carole Pateman, and Robin West have criticized the "add women and stir" approach to incorporating women's concerns in purportedly neutral accounts of equality. Some political philosophers have not even included women in their theories in this superficial way.[17] Likewise, critical race theorists such as Derrick Bell, Kimberlè Crenshaw, Mari Matsuda, and Charles Lawrence have shown how supposedly neutral discourse disguises real biases and ignores or discounts the experiences of minorities. Whereas such concerns and experiences were previously dismissed in theoretical work (even by many women and people of color) they are now given voice—and given credence. Feminist theory, for example, continues to be informed by a method common to activists, but still shunned by academics, that of consciousness-raising, which, as Ann Scales describes it, "means that dramatic eye-witness testimony is being given; it means, more importantly, that women now have the confidence to declare it as such. We have an alternative to relegating our perception to the realm of our own subjective discomfort. Heretofore, the tried and true scientific strategy of treating non-conforming evidence as mistaken worked in the legal system. But when that evidence keeps turning up, when the experience of women becomes recalcitrant, it will be time to treat that evidence as true."[18]

Methods such as consciousness-raising and first person storytelling have been instrumental in the undermining of the dichotomy between the private and the public[19] as well as other dichotomies that arose out of the devaluing of the perspectives of those not doing the theorizing. Two decades of feminist theorizing about gender and the family have brought to the fore issues once considered too personal to warrant philosophical attention. Still, most mainstream political theorizing continues to ignore feminist theory[20] and Waldron minimizes the importance of the issues raised by it by making disparaging comments about the recent philosophical focus on such public policy issues as child care. Why issues such as child care are of *philosophical* importance is evident once one realizes that, as Carole Pateman put it, "Feminists are trying to develop a theory of a social practice that, for the first time in the Western world, would be a truly general theory—including women and men equally—grounded in the interrelationship of the individual to collective life, or personal to political life, instead of their separation and opposition. At the immediate practical level, this demand is expressed in what is perhaps the most clear conclusion of feminist critiques; that if women are to participate fully, as equals, in social life, men have to share equally in child-rearing and other domestic tasks."[21]

Theories that are informed by practice gain acknowledged bases in actual experience and explicit (rather than hidden, unspoken) perspectives. Even if what we are aiming for is an objective theory applicable to all human experience, as Thomas Nagel points out, "Objectivity needs subjective material to work on, and for human morality this is found in human life."[22] Political theory divorced from practice, as advocated in Waldron's article, lacks the "subjective material" needed for adequate theorizing. Practice brings us closer to being able to grasp the particularity of others' experience, which, in turn, enables us to do justice to difference.

IV. Changing the World and Being Changed by It

Activist-theorists not only consider their theorizing to have the potential to help change the world, they also are acutely aware of the way their experiences in the world have changed them and influenced their theories. Their membership in oppressed groups has forced them to pay attention to discrimination, poverty, harassment, and hate-motivated violence, and they consciously bring their perspectives as outsiders to theorizing about these issues.

Mari Matsuda has advocated the use of what she calls "multiple consciousness"[23] as a method for theorizing about law and politics, one that draws on the experiences of those, such as women of color, who are forced by the split between their cultural awareness and their professional status to see the world in shifting perspectives. Matsuda presents as an example a student with "woman-of-color consciousness" in a law school class listening to a professor who "sees his job—and I use the male pronoun deliberately—as training the students out of the muddleheaded world where everything is relevant and into the lawyer's world where the few critical facts prevail." While the professor lectures on a *Miranda*-type case involving a man charged with rape, the student "wonders whether the defendant was a person of color and whether the police officer was white. . . . [She] wonders about the race of the victim . . . [and] thinks about rape—the rape of her roommate last year, and her own fears." Some of her classmates have been raped, and "[s]he wonders how they are reacting to the case, what pain it resurrects for them."[24] In contrast to the professor in this scenario who considers such questions irrelevant to the issues at hand, Matsuda argues that we all could—and should—take the "outsider's perspective" seriously in our teaching and writing about political and legal theory. She urges legal theorists to make "a deliberate choice to see the world from the standpoint of the oppressed," a standpoint she considers to be accessible to all of us through "reading, studying, listening, and venturing into different places. For lawyers, our pro bono work may be the most effective means of acquiring a broader consciousness of oppression."[25]

And, as Marge Piercy has written, "If what we change doesn't change us then we are just playing with blocks."[26] If what we see doesn't change us, then perhaps we are just not paying attention. That's the charitable interpretation. We may be willfully resisting changing our theory to accommodate our perceptions of the world. Or we may be all too willing to jettison a theory if it challenges too radically our conception of what ought to be done. As shown by a common reaction to Peter Singer's article, "Famine, Affluence, and Morality," taking it to be a *reductio* argument against utilitarianism, one philosopher's call to action is another's counterexample. I do not mean to be taken as advocating that political philosophers aspire to moral sainthood. Just as an ethical theory should not require us to be Mother Teresa, a political theory should not require us to be Martin Luther King, Jr. We have our limits and they are not (all) weaknesses. But one sort of limitation—that imposed by our own context-determined perspective—ought to be overcome, and it can be if we pay greater attention to the contexts in which others live, engage in political practice, and theorize.

Some of us, like the woman of color in the law class on rape, have no choice but to take our own contexts into account. Others, whose own perspectives coincide with those deemed universal, have the luxury of being able to ignore context in theorizing. Those who neglect context, however, risk committing the same anachronistic fallacy Waldron decries in readings of the canon that pay, on his view, undue attention to racist and sexist pronouncements of the authors. Waldron argues that our focus on such current concerns leads to anachronistic, misleading, and unhelpful readings of the canon. However, Waldron's assumption that we can arrive at useful insights about political life without taking into account the contexts in which the great political theorists wrote can also lead to anachronist readings, ones that neglect the essential roles that patriarchy and racial hierarchy played in the development and justification of the theories themselves.

Perhaps mainstream political philosophers are prepared to dismiss racism and sexism in the canon as irrelevant idiosyncrasies because they, like their predecessors, view philosophy by definition as unconcerned with such personal traits as race and sex and such historical accidents as racism and misogyny. This traditional view of the enterprise of philosophy as abstracting from the particular circumstances of its practitioners is exemplified by this passage from Bertrand Russell:

The free intellect will see as God might see, without a *here* and
now, without hopes and fears, without the trammels of customary
beliefs and traditional prejudices, calmly, dispassionately, in the
sole and exclusive desire of knowledge—knowledge as impersonal, as purely contemplative, as it is possible for man to attain.
Hence also the free intellect will value more the abstract and
universal knowledge into which the accidents of private history
do not enter, than the knowledge . . . dependent . . . upon an
exclusive and personal point of view."[27]

Critical race theorists and feminist theorists argue, in contrast, that we all theorize from a "positioned perspective."[28]
This is not obvious to all, but those of us who have been outsiders have been forced to be aware of this. For others, the process
of "contextualizing" legal and political theorizing can expose the
biases inherent in supposedly neutral theories. As an antidote to
our illusion of neutrality Seyla Benhabib, for example, urges us
to adopt what she calls "the standpoint of the concrete other"
which, in contrast to that of the "generalized other" employed
in mainstream political theory, "requires us to view each and
every rational being as an individual with a concrete history,
identity, and affective-emotional constitution. In assuming this
standpoint, we abstract from what constitutes our commonality."[29] Others have argued for the value of empathy for those
different from ourselves as an important element in understanding legal and political issues.[30] Both are ways of acknowledging and trying to compensate for the limitations to understanding that follow from the fact that we are situated beings.

V. Taking Our Conclusions Seriously

Peter Singer asked, in "Famine, Affluence, and Morality,"
"What is the point of relating philosophy to public (and personal) affairs if we do not take our conclusions seriously? In this
instance, taking our conclusion seriously means acting upon
it."[31] I have been arguing that theory should begin (as well as
end) in practice. If we accept that conclusion, how do we take it
seriously? How can we put it into practice?

The considerations I have been raising point to new ways of
reading, teaching, and doing political philosophy. At the very

least, we should pay more attention to the perspectives of formerly excluded groups. We should not assume that it is possible to theorize in a universal voice and that only those who are "different" (that is, different from us) are viewing the subject matter from a particular perspective. It takes a perspective to see a perspective.[32]

Waldron gently ridicules his students (and some of his colleagues) who not only condemn the sexist and racist views of some of the great figures of political philosophy, but also find in these benighted views reason to suspect other aspects of the theories in question. A theory of citizenship, for example, is viewed as suspect if its author took slavery for granted, and an account of natural rights is discredited if it did not accord such rights to women: "like the thirteenth chime of a crazy clock, the policies call not only themselves, but everything that went before into question."[33] Waldron argues that such suspicions are unwarranted. It is not that he thinks such views are correct, or even tolerable. But we must, it seems, do our best to avert our gaze, so as not to be distracted by such irrelevant rantings. He assumes both that we are in agreement about what is relevant and what is irrelevant to our properly philosophical interest in these figures and that we can—and should—simply ignore (or perhaps pause long enough to quickly lament) what's deemed "irrelevant." But should we ignore or consider irrelevant the sexism and racism of these figures? Is this *possible*—even for those who are philosophically disenfranchised by these very attitudes (which persist in the profession, although they are now held unconsciously and expressed in subtler, more insidious ways)?[34]

While those of us in the profession of political and legal philosophy claim to be making an effort to attract more women and people of color into the field, most of us are prepared to gloss over the sexist and racist pronouncements of the great philosophers, paying about as much attention to them as we might to their antiquated prose style or to typos in editions of their work. So we expect our female students and colleagues to consider irrelevant (or an occasion for a bemused chuckle) Aristotle's view that "the courage of a man is shown in commanding, of a woman in obeying. . . . All classes must be deemed to have their special attributes; as the poet says of women, 'Silence is a woman's glory,' but this is not equally the glory of man."[35]

Most would also have us ignore or smile at Rousseau's views about the difference between man and woman "in their moral relations," that "the man should be strong and active; the woman should be weak and passive; the one must have both the power and the will; it is enough that the other should offer little resistance."[36] Such prescriptions, if noticed at all, are to be viewed as quaint anachronisms, evidence that even as eminent a thinker as Rousseau was still, to that small extent, a product of his time (never mind that some of his predecessors managed not to succumb to such historical conditioning).

But women are becoming less inclined to take their (male) colleagues' and professors' advice about what is relevant and what is not, what is evidence of a serious failure of "understanding" and what is trivial, what is condemnable as sexism or racism and what is to be laughed off or ignored. Just as we have come to view sexual harassment and assault as serious (and no longer laughing matters) now that we can see them from women's perspectives, we should come to see gender and racial biases in the canon as serious enough to warrant our attention. Why consider trivial and irrelevant in the great philosophers the very attitudes that we would not tolerate in ourselves or in our colleagues?

We should put ourselves in the position of our students of color when we read the following quote from Hume: "I am apt to suspect the negroes, and in general all the other races and species of men (for there are four or five different kinds) to be naturally inferior to the whites. There never was a civilized nation of any other complexion other than white, nor any individual eminent either in action or speculation."[37] And we should try to imagine how our African-American students respond to Kant's pronouncement on the worth of the opinion of a Black person: "And it might be said that there was something in this which perhaps deserves to be considered; but in short, this fellow was quite black from head to foot, a clear proof that what he said was stupid."[38] If our colleagues said such things, we would hardly let them go unchallenged. We would surely have serious doubts about their ability to do philosophy. Why *shouldn't* our students view such pronouncements as calling into question other aspects of these philosophers' theories? Waldron thinks we "run a great danger" if our readings of the canon—and our own normative theorizing—are too closely bound up with "political advocacy" and "wish-lists." The danger is that we will be led astray—away from the true nature of political theory. "We should think of it instead," Waldron urges, "literally as political *philosophy*—a deepening of our insight into the realm of the political and of our understanding of what is involved in making judgments and decisions in that realm."[39] His emphasis on what "political *philosophy*" means *literally*, should not, however, be interpreted as a call to return to ordinary language philosophy, to the "sterile analysis of concepts" that he condemns. Nevertheless, he does argue that the proper goal of philosophy should be achieving a better understanding of "the concepts of politics—like *power, the state, politics, civil society, community, morality, violence, justice, democracy, order, freedom* and *law*."[40] It is not a coincidence that he leaves out of this august list such concepts as *the family, gender,* and *race,* which are the concepts that so exercise his female and minority students and colleagues. Attempts to clarify these concepts would presumably get us mired in such (on Waldron's view) unphilosophical public policy questions as whether there is a right to abortion or what are equitable child care arrangements or how severe are the harms of racist hate speech.

But the assumption that the concept of gender or of race is less central to political philosophy than the others listed above, and the corollary that the above concepts could be clarified without reference to gender or race reveals a bias that should be questioned. As Waldron himself points out, "An area of inquiry cannot become *philosophy* until people have seen reason to throw its fundamental presuppositions into doubt."[41] This philosophical enterprise is precisely what feminist theorists and critical race theorists are engaging in as they seek to expose the biases in traditional legal and political theory, including the privileging of the universal and abstract over the particular and concrete, the public and the political over the private and personal. They are challenging the legitimacy of these very distinctions, and along with them, the distinction Waldron assumes between political philosophy and public policy. Their aim is, in Adrienne Rich's words, "To question everything. To remember what it has been forbidden even to mention. To come together telling our stories."[42]

One of the forbidden questions activist-theorists are daring to ask is: why do legal and political philosophy? Is the goal to further some political agenda (while navigating between the Scylla of debilitating scepticism and the Charybdis of dogmatic proselytizing)? To "understand" the nature of political life (and other perennial problems)? To interpret the canon (in order to arrive at the truth about what so-and-so said—or, even, to arrive at *the truth*)? To train our students in the history and methods of our discipline? To encourage our students to question and subvert these academic presuppositions? To get good academic jobs? To impress our colleagues with our cleverness?

We should not expect a unitary response to these questions, since "we" are not all in this line of work for the same reason. As Charles R. Lawrence, III, writes: "I am struck by the strong sense of alienation that I have felt from the role of 'scholar.' " The scholar, as depicted by Lawrence, "is 'objective.' He views his work as a value-free inquiry, an effort to clarify the world rather than to change it. He is guided by an orthodoxy that equates objectivity with emotional disengagement, cognitive distance, and moral indifference. It is the work of those who remain cool and distant in the face of suffering or anger because it is not their liberation, their humanity, which is at stake."[43]

It is a bit harsh to say that the work of more traditional scholars is motivated or characterized by moral indifference. However, personal detachment (in the guise of objectivity) and disdain for practice (in the dedicated pursuit of theory) are, if not academic prerequisites, professionally rewarded attitudes. In spite of the many articles cited by Waldron dealing with public affairs, the profession still assumes a split between political philosophy and political activism and forces a choice between theory and practice. In "What Plato Would Allow," Waldron seems to endorse Plato's vision of the philosopher who remains untainted by the sordidness of political life. Those who have, as Plato put it, "tasted the happiness of philosophy and seen the frenzy of the masses, understand that political life has virtually nothing sound about it." The best they can do, in this imperfect world of ours, is to "live quietly and keep to themselves, like a man who stands under the shelter of a wall during a driving storm of dust and hail; they see the rest of the world full of wrongdoing, and are content to keep themselves unspotted from the wickedness and wrong in this life, and finally leave it with cheerful composure and good hope."[44] Plato's image of philosophy as providing a wall between the theorist and the harsh realities of political life illustrates what activist-theorists find most maddening about our profession. Who among us, having "tasted the happiness of philosophy," can, when confronted with the problems of famine, war, AIDS, sexual violence, racist hate crimes, just to name a few public policy issues, "live quietly," keeping to oneself, as Waldron claims Plato advises? Either philosophy would have to be a lot more consoling, or political advocacy more demoralizing, for us to imagine ourselves, at the end of such a cloistered life, filled with the "cheerful composure and good hope" Plato describes.

There is, nonetheless, in the field of philosophy, an academically rewarded indifference to real-world concerns. Political philosophy can function as a kind of glass wall, providing us not only with the illusion of clear vision and shelter from the storm but the sense of a lack of responsibility that comes with enforced distance. The glass wall provides even better protection than Gyges' ring against being pressed into public service. It is not that we are invisible, which would give us a choice about whether to be moral or, in this case, politically active. We are impotent, so the whole matter is taken out of our hands. Qua philosophers, anyway, if not qua citizens or moral agents, our political inertness is not merely excusable but imperative, at least if we are to do respectable work. Meanwhile, those who— through personal trauma or overactive imaginations that make unbearably vivid others' suffering—can find no refuge behind Plato's wall are considered morally benighted or, simply, not very bright.

Waldron's view of philosophy vacillates between finding it a blessing (as in the passage from Plato) and considering it a curse (as in his contrast between those of us "cursed with philosophical pretensions" and those eager to know what difference our work might make). This curse condemns philosophers to grapple with conceptual puzzles "long after the point when a man of good sense would have put down his *Logic* and gone home to play backgammon."[45] But we should add to Waldron's characterizations of philosophy as blessing and as curse that, above all, it's a luxury, not merely in the obvious material sense that it can be done only if one has one's basic needs met, but also in a psychological sense. If one is dealing, on a daily basis, with pressing social issues, such as sexual and racial harassment and assault, abortion, child care, discrimination, marginalization, it is hard to focus on "pure" theory. These, not a warm fire and a game of backgammon, are the distractions from philosophy that activist-theorists face, and not only when they go home. If, in addition, the assumptions made in the theory itself are experienced as yet another form of harassment and marginalization (as the sexist and racist quotes from the canon above might well be), working within the theory can be accomplished only at the painful cost of denying one's own worth as a theorist.

I began this section by talking about taking our conclusions seriously, and I want to end by urging us to take our starting points seriously. We should question our motives, our biases, and our most fundamental presuppositions. One such assumption is that only after getting the theory right can we then go on to apply it to practical concerns. In *Life's Dominion*, Ronald Dworkin presents a different model, which he calls doing "philosophy from the inside out," beginning with "practical problems, like the question of whether the law should ever permit abortion or euthanasia," then asking "which general philosophical or theoretical issues we must confront in order to resolve those practical problems." He argues that this strategy, one that "engages theoretical issues but begins with, and remains disciplined by, a moral subject of practical political importance" yields results no less "deep" and philosophical than those arrived at by theory-driven approaches.[46] This approach to theory, like that advocated by critical race theorists and feminist legal theorists, if pursued conscientiously, requires us to listen to others' voices and to take seriously their perspectives. Dworkin advocates such an approach because it "may be more likely to succeed in the political forum."[47] But even those (if they exist) who consider themselves to have a purely theoretical interest in the discipline should pay more attention to practice from the outset, if only for the sake of their theories.

NOTES

I would like to thank Judith Wagner DeCew, Margot Livesey, and Thomas Trezise for their encouragement and for their insightful comments on an earlier draft.

1. This volume, 138–178.

2. For an elabortion of the ways in which practice is dependent upon theory, see Cass Sunstein's contribution to this volume, 267–287. See also Ronald Dworkin's discussion of the centrality of theories of interpretation in legal practice in *Law's Empire* (Cambridge, Mass.: Harvard University Press, 1986).

3. Mari J. Matsuda, Charles R. Lawrence, III, Richard Delgado, and Kimberlè Williams Crenshaw, eds., *Words That Wound: Critical Race Theory, Assaultive Speech, and the First Amendment* (Boulder, Colo.: Westview Press, 1993), 3.

4. Martha Albertson Fineman, "Introduction," in *At the Boundaries of Law: Feminism and Legal Theory,* ed. Martha Albertson Fineman and Nancy Sweet Thomadsen (New York: Routledge, 1991), xi–xii.

5. In *Political Liberalism* (New York: Columbia University Press, 1993), Rawls does not cite Susan Moller Okin's or other feminist critiques of *A Theory of Justice,* although much of the book is devoted to elaborating his theory in response to other recent developments in political theory. For Okin's critique, see her book, *Justice, Gender, and the Family* (New York: Basic Books, 1989).

6. Jeremy Waldron, "A Right-Based Critique of Constitutional Rights," *Oxford Journal of Legal Studies* 13 (Spring 1993): 35.

7. Ibid.

8. Waldron, "What Plato Would Allow," this volume, 171.

9. Harry Frankfurt, *Iyyun: The Jerusalem Philosophical Quarterly* 41 (January 1992): 3–19.

10. Iris M. Young, among others, has noted the ways in which the women's movement has made public issues out of such "private" practices. See her "Impartiality and the Civic Public," in Seyla Benhabib and Drucilla Cornell, eds., *Feminism as Critique* (Cambridge: Polity Press, 1987), 74.

11. See Dworkin's chapter, "Do We Have a Right to Pornography?" in *A Matter of Principle* (Cambridge: Harvard University Press, 1985), 335–72 and his essay, "Pornography, Feminism, and Liberty," *New York Review of Books* (August 15, 1991).

12. *Life's Dominion: An Argument about Abortion, Euthanasia, and Individual Freedom* (New York: Knopf, 1993). I am not arguing that Dworkin actually succeeds in treating public policy issues concerning abortion and euthanasia in a way that is not dictated by his theory. But his attempt to do this is novel and noteworthy.

13. Robin West points out the dangers of taking even certain uncontroversial constitutional rights, such as the right to free speech, as morally justifiable, since doing so can blind us to the ways in which people are harmed by the exercising of such rights. She defends "normative constitutional scepticism" as an antidote to the unquestioning faith in the rightness of the (properly interpreted) Constitution. Robin West, "Constitutional Scepticism," in Susan J. Brison and Walter Sinnott-Armstrong, eds., *Contemporary Perspectives on Constitutional Interpretation* (Boulder, Colo.: Westview, 1993), 234–58.

14. "What Plato Would Allow," this volume, 148.

15. For example, Seyla Benhabib points out a problem with Rawls's strategy for capturing impartiality in the original position: according to Rawls, "moral reciprocity involves the capacity to take the standpoint of the other, to put oneself imaginatively in the place of the other, but under conditions of the 'veil of ignorance,' the *other as different from the self* disappears." Benhabib, "The Generalized and the Concrete Other," in Seyla Benhabib and Drucilla Cornell, eds., *Feminism as Critique: On the Politics of Gender* (Minneapolis: University of Minnesota Press, 1987), 89.

16. Martha Minow, "Justice Engendered," in Brison and Sinnott-Armstrong, *Contemporary Perspectives on Constitutional Interpretation,* 174. The quote from Audre Lorde is from "The Master's Tools Will Never Dismantle the Master's House," in C. Moraga and G. Anzaldúa, eds., *This Bridge Called My Back: Writings by Radical Women of Color* (New York: Kitchen Table Press, 1981), 98.

17. For an insightful analysis of several contemporary political philosophers who neglect women in their theories see Susan Moller Okin, *Justice, Gender, and the Family* (New York: Basic Books, 1989).

18. Ann C. Scales, "The Emergence of Feminist Jurisprudence: An Essay," *Yale Law Journal* 95 (1986): 1402.

19. As Carole Pateman has noted, "[t]he dichotomy between the private and the public is central to almost two centuries of feminist

writing and political struggle; it is, ultimately, what the feminist movement is about." *The Disorder of Women: Democracy, Feminism and Political Theory* (Cambridge: Polity Press, 1989), 118.

20. For a critical discussion of the ongoing neglect of feminist theory, see the afterword in the 1992 printing of Susan Moller Okin, *Women in Western Political Thought* (Princeton: Princeton University Press, 1979), 309–40.

21. Pateman, 135.

22. Thomas Nagel, *The View from Nowhere* (New York: Oxford University Press, 1986), 186. Nagel, however, goes on to say that ethics "requires a detachment from particular perspectives and transcendence of one's time and place." (187) I would argue, however, that since this is impossible to achieve, we should instead aspire to the more realistic goal of what Amartya Sen calls "transpositional objectivity." For an elaboration of this notion, see Sen, "Positional Objectivity," *Philosophy and Public Affairs* 22:2 (Spring 1993): 126–45.

23. Mari J. Matsuda, "When the First Quail Calls: Multiple Consciousness as Jurisprudential Method," *Womens' Rights Law Reporter* 11 (Spring 1989): 7–10.

24. Ibid., 7.

25. Ibid., 9.

26. Quoted by Martha Minow in "Justice Engendered," 180.

27. Bertrand Russell, *The Problems of Philosophy* (New York: Oxford University Press, 1969), 160.

28. Charles R. Lawrence, III, "The Word and the River: Pedagogy as Scholarship as Struggle," *Southern California Law Review* 65 (1992): 2252.

29. Seyla Benhabib, "The Generalized and the Concrete Other," in *Feminism as Critique*, 87.

30. See Jane Mansbridge, "Feminism and Democratic Community," in John W. Chapman and Ian Shapiro, eds., *Democratic Community: Nomos* XXXV (New York: New York University Press, 1993), 347–61; Lawrence, 2275; Diana Meyers, "Social Exclusion, Moral Reflection, and Rights," *Law and Philosophy* 12:2 (May 1993): 125–26.

31. "Famine, Affluence, and Morality," *Philosophy and Public Affairs.* 1:3 (Spring 1972), 242.

32. This was a frequently articulated theme at the "Speech, Equality, and Harm" conference at the University of Chicago Law School, March 1993.

33. Waldron, this volume, 140.

34. For an illuminating discussion of the insidiousness of racism see

Charles R. Lawrence, III, "The Id, the Ego, and Equal Protection: Reckoning with Unconscious Racism," *Stanford Law Review* 39 (1987): 317.

35. Aristotle, *The Politics*, ch. XIII, quoted in Jane English, *Sex Equality* (Englewood Cliffs, N.J.: Prentice-Hall, 1977), 29–30.

36. Jean Jacques Rousseau, *Emile*, quoted in Jane English, *Sex Equality* (Englewood Cliffs, N.J.: Prentice-Hall, 1977), 43.

37. David Hume, "Of National Characters," in *The Philosophical Works of David Hume*, ed. by T. H. Green and T. H. Grose (London, 1882). Quoted in Howard McGary, "Philosophy and Diversity: The Inclusion of African and African-American Materials," *APA Newsletter on Feminism and Philosophy* 92:1 (Spring 1993): 52.

38. Immanuel Kant, *Observations on the Feeling of the Beautiful and Sublime*, trans. John T. Goldthwait (Berkeley: University of California Press 1965), 113. Quoted in McGary, 52. See McGary's article for other racist comments from the canon, as well as for suggestions for making philosophy more inclusive.

39. Waldron, "What Plato Would Allow," this volume, 143.

40. Ibid., 166.

41. Ibid., 170.

42. Adrienne Rich, "Natural Resources," in *The Dream of a Common Language: Poems 1974–1977* (New York: Norton, 1978), 66.

43. Charles R. Lawrence, III, "The Word and the River: Pedagogy as Scholarship as Struggle," *Southern California Law Review* 65 (1992): 2238.

44. Plato, *Republic*, book 6, 292 (496c–e), quoted by Waldron in this volume 154. Waldron's interpretation of this passage from the *Republic* is also questionable. See Martha Nussbaum's contribution to this volume.

45. Waldron, "What Plato Would Allow," this volume, 171 (with obvious reference to Hume).

46. Ronald Dworkin, *Life's Dominion: An Argument about Abortion, Euthanasia, and Individual Freedom* (New York: Knopf, 1993), 28–29.

47. Ibid., 29.

8

AVOIDABLE NECESSITY: GLOBAL WARMING, INTERNATIONAL FAIRNESS, AND ALTERNATIVE ENERGY

HENRY SHUE

FOUR QUESTIONS OF FAIRNESS

A wide international consensus of scientists is convinced that this planet faces serious danger from changes in temperature and other aspects of weather to which agricultural systems probably cannot adjust with the speed that would be necessary in order to avoid serious disruptions in food supplies for millions of vulnerable humans.[1] In order to reduce the magnitude of this danger, which is generally referred to as "global warming" (in spite of the fact that temperature is only one of its many aspects), it would be necessary to have comprehensive international cooperation, cooperation that might not need to be literally universal across countries but would certainly need to include both the richest industrialized countries, whose emissions of "greenhouse gases" are the main current sources of global warming, and the most populous less-industrialized countries, whose emissions will be the main future sources of warming if they try to follow the model of industrialization pioneered by the now-rich. If this scientific consensus is even roughly correct, one of the most important issues facing humanity is: on what terms can rich and poor, industrialized and less-industrialized, cooperate in dealing with this common global threat?

Unfortunately, we face here not simply one question about fairness, but at least four questions, the answers to which must in the end nevertheless be coordinated. For the sake of a clear analysis, we need initially to see that at least four different issues of fairness must be handled by any cooperative international arrangement. For the sake of effective action, we then need ultimately to tie the answers to the four questions together into a single coherent package. At greater length elsewhere I have explained why I believe that all the following four questions must be answered before we can know how to proceed fairly:

1. What is a fair allocation of the costs of preventing the global warming that is still avoidable?;
2. What is a fair allocation of the costs of coping with the social consequences of the global warming that will not in fact be avoided?;
3. What background allocation of wealth would allow international bargaining (about issues like 1. and 2.) to be a fair process?; and
4. What is a fair allocation of emissions of greenhouse gases (A) over the long-term and (B) during the transition to the long-term allocation?[2]

In this chapter I will try to begin to answer question (4A), by discussing what the allocation of emissions should ultimately become; I will not tackle the other crucial, and of course practically more immediate, issue of how rapid should be the transition from the current allocation to a fair one.[3]

IDEAL BEFORE NON-IDEAL?

This is a messy chapter in at least the following sense: in addition to recognizably normative discussion about fairness and inequality, essential reference is also made not only to various elements of the scientific consensus about the problem of global warming but also, in the defense of practical judgments among alternative solutions, to supposed aspects of human psychology and even speculations about U.S. politics. Those influenced by the magisterial work of John Rawls, among others, may well feel that this is a muddled manner in which to proceed, especially perhaps on issues about fairness to which Rawls has contributed so much. In particular, it might be thought wiser first to establish what the ideal arrangements would be and then gradually to factor in the relevant psychological, political, and other empirical elements needed to decide what to do in the thoroughly non-ideal situation that everyone, Rawls included, is well aware we face.

A firm believer in the principle that the proof of the pudding is in the eating thereof, I will not offer a general defense of my method in advance and in the abstract but will leave readers to judge its persuasiveness and fruitfulness in the concrete. I would, however, like to make one preliminary critical comment about the much neater sounding thought that one should engage in ideal theory first and only then move, compromising as one goes, into non-ideal theory. The critical comment is that, at least in Rawls's original formulation, the line between ideal theory and non-ideal theory is indeterminate.

Famously, the construction of the argument by Rawls in *A Theory of Justice* has four stages: original position, constitutional convention, legislative stage, and application of rules to particular cases.[4] In the original position use is made of general truths, but not of knowledge about particular contingencies; in stages two through four the particular contingencies are gradually fed back in and—it would seem to me—some of the general truths fall out (since we do not in reality know all the general theoretical truths that in the original position we are hypothetically assumed to know). The four-stage sequence gives us "a schema for sorting out the complications that must be faced"; at each stage "the veil of ignorance is partially lifted."[5] Thus, at, for instance, the second stage (of the constitutional convention),

> in addition to an understanding of the principles of social theory, they now know the relevant general facts about their society, that is, its natural circumstances and resources, its level of economic advance and political culture, and so on.[6]

And Rawls shortly adds:

> I imagine then a division of labor between stages in which each
> deals with different questions of social justice. This division
> roughly corresponds to the two parts of the basic structure. The
> first principle of equal liberty is the primary standard for the
> constitutional convention. . . . The second principle comes into
> play at the [third] stage of the legislature.[7]

To put it unkindly, we have just been told that the constitution
is to be written with no attention to its economic and social
implications, since neither the relevant (second) principle nor
the relevant information—"the full range of general economic
and social facts"—become available until the constitution is fin-
ished and the third (legislative) stage begins. Many reasons have
been given during the succeeding two decades of debate why
this picture of the relation of constitution and legislation—resting upon a sharp division between liberties, on the one hand,
and everything else, on the other—is profoundly misguided.[8]
But it does at least appear to be clear.

Not so. At *every* one of the four stages of construction, including the original position, one may conduct two kinds of inquiry,
ideal and non-ideal; and within non-ideal inquiry two kinds of
compromise principles are needed:

> One consists of the principles for governing adjustments to natu-
> ral limitations and historical contingencies, and the other of prin-
> ciples for meeting injustice.[9]

Most references to Rawlsian non-ideal theory that I have
encountered make it sound as if compromise is allowed only to
deal with partial compliance, the second of the two kinds of
compromise expected in non-ideal contexts. That Rawls is not
in the sentence quoted simply overindulging in the creation of
typologies by mentioning a different, first kind of non-ideal
theory is indicated by his having just previously made precisely
the same distinction on the issue of supreme importance to him,
restrictions on liberty:

> There is, however, a further distinction that must be made be-
> tween two kinds of circumstances that justify or excuse a restric-

tion of liberty. First a restriction can derive from the natural limitations and accidents of human life, or from historical and social contingencies. . . . For example, even in a well-ordered society under favorable circumstances . . . the principle of participation is restricted in extent. These constraints issue from the more or less permanent conditions of political life. . . . In the second kind of case, injustice already exists, either in social arrangements or in the conduct of individuals. The question here is what is the just way to answer injustice.[10]

Here too, Rawls distinguishes the subsequently much more widely discussed (second) case of partial compliance, or departures from justice, from the (first) case of natural limitations and historical and social contingencies.

Now, these remarks by Rawls raise several kinds of important issues that I cannot pursue, and I will call attention to only one. For purposes even of *ideal* theory at the constitutional (second) stage of construction, people know "the relevant general facts about their society, that is, its natural circumstances and resources, its level of economic advance and political culture, and so on." For purposes of *non-ideal* theory at the same constitutional (second) stage, restrictions specifically in liberty "can derive from the natural limitations and accidents of human life, or from historical and social contingencies." I submit that there is no clear commonsensical answer and no clear answer within Rawlsian theory to the question: where is the line between "the relevant general facts about their society" (ideal theory) and "historical and social contingencies" (non-ideal theory)? That means that there is no systematic way to know which information is appropriately invoked in arguments within ideal theory and which is appropriately invoked in arguments within the first of the two kinds of non-ideal theory. One is left, I think, to muddle through, judging relevance as one goes. It will turn out below, in the case at hand, that empirical judgments about what is in fact avoidable and what is not avoidable are integral to the argument for a standard of fairness and that judgments about what is politically and ideologically palatable are crucial to the choice of what specifically to do.

GLOBAL WARMING: NOT YOUR USUAL PROBLEM

Global warming, which is almost certainly not yet occurring, will be produced here on the surface where people live by the accumulation of unprecedented amounts of greenhouse gases in the atmosphere a few miles above. A greenhouse gas just is a gas that to some significant degree holds heat on the planet by reflecting heat back from the atmosphere toward the surface. Water vapor, which humans cannot control, is a major greenhouse gas, as are CFCs, which we could control (and which we invented), and to some extent are controlling. By far the most important greenhouse gas produced by humans is carbon dioxide. All fossil fuels—coal, oil (including of course the gasoline refined from oil), and natural gas—are carbon-based, and burning any fossil fuel for energy thrusts carbon dioxide into the air. Carbon that had been, as the scientists say, "sequestered"—taken out of circulation—for thousands of millennia in coal, gas, and oil is now suddenly being flooded in torrents into the atmosphere as carbon dioxide. It would be extraordinary indeed if this sudden, massive, and increasing rush of carbon dioxide into the upper atmosphere had no effect here on the surface. And there is indeed plenty of reason to think that, roughly, once the concentration of carbon dioxide doubles, which will not take much longer at current rates, the surface temperature of the earth will rise enough to affect the volume of sea-water and thus the location of high-tide (water expands with rises in temperature), the top velocity of hurricane winds (the maximum speed rises with the temperature of the underlying ocean water), and many other aspects of the weather vital to agriculture and human food supplies, especially the supplies to the poorest people.[11]

Nothing that is done by way of the atmospheric mechanism behind global warming can have any effect here on the surface until many years after it is done. The delay between cause and effect in this case spans decades. This is an utterly critical, and quite unusual, fact about the greenhouse effect. What has to be changed in order to affect global warming is the accumulated total of gases at certain levels of the atmosphere, but what atmospheric scientists call the "residence times" of the critical gases are, in the case of carbon dioxide, several generations—about a century—and even in the case of one of the shortest-lived ones, methane, a full generation (fifteen years). Needless to say, atmospheric chemistry is exceedingly complex and lively (far beyond anything I know about): no gas particle simply floats in place for one hundred years and then evaporates. Nevertheless, generally speaking it would be the case that if, *per impossible*, we could avoid adding any carbon dioxide to the earth's atmosphere for an entire year, the atmosphere would at the end of the year contain all the carbon dioxide it had contained at the beginning except for the last of the carbon dioxide emitted around 1895, which would finally have played itself out at that location. Most of the vastly greater quantities of carbon emitted in the unprecedented burst of industrial activity since World War II, most notably, is continuing to be active in one way or another, especially since more is emitted every year than was emitted the year before. The carbon dioxide emitted in 1995 will mostly still be very active in, say, 2050. Consequently, we could by beginning now significantly affect the temperature and weather in 2050, but there is next to nothing that we could do now to change the temperature in 2000. That die has been cast. Global warming is the ultimate case of the prevention being easier than the cure.

Consequently, the argument that we should not take any action until we have observed global warming is a little like the argument that one should not stop smoking until one has seen tumors in one's lungs. It is admittedly possible for one to smoke all one's life and not get lung cancer. Consequently, it is true that one might give up smoking "for nothing" in the sense that one might never have developed cancer (or any of the other serious diseases that are provoked and promoted by smoking) even if one had never given up the smoking. To be fully analogous, however, the cigarette smoke would have to remain trapped in one's lungs for up to, say, fifty years after one stopped smoking so that if one wanted to be free of continuing effects of the smoke at age sixty-five, one had to stop smoking when one was fifteen. Some aspects of nutrition are exactly like this: a child whose nutrition up to about age two does not permit adequate bone development will suffer from fifty-five to sixty in ways that cannot then be undone (one of many reasons why the levels of childhood malnutrition that we routinely tolerate in the Third World are criminal).

In fact, insofar as those harmed by the effects of any given emissions are not the members of the emitting generation but are instead the members of succeeding generations, the analogy with smoking would become still closer if it were the case that the "passive" smoke from the cigarettes of one generation collected and remained in the lungs of their grandchildren to do damage there decades after its emission.

Consequently, we face what might be called quasi-irreversibility. One of the reasons why the extinction of plant and animal species is such a serious matter is that extinction is strictly irreversible; one cannot bring a species back once it is gone. It is, by contrast, perhaps not the case that once global warming has been set in motion it literally cannot be reversed, although we should not glibly assume that no reverberating cycle of positive feedbacks, making the warming worse and worse, will be unleashed beyond some unknown threshold.[12] For the same reason, namely that no one knows nearly enough, we cannot be certain that negative feedbacks would not correct any warming that occurs; higher temperatures might, for example, lead to additional water vapor in the atmosphere in the form of clouds that would block enough incoming sunlight to restore the temperature to its former level, and so forth. Because clouds, in particular, are so little understood, we really do not know what to expect: "Most of the variability between global climate models can be traced to differences in cloud radiative feedback."[13] While this wonderfully curative response to unprecedented human activity is not inconceivable, it is important to note that we lack adequate empirical grounds for counting on it and that, if it were to occur, it would be entirely outside human control and would have many other effects as well, not necessarily all positive from a human point of view. Basically we are blithely unleashing planetary forces that we do not understand and that we have no reason to believe we can tame.

LESS ECONOMIC ACTIVITY OR DIFFERENT
ENERGY SOURCES?

The main challenge, then, is to reduce new emissions of carbon dioxide to a level that will allow the atmospheric concentration to stabilize at a quantity that is not too much higher than the quantity we are accustomed to living with and for which agriculture has evolved. Obviously, there are two broad possibilities. First, without necessarily using any less energy, and therefore without necessarily reducing our standard of living, we could use energy from sources other than fossil fuels; possibilities include nuclear (fusion as well as fission), hydroelectric, geothermal, wind, passive solar, and photovoltaic. Remarkably little interest has been shown—and a pitifully small proportion of the gigantic public subsidies for energy has been spent—on energy sources other than fossil fuels and nuclear fission by the current political structure.

The second possibility is to continue using fossil-fuel as our predominant source of energy but reduce our consumption of energy, which will sooner or later mean reducing our standard of living.[14] This is complicated since "standard of living," as conventionally measured, and quality of life are, I think, two different matters. Every time someone wastes a tank of gasoline in pointless driving, the GNP goes up, along with the carbon dioxide. To some extent, reductions in standard of living could improve quality of life. On the other hand, advanced medical technology is possible only on the basis of considerable societal wealth. In addition, people do need jobs in order to support themselves, so net reductions in standard of living must generate jobs, which is quite possible (if, for example, production becomes less energy-intensive and more labor-intensive). I have neither the space here nor the competence to pursue this controversial (and ethically charged) but important matter. For simplicity, then, I will talk as if reductions in standard of living are always a problem, as they are now widely perceived to be and are always treated by conventional economists as being.

Basically, then, we can either switch energy sources, away from fossil-fuels, or we can reduce energy consumption and thereby reduce standards of living. Since our political leaders have so far steadfastly ignored the former option of changing our source of energy, I will in most of the rest of this chapter explore the latter option, returning to reconsider alternative energy sources only at the end in the light of how the main argument develops. For now and through most of the remaining discussion, then, I will assume (1) that if we are going to reduce carbon emissions, we will have to make sacrifices in our standard of living through reducing economic activity. As I indicated in the previous paragraph, I will also assume (2) that making sacrifices in our standard of living is bad. Making sacrifices in our standard of living, I am thus assuming in company with the vast majority, would mean making sacrifices in our self-interest.

Even so, there is one other complication that is most fortunate for us in the rich industrialized countries. Much of the carbon emissions by the rich countries are from energy that is entirely wasted. These emissions are the product of sheer inefficiency. (Not to mention that carbon-emitting fossil fuel is used when non-carbon-based fuel could easily have been substituted.) We are failing to make what have become popularly known in the public-policy community as "no-regrets" emissions reductions. A politically broad-based and authoritative consortium of public interest groups said: "Our conclusion: whether one simply wants to minimize costs to consumers, or to mitigate global warming, vigorous adoption of energy-efficiency measures and accelerated use of renewable energy sources make sense. . . . Current government policies and the marketplace are structured in a way that encourages the wasteful use of fossil fuels, not the efficient use of all available energy sources."[15] Only appalling indifference to the fate of future generations, our own and other peoples', allows this part of the rich country emissions. We could actually save money for ourselves while improving conditions for the future. Our remarkable failure to do so reflects political incompetence and social irrationality of a high order, in addition to flagrant disregard of the environment itself and of future generations as well as a craven degree of subservience to the entrenched interests of fossil-fuel firms. In these respects, all that we have to do is to stop shooting ourselves in the foot with bullets that ricochet and harm others as well. This part of the current behavior of the rich is utterly feckless.

The "no-regrets" reductions in carbon emissions could actually enable us in the rich countries to raise our living standards if we invested the savings from the increased energy efficiency into improvements for ourselves. Not everything that needs to be done to minimize global warming can be done at a profit, of course. Additional measures would actually require reductions in the living standards of the rich. Presently we will move on to the emissions reductions that would reduce our living standards, that are definitely contrary to at least our immediate self-interest (continuing to ignore any divergence between standard of living and quality of life). The costs to rich countries of these reductions would represent a genuine contribution by us to the cost of mitigating global warming. Where true sacrifices must be made, questions of fairness arise about who should make them.

CURRENT CARBON EMISSIONS

Who ought in fairness to make which sacrifices for the sake of combatting global warming depends upon several factors. For a final decision I believe that one needs the answers to at least the first and second, as well as the fourth, of the questions listed at the beginning of the chapter; one would not in practice need the answer to the third if the parties were willing to decide the terms of cooperation on principle rather than to engage in no-holds-barred bargaining based on current power. Certainly the answer to the fourth question, what is a fair allocation of emissions of greenhouse gases? is crucial because, other things equal, the allocation of the costs of resisting global warming ought to move the allocation of emissions in the direction of a fair allocation.[16] That is, if the current allocation is unfair because some countries' emissions now exceed their fair share, and if some emissions need to be cut in order to prevent or reduce global warming, then, other things equal, the emissions to eliminate are the ones that are already excessive, the ones that go beyond a fair share.[17] So we need to know what a fair share would be in the end. But first we should take note of actual shares.

How do the current carbon emissions of the rich and poor countries compare? The electrifying fact about current rich-country carbon emissions is that they constitute almost half the emissions by all humanity, while the residents of the rich countries are only about 16 percent of the human population: 15.7 percent of the people are producing 48.5 percent of the carbon emissions.[18] Thomas E. Drennen, who made the calculations just cited, also puts the comparison in per capita terms: "Citizens of the industrialized world are responsible for emitting 11.9 tons of CO_2 per capita per year, ten times more than their counterparts in developing countries (1.1 tons)."[19]

Drennen's ratio of 10:1 is an extremely conservative (from the point of view of the rich) calculation. A ratio of 8150:1, for U.S. to Indian citizens, in *net* emissions of *all* greenhouse gases has been calculated by Anil Agarwal and Sunita Narain of the Centre for Science and Environment in New Delhi.[20] Obviously these two ratios are not comparable: the particular figures I am citing from Drennen concern carbon dioxide only, not all greenhouse gases, and they are gross, not net. I am persuaded by Drennen's arguments that figures on biological emissions, most notably methane emissions, are not firm enough to be relied upon yet and that for this and other reasons we should in the immediate future concentrate upon carbon dioxide.[21] There is also no doubt that carbon dioxide is the single most important anthropogenic greenhouse gas, whether or not one should focus on it exclusively.[22] I am, in addition, dubious about the nationalistic allocation of sources and sinks that underlies this particular result drawn from Agarwal and Narain. In any case, a ratio of 10:1 may already cry out sufficiently loud for correction before one even contemplates allegedly still more unequal ratios, especially when one considers the role of carbon emissions in everyone's life.

EQUAL MINIMUM OF THE ESSENTIALS

The making of per-capita calculations implicitly assumes that equal shares per capita are at the very least a relevant benchmark, if not a moral requirement. I would like now to examine a little more fully the question of per capita equality in carbon emissions. Some discussions seem to assume—although perhaps no one has actually put it quite so crudely as I now will—that if "all men are created equal," then each is entitled to an equal share of emissions. That, however, by no means follows. This is another case in which the specific facts about something, namely carbon emissions, are highly relevant to how they should be viewed morally, namely whether it is or is not the case that they are among the things that ought to be distributed equally. We need to know what role carbon emissions play in life as it is actually lived today.

That all persons are fundamentally equal has to imply that they have important equal entitlements, but it need not imply that they have equal entitlements in everything or even in most things. Some things should not, or cannot, be distributed centrally, and consequently cannot be guaranteed any particular kind of distribution. Some things would lose their value if they were equally distributed. And so forth. Belief in fundamental human equality still leaves open what shape, if indeed any particular shape, the distributions of many things should have.[23] So, any position on the distribution of something as particular as greenhouse-gas emissions requires specific, factually informed argument.

And it is argument that is entirely dependent on distinctive features of the stage of economic history in which we find ourselves. It happens to be the case that a single form of industrial society has spread throughout the globe and that this dominant form of industrialization is overwhelmingly dependent upon energy obtained from burning fossil-fuels, which of course emits carbon dioxide in huge amounts. The poor and powerless confront industrialized or industrializing societies in which engaging in enough economic activity to support oneself and one's family requires the emission of carbon. In the fossil-fuel dependent economies into which poor people are born, people can survive only through activities that generate carbon. Significant carbon emissions are a necessity of life, given the energy sources made available to the poor by those who control energy policy. For as long as these emissions are a necessity of life—for as long as those who control the economy, and energy policy in particular, choose to rely heavily on fossil-fuel—everyone ought to be allowed at least an equal minimum amount of emissions sufficient for at least a decent life. Several points about this need to be noted.

First, while it may be obvious, it is also important that an equal minimum is not full equality. It is not my contention that there ought to be no departures from equality in possession of necessities of life—I am not suggesting that there is an objection to anyone's having more of one of the necessities of life than anyone else has when the total supply of the commodity or capacity in question is more than adequate for everyone's needs.

Second, I am not asserting, nor am I denying, the perfectly general thesis that if something is a necessity of life, every person is entitled to at least an equal minimum amount of it. Considerable discussion, in which I have participated, has occurred in recent years at that level of generality; here I want to concentrate on a more specific case.[24]

Third, the critical special feature of the case of carbon emissions is that its becoming zero-sum, or more precisely its mattering that it would become zero-sum, is the result of social choices not made by the poor. Whenever it is decided that, because of the threat of global warming, the global total of annual carbon emissions must be capped, carbon emissions become zero-sum. Once the total is frozen, every emission produced by someone is an emission that cannot be produced by anyone else. This only matters because the rich and powerful have allowed fossil fuels to become so inordinately important to all economies. I will attempt now to explain this crucial third point more fully.

Making a Zero-Sum Capacity Essential to Life

A strong international scientific consensus holds that the global total of annual emissions must not merely be capped but must be reduced; the original report of the Intergovernmental Panel on Climate Change considered that in order to stabilize the atmospheric concentration of carbon dioxide, annual emissions would have to be cut more than 60 percent below 1990 levels![25] Thus, if the politicians ever act upon the available scientific knowledge, we will have a *shrinking zero-sum:* a timetable for annual reductions in the global total. Then, not only will it be the case that every emission produced by one source is an emission that may not be produced by another, but some of the emissions permitted in a given year will have to be foregone by everybody in the subsequent year. The annual total would have to be reduced in order to prevent expansion of the accumulated concentration in the atmosphere. The relation between the annual emissions and the atmospheric concentration is just like the relation between the budget deficit and the national debt (and will, heaven help us, take similar leadership and courage to be dealt with). The national debt continues to *rise* even in years in which the budget deficit is *reduced* because even a reduced deficit adds to the total debt; its being reduced merely means that it does not add as much as it otherwise would have added. Reduced annual carbon emissions similarly continue to add to the atmospheric concentration as long as the annual emissions exceed the earth's capacity to recycle them before they reach the atmosphere; therefore, we can reduce total global emissions and still continue to expand the atmospheric concentration (but less rapidly than before) if we do not reduce emissions to a sustainable level.

Moreover, even if we were to reduce current emissions to a sustainable level (comparable to a balanced budget), that would still do nothing to *reduce* the atmospheric concentration (comparable to the national debt). The national debt does not go away simply because one balances some or all annual budgets; neither does the atmospheric concentration.[26] Worse, the longer one waits to attain annual balance, the higher the level at which the national debt/atmospheric concentration stabilizes. Global warming is caused, not directly by the level of annual emissions, but by the level of the atmospheric concentration. Stabilization at, for example, a doubled concentration of carbon dioxide can be expected to mean warmer temperatures (worse hurricanes and the rest) for a long time. Worse still, the longer our "leaders" wait to deal with the problem, (1) the greater the concentration of greenhouse gases in the atmosphere will be (since it is now ballooning every year because the annual total every year is greater than the sustainable amount) and (2) the larger the human population—the "emitters"—will be (population too will stabilize at a higher absolute number the longer it takes to stabilize it).

In spite of what I have just noted, in order to keep the assumptions of my argument as weak as possible, I will appeal merely to the fact that total tolerable emissions will, if ever we get organized to deal with global warming, be zero-sum. This alone will already produce extraordinary stringency, unprecedented except possibly during wartime. If, as I have noted in the last few paragraphs, we must in fact have a total that is a shrinking zero-sum, the stringency will, I fear, be more than humans can bear. On the assumption that the shape of the problem, although not its urgency, is the same with a simple zero-sum as with a shrinking zero-sum, I will appeal in subsequent argument here only to the former.

Now, whatever may be the case in general about whether every human being is entitled to an equal minimum share of all necessities for life, I submit that every human being is definitely entitled to an equal minimum share of an essential zero-sum capacity like carbon emissions, and all the more so if the capacity was made essential for the powerless by decisions by the powerful.

Consider again the difference between what makes carbon emissions essential—what makes them a necessity of life—and what makes them zero-sum. Carbon emissions are currently *essential* because those who control energy policy have failed to fund the research and development of sources of energy alternative to fossil-fuel (that are safe, affordable, and so forth).[27] The day may come when the bulk of carbon emissions become thoroughly unnecessary through the availability of safe, affordable alternatives, but this is certainly out of the hands of the poor people of the Third World. We in the countries that dominate the global energy regime present them with a world in which one can live above medieval subsistence standards only by means of carbon emissions. Carbon emissions must become *zero-sum* because the surface temperature of the planet will rise with effects harmful to human beings unless the concentration of greenhouse gases, especially carbon dioxide, is (1) stabilized at (2) a level that is not too much higher than preindustrial levels (obviously no one is claiming to know exactly where this level is).

There is a sense in which both characteristics, the necessity and the zero-sum character, would be the result of human choice. Carbon emissions will not be zero-sum unless (and until) a decision is made by the international community to specify and enforce a global cap. Yet it is seriously misleading, I think, to stress the extent of choice about making emissions zero-sum. If the international consensus of scientists is correct, we have no choice, in the usual sense of that phrase, that is, we have no good alternative. We could go ahead and allow carbon emissions to continue to compound decade after decade as we have in fact done since the beginning of the Industrial Revolution, although faster still as the billions in the Third World industrialize using fossil-fuel, and just let the temperature rise (the hurricanes intensify, the sea-level rise, and so forth), attempting to cope with the effects directly and efficiently after they occur rather than attempting to prevent or at least reduce them before we are certain of their nature or extent. Such a wait-and-see approach has its advocates among economists.[28]

This is not the place for a full-scale discussion of adaptation versus mitigation. Simply in summary, I believe that the strategy that counsels wait-and-see what happens and then adapt to it, using all the wealth we will by then have accumulated by not having been earlier panicked into premature and wasteful mitigation strategies, fails to give sufficient weight to, among other things, (1) the vulnerability of the poorest to even small "temporary" changes in food supplies, (2) the slowness with which agriculture can adapt to climate change (not only temperature itself, but length of season, amount of rainfall, timing of rainfall, evaporation rates, etc.), and (3) the extinction of species of plants and animals that could not adapt rapidly enough.[29] It might be that wealthy people could, at great expense, adapt rapidly enough after changes in climate had occurred, but poor people and many species of plants and animals could not. Consequently, I would judge the *zero-sum* character of future carbon emissions to be basically the *unavoidable* response to the facts about complex natural mechanisms that humans are unable fundamentally to modify.[30]

Carbon emissions are essential, by contrast to zero-sum, only as long as we choose to rely heavily on fossil-fuels. Indeed, if gasoline for automobiles were priced to internalize the phenomenal environmental and health effects of combustion-engine driven transportation, solar energy would instantly become overwhelmingly competitive in the market. Problems, like what to do about batteries for electric cars that could be recharged by the sun but that would not power cars for trips as long as we sometimes like to take, would be solved in profitable ways in a flash if gasoline and gasoline-powered car prices reflected even a small fraction of the environmental destruction they are wreaking. An adequate gas tax could have revolutionary technological effects. Consequently, I would judge the *essential* character of future carbon emissions to be an easily *avoidable* social choice resulting from vested economic interests in fossil-fuels and combustion engines and from political failure to have the courage to confront the interests and to have the imagination to construct the alternatives.

Further, it is only because we chose to travel behind combustion engines and to generate so much of our electricity with coal, oil, and gas that carbon emissions must be capped and become zero-sum. If total demand for carbon emissions fell well below the recyclable level because so much of our activity was powered by other energy sources, usage would probably no longer be zero-sum either. That is, if they stopped being essential, they would probably soon stop being zero-sum as well because demand would fall so far below any cap that would have needed to be enforced.

The significance of the discussion of the essential and therefore zero-sum character of carbon emissions is this: it is technological choices by the rich and powerful, most notably the choice to remain dependent upon fossil-fuels, that makes carbon emissions a zero-sum matter. It is of course a natural fact that atmospheric concentrations beyond a certain level will produce rises in surface temperature of a certain number of degrees (and, I have suggested without full argument, that the resulting effects could be successfully adapted to only by people with levels of wealth most people are unlikely to command at the time). This fact has human significance, however, only because we, with the ability to influence energy policy, make carbon emissions essential to life by choosing not to pursue alternative energy sources aggressively. Therefore, carbon emissions will become zero-sum if we choose to resist unlimited global warming, but they will become zero-sum only because (and as long as) we choose to rely upon fossil-fuel. If, on top of all this, we ourselves used up so much of the allowable total of carbon emissions that the poor of the world did not have available the minimum amount needed for a decent life, we would have (1) created a politico-economic system in which carbon emissions were zero-sum and then (2) used so much of the total that there was not enough left for the survival of others. We would, in other words, first have created the scarcity and then consumed so much that even minimal amounts did not remain for others. That would be truly unconscionable, and it is precisely what we are doing. We, with influence over energy policy, have made a world in which everyone can survive only if each restricts himself or herself to a fair share of something we have allowed to become essential to life, carbon emissions, and now we are proceeding to consume vastly more than our share, leaving grossly inadequate amounts for others.

SHRINKING OUR ECONOMY?

Presidents of the United States tend to propose solving our problems by "growing" our economy. The problem of global warming cannot be solved by "growing" any economy fueled by fossil-fuels, unless some now unforeseen technology for recapturing the carbon is created and made economically feasible very rapidly. Carbon emissions must be reduced; the only way to do that is to use less carbon-based fuel, as long as there is no recapture technology in place. The only way to do that, as long as the economy is overwhelmingly dependent upon fossil-fuels, is to shrink the economy. As long as fossil-fuels are essential, choosing to resist global warming means their usage becomes zero-sum. If we are not to deprive the poor and powerless of the planet of an essential of life (carbon emissions) by using vastly more than our share of it, we ought to reduce our usage enough to shrink it to our share of the constricted total for the globe. This means shrinking our energy usage, and thereby our economy, vastly. These are the required reductions in the living standards of the rich to which I referred earlier.

No way! Right or wrong, we will not do it! No U.S. president is likely to suggest it. If a President were politically foolhardy enough to suggest shrinking the economy, the U.S. populace would drive him or her out of office, even if he or she could correctly say that the number of jobs would not shrink. We will disrupt the climate for everyone before we will willingly accept a lower standard of living for ourselves. Fairness to "foreigners" simply does not today move enough people to sacrifice their own interest. I would guess that few would deny this judgment about the practical persuasiveness of the kind of argument I have given, its theoretical merits aside. Explaining the roots of the unshakable attachment to "economic progress" would be much more challenging. Perhaps the ideology of modernity that structures the thought of our era contains so deep a commit-ment to endless economic growth that attempts to challenge the growth automatically disqualify the challenger from being taken seriously.[31] No one in the mainstream advocates limits to growth because as soon as someone advocates them, he or she is no longer in the mainstream; only Thoreauvian cranks think that we should not "grow" the economy. One could hope that arguments about the difference between standard of living and quality of life, which I have left aside, can have some bite here, but I am not optimistic.

What then? I leave aside recapture technology, which would allow us to continue our love affair with gas and oil but reduce the carbon emissions anyway by extracting them before they are released into the air. Journalistic accounts report some research underway, mostly in Japan, but I do not know of any reason to be hopeful that such a technology will in fact be developed soon enough to keep atmospheric concentrations from becoming high enough to cause temperature rises at surface level. Recap-ture aside, we have three options: (1) go ahead and produce global warming, thereby avoiding any decision to make carbon emissions zero-sum; (2) reduce our economic activity and standard of living, thereby living within our fair share of a zero-sum emissions total; or (3) develop non-carbon-based energy sources, thereby making carbon emissions nonessential and making any zero-sum total set to resist global warming irrelevant to most people's lives, thereby defusing this issue of fairness. I believe the first option is dangerous and irresponsible toward future generations, although I have not tried to argue for that here but have simply assumed it, along with most of the scientists who study the phenomena and their likely social effects. I believe the second option is politically and psychologically impossible; I have not argued for this either, but I think that, however much I wish otherwise, an examination of the ideology of our time would support my political pessimism.

That leaves the third option as the only practical hope. If gas and oil were taxed heavily enough to incorporate the costs of their harmful effects, solar technology would immediately be competitive.[32] Other non-carbon-based energy technologies should be vigorously researched as well. Economic growth could continue, undisturbed by concern about carbon. Even so, this option means taking on the oil companies and the automobile companies, and millions of affluent consumers, who have given a new meaning to "autocracy" (or could quiet, electric-powered vehicles somehow still give the sense of power now derived from roaring combusion engines?) Is this too politically and psychologically impossible? If so, we rich, and our children, and their children, appear to be headed for a destabilized climate; the children of the poor seem headed for "temporary" disruptions in food supplies. If even narrow political change concentrated upon the energy regime is impossible, climate change is likely, hastened and exacerbated by extreme unfairness.[33]

NOTES

1. See J. T. Houghton, G. J. Jenkins and J. J. Ephraums, eds., *Climate Change: The IPCC Scientific Assessment* (New York: Cambridge University Press for the Intergovernmental Panel on Climate Change [WMO/UNEP], 1990); the brief "Policymakers' Summary" is also avail-

able in a separate and more colorful form as *Scientific Assessment of Climate Change: The Policymakers' Summary of the Report of Working Group I to the Intergovernmental Panel on Climate Change* (Geneva: Intergovernmental Panel on Climate Change [WMO/UNEP], 1990). Also see J. T. Houghton, B. A. Callander and S. K. Varney, eds., *Climate Change 1992: The Supplementary Report to the IPCC Scientific Assessment* (New York: Cambridge University Press for the Intergovernmental Panel on Climate Change, 1992).

2. Henry Shue, "Subsistence Emissions and Luxury Emissions," *Law & Policy* 15:1 (January 1993): 40. The heart of this analysis has also appeared as Henry Shue, "Four Questions of Justice," in *Agricultural Dimensions of Global Climate Change,* ed. Harry Kaiser and Thomas Drennen (Delray Beach, Fla.: St. Lucie Press, 1993), 214–28.

3. I have already attempted to show that the answer to question (4A) has strong implications for the answer to question (1)—see Henry Shue, "After You: May Action by the Rich Be Contingent Upon Action by the Poor?" *Indiana Journal of Global Legal Studies* 1:2 (1994): 343–366—and am beginning to consider question (4B)—see "Environmental Change and the Varieties of Justice," a paper prepared for a conference on "Global Environmental Change and Social Justice," Peace Studies Program, Cornell University, photocopy. In addition, I have argued that the answers to questions (1) and (2) are mutually dependent—see Henry Shue, "The Unavoidability of Justice," in *The International Politics of the Environment,* ed. Andrew Hurrell and Benedict Kingsbury (New York: Oxford University Press, 1992), chap. 14.

4. John Rawls, *A Theory of Justice* (Cambridge: Belknap Press of Harvard University Press, 1971). Obviously too important to be taken up here is the question of the nature and the significance of the methodological differences displayed by John Rawls, *Political Liberalism,* The John Dewey Essays in Philosophy, 4 (New York: Columbia University Press, 1993). The methodology of Rawls's later work is the subject of Frank I. Michelman, "On Regulating Practices with Theories Drawn from Them: A Case of Justice as Fairness," this volume.

5. Rawls, *A Theory of Justice,* 196, 197.

6. Rawls, *A Theory of Justice,* 197. It is the reasoning that would be done in the constitutional convention that is the primary focus of Michelman, "On Regulating Practices with Theories Drawn from Them," this volume.

7. Rawls, *A Theory of Justice,* 199.

8. A perceptive early critique of the sharp split between two clusters of primary goods is Norman Daniels, "Equal Liberty and Unequal Worth of Liberty," in *Reading Rawls: Critical Studies on Rawls' 'A Theory*

of Justice', ed. with a new Preface by Norman Daniels, Stanford Series in Philosophy (Stanford, Calif.: Stanford University Press, 1989), 253–81. For a later more comprehensive argument see Thomas W. Pogge, *Realizing Rawls* (Ithaca, N.Y.: Cornell University Press, 1989), 109–60.

9. Rawls, *A Theory of Justice*, 246.

10. Rawls, *A Theory of Justice*, 244–45.

11. See Cynthia Rosenzweig and Martin L. Parry, "Potential Impacts of Climate Change on World Food Supply: A Summary of a Recent International Study," in *Agricultural Dimensions of Global Climate Change*, ed. Harry Kaiser and Thomas E. Drennen (Delray Beach, Fla.: St. Lucie Press, 1993), 87–116; and, for fuller detail, C. M. Rosenzweig, *et al.*, *Climate Change and World Food Supply* (Oxford: Environmental Change Unit, 1993). Temperature changes are expected to be least at the equator and greater as one moves toward the poles. It is often speculated that, therefore, people in the tropics will suffer least. Rosenzweig and Parry indicate that this is completely unfounded and that the impoverished residents of the tropics, who live closest to the margin, will probably suffer most. On the significance of the study, which was funded by the EPA, see "Warming Will Hurt Poor Nations Most," *Science News* 142:8 (22 August 1992): 116. Also see M. Lal, ed., *Global Warming: Concern for Tomorrow* (New Delhi: Tata McGraw–Hill, 1993).

12. Or that a significant rise would not unleash a precipitous fall in temperatures—precedents for sharp reversals have now been documented. See Greenland Ice-core Project (GRIP) Members, "Climate Instability during the Last Interglacial Period Recorded in the GRIP Ice Core," *Nature* 364 (15 July 1993): 203–7. These scientists warn that the stability of climate during the years of human civilization so far is extraordinary: "Given the history of the last 150 kyr, the past 8 kyr has been strangely stable" (207). They also note that "mode switches" from warming to cooling "may be completed in as little as 1–2 decades and can become latched for anything between 70 yr and 5 kyr" (207). The science correspondent for the *New York Times* observed: "The data are likely to bolster concern that future changes in climate might not be spread over many centuries, allowing farmers to adjust to altered growing conditions and coastal cities to deal with rising sea levels, for example"—see Walter Sullivan, "Study of Greenland Ice Finds Rapid Change in Past Climate," *New York Times* (15 July 1993): A1 and B9.

13. Martin I. Hoffert, "Climate Sensitivity, Climate Feedbacks and Policy Implications," in *Confronting Climate Change: Risks, Implications and Responses*, ed. Irving M. Mintzer (New York: Cambridge University Press for Stockholm Environment Institute, 1992), 42.

14. Obviously, I am speaking in general terms about very compli-

cated matters. For example, in 1980 the United States ranked eleventh in the world in GNP per capita (at $11,360) but was second only to Canada in 1979 energy consumption per capita (at 308 MBtu), while Switzerland ranked third (behind only the United Arab Emirates and Kuwait, which just sit and rake in monopoly profits on oil) in GNP per capita (at $16,440) with energy consumption of only 128 MBtu per capita—Duane Chapman, *Energy Resources and Energy Corporations* (Ithaca, N.Y.: Cornell University Press, 1983), 281, Table 14–1.

15. Alliance to Save Energy, *et al.*, *America's Energy Choices: Investing in a Strong Economy and a Clean Environment* (Cambridge, Mass.: Union of Concerned Scientists, 1991), 2.

16. Other things that might not be equal are the answers to the other questions, about the costs of prevention as such and the costs of mitigation as such. I, in fact, think that *all* the answers to *all* the questions line up in the same direction, but the arguments have to be made one at a time—see my other essays on this subject cited above. I hope to bring all these arguments together under the working title, *Compound Injustice*.

17. The opposite, more efficient strategy is: make the lowest cost reductions in emissions first, irrespective of whose emissions they are. The now-popular strategy of "joint implementation" is claimed by some proponents to combine fairness and efficiency by making lower-cost reductions in emissions in poor countries (for efficiency) and having them paid for by rich countries (for fairness) with funds that would otherwise have produced smaller, more expensive reductions in their own emissions. This strategy is in danger, however, of freezing international inequalities in standards of living into place. I believe it is essential to take into account the human function of the activities that produce the emissions—see Shue, "Subsistence Emissions and Luxury Emissions," 54–58; and Onno Kuik, Paul Peters, and Nico Schrijver, eds., *Joint Implementation to Curb Climate Change* (Boston: Kluwer Academic Publishers, 1994).

18. Thomas E. Drennen, "Economic Development and Climate Change: Analyzing the International Response" (Ph.D. diss., Cornell University, 1993), 142 (Table 6.5).

19. Drennen, "Economic Development and Climate Change," 8.

20. Anil Agarwal and Sunita Narain, *Global Warming in an Unequal World: A Case of Environmental Colonialism* (New Delhi: Centre for Science and Environment, 1991), 18. This publication often appears in bibliographies as an example of "egalitarianism," but neither its empirical calculations nor its ethical theses are often examined. Also see Gilberto C. Gallopin, *et al.*, "Global Impoverishment, Sustainable De-

velopment and the Environment," *International Social Science Journal* 121 (1989): 375–97; Alvaro Soto, "The Global Environment: A Southern Perspective," *International Journal* 47 (Autumn 1992): 679–705; and J. K. Parikh, "IPCC Strategies Unfair to the South," *Nature* 360 (December 1992): 507–8.

21. Drennen, *Economic Development and Climate Change,* ch. 4, "The Role of Biological Emissions"; an earlier version appeared as Thomas E. Drennen and Duane Chapman, "Negotiating a Response to Climate Change: The Role of Biological Emissions," *Contemporary Policy Issues* 10:3 (July 1992): 49–58.

22. I have argued for a slightly different position from Drennen's in Shue, "Subsistence Emissions and Luxury Emissions," 54–58.

23. Michael Walzer has argued eloquently for the diversity of goods and the diversity of distributive arrangements in *Spheres of Justice: A Defense of Pluralism and Equality* (New York: Basic Books, 1983). I believe that the diversity across goods is clearer than the diversity across societies for the same good.

24. It is noteworthy that Rawls now explicitly acknowledges fundamental economic rights—see John Rawls, "The Law of Peoples," in *On Human Rights,* ed. Stephen Shute and Susan Hurley (New York: Basic Books, 1993), 62.

25. J. T. Houghton, *et al.,* eds., *Climate Change: The IPCC Scientific Assessment,* xviii, table 2.

26. There is the qualification that the atmospheric residence time of every gas is finite, so that gradual natural diminutions occur. However, the atmospheric residence time of CO_2 is on the order of a century so the real value of the national debt may well be reduced by inflation faster than the accumulation of CO_2 will be reduced by natural attrition.

27. Even conservative business groups now realize that the neglect of research and development on alternative energy has been excessive: "CED believes that federal support for renewable energy R&D should be given a higher priority than it was during the 1980s"—Committee for Economic Development, Research and Policy Committee, *What Price Clean Air? A Market Approach to Energy and Environmental Policy* (New York: Committee for Economic Development, 1993), 80–81.

28. See Wilfred Beckerman, "Global Warming and International Action: An Economic Perspective," in Hurrell and Kingsbury, ch. 10.

29. On the food supplies, see Rosenzweig and Parry, "Potential Impacts of Climate Change on World Food Supply," in Kaiser and Drennen.

30. If, contrary to what I have just argued, this were a relatively

unconstrained social choice, my argument that the powerless are at the mercy of discretionary choices by the powerful would be doubly strong.

31. A sophisticated explanation along these lines is currently being worked out by Chris Reus-Smit; see his paper, "The Normative Structure of International Society and the Justice of International Environmental Accords," prepared for a conference on "Global Environmental Change and Social Justice," Peace Studies Program, Cornell University, photocopy.

32. The most positive recent development is a "conceptual breakthrough" in solar technology made at the University of New South Wales—Matthew L. Wald, "New Design Could Make Solar Cells Competitive," *New York Times*, 14 June 1994, C9.

33. While this volume has been in press, a highly accessible account of the scientific issues, written for laypersons, has been published by the chairman of the Science Working group of the IPCC. See John Houghton, *Global Warming: The Complete Briefing* (Elgin, Ill.: Lion Publishing, 1994).

PART IV

THEORY AND PRACTICE IN THE LAW

9

ON LEGAL THEORY
AND LEGAL PRACTICE

CASS R. SUNSTEIN

Law is a normative enterprise; it is inevitably philosophical. For this reason, the distinction between legal theory and legal practice is at most one of degree. Certainly it can be shown that much legal practice takes theoretical issues for granted, but this does not mean that it is not pervaded by theoretical claims. On the other hand, there are real hazards for lawyers who use political philosophy to inform legal practice, especially when the philosophy is designed for a first-best world, or when it rests on assumptions that do not hold for us. Moreover, legal practice might seek to bracket philosophical questions, in order to facilitate change over time, to allow an incompletely theorized agreement on particular outcomes among people who disagree on first principles, and to avoid various forms of hubris.

These will be my basic claims in this essay. In part 1, I briefly support the view that even mundane claims about the content of law have large-scale theoretical components. In part 2, I discuss some of the problems that arise when lawyers rely on what philosophers think. In part 3, I explain why a system of legal practice might limit its philosophical ambitions, in the process contrasting an antitheoretical, highly practical judge— Justice John Marshall Harlan—with Ronald Dworkin's Hercules. An important point here is that people who diverge sharply on large principles might well be able to agree on specific cases. This point helps explain why in a heterogeneous society, a normative practice, including law, might seek to bracket philosophical questions, and do so successfully.

I. How Law Is Philosophical

All descriptive claims about the content of law depend in some important way on ideas about the right, the good, or both. When we read Supreme Court opinions or appellate briefs, or if we listen to how lawyers discuss their cases, we find many claims about liberty, rights, equality, and justice. For example, the Constitution says that no state shall deprive any person of the equal protection of the laws. What does this mean? How do we even go about knowing what it means? Suppose that a state discriminates against homosexuals, fails to provide welfare benefits, creates an affirmative action program, or stops people under eighteen from voting. Has there been a constitutional violation?

Begin with the text. Very rapidly it becomes clear that the word "equal" has multiple meanings. The term could be a prohibition on irrational differentiation; it could guarantee minimally decent conditions for all; it could forbid caste systems; it could require a legitimate public purpose for all laws; it could forbid large disparities in wealth. Because of the multiplicity of textually plausible readings, we will be forced to resort to something supplemental to text in order to bring it to bear on disputed cases. Unless we can get help elsewhere, it will be necessary to make some substantive judgment about the appropriate conception of equal protection under the Constitution.

We might then try another route. We might ask some questions about the understanding of the people who wrote the provision. Suppose that they intended to prohibit all discrimination against blacks but to do nothing else. (Let us put to one side the many complexities in the notion of an "intention" or an "understanding" of a collective decision-making body.) Then it becomes necessary to ask whether this intention is binding. How will we resolve this question? Without circularity we cannot say that the intention is binding because the framers intended it to be binding. Before long, we will have to say something about democracy, majoritarianism, rights, and much else. Here too, large-scale theoretical claims seem unavoidable.

We might turn then to the judicial precedents, at least if we have some. The first question is: On what principle of equality are those precedents based? But this question will not be easy to answer. Suppose, for example, that the Court has forbidden school segregation. How does this precedent bear on affirmative action or substandard welfare benefits? To decide, we will have to choose how to characterize the precedents, and to do that, we will have to say something substantive about the appropriate equality principle. Precedents are not brute facts. And if the precedents are genuinely helpful, we have to ask whether they should be binding. And to answer that question, we will have to discuss the need for stability in law, the possibility of mistake, the potential for democratic correction, and so forth.

I think that this example shows the extent to which people engaging in the practice of law must make theoretical claims. The line between legal practice and legal theory is blurry. The point is not limited to the sometimes exotic area of constitutional law. Suppose, for example, that someone claims that he need not comply with his contractual obligation to sell one thousand barrels of widgets for one hundred dollars, because the price of widgets has risen so unexpectedly in the past week as a result of a strike in the widget factory. A legal system must answer this question by reference to something—and that something must be a conception of autonomy, or utility, or efficiency, or welfare, or something else. Even mundane areas of the law of contracts are thus pervaded by theoretical claims about the reasons for social obligations. The familiar notion of "party autonomy" hardly makes such claims unnecessary; it is merely a resort to a certain kind of theoretical claim.

Much the same is true of tort law, which has to decide on appropriate spheres of human action. Judgments about causation are of course rooted in theories of moral responsibility. Nor can judges say whether there is an act or an omission—a relevant distinction in many areas of the law—without positing a morally privileged state of affairs. To do that, we will have to discuss theoretical questions. Similar things can be said about criminal law, which is pervaded by issues of intention, fault, and responsibility; these issues cannot be approached without theoretical claims.

It is sometimes thought that those engaged in law may often bracket such claims and that they must speculate on abstract matters only on issues at the frontiers of the law, when existing legal materials are not decisive. Such "frontiers" cases, it is said, are rare. But even the easiest cases present theoretical issues. Jones is said to have violated the law fixing a speed limit of fifty miles per hour. Perhaps Jones was trying to get to the hospital; perhaps he was late for work; perhaps his mind wandered. In any of these cases, should the judge convict Jones? If the answer is yes, it is for reasons that have to do with, among other things, the appropriate role of judges in a democracy, and this is a substantive view that should be defended even if now uncontroversial. Easy cases can claim to be easy only on the basis of reasons.

These ideas do not need to be belabored. Much of the change in legal education in the last decades has stemmed from work by economists, philosophers, and others who have shown that many of the conventional legal categories—even conventional conceptions of how to describe "the facts"—turn out to depend on philosophical claims, and often on controversial ones. In this sense, legal practice has inescapable theoretical dimensions.

It may well be unfortunate if those who practice law are not self-conscious about this fact. Sometimes the claims that underlie law are taken as self-evident—as in the view that an abortion is an act rather than an omission, or that the meaning of a text is determined by investigating the views of its drafters, or that emotion and reason are at opposite poles, or that democracy and majoritarianism are the same thing, or that there is sharp distinction between "words" and "conduct." Such claims depend on complex theoretical judgments that ought to be brought into the open and evaluated as such.

II. How Lawyers Misuse Philosophy
and Philosophers

None of this necessarily means that lawyers should turn to philosophy or to great philosophers for the answers to their questions. There are several characteristic risks with efforts of this sort. First, lawyers may misunderstand philosophers (as they sometimes misunderstand economists). Here as elsewhere, a little knowledge may be a dangerous thing. Second, and more interestingly, lawyers may fail to understand the difficulties in bringing philosophical arguments to bear on concrete legal disputes. The application may seem mechanical, but it usually requires an act of translation, and one that involves a large element of construction. Suppose that we seek to be good Lockeans, and that we want to know how to deal with the question whether government should forbid private race discrimination. When a private employer refuses to hire blacks, the employer has not committed any act of conventional force or fraud. Does this mean that Locke is opposed to the Civil Rights Act of 1964? It should be obvious that there is no purely factual answer to this question. Instead, lawyers will be forced not to try to uncover some fact, but to offer the best constructive interpretation of Locke, recognizing that the relevant interpretation is neither pure discovery nor pure invention. The Lockean who approves or disapproves of Civil Rights Acts is hardly the historical Locke. Even when a philosopher makes explicit claims about a topic, the application can be far from clear. The Lockean proviso about the need to leave "enough and as good for others" cannot realistically be said to decide questions about welfare entitlements.

There is a third problem, having to do with the need for legal solutions to operate in a world with distinctive limitations. Let us suppose, for example, that philosophers have persuasively shown that wealth maximization is a philosophically indefensible ideal, and that a just state should be concerned instead with utility, with human flourishing, or with protection of a category of basic rights. It might be clear, for example, that the maximization of wealth is too crudely connected to anything that human beings do or should really care about. Have we therefore shown that lawyers should reject the pursuit of wealth maximization through the law of contract and tort? Not necessarily. It may be that wealth maximization is the approach to contract and tort law that best combines the virtues of substantive plausibility and real-world administrability. Even if wealth maximization is not in the end a good approach to justice, it might be shown that greater social wealth is at least roughly connected with the achievement of important human values. And if those other values cannot easily be promoted by common law courts—consider utility—perhaps wealth maximization is not so bad after all.[1] In any case the philosophical defects with wealth maximization, even if they run deep, may not be decisive for law.

The example is not exotic. Some philosophers think that a free speech principle that places a special premium on political discussion is extremely attractive.[2] But perhaps this approach would be too readily subject to abuse in the real world. Perhaps any institutional judgments about the category of what counts as "the political" would be too biased and unreliable to be acceptable. For good institutional reasons, we might adopt a free speech principle of a philosophically inadequate sort, simply because that inadequate approach is the only one that we can safely administer.

To take another example: Some philosophers believe that emotions have important cognitive dimensions, or that they are a form of cognition, and indeed it seems clear that various emotions—grief, hate, love—are based on judgments of value.[3] But a democratic society might still decide that emotions are so likely to be partisan or parochial, or to go wrong in some predictable way, that they should be excluded from certain areas of law. The exclusion might be based not on a philosophical mistake about the distinction between reason and emotion, but instead on an awareness of institutional limits faced by human beings in certain situations.

One final example: Suppose that we wanted to ensure that confessions are made under circumstances in which they are truly voluntary. Suppose that we can generate a philosophically adequate account of voluntariness, and that with respect to that account, some confessions that come after the *Miranda* warnings are involuntary, while some confessions that are given without those warnings turn out to be voluntary. The *Miranda* rules, in short, turn out to be both overprotective and underprotective with reference to the best philosophical understanding of voluntariness. Do we have a sufficient reason to abandon *Miranda*?

Surely not. The *Miranda* approach may be the best means of combining real-world administrability with substantive plausibility. If so, it may be more than good enough despite its philosophical inadequacy. The phenomenon of philosophically inadequate but nonetheless justified legal strategies seems to be a pervasive part of a well-functioning system of law.

This leads to a final point, having to do with the complex connection between theories of the good or the right on the one hand and concrete legal disputes on the other. Perhaps the point emerges most simply by thinking about works of literature that seem to have political components. Dickens and James are obvious examples. It would be obtuse to ask whether Dickens favors worker ownership of plants, or whether James believes that any real revolution must occur quickly or instead in short steps. The problem is not that the works of Dickens and James do not bear on these issues. It is that Dickens and James may greatly deepen understanding of capitalism or of the revolutionary sensibility without at the same time telling us about what sorts of legal reforms and approaches make sense.

Some of these same things may also be true of Hobbes, Locke, Rousseau, or Rawls and Raz. The relationship between any philosophical account of (say) justice and liberty need not lead to any particular specification of outcomes in disputed cases in law. We may believe, with Raz, that human values are not commensurable[4] without having endorsed a position about prostitution and surrogacy, about the appropriate remedy for natural resource damages, or about the relationship between specific performance and monetary damages in tort cases. Of course, views about commensurability may influence these debates. But the philosophical claims cannot be decisive, because there is much else of which real-world institutions must take account. We may think, with Rawls, that the difference principle is required by good thinking about justice, without believing that the Constitution mandates that principle, or even that the United States Congress should pursue that principle in light of the multiple constraints that it faces. In this way philosophical commitments may inform understandings about law without leading to particular judgments about legal disputes.

III. PHILOSOPHY VS. LAW? OF HARLAN
AND HERCULES

Legal positivists sometimes think that law has nothing to do with philosophy, at least in the quiet narrow sense that the legal enterprise can often operate without offering any philosophical or theoretical claims at all.[5] In this way, positivists believe that legal practice and legal theory can be sharply distinguished. As against the positivists, Ronald Dworkin famously argues that there is an inevitable evaluative or normative dimension to statements about what the law is.[6] Often, at least, one cannot say "what the law is" without also saying something about "what the law should be." That is, when lawyers disagree about what the law is with respect to some question—can the government ban hate speech? cross-burning?—they are disagreeing about "the best constructive interpretation of the community's legal practice."[7] Thus Dworkin argues that interpretation in law consists of different efforts to make a governing text "the best it can be." This is Dworkin's conception of law as integrity.

Hercules, Dworkin's infinitely patient and resourceful judge, approaches the law in this way. Here we have an interesting view of the relationship between legal theory and legal practice. Is Hercules a theorist or a practioner? The answer is that he is neither and both. Hercules is a practitioner insofar as he takes legal practice—in the form of the existing legal materials—very seriously indeed. People's legal rights may well be different from the rights that would be yielded by the best abstract theory. Dworkin thus places a large emphasis on "fit" with existing materials as a criterion for correctness of legal outcomes. The lawyerly virtue of integrity is connected with achievement of principled consistency among similar and dissimilar cases; principled consistency may generate outcomes that diverge from what justice requires if it is understood as an independent ideal. Thus justice and integrity are not the same thing. On the other hand, Hercules is a theorist too. To know what the law is, the judge has to cast the existing materials in their best light, and to do this, the judge must often (and perhaps always) take a stand on some large theoretical questions.

We might compare Hercules' conception of the judicial role

with the search for reflective equilibrium in politics and ethics.[8] Much of practical reasoning, in law and elsewhere, entails an effort to produce general theories by close engagement with considered judgments about particular cases. Those judgments may serve as provisional "fixed points" for inquiry, in the sense that we have a high degree of confidence in them and cannot readily imagine that they could be shaken. In searching for reflective equilibrium, what we think tentatively to be the general theory is adjusted to conform to what we think to be our considered views about particular cases. The particular views are adjusted to conform to the general theory and vice versa.

There is a close relationship between the search for reflective equilibrium and Hercules' approach to law. Hercules also attempts to go back and forth between particular judgments—reflected in judicial holdings—and the various theories that account for them. The general theory is adjusted to conform to the holdings. This search for an equilibrium between "fit" and "justification" might be understood to be the practical lawyer's analogue to this conception of the philosopher's project.

Here we have a distinctive picture of the relationship between practice and theory in law. The picture helps show how the lawyer's task is both similar to and importantly different from that of the philosopher. It is also true that a statement describing the law is not a statement about some "plain fact"; when it comes to interpretation, there is often a large evaluative dimension to positions about what the law is.[9] Often the disagreement really rests on what approach makes for the best system of law—which is not the same as saying that it rests on an independent judgment about the best theory.

Many lawyers, however, wonder whether Dworkin fully describes how lawyers think, and their puzzlement says something important about the relationship between theory and practice in law. A serious problem has to do with the practice of analogical reasoning, which lies at the heart of how lawyers (and many ordinary people) proceed. In Dworkin's hands, theories are produced in the large, on the basis of fairly abstract moral theory (so long as the judge respects the duty to fit the cases). These theories are then brought to bear on particular problems. Consider, for example, Dworkin's description of how judges should think about free speech law.[10] Dworkin begins with a noninstrumental, "constitutive" conception of free speech, in accordance with which speech is protected because of the need to respect the moral autonomy of the citizenry. On Dworkin's view, moral autonomy is insulted whenever government attempts to prevent people from hearing things that they find persuasive.[11] Dworkin brings this idea to bear on the area of libel; he concludes that the Constitution imposes firm barriers against liability for public or private libel. Or consider the area of race discrimination. On Dworkin's account, the judge must ask: Does the legal prohibition on race discrimination reflect a category of suspect classifications stemming from a general right to be treated as equals; or a right against the use of certain banned categories; or a right not to be subject to prejudice? Dworkin concludes that the third theory is best and that affirmative action is therefore constitutional.[12]

Dworkin emphasizes that in answering such questions, lawyers will not be pure philosophers. They do not simply develop the best theory from the standpoint of principle; they must offer their answers in a way that is attuned to the need for "fit" and to the courts' proper role. But this concession may be insufficient. In deciding whether, for example, a restriction on private libel offends the first amendment, lawyers usually do not ask which interpretation makes the amendment the best it can be. They do not begin or end with a high-level conception of the values promoted by the amendment. These are broad and abstract questions. They are too hard, large, and open-ended for legal actors to handle. They call for responses that are, in one sense, too deeply theorized.

We might think here about Justice John Marshall Harlan, a very different judge from Hercules. I cannot discuss Harlan's opinions in detail here, but let me offer a few observations. Harlan was an extraordinarily skilled but in many ways a highly conventional common lawyer.[13] Harlan's approach to law was at most intermittently theoretical. He avoided large claims. He was a great analogizer. He was closely attuned to connections among cases without attempting high-level theories about the right or the good. And here, I think, we can find a conception of legal practice that at least attempts to be divorced from legal theory.

That is, Harlan's writings show the possibility of a form of what we might call low-level normative practice, diverging from full-scale normative theory.

Harlan was an especially distinguished judge, but his approach to law is far from unfamiliar. In thinking about free speech issues, lawyers engaged in ordinary practice do not generate large-scale theories about the meaning of (for example) free expression in a democracy. Instead, they ask what particular sorts of practices clearly seem to violate the first amendment, or the principle of free expression, as these are understood through our practice. Then they ask whether a restriction on (for example) private libel is relevantly similar or relevantly different. The same is true of much judicial work in private law; it is also true of statutory construction, at least in difficult cases, where the issue is whether the case at hand resembles the cases at which the statute is unambiguously aimed. Of course, the description of relevant similarities and differences will have evaluative dimensions, and these should be made explicit. But lawyers and judges will not engage in anything like general moral theorizing. If a distinction between legal practice and legal theory is to be sustained, I think that this is the place to start. Everyday legal thinking proceeds without taking high-level stands on questions of the right or the good.

Is this project possible or worthwhile? From the standpoint of Dworkin's Hercules, we might respond in the following way. A judge who operates in this apparently conventional way might end up being Herculean, too. At least he had better have that aspiration in mind. When our modest judge—Harlan rather than Hercules—uses analogical reasoning to say that case *A* is like case *B*, he has to rely on a principle. If he is reasoning well, he will have before him a range of other cases, *C* through *Z*, in which the principle is tested against others and refined. At least if he is a distinguished judge, he will experience a kind of "conceptual ascent," in which the more or less isolated and low-level principle is finally made part of a general theory, or of reflective equilibrium. On this view, Harlan should be seen as someone who engages in a truncated form of what Hercules seeks to do, with the truncation starting at just the point when things start to become interesting or difficult. Little can be said

for something as modest and cautious as that. It might therefore be concluded that legal practice is simply a form of legal
theory without the requisite self-consciousness or ambition.

There is some truth in this response. Any claim that one case
is like another does depend on the implicit or explicit invocation
of a principle. We cannot tell whether a ban on private libel is
like a ban on commercial speech, or like a ban on attempted
bribery, without a principle enabling us to know what is similar
to what. The principle should of course be identified. Once we
know what it is, we might want to test the principle by seeing
how it coheres with all of the existing legal materials (or with a
theory independent of those materials). Thus far, then, Harlan
does not seem to be a worthy competitor to Hercules, but
merely a somewhat lazy imitator.

But this view is incomplete. We can identify a number of
distinct advantages to what I am describing as a form of practice
that is in important respects independent of theory. Each of
these advantages is especially important for people engaged in
legal reasoning.

First, this form of reasoning may be the best approach that is
available for people of limited time and capacities. The search
for reflective equilibrium, or for vertical and horizontal coherence, may be simply too difficult for participants in law (or for
others engaging in practical reasoning in an attempt to think
through difficult problems). Often there are too many real-
world constraints to work out a fully general theory. And when
compared with the search for reflective equilibrium, analogical
reasoning has the advantage, for ordinary lawyers and judges,
of humility and modesty. To engage in analogical reasoning,
one need not take a stand on large, contested issues of social
life, some of which can be resolved only on a sectarian basis. For
this reason, we might think that practical reasoning in law of the
sort I am now describing can claim to avoid the risk of hubris.

Second, reasoning by analogy may have the large advantage
of allowing a convergence on particular outcomes by people
unable to reach anything like an accord on general principles.
Sometimes it is exceedingly difficult to get people to agree on
the general principles that account for their judgments. But

sometimes it is possible to get them to agree on particular solutions or on low-level principles.[14] An incompletely theorized agreement[15] is often possible on the view that case *A* is relevantly similar to case *B*—even if those who join the agreement could not decide as between utilitarianism or Kantianism, or come to closure on the appropriate role of religion in society. This is especially important in a legal system, for people must be able to converge on particular judgments even if they disagree on matters of high principle. It might even be said that allowing this form of convergence is one of the most crucial tasks for a system of adjudication in a liberal democracy.

There are many examples inside and outside the law. Consider the enormous difficulties that would arise if any heterogeneous faculty attempted to set out the appropriate general principles by which to decide issues of faculty diversity. It is certainly possible that no such principles could command consensus, or indeed, that the effort to reach consensus would produce acrimonious and only mildly productive debate. But even such a faculty might well be able to agree on a wide range of particular appointments cases, with its agreement on outcomes supported by diverse (and incompletely debated) justifications. This example may serve as a metaphor for how legal arguments—and perhaps day-to-day normative practice—really work. People who could not reach agreement on high-level principles, or theorize about their judgments without collapsing into sectarianism, might nonetheless be able to engage in productive, low-level debates, and precisely because particular judgments can be supported by a range of diverse principles on which no stand need be taken. This is what happens with most disputes in both public and private law.

Third, analogical reasoning may be especially desirable in contexts in which we seek moral evolution over time. If the legal culture really did attain reflective equilibrium, it might become too rigid and calcified; we would know what we thought about everything, whether particular or general. By contrast, Harlan's method has the important advantage of allowing a large degree of openness to new facts and perspectives. It enables disagreement and uncertainty to turn into consensus. This is a large advantage of a form of day-to-day normative practice that is distinct from abstract and general normative theory.

Fourth, analogical reasoning in law operates with precedents that have the status of fixed points. This is so even for people who disagree with those precedents as a matter of principle. In searching for reflective equilibrium, by contrast, everything is revisable. (Here, there is a contrast as well between Dworkin's approach and the search for reflective equilibrium; because Hercules places a high premium on fit, it seems clear that he must take cases as given even if he would not agree with them in principle, though Dworkin is not entirely clear on this point.) The fact that precedents are fixed points helps to bring about an incompletely theorized convergence as well, by constraining the areas of reasonable disagreement. In this way, analogical reasoning introduces stability and predictability, which are important virtues for law.

There is a larger point here. Lawyers could not try to reach reflective equilibrium without severely compromising the system of precedent. The judgments at work in the search for reflective equilibrium are subject to critical scrutiny, and any of them might be discarded. The point helps explain Rawls's suggestion that "for the purposes of this book, the views of the reader and the author are the only ones that count. The opinions of others are used only to clear our own heads." [16]

In a legal system, precedents are far more than an effort "to clear our own heads." If a judge or a lawyer is to attempt to reach reflective equilibrium, precedents will have at most the status of considered judgments about particular cases, and these might be revised when they run into conflict with something else that he believes and that is general or particular. In the legal system, precedents have a much firmer status. To be sure, precedents are not immune to revision, but the principle of stare decisis ensures that they operate as relatively fixed points.

I conclude that the search for reflective equilibrium is a misleading description of law, and in some ways an unattractive prescription, for participants in a legal system aspiring to stability should not be so immodest as to reject judgments reached by others whenever those judgments could not be made part of reflective equilibrium for those particular participants. Of course, it is only a mixed blessing to have fixed points that may be wrong as a matter of principle. For this reason, observers of or participants in the legal system may be pushed in the direction of theoretical challenges to current legal materials. These challenges should hardly be disparaged; sometimes they prevail, and rightly so. But legal practice often operates with a kind of consensus on theoretical issues, a consensus in which people who diverge on large-scale issues can agree on how to approach particular controversies.

Now let us return to Hercules, who does not seek to achieve reflective equilibrium of the ordinary sort, acknowledging as he does that the existing legal materials must usually be accepted even if they seem wrong. Does Harlan have some advantages over Hercules? I think that he does. Insofar as Harlan avoids resort to large-scale theory, he not only avoids unrealistic expectations for people engaged in law, but also promotes a system in which people who disagree on a great deal can converge on the particular judgments of which a system of adjudication must consist. This too is at best a mixed blessing. It may perpetuate errors. It may tolerate inequality and unfair treatment. But a blessing that is mixed is a blessing nonetheless.

One additional note: Dworkin's conception of law contains an interesting account of what it means for law to be legitimate. Hercules can produce vertical and horizontal consistency among judgments of principle; Harlan can offer nothing so bold. A legal system that is incompletely theorized will not yield anything like coherence, and perhaps this is a decisive defect.

A complete response would require more detail than I can offer here, but a few remarks are in order. Full theorization consists of much more than a legal system of numerous, heterogeneous, hierarchically arranged courts can be expected to offer. Because of the need for predictability and stability in law, judges must reason from cases with which they disagree, and the resulting judgments are unlikely to be fully theorized. If this is so, a system of legal practice may well be able to claim the requisite legitimacy if it is democratic (broadly speaking) and if individual judges seek to produce the limited but important sorts of consistency that Harlan can yield. If this is correct, a system in which judges reason by analogy, and do not seek

reflective equilibrium, might itself be justified as part of the
reflective equilibrium reached by informed observers who take
institutional issues into account.

IV. A Final Challenge for Legal Practioners

There is a final challenge to what I am describing as Justice
Harlan's method, and this challenge bears directly on the relationship between theory and practice in law. The challenge
would emphasize that Harlan's method, and especially his emphasis on incompletely theorized particulars, is necessary only
because of our failure to develop general principles, which
ought to be evaluated in their own right. The method of analogy, for example, is based on the question: Is case *A* relevantly
similar to case *B*, or not? Is a ban on homosexual sodomy like a
ban on the use of contraceptives in marriage, or like a ban on
incest? We have seen that to answer such questions, one needs a
theory of relevant similarities and differences. By itself, analogical reasoning supplies no such theory. It is thus dependent on
an apparatus that it is unable to produce.

In short, everything is a little bit similar to, or different from,
everything else. Perhaps better: everything is similar in infinite
ways to everything else, and also different from everything else
in the same number of ways. Without a set of criteria to engage
in analogical reasoning, one has no idea what is analogous to
what.

The first and most modest response to this idea is that judgments in particular cases may be an important part of the development of governing principles, which are often low-level. For
example, it will be very hard to develop criteria or general
theory without looking at the wide range of cases that raise free
speech issues. This is certainly so for judges in a system of
adjudication, and even more in a legislature during a period of
enthusiasm for general rules. Specification of the general theory
will be an extraordinarily difficult task. Often it cannot be described, except at an uninformatively high and crude level of
abstraction, in advance.

Thus far I have suggested that Harlan's approach is helpful
even if the criticism is fundamentally right: we do need princi-

ples to decide cases; but this is not an objection to reasoning from particular cases, which helps us to decide what our (low-level) principles are. But this humble point may establish only that analogies help us discover principles, which are in an ultimate sense freestanding. In Kant's formulation, examples may be like walkers for children, helping people who are ethically immature to begin to orient themselves like adults.[17] Thus "casuistry is most suitable to the capacity of the undeveloped and so is the most appropriate way to sharpen the reason of young people in general."[18] Convictions about particular cases—the stuff of practice—are like a ladder that can be discarded once we have climbed to the top.

I think that this metaphor is misleading, because it suggests that the relevant convictions are dispensable in a way that they are not; particular judgments are not a ladder to be tossed away, but an important basis for our general principles. And as many have emphasized, some faculty is necessary to bring general rules to bear on particular cases; often the application is far from mechanical. But a fuller response to this criticism will have to go deeper. I must be tentative about the point here, but the fuller defense would start with the claim that particular judgments about particular cases have a kind of priority in deciding what the law is or should be. My speculative suggestion is that correct answers in law might consist precisely of those particular judgments and these low-level principles, once these have been made (maximally) to cohere. The claim may extend beyond law to ethics and politics as well.[19]

The claim may be right even if we acknowledge, as we should, that the effort to develop broader levels of abstraction is often a check against partiality and error in particular cases. In ethics as in law, judgments about particulars should be provisional in the sense that sometimes they must be revised precisely because they cannot be squared with other judgments that are particular and general; but in certain endeavors, those particular judgments may deserve a kind of priority. They may deserve priority because they are more fully and carefully attuned to the multiple considerations likely to be at stake, and because general rules may be so broad and abstract as to ignore pertinent features of good judgment. Of course, nothing in this view amounts to a denial of the need for general principles and rules, to counteract bias, to minimize costs of decision, and to bring about the various virtues associated with the rule of law.

Often, at least, general principles do seem inadequate to the matter at hand. Too many factors will be relevant, and too many variations will be possible, to allow a general formulation adequately to capture the range of right results in the cases. Sometimes any general theory will be too rigid and too inflexible. Part of the reason is that the relevant goods are diverse and plural, and most general theories are poorly attuned to this fact. In the law of free speech, for example, the Supreme Court has not offered a theory to account for its judgments. It has not explained what speech counts as "high value" and what speech falls in a lower tier. It is tempting to say that this is a major failure in constitutional law, and that the Court would do much better to tell us in plain terms what "test" it is using. But perhaps any test, described at a high level of generality, will be subject to decisive counterexamples, and will therefore be inadequate to the task.

Perhaps this is true partly because of the diversity of goods served by free speech—autonomy, development of the capacities, political liberty—and because diverse goods are unlikely to be well-captured by a highly general theory. Perhaps this is not true for the first amendment; it is possible that (1) if we thought well enough, we would come up with a perfect general theory, or—a quite different point—that (2) the advantages of an inadequately precise test might outweigh the disadvantages of having no general theory at all. All I mean to suggest is that sometimes analogical reasoning might, in principle, be preferred to a general theory, simply because no such theory can adequately account for particular convictions, and because those convictions, responsive as they are to the full range of interests legitimately at stake, deserve priority in thinking about good outcomes in law.

This claim may be wrong; certainly I have not defended it adequately here. But if it is right, it may have large and incompletely explored implications for the relationship among normative theory, operating through general theories, and what I am calling normative practice, operating modestly with low-level convictions.

CONCLUSION

The practice of law is theory-laden. In their day-to-day work, many lawyers and judges are actually making theoretical claims. In some ways, it is most unfortunate that this point is not recognized more often. The absence of self-consciousness about the theoretical claims may conceal those claims from view and make it harder to see that they represent a choice among plausible alternatives. The attack on legal formalism is above all an insistence that legal work that purports to be mechanical is actually based on controversial substantive claims. Those claims ought to be brought out into the open and evaluated.

But there are some advantages to the divorce of legal practice from legal theory. Analogical reasoning might be taken as a model for a process of thinking that is appropriately nonsectarian and that tries to avoid large-scale claims about the right or the good. This approach is especially promising in light of the fact that it accomplishes a central task of a legal system and perhaps of normative practice generally: It enables people to converge on particular outcomes even though they disagree sharply on first principles. We might go further: Judgments about particular cases might deserve a kind of priority, or at least a distinguished place, in our thinking about law or even justice. It is unclear whether it is possible to have a form of legal practice that is agnostic on or largely independent of legal theory. But if this is possible, I contend that something of the sort suggested here is the place to start.

NOTES

1. As contended in Richard A. Posner, *Problems of Jurisprudence* (Cambridge: Harvard University Press, 1990).
2. Alexander Meiklejohn, *Free Speech and Its Relations to Self-Government* (New York: Macmillan 1948).

3. See Ronald de Souza, *The Rationality of Emotion* (Cambridge: Cambridge University Press, 1989); Martha Nussbaum, *The Therapy of Desire* (Princeton: Princeton University Press, 1994).

4. See Joseph Raz, *The Morality of Freedom* (Oxford: Oxford University Press, 1986), ch. 13.

5. I draw in this section on Cass R. Sunstein, "On Analogical Reasoning," *Harvard Law Review* 106:741. I discuss these issues further in "Political Conflicts and Legal Agreements," forthcoming in the 1995 Tanner Lectures in Human Values, ed. S. McMullin.

6. See Ronald Dworkin, *Law's Empire* (Cambridge: Harvard University Press, 1986).

7. Ibid., 224.

8. See John Rawls, *A Theory of Justice* (Cambridge: Harvard University Press, 1971), 19–22, 46–51, and "The Independence of Moral Theory," *Proceedings and Addresses of the American Philosophical Association* 75 (1974–75): 5.

9. This issue is discussed in chapter 4 of Cass R. Sunstein, *The Partial Constitution* (Cambridge: Harvard University Press, 1993).

10. See Dworkin's discussion of free speech, in "The Coming Battles Over Free Speech," *New York Review of Books,* (11 June 1992): 55, where the governing theory is also developed at an exceedingly high level of generality and where analogical reasoning plays no role. In fact, many of Dworkin's particular discussions are based on a form of deduction, in which he develops a general theory and evaluates particular cases by reference to that theory.

11. The idea first appears in T. M. Scanlon, "A Theory of Freedom of Expression," *Philosophy and Public Affairs* 1 (1972); 204. Scanlon significantly revised his theory in "Freedom of Expression and Categories of Expression," *University of Pittsburgh Law Review* 40 (1979): 519.

12. *Law's Empire,* 393–97.

13. See Bruce Ackerman, "The Common Law Constitutionalism of John Marshall Harlan," New York Law School L. Rev. 5: 1 (1992).

14. See the discussion in Albert Jonson and Stephen Toulmin, *The Abuse of Casuistry* Berkeley: University of California Press (1988), 16–20. See also my "Political Conflicts and Legal Agreements," supra note 5.

15. Cf. John Rawls, "The Idea of an Overlapping Consensus," *Oxford Journal of Legal Studies* 7 (1987): 1.

16. Rawls, *A Theory of Justice,* 50. I do not claim that the only function of this statement is to point to revisability. In the relevant section, Rawls is discussing the analogy between the sense of grammar

and the sense of justice, and suggesting that a knowledge of one person's sense of either would be a good beginning.

17. See the instructive discussion is Onora O'Neill, "The Power of Example," in her *Constructions of Reason* (Cambridge: Cambridge University Press, 1989).

18. Ibid., 168.

19. Compare John Rawls, *Political Liberalism* (New York: Columbia University Press, 1993), who suggests that in the search for reflective equilibrium, judgments at all level of generality are provisional and that no level has priority.

I do not deal here with the fact that analogies may sometimes be a result of patterns that reach deep into cognitive processes, and that there is no identifiable "principle" to make one thing analogous to another but instead patterns that are constitutive of human reasoning. The cognitive role of judgments of analogy would take me far beyond the present discussion.

10

RELIGIOUS RESISTANCE TO THE KANTIAN SOVEREIGN

STEPHEN L. CARTER

My topic—inspired by Jeffrie Murphy's chapter—is how a Kantian sovereign, mindful of Kant's disdain for the theory/ practice distinction raised by his critics, should deal with the puzzling phenomenon of religious resistance. By religious resistance, I mean the decision by a religious community to struggle against the authority of the sovereign on the ground that on the particular issue in question, the community is required by its faith tradition to follow the very different commands of a separate, higher sovereign. This small but vital aspect of the problem of civil disobedience is insufficiently discussed in philosophical literature; it turns out, however, that Kant's essay on theory and practice sheds surprising light on the sovereign's proper response. Unfortunately, the light that it sheds reveals a sovereign who is necessarily a tyrant when confronting such claims. In this chapter, I try to outline an escape from this tyranny. I then translate this method into constitutional law, and suggest how the courts might do a better job of keeping the religions free.

One refreshing aspect of addressing this problem is that it has required me to go back and read the full text of Kant's essay on theory and practice again. And although, unlike Murphy, I have no German, I rather like the slightly different and more colloquial translation of Kant's title in the Ashton translation:

On the Old Saw: That May Be Right in Theory, But It Won't Work in Practice.[1] "Old Saw" seems to me to capture better than "Proverb" just what Kant has in mind, because he ultimately thinks the challenge not just wrong but even a little silly, something that is said without thinking.

I would like to focus on one small area of Kant's concern, an area that Murphy also finds intriguing, and one with useful— dare I say *practical* implications for the field in which I work. I refer to the idea that the reason to struggle against the theory/ practice distinction is in order to enable a moral critique of political institutions. I am, for the moment, indifferent as to the *content* of the moral critique. The point here is that the theory/ practice distinction is often used as a way of making moral critique seem irrelevant.

Murphy sees in Kant an early version of the conversational accounts of justice that would later fascinate such theorists as Rawls. He draws this, sensibly, from Kant's difficult criterion that a just law is one to which all citizens might possibly be convinced to assent. The notion of convincing someone else, even in theory, carries an implication of talking her into accepting your point of view, a proposition that is much the rage in contemporary philosophy. I will confess that liberal conversational accounts of justice have always left me a little bit cold— cold as in scared—not only because of my empathy with those who tend to be left out of the conversation, but also because, as the title character says in John Sayles's film *Lianna,* "Just because you can argue better than me doesn't mean you're right."

But that is for another day. What I want to do here is to point out an important way in which Kant's theory is limited. I refer to his easy assumption that since the conversation he envisions is about the justice of the policies of the sovereign, we know who the sovereign is. Indeed, Kant tells us who the sovereign is, in the second section of his essay ("*Contra* Hobbes"): the head of the state is the lone person or institution "excepted" from legal coercion and "capable of exerting" it (291, 59).

Capable of exerting coercion, indeed! This account of sovereignty is about power: the sovereign, ultimately, is the one with the guns. However, it is entirely possible to imagine Kantian citizens who do not so readily acknowledge the sovereignty over all matters of the one with the effective legal power to coerce. In particular, one may easily imagine citizens who are moved by their religious traditions to accept, with respect to certain questions, a divine rather than a secular sovereignty, even when this leads them into direct conflict with the coercive authority of the secular state. In this chapter, I will suggest that the answers to this difficulty implied by Kant and made explicit by contemporary liberal philosophers are potentially quite tyrannical, and that present-day constitutional law, although sharing some of the same weaknesses, contains at least the seeds of a richer solution.

I

The liberal theory of the state works best if an institution exists to which all citizens agree to defer. Then all that theorists need argue about is justice. Civil disobedience poses a sharp challenge to theory in the best of cases, but the challenge may be insuperable when it rests on a question, not about the morality of a policy or the authority of the sovereign, but the identity of the sovereign itself. Religious resistance is frequently of this sort, and it often raises more troubling questions than resistance of other kinds.

Take the case of the Jehovah's Witnesses, pacifists who refuse to fight. During World War II and the Korean war, the federal government made examples of a few Witnesses, jailing them for refusing to register for the draft. (The law permitted the Witnesses, as conscientious objectors, to refuse military induction, but not to refuse to register.) When I say "the federal government," I obviously have in mind what most of us would take to be "the sovereign" in Kantian terms. But the Jehovah's Witnesses who refuse the government's command may not be so sure. The Witnesses, in resisting government command, even command backed by threat of force, are in effect adhering to the perceived command of a separate sovereign; they are, they believe, following divine will.

The theologian David Tracy has suggested that religions "live by resisting."[2] This insistence on resisting state coercion because of the perceived commands of a separate sovereign makes religions valuable in the liberal state, because by it they become buffers against state power. Religions, as Alexis de Tocqueville realized, fill the important space between sovereign and citizen, reducing the scope of government authority by splitting the allegiance of the devout.[3] Moreover, as communities of corporate worship, religions supply for their adherents a vision of reality—a meaning—that will often be different from the meaning assigned by the powerful but separate group of individuals who run the apparatus of the state.[4]

The religions, in Paul Tillich's famous phrase, focus on what are for human beings matters of "ultimate concern"—and if the concerns with which religion deals are ultimate, the meanings that the religious discover can quite plainly displace in the religious mind the perhaps quite different meanings assigned by the Kantian sovereign. This often leads the religiously devout to acts of resistance against the state's efforts to enforce its meanings as laws. In America, one thinks not only of the resistance of the Witnesses, but also of the abolitionists, the civil rights movement, and, more recently, what has come to be called the sanctuary movement. Even if the religious resistance to state authority is sometimes pressed in causes that seem illiberal—one thinks for example of Operation Rescue, the activist anti-abortion group—it remains a species of the same animal. In every case, the religiously devout are responding to the command of a different sovereign than the one that Kant would likely designate. And in every case, the state that perceives the religious resisters as a threat must act, with threat of force, to protect its policies.

But look how this changes matters. Now, suddenly, the state is involved not merely in a conversation about the *justice* of its policies—about whether its institutions or rules accord with moral theory—but in a conversation about the *allegiance* of its members. This, of course, is the problem faced by all liberal theories: they presuppose a certainty about the identity of the sovereign. But the existence of the competing sovereignty of religion—or of any other sovereign that battles for the loyalty of humans—complicates the liberal task.

The task becomes complicated for two reasons. First, and more obviously, if two people involved in a dispute do not agree on the identity of the institution empowered to adjudicate it, one can safely predict that if some institution sets itself up as the "sovereign" and tries to adjudicate it, the loser will refuse to acknowledge the institution's authority. Second, and more subtly, when the refusal to acknowledge the sovereign rests on a religious conviction, the Kantian will understandably become concerned about whether the resister will accept the premises or forms of argument to which believers in liberal dialogue tend to be committed.

It is important to distinguish the objection that denies the legitimacy of a particular policy from the objection that denies the authority of the putative sovereign. Moral analysis and, in the United States, constitutional analysis, can be used to resolve the first objection. The second objection—the one that concerns us here—might seem to require that we consult first principles, reminding the resister (and ourselves) how it is that governments come to be constituted. The trouble is that the first principles, when we return to them, cannot possibly answer the objection, because it is the first principles themselves that are the subject of the objection.

However, Kantian liberalism has a solution, even if it is not a pretty one. And the solution is foreshadowed by Kant himself. Jump, as it were, to the back of the book, where Kant faces the problem of the opposing interests of states, and dismisses it as blithely as liberalism too often discusses the opposing interests of human beings—that is, by suggesting that the battling individuals (or, here, the battling states) must improve themselves, but that, in the meanwhile, the answer is regulation: "Just as universal violence and the resulting distress were finally bound to make a people decide that they would submit to the coercion of public laws, which reason itself prescribes for them as remedy, and found a state under a *civil constitution*, even so the distress of ceaseless warfare, in which states in turn seek to reduce or subjugate each other, must eventually bring the states under a *cosmopolitan* constitution even against their will" (310–11, 78–79).

"Even against their will," says Kant. Here we see what might be described as the seed of the bureaucratic mentality: If citizens collide, we are told, put a sovereign over them to make them do the right thing. If states collide, put a sovereign over them, to make them do the right thing, too. Which suggests that if religion (or anything else) offers a competing—that is, colliding—sovereignty to that of the state, either religion must yield or another superior sovereign must be placed over both.

Now, in principle, what is wrong with this solution? One might answer by using the central proposition of Kant's thesis—that is, one might suggest that the solution is bad because it can't work. After all, if religion-as-resistance counsels the faithful to ignore the commands of State A, thus creating the competition in the first place, the establishment of State B as a putatively superior sovereign will not avoid the problem. The resisting faithful will simply transfer their resistance from the old State A to the new State B.

That, again, is a merely practical objection. But it does help suggest why, Jeffrie Murphy's defense notwithstanding, there is more force than might first appear in the criticisms of Kant (and neo-Kantian followers) for imagining the possibility of a non-situated self. The reason for this is not, as some critics say, that one needs to be inclusive of diverse perspectives, nor even that we cannot really, in our situatedness, imagine what we would think or believe—that is, how we would reason—if not situated. No, the reason that there is force in the criticism rests on Murphy's convincing critique of Kant's evident view that his test for the justice of state policy—that it is possible that all citizens could be convinced to consent—is foundational. In truth, Murphy tells us, it isn't foundational at all because it requires a background value in order to help us decide which policies resting on consent—imagined, tacit, or actual—are to be respected and which are not.

Murphy argues that the best candidate for this role of background value is an account of human good, which is why he rejects neutralist accounts of liberal theory. Without a background theory of the human good to enable one to sort among the various actions to which the citizens might consent, in other words, consent-based theories offer little guidance—or, at least, little guidance that a good Kantian should feel bound to respect.

But here is where the adherents of a religion that preaches resistance will also make their stand. "We come to the table," they will say, "already armed with a theory of human good. We draw it from our religious traditions." The religious tradition in question might teach, for example, hospitality to strangers, which is why one finds many Mennonites, who share a tradition that teaches precisely that, involved in the sanctuary movement, through which the religious shield refugees from a government that might deport them. Plainly, religionists who are so moved are ignoring the state command. But they do so by appealing to a competing theory of the human good—a theory, in turn, that derives from a religious tradition that offers a set of meanings different from those imposed by the state and therefore serves to split the adherents' loyalties between competing sovereigns.

Political theorists who are busy trying to cabin the role that religiosity might play in public debate often fail to respect its all-encompassing character for one who is devout. To the believer, religion is neither a lifestyle nor a prejudice. It is not simply a source of moral norms.[5] It is, rather, a submission to divine authority and a way of understanding all of one's life and re-sponsibilities. In this sense, a religious tradition may be totaliz-ing within the life of the individual adherent. But, as countless theologians have affirmed, the submission is also liberating, pre-cisely because it enables the believer to see things as they truly are.

To the extent that religious traditions influence only the behavior of the religionists, in ways not touching the freedom of others, the Kantian sovereign is not much threatened, and most contemporary liberal theories will therefore make space for them. Thus, the Jehovah's Witnesses may refuse to serve in the armed forces, the Old Order Amish may refuse to send their children to school after eighth grade, and (in many juris-dictions, but not all) Native Americans may use peyote in reli-gious rituals. In other words, laws of general application may be drafted or interpreted in a way that circumvents the battle over which sovereign's commands really count. True, these excep-tions—or accommodations, in modern parlance—might seem to give the lie to Kant's desire for even hypothetical unanimity; but, as Murphy points out, we can make moral absolutes more complicated by adding exceptions and qualifications and still preserve their status as absolutes.

Thus, one might summarize the principal point this way: If a citizen objects to a command of the sovereign on the ground that with respect to that subject, the citizen recognizes a different sovereign, tyranny is avoided only if the sovereign is prepared, if possible, to accommodate that objection. Otherwise, the conversation is about power, and the answer is about guns.

II

The federal courts show intermittent understanding of this point, for they occasionally grant accommodations on religious grounds to laws of general application, grounding their decisions in the free exercise clause of the First Amendment. For example, the exemption to the Old Order Amish came in response to court order.[6] More often, they deny accommodations, as the Supreme Court did when adherents of the Native American Church challenged a law of the state of Oregon, one of the few jurisdictions that does not grant the group a statutory exemption from its drug laws for the religious use of peyote.[7] (Legislative exemptions of religious groups, although sometimes under fire from scholars,[8] are routinely upheld by the courts.)

Indeed, the Court's refusal to create an exemption for the use of peyote by members of the Native American Church in *Employment Division v. Smith*[9] is particularly instructive, for the rationale offered by Justice Scalia for the majority makes an argument that Kantians probably should appreciate but that fills many religionists with despair. Scalia concluded that such exemptions must be sought, if at all, through the political process, thereby tossing the problem out of the realm of free exercise rights and into the world of majority rule. This solution would, he conceded, "place at a relative disadvantage those religious practices that are not widely engaged in." But that result, he said, is an "unavoidable consequence of democratic government."

The *Smith* opinion presupposes—as judicial decisions must, by their nature—agreement on the identity of the sovereign. Otherwise, it makes no sense to speak blithely of "democratic government." But this response to the demand for accommodation precisely misses the point of the sovereignty objection. To one who does not accept the legitimacy of the sovereign with respect to the subject in question—here, the matter of the religious practices of the Native American Church—the government cannot possibly appear to be democratic. Indeed, with respect to that citizen, the government is *not* democratic, because it is seeking to control matters over which the citizen recognizes the authority of a competing sovereign.

Consider by analogy the problem raised by R. Lea Brilmayer of whether a democratic state, when it makes foreign policy that affects the people of an undemocratic state, can sensibly speak of the policy as democratically determined with respect to those outside of its borders.[10] Suppose that the democratic State A decides to make war on the undemocratic State B. The citizens of the democratic State A will understandably insist on the superiority of the system through which their government reaches its decisions, but this will not satisfy the citizens of the undemocratic State B. The people of State B have no say in the decisions of State A, which means that, with respect to the people of State B, the decision of the putatively democratic State A to make war turns out to be undemocratic. This in turn means that the democratic nature of the manner in which State A has decided to go to war provides no democratic justification for the imposition of that policy on the citizens of the undemocratic State B.

When the religious citizen challenges the sovereignty of the democratic state over a particular issue (think once more of the pacifist Jehovah's Witnesses who object to draft registration), she raises an analogous challenge. On this issue, she argues, the policy has not been made in the proper manner, because the state that has made the decision has no power to bind her; it is, the religionist argues, the wrong sovereign.

Of course, there is an important and obvious difference: when the religionist objects to a state policy and demands an exemption, she is not calling for a broader democracy in the usual sense. Indeed, the fact that she *does* have a say in the development of state policy (even if her side happens to lose) forms the heart of Justice Scalia's rejection of the claims of the

Native Americans in *Smith:* the fact of her defeat, Scalia implies, simply means that the other side had more votes. However, as he correctly notes, if a citizen is entitled to an exemption simply because she wanted a different outcome—that is, because her side lost—the entire project of democratic government begins to founder. The majority must be able to bind the minority; that is why we bother to count the votes.

Moreover, although the religionist insists that the nature of her claim is different—that she is not simply disgruntled with the result but actually challenges the sovereignty of the state over the issue in question—the tacit consent theorists would insist that her denial of sovereignty does not matter, that she cannot pick and choose which aspects of state sovereignty to acknowledge. But the argument is a distraction, for two reasons. First, tacit consent theories suffer a statist bias that presupposes the state and is not seriously interested in deriving legitimate state powers from an original compact (which is unlikely to include very strong powers to intrude on religious practices). Second, and more important, even if tacit consent theory adequately establishes the ultimate legitimacy of the state's use of its coercive authority to force the dissenting religionist to yield to her fellow citizens, it carries no normative content: it does not say whether the state *should* do so or not.

Consequently, when Justice Scalia remands the adherents of the Native American Church to politics—sending them back to the place where their claims have already been rejected—he implicitly endorses a statist model of the relationship of the government to religion. It is not simply that his argument rejects, as a court probably must, the religionist's claim to serve two sovereigns; nor is it simply that the argument countenances the legislature's prior decision to reject the claim; rather, the problem is that the argument does not require the state to *do* anything in particular in order to justify its refusal to make life any easier for those of its citizens who are religiously compelled to dissent.

Even the true Kantian might have trouble with this result, and certainly the neo-Kantians who predominate on constitutional law faculties registered little enthusiasm. Academic critics of *Smith* (myself among them) have argued that the Court should have required the state to demonstrate that its drug policy was necessary in order to serve a compelling interest, rather than simply allowing the argument from democracy to resolve the matter.[11] But the academic criticism rests on a substantive theory of human good—not derived from Kant, to be sure—that allows a greater sweep of individual liberty when no threat to others exists. It is, in other words, because of a special solicitude for the individual and for what we have come to think of as matters of private conscience. It has nothing to do with religion as such.

This distinction matters because contemporary constitutional theory seems to embody what Mark Tushnet has called "the reduction principle"—the tendency to assume that religion is just like any other belief, and entitled to protection in the same way.[12] The jurisprudential trend has been to grant to religious freedom as much protection as—but no more protection than—other First Amendment rights receive. Thus, freedom to *preach* has been given substantial protection,[13] but freedom to *act* on what is preached has not. The first is classic free speech activity and would be protected even were there no free exercise clause; the second, however, is crucial to religious autonomy. A religion, as I have already explained, is more than simply a belief; it involves a faith tradition that infuses the personality and moves the believer to act in the world. If faith-acts are entitled to no special judicial solicitude, if they are treated as a matter of constitutional law in the same way as acts of any other kind, it is difficult to see how the free exercise clause actually does any work. Yet only a somewhat blinkered vision of legislative drafting could propose that the reason the founders placed the free exercise clause in the First Amendment before the free speech clause was in order to emphasize the relative unimportance of the first and the priority of the second.

To be sure, some observers believe that the Supreme Court Justices have retreated a bit from the strict separationism of *Smith* in their more recent decision in *Lukumi Babalu Aye v. City of Hialeah* (1993),[14] in which the Court unanimously struck down a municipal ordinance banning the killing of animals as part of the practice of the religion of Santería but permitting it for almost every other purpose. Santería, a fusion of Roman

Catholicism and Yoruba religious traditions, uses animal sacrifice for several purposes and often involves the consumption of the animals that are killed. *Lukumi Babalu Aye,* however, was quite an easy case, for the church did not really seek an exemption from a law of general application; on the contrary, no one could read the record without concluding that the ordinance in question was aimed at suppressing a particular religious tradition—Santería—and nothing else.

Besides, even if *Lukumi Babalu Aye* represents a softening of the *Smith* approach, the courts can retreat only so far. If the courts were to acknowledge the possible existence of a multiplicity of sovereigns within the personality of a single citizen, their own authority would plainly come into question. After all (although constitutional theorists, and even judges, often write as though they have forgotten it) the courts are an arm of the state, and the legitimacy of their authority, too, depends on an acceptance of the single Kantian sovereign. Thus, the argument that a higher (divine) sovereign commands something different than what a *court* thinks best is profoundly threatening—as it was, for example, when the Supreme Court upheld the contempt citations for Dr. Martin Luther King, Jr., and other leaders of the Southern Christian Leadership Conference who defied a court order and marched in Birmingham, Alabama, as they believed they had to, on Easter Sunday.[15] For the Court to have done otherwise would have been to acknowledge (impossibly) the struggle between competing sovereigns that often characterizes the relationship of the religionist to the larger political society.

At times, the threat of this struggle has seemed to deter the courts from granting even accommodations that would cause little societal disruption. In *Smith,* when Justice Scalia warned of the slippery slope, one could almost hear in the background the sense that the courts, too, were under threat. Still, some courts—and some legislators—have granted special exemptions to religionists when no one else in the society appears to be at risk. For example, when the Supreme Court allowed the Old Order Amish to keep their children out of school after the eighth grade, it relied heavily on its understanding of the Amish faith-world—"a highly successful social unit within our society,

even if apart from the conventional 'mainstream,' " the majority
called it—which preaches a separatism that, as the Justices
seemed to understand it, made it quite unlikely that any of these
less-educated youngsters would burden, or even interact much
with, the larger society.[16] This, indeed, is how the political system seems to like its ardent religionists: bothering nobody but
each other.

III

The trouble arises when the religious resistance takes the form,
not of seeking an exemption for the devout from a law of
general application, but of insisting that the sovereign use its
coercive power to make others follow the rule that the religious
tradition—the competing sovereign—dictates. The religious
resistance is therefore aimed at *substituting* its set of meanings
for the meanings that would otherwise be imposed by the state.

Consider Harold J. Berman's wonderful description of the
Christian understanding of the function of law: "[L]aw, understood in a Christian perspective, is a process of creating conditions in which sacrificial love, the kind of love personified by
Jesus Christ, can take root in society and grow."[17] Note that he
is not necessarily calling for the imposition of a particular doctrine as law; in the same essay, he distinguished the "minimum
standards" of good that law imposes from the "maximum standards" of good that God imposes. Law, says Berman, makes the
second possible, but only requires the first. Nevertheless, the
law that his description envisions would plainly be a law driven
by a set of religious meanings: the meanings that are, for Christians, exemplified by the life and ministry of Jesus Christ. Although many would insist that such religiously motivated law-
making is plainly unconstitutional, I would respectfully
disagree.[18] And in a religiously devout and religiously pluralistic
nation, the question of how to deal with religious resistance
aimed at coercion is one that obviously recurs.

Probably the most controversial contemporary example is the
religious wing of the anti-abortion movement, which is quite
explicit in its desire to order the society according to its tenets.
Of course, there are as many examples of coercive religious

resistance in liberal causes: the civil rights and abolitionist movements are only the most obvious historical episodes. (Lest one protest that these movements were not coercive, bear in mind that slaveholders argued that they owned the people that the abolitionists wanted to free, and the proprietors of the lunch counters that the civil rights movement fought to desegregate argued that they should be able to use their property however they pleased. Coercion in a good cause is no less coercive.)

Consider how the situation is now different. In the case of the Old Order Amish—or, for that matter, the adherents of the Native American Church who wanted to use peyote—the Kantian sovereign can content itself with the assurance that permitting an exemption for the particular conduct at issue will have little if any effect on anybody else. In the Millian sense, no harm is done. But when the dissenting religionist demands a ban on abortion (or, for that matter, a ban on segregation), not only is there an effect on others—the policy is *designed* to have an effect on others. The pro-life activist *wants* to prevent those who do not share her theology from having abortions. The civil rights activist *wants* to prevent those who do not share her theology from segregating their lunch counters and hotels.

The pro-choice activist will answer (as, in an earlier era, pro-segregationists did) that the religionist is interfering with a fundamental right. Nowadays, if opinion surveys are correct, most Americans would probably agree with that contention in the case of the effort to ban abortion and disagree in the case of the effort to ban segregation, and there are sensible moral reasons for drawing the distinction. But the significant moral differences between the goals of the two movements should not blind us to the simple proposition that both involve religious resistance. Both demonstrate the capacity of the religionist to deny the secular state's sovereignty over a particular issue, insisting instead on giving allegiance to a separate (the religionist would say *higher*) sovereign that has set forth a different command, and then to insist that the secular state be guided by the religious meaning. The state has sought to impose one set of moral meanings on the world, but the separate sovereign of the dissenting religionist responds with the command that the state impose another.

How does the Kantian state sort out these religious efforts to impose substitute meanings? The easy answer is that it does not. Having established a rule of recognition for the identity of the sovereign, the Kantian can hardly start the same argument over again from scratch. Of course, the argument then becomes engagingly tautological: you cannot challenge the identity of the sovereign because the sovereign is already identified. So baldly put, the proposition will hardly persuade the dissenting religionist to abandon resistance. It hardly advances matters to further respond with a mumble about consent—to suggest that we simply count the votes—since we have already decided that a background value, probably a theory about the human good, is necessary to make consent theories work. Consequently, one must answer that the religious tradition in question, the one that offers a competing theory of the human good, cannot lay claim to the coercive authority of the state unless it accords with the supervening theory of the human good—even if it can lay claim to the unanimous, or near-unanimous, consent of the citizenry.

Now the Kantian house of cards is very close to collapse. The reason is old and familiar: in the crunch, consent theory does none of the work. (In other words, it doesn't even work in theory, to say nothing of practice.) The underlying theory of the human good—the one that allows us to judge how reasonable the arguments advanced to gain consent are—turns out to be doing all the work. Which means that Kant ends up precisely where he did not want to be—with a theory of the liberal state that ultimately rests very little, if at all, on the consent of free and equal citizens.

This, of course, is precisely the crisis that afflicts modern constitutional law, which, one might say, currently suffers overmuch from the effort to fit practice too closely to theory. The traditional justifications for allowing courts to supplant the commands of the elected branches of government with commands of their own is that the exercise is necessary in order to avoid allowing temporary political majorities to run roughshod over fundamental constitutional principles. Contemporary theorists, however, have made hash of every effort to supply principles dependent on something called "the Constitution," if the document is treated as somehow acontextual and unsituated. Perhaps as a consequence, we now live in a political world in which right and left alike, whatever their differences on other matters, appear to be united in the conviction that the reason that constitutional law exists is not for so mundane a purpose as trying to apply even an interpreted version of the Constitution's language or the relevant precedents; instead, the reason that constitutional law exists is to supply a theory of human good that can then guide the sovereign in the exercise of its coercive powers over its squabbling, morally and politically contentious *subjects,* who, when facing the courts, lose the more lofty role of *citizens* in the Kantian trichotomy of roles.

Another way of putting the point is this: it turns out that the practice of constitutional law has less to do with precedent, language, or history than with the selection and implementation of a theory of human good. Majoritarian decisions consistent with the judicially selected theory are appropriate; majority decisions inconsistent with it are unconstitutional. (I should add that I do not necessarily decry this state of affairs; I simply describe it.)

All of which leads us to one of the final published works of the late legal theorist Arthur Leff. In his famous review essay "Economic Analysis of Law: Some Realism about Nominalism"—which many have dismissed as nihilistic—he raised what might be called the democratic liberal challenge to the autocracy, as he apparently conceived it, of law and economics.[19] The discipline of law and economics, Leff noted, seeks to push our law in the direction of greater efficiency. Leff ridiculed this notion, suggesting that in a democratic polity we probably have pretty much the degree of inefficiency we want. Were our laws made more efficient, Leff argued, they might move away from where the consensus among *citizens* (not subjects now) would place them.

The reason this matters is that governmental institutions, especially those of great complexity, seem to follow an organizational version of the Second Law of Thermodynamics. They tend toward entropy—that is, toward disorder. In the Kantian tradition, the contemporary liberal solution to this is to slap another layer of control—another sovereign—atop each disorderly bureaucracy, in an effort to bring it under control, a process to which we refer, no doubt through force of habit, as reform. On welfare state issues, this tends to be my reaction as well: unlike conservatives, I tend to think that government is important and, with the Kantians, I tend to think that if we are going to do it, we certainly ought to do it right. And so I tend to join the very practical game of the Kantian reformer, trying to nudge our institutions (in my work, our legal institutions) closer to a theoretical ideal. If we can't do it right in n iterations, then I'm usually all for $n+1$.

Moreover, in the case of religious resistance, this response is fairly standard among today's neo-Kantians. The superior sovereign that contemporary liberalism supplies is the Supreme Court of the United States, which is encouraged to enforce the Establishment Clause in a manner that will make it difficult for the religionists to form effective communities of resistance. The precise methodology of the preferred jurisprudence is often quite unclear; at the very least, however, a minor trend in the cases and a substantial trend in the literature propose that the government should not be able to act without an articulated secular (sometimes called "neutral") justification for its action. A religious justification is then impermissible.[20] In this way, the dissenting religionists who question the *identity* of the sovereign are prevented from capturing, even for a limited purpose, the sovereign that already exists.

But this, as Michael Perry has effectively argued, is not an attractive solution.[21] It requires the religious citizen to split off a part of her personality—the religious part—in order to translate her arguments into a secular dialogue resting on premises that all good citizens presumably share. But because her religiosity may be (probably is) a genuine expression of her personality, this splitting has the effect of trivializing what is for her vital. Even to imagine that she can split herself entirely from it is to suppose that her religious self is less important than other aspects of her self. And that assumption, in turn, sends a message about the value of religion.

Some contend that the reason for these dialogic rules is the fear that religious dialogue as a basis for state action will lead to regressive results—the triumph of the much-feared, but weaker than imagined, religious right. But it is bizarre, and certainly ahistorical, to construct an entire philosophy on the basis of what has happened lately. It is hardly the fault of the religious right that the secular left has been shedding religious rhetoric over the past two decades. Until the 1970s, the reliance on religious rhetoric was a key feature of nearly every movement for social change in the United States. During the civil rights movement, the rhetoric was even used on the floor of the Congress to justify votes in favor of the key statutes of the Second Reconstruction. To craft rules making it harder to engage in religious resistance, then, is not only to alienate the tens of millions of Americans for whom religious traditions are crucial to moral and political decisions, but to deny the nation the progressive fruits of the alternative meanings that resisting religions propose.

True, today's liberals are understandably worried about the rhetoric—and, thus, the politics—of the religious right. To encourage religious resistance to the sovereign, they fear, would be to encourage victory by forces that many liberals deem regressive. But this abortion-centered worry ignores current sociological data. The much-feared Christian evangelicals are hardly the rightist automatons that much contemporary rhetoric suggests. To take but a single intriguing example, support for income redistribution and other progressive economic schemes turns out to be *positively* correlated with the degree of belief in Biblical literalism.[22]

But the most important reason for a sensible reluctance to endorse the Kantian solution of placing a fresh sovereign over the competing factions and having it sort things out is that it is potentially the enemy of democracy. Put aside now my main concern—the liberal tendency to overrule automatically the objections of the religionists who press a competing version of the human good. Consider only the more general proposition, that the way to overcome dissent against the old sovereign is to create a new sovereign that can make a decision and force all the dissenters to comply. We should make any pretense that this particular effort to fit theory to practice has much to do with democracy. As Arthur Leff might have said, we must not overlook the possibility that Americans *like* their government lumbering, inefficient, theoretically incorrect, stumbling toward entropy. Thus, it is not possible, I would suggest, to give a coherent theoretical account of the current regressive Social Security system, whatever neat theory might have been available at its creation. But trying to alter the system in more than its most abstruse details is the easiest way I know to be reminded just how powerful the aroused beast of democratic objection can be. All successful politicians understand this, which is why every academic theory on reforming Social Security is transformed, in the crucible of practice, into a rather different theory, and a politically harmless one.

I do not mean by any of this to challenge what seems to me Kant's central proposition—that the philosopher should never shrink from moral criticism of policy simply because of apparent practical barriers to change. Rather, I suggest that the philosopher too often is engaged in a liberal philosophic project that is less about the proper structure of a democratic polity than about the set of results that the political processes should dictate. Surely this is Kant's contradiction: that Kantian philosophers can reason their way to the point that Kant forbids, the point where respect for the co-equal voices of people as citizens is submerged beneath a theory of the good that treats them as subjects to be coerced. It is at this point that the philosopher should be reminded of the corollary to Kant's thesis: the greater the practical difficulties in implementing the theory, the greater the likelihood that the theory itself is wrong. Today's critics of Kantian liberalism, armed with stories of false consciousness, or racial subjugation, or male dominance, understandably scoff at this claim, and nothing written here is likely to change that. They will say that the difficulties of fitting theory to practice show problems not with theory, but with practice—that is, with people—so that it is not the theory but the practice—the people—that must yield. To the Kantian, that should seem a dangerous proposition, which is why today's liberals, even if armed with what they think to be a valid theory of human good, must strive mightily to avoid walking into the same trap. A theory of politics, as Kant reminded us in his sensible hours, must ultimately be a theory of mutual respect among persons; today's neo-Kantian philosopher must remember that respecting people does not mean thinking up ways to be sure that only the people with whom the philosopher agrees have the chance to win. If people matter, the philosopher's own ideas must bear the risk of defeat. Only in this way can liberalism, or any political theory, become the salvation rather than the enemy of democracy.

Oh, and what happened to those Jehovah's Witnesses who resisted draft registration and were sent to jail? Their story, like Kant's, has a happy ending. On Christmas Eve of 1992, hidden behind the brouhaha over President George Bush's pardons for government officials accused of breaking the law in the Iran-Contra scandal, the Witnesses, too, received full, free, and absolute pardons for their crimes. The Witnesses' offense, as I explained at the outset, was essentially a political one, the choice to serve a different sovereign than the one holding the secular power to punish. But they were guided in their choice by a clear perception of moral duty. Surely, then, their pardons give all true Kantians reason to cheer.

NOTES

I am grateful for the comments of Enola Aird, Judith Wagner DeCew, Kent Greenawalt, and Ian Shapiro.

1. Immanuel Kant, *On the Old Saw: That May Be Right in Theory, But It Won't Work in Practice,* trans. E. P. Ashton (Philadelphia: University of Pennsylvania Press, 1974). All page numbers in the text are from the Ashton translation.

2. David Tracy, *Plurality and Ambiguity: Hermeneutics, Religion, Hope* (Chicago: University of Chicago Press, 1987), 83.

3. See Alexis de Tocqueville, *Democracy in America,* trans. George Lawrence (Garden City: Anchor Books, 1969), 291–95.

4. This may hold true even when the individuals discovering a different meaning are not treated as citizens, as, for example, with the religious understandings of the world by those whom America enslaved. See, for example, the discussion in Eugene D. Genovese, *Roll, Jordan, Roll: The World the Slaves Made* (New York: Vintage Books, 1976), 159–284.

5. For effective criticism of the image of the state of being reli-

gious as simply reflecting the choice to live according to a set of moral rules, see Karl Rahner, *Foundations of Christian Faith: An Introduction to the Idea of Christianity*, trans. William V. Dych (New York: Crossroad, 1986), 405–11.

6. *Wisconsin v. Yoder*, 406 U.S. 205 (1972).

7. *Employment Division v. Smith*, 494 U.S. 872 (1990).

8. For examples of scholarly criticism of legislative exemptions, see Philip Kurland, "Of Church and State and the Supreme Court," 29 *University of Chicago Law Review* 1 (1961); and Ira C. Lupu, "Reconstructing the Establishment Clause: The Case Against Discretionary Accommodation of Religion," 140 *University of Pennsylvania Law Review* 555 (1991).

9. 494 U.S. 872 (1990).

10. R. Lea Brilmayer, *Justifying International Acts* (Ithaca, N.Y.: Cornell University Press, 1990).

11. My own criticism of the decision on this ground, and citations to some other critics, may be found in Stephen L. Carter, *The Culture of Disbelief* (New York: Basic Books, 1993), 124–35.

12. Mark Tushnet, *Red, White, and Blue: A Critical Analysis of Constitutional Law* (Cambridge, Mass.: Harvard University Press, 1988), 257.

13. See *Murdock v. Pennsylvania*, 319 U.S. 105 (1943); and *Kunz v. New York*, 340 U.S. 290 (1951).

14. 113 S. Ct. 2217 (1993).

15. *Walker v. City of Birmingham*, 388 U.S. 307 (1967).

16. *Wisconsin v. Yoder*, 406 U.S. 205 (1972).

17. Harold J. Berman, "Law and Love," in *Faith and Order: The Reconciliation of Law and Religion* (Atlanta, Ga.: Scholars Press, 1993), 313.

18. For some of the reasons for my disagreement, see Stephen L. Carter, "Evolutionism, Creationism, and Treating Religion as a Hobby," 1987 *Duke Law Journal*.

19. Arthur Allen Leff, "Economic Analysis of Law: Some Realism about Nominalism," 60 *Virginia Law Review* 451 (1974).

20. See, for example, Bruce Ackerman, *Social Justice in the Liberal State* (New Haven, Conn.: Yale University Press, 1980); Bruce Ackerman, "Why Dialogue?" 86 *Journal of Philosophy* 5 (1989); Thomas Nagel, "Moral Conflict and Political Legitimacy," 16 *Philosophy and Public Affairs* 215 (1987).

21. See Michael J. Perry, *Love and Power: The Role of Religion and Morality in American Politics* (New York: Oxford University Press, 1991).

22. See the discussion in Stephen Hart, *What Does the Lord Require? How American Christians Think about Economic Justice* (New York: Oxford University Press, 1992).

11

ON REGULATING PRACTICES WITH THEORIES DRAWN FROM THEM: A CASE OF JUSTICE AS FAIRNESS

FRANK I. MICHELMAN

There are such things as wide or pervasive social practices. (Think of constitutional democracy.) It seems we can approach them as stores of clues to reasons and the reasonable. From the empirical run of our own practice, we can try to distill a set of inner, mental grounds and sources of it: representations and worldviews, conceptions and beliefs, desires and ideals. We thus (insofar as we succeed) put on display our own reason, or at any rate a side of it, some way we have of being reasonable.

Is this like catching your shadow? Can we really do it? Can we in this way make practice yield up regulative guides to the further conduct and improvement of itself? Here, I pursue these questions using as a case in point John Rawls's theory of justice as fairness, especially as developed in writings since 1980.

I. Interpretation and Consensus in Justice As Fairness

A. *Interpretative Theories of Practices*

Social practices are normatively constituted activities. Every distinguishable practice is informed by some assemblage of vocabularies and significations, cues and expectations, rules and standards. This assemblage is cultural. It is accessible to reflective practitioners, although doubtless some parts are tacit and hard to describe. Now, to be fully in on this cultural assemblage isn't yet to have an interpretative theory of the practice. From the standpoint of interpretation, a practice's informing cultural assemblage, far from constituting its theory (its interpretation), constitutes itself; the cultural assemblage is very much a part of the thing to be theorized (to be interpretatively clarified). Interpretative theories are *abstracted* from practices thus richly conceived.

Perhaps we think that standing somewhere behind the practice's directly accessible cultural constitution are more primitive, organizing "takes" on reality and world, society and self, possibility and necessity, significance and value. Starting from our observation of the empirical practice, but inevitably bringing to the work some measure of our own ineluctable common sense, we strive to discern and perspicuously display the parts of this more remote mental set. Necessarily, we construct the set to fit both the core features of the practice and those parts of our own common sense that stay unshakably fixed in the face of what we observe.[1] Which features of the practice *are* the core of it is part of what we come to discern—some would say construct—in the process of interpretatively theorizing it.

B. *Justice as Fairness and Interpretative Theory*

Now consider John Rawls's recent writings on political liberalism.[2] In these writings, Rawls is concerned to defend as reasonable a somewhat contentiously egalitarian conception of political justice—that is, the conception of justice "as fairness" formulaically represented by the famous two principles of justice.[3] In order to be reasonable, Rawls posits, a conception of justice has to be stable; it must command support from all the diverse, reasonable "comprehensive views"—bodies of ethical and moral understandings—that may be expected to arise and persist in a society effectively governed by the conception. Stability does not, however, require a constant, present agreement on the theory's specific normative formulations. What's required is that the conception's normative formulations be plainly defensible by good arguments proceeding from *grounds* that would be found morally compelling by followers of each one of the reasonable comprehensive views.

Here I want to focus on these requisite common grounds or what Joshua Cohen calls a shared terrain of political-moral argumentation, made up of a complex of views of persons and society, reality and value.[4] Rawls explicitly "draws" the specific grounds of justice as fairness from a certain empirical practice, one he calls constitutional democracy; he produces the shared terrain, we may fairly say, as an interpretative theorization of the ongoing historical practice of constitutional democracy. And this drawn-from-practice credential is indispensable, I suggest, from Rawls's full philosophical argument for the moral appeal-cum-stability of justice as fairness.

Justice as fairness, Rawls writes, "starts from within [the constitutional-democratic] tradition" and strives "to draw solely upon basic intuitive ideas"—like religious toleration and anti-slavery—"that are embedded in the political institutions of a constitutional democratic regime" along with "the historical [public] traditions of their interpretation." Down deep in these embedded intuitions, organizing them, Rawls finds (or does he posit?) a more abstract idea of society as a fair scheme of cooperation over a complete life among persons conceived as free and equal.[5] And by further analyzing this abstract idea, Rawls recovers a distinctive "political" conception of the person.[6]

> Since we start within the tradition of democratic thought, we also think of citizens as free and equal persons. . . . Since persons can be full participants in a fair system of social cooperation, we ascribe to them . . . two moral powers connected with . . . the idea of social cooperation . . . : namely, a capacity for a sense of justice [that is, to understand and act from some public concep-

tion of justice that fixes fair terms of cooperation] and a capacity
for a conception of the good [that is, to form, revise, and rationally pursue a conception of one's good].

So here we have this special conception of persons, politically
speaking, as possessed of the two moral powers. And not only
as possessed of them, but—correspondingly—as moved by
higher-order interests in the exercise of them.[7] Here we have
Rawls "drawing" this special—this moralistic—conception of
the person from the empirical political practice of democratic
constitutionalism, construed as a complex of characteristic institutions and interpretive traditions. This drawn-from-practice
political conception of the person thenceforward fundamentally
both shapes and supports the construction of justice as fairness.
It does so in at least two ways. A first way is by guiding the
design of the heuristic "device of representation" or "procedure
of construction" used to select among candidate principles of
justice, that is, the original position.[8] A second way, less precise
in Rawls's texts but more deeply layered into his argument, is
by explaining how the fact of a society's being well-ordered by a
public conception of justice (and specifically by the conception
of justice as fairness) carries a special, intrinsic value for every
person in the society. As we will see, this idea of the intrinsic
value accruing to each person from a well-ordered social state is
required for the complete philosophical justification of justice
as fairness as both *a* reasonable political conception of justice
and *the most* reasonable conception for us.

Now, a special conception of the person may be used in the
first way I mentioned, in the design of an heuristic procedure
of construction, regardless of whether the conception is already
found latent in any particular practice. But when it comes to
defending a particular conception of justice by appeal to that
conception's unique value for persons conceived in a certain
special way, then the strength of that defense may very well
come to rest on people's ability to recognize as their own—as
already contained in their own practice—that special notion of
the person. It does come to rest there in Rawls's argument, as
we are now about to see.

C. Consensus in Justice as Fairness

Rawls avowedly intends a regulative mission for justice as fairness. The empirical practice of constitutional democracy has well-settled parts (else we couldn't see it as a distinct practice), but many important issues within this practice remain obstinately unsettled. One task of political philosophy, Rawls says, is to examine whether some underlying basis of agreement can be uncovered for resolving some of these questions or at least for narrowing disagreements.[9]

Philosophy's task of uncovering such a basis of agreement ties directly into the abstractive movement that makes an interpretive theory a theory and not just a description (or version or rendition). As a conception of justice "elaborated" from the fundamental intuitive constitutional-democratic idea of society as a fair system of cooperation, justice as fairness is "abstract: that is, it singles out, or focuses on, certain aspects of society . . . and leaves others aside." Only thus, Rawls explains, can a conception of justice hope to achieve its regulative aims.[10] When we are striving to resolve disagreements with others, Rawls says, we must look for premises that both we and the others can accept "for the purpose of establishing a working agreement." To that end, it can sometimes be helpful to postpone concrete issues pending establishment of common ground at higher levels of abstraction.[11]

Rawls, of course, is also highly sensitive to a converse point: that parties who disagree hopelessly over "the highest things" may happen to find an intersection (overlapping consensus) on a range of derivations respectively subsumed by their diverse comprehensive views; "different premises," as Rawls writes, "may [support] the same conclusions."[12] In constitutional-democratic societies, Rawls believes, we have the best chance of finding this sort of mid-level overlap when we focus on the main political, social, and economic institutions of the regime, its "basic structure."[13] The consensus-starting objective thus suggests that a publicly affirmable conception of justice should aim in the first instance at criteria for the basic structure, framed at a moderately high level of abstraction (witness the two principles of justice).

A political conception of justice, such as justice as fairness, is meant to supply highest-order public justificatory criteria for lawmaking, both constitutional and ordinary.[14] Given what Rawls calls the general fact of reasonable pluralism—the fact, that is, that liberal practice itself sustains a plurality of reasonable but conflicting comprehensive ethical and metaphysical doctrines[15]—Rawls thinks the best way to find consensus on a public regulative conception is to confine the conception's scope to the basic structure. He hopes it is possible to "work out" a moderately abstract, regulative conception for the confined subject matter of the basic structure without having to take positions on ethical and metaphysical issues over which the comprehensive doctrines cannot avoid division and conflict.[16] A further hope is that if we can find, for a highest-order public conception of political justice to govern the basic structure, a moderately abstract, clear and simple expression that is acceptable to every reasonable comprehensive view, then the results issuing from a politics visibly conducted in accord with that expression should be broadly acceptable.[17] ("Visibly" will become important later, when we come to speak of public reason.)

Now, one way in which Rawls seeks to nourish all these hopes is to draw the regulative conception for the basic structure as far as possible from ideas already cognizable in the empirical practice and attendant public culture of constitutional democracy[18]—ideas such as (perhaps) the conception of persons, politically speaking, as constituted by the two moral powers and higher-order interests in their exercise. In order to grasp fully the import of such cognizability in Rawls's total argument, we need a closer look at the Rawlsian notion of liberal consensus.

Consensus, obviously, is a pivotal idea in Rawls's argument. Yet Rawls is emphatic that a political conception of justice, such as justice as fairness, does not aim at consensus for the sake of peace or *modus vivendi.* To organize a construction of (so-called) justice around pursuit of consensus as *modus vivendi,* which is to say accommodation or compromise, makes the resultant conception what Rawls calls political in the wrong way.[19] *Modus vivendi* suggests imposition by dominant forces on some who hold different but not-unreasonable views, requiring the latter, for the sake of (so-called) justice, to get along by going along.

Commentators have very incisively questioned whether there is finally any difference between a Rawlsian overlapping consensus and a *modus vivendi*.[20] There is no difficulty, though, in conceptually distinguishing the two. What makes an agreement a "mere" *modus vivendi* is that each party regards the agreement as strictly instrumental to a good of his or hers that lies entirely beyond the agreement itself (namely, in this case, relatively unobstructed pursuit of his or her determinate conception of the good). What would make an overlapping consensus different would be that the parties regarded participation in the consensus as a moral good and hence as good for them already, as good in itself. The participants would in that way regard the achievement and maintenance of the consensus as a common aim or social good that is at the same time a constituent of each of their goods taken severally. It is (in part) in this special way that overlapping consensus is supposed to support the stability of justice in a well-ordered society.[21] Conceptually, the difference from a strictly instrumental agreement seems plain.

What is not, however, quite so immediately plain is how it might possibly be that people would find *intrinsically* (not just instrumentally) valuable the existence of a social consensus over principles to regulate the basic structure of their society. We need to ask, on what prior (political) understanding of these people's natures would it make sense for them to find intrinsic value in this sort of agreement? On what prior understanding of their goals or ends could a political philosopher publicly explain to his constituency his attribution to them of intrinsic ethical interests in such a consensus?

The questions are apt. Is not an answer at hand? The responsive prior understanding is contained in the special conception of citizens as constituted, politically speaking, by the two moral powers and higher-order interests in the exercise of them both. On that understanding, overlapping consensus on a public regulative conception of justice is an intrinsic good because it puts within reach a certain " 'meta-value,' "[22] an enabling condition for a good life, politically speaking. It enables satisfaction of a "conception-dependent desire" to realize in one's person an ideal conception of liberal citizenship.[23] Overlapping consensus is the condition upon which it can be true for the generality of persons that the first moral power, that of grasping and acting upon a public conception of justice, can actualize itself without grievously infringing on the second moral power, that of holding to one's own autonomously determined conception of the good. This possibility corresponds to the state of the person that Rawls calls full autonomy.[24]

No doubt the resulting position is complex. On the one hand, the claim that justice as fairness has regulative force for any group is seen to rest heavily on the claim that justice as fairness supports a special kind of consensus that members of that group have good reason to value intrinsically.[25] On the other hand, the claim that any sort of consensus can possibly have intrinsic value for anyone depends on what appears to be a quite specific and distinctly moralistic conception of the person. In conjunction and taken seriously, these two features of the total position would mean that the full regulative force of justice as fairness is available only to those for whom this specific conception of the person is correct or compelling.[26]

Accordingly, the question looms: In virtue of *what* is this specific conception of the person supposed to be *commonly* compelling upon interlocutors *coming from a deeply divided plurality* of comprehensive ethical and metaphysical views? What—it is reasonably asked—is the "political method" of soliciting endorsement, from such a diverse constituency, of principles geared to such a specific conception of the person?[27]

For answer to this question, Rawls relies on the hope or expectation that the conception is *cognizable* by diverse parties as already there, ensconced in their practice and public culture of constitutional democracy. But now let us proceed with care. To establish the stability of the conception of justice as fairness, one need not claim that *today's* citizens of *actual* constitutional democracies would (with a little prompting) converge on a shared recognition of the moralistic conception of persons, politically speaking, as latent in their practice. To establish stability, it is enough to show that such a convergence hypothetically would hold among participants in a public culture of constitutional democracy *already effectively governed* by the conception of justice as fairness. Establishing the stability of a public conception of justice as fairness does not—at least not directly—depend on an interpretative theorization of any historically actual or contemporary practice.

However, stability is not all there is to justification of a particular conception of justice. Stability is a second-stage test for a conception that has already been found "in other respects attractive" in that it "organizes a set of fundamental political values in a plausible way."[28] *What* set of values? In the writings here examined, Rawls takes as given a specific set of fundamental political values to be organized, namely, those characteristic of empirical constitutional democracy; he aims to produce a conception that attractively organizes that specific set of values. Now, if a political conception cannot hold the freely given loyalties of adherents to all the moral and metaphysical doctrines that survive critical reflection in the culture that the conception itself sustains, then that conception is to that extent not a reasonable one at all; that is the question of stability. But neither is a political conception reasonable "for us" (that is, for contemporary inhabitants of actual constitutional democracies) unless it can draw our freely given support; that is the question of attractiveness.

Moreover, there is a strong inferential connection between the hypothetical ability of those living under justice as fairness to converge on the moral rightness of its grounds and "our" ability now to discern those grounds as latent in our own empirical constitutional-democratic practice. The conception of justice as fairness, after all, is supposed to represent an attractive, compelling organization of fundamental values—which is to say, values whose fundamental status is inferred from the empirical practice of constitutional democracy. The conception of justice as fairness is in that sense to be a clarification of extant constitutional-democratic political culture. We therefore have reason to expect that something resembling the extant range of comprehensive views would flourish under justice as fairness. It follows that if the moral grounds of justice as fairness (including its companion political conception of the person) were not already convergently cognizable by various of "us" as latent in the constitutional-democratic practice that we share, the claim that justice as fairness is a stable conception would be called into serious question.[29]

One can see, then, why Rawls writes that what ultimately justifies a conception of justice politically is "congruence with our deeper understanding of ourselves and our aspirations, and our realization that, given our history and the traditions embedded in our public life, it is the most reasonable doctrine for us."[30] Rawls asks us to imagine not that citizens "choose" these aspirations but rather that they discover themselves already "holding" them as "ideals that they have taken in part from the culture of their society." "Society's main institutions, and their accepted forms of interpretation," Rawls writes, "are seen as a fund of implicitly shared ideas and principles."[31] In other words, the citizens *recognize* justice as fairness, because justice as fairness derives from a valid interpretative theorization of their practice.

II. LIMITS TO IMMANENCE?

A. *Fairness and Moral Motivation*

It is an intriguing question whether an interpretative theory of a political practice must, in order to fulfill its regulative ambition, contain normative elements drawn from sources external or "transcendent" to the empirical political practice it theorizes. What about justice as fairness? Consider this remark by Rawls, to which we shall return at the end:

> In [exhibiting the possibility of an overlapping consensus in a society with a democratic tradition characterized by the fact of pluralism], political philosophy assumes the role Kant gave to philosophy generally: the defense of reasonable faith. . . . [I]n our case, this becomes the defense of reasonable faith in the real possibility of a just constitutional regime.[32]

Rawls does not himself explicitly pick out, as prompted by faith, any element of his interpretative theorization of constitutional democracy. Still, he could be read as providing some pointers. In commending the "method of avoidance"—that is, the effort to frame the question of justice with a constant eye to overlapping consensus[33]—Rawls writes that this method may let us catch a glimpse, at least, of how, "given a desire for free and uncoerced agreement," our liberally pluralized society could conceivably sustain some basis for mutually respectful social cooperation. ("Until we bring ourselves to conceive how this could happen," Rawls tartly adds, "it can't happen."[34]) Such remarks suggest that justice as fairness reaches (or reaches across) the bound of the empirical when it conceives of persons as constituted, politically speaking, by the two moral powers and higher-order interests in their exercise.

More precisely, such remarks suggest that the bound is reached (or breached) by that conception's parent notion of society as a fair scheme of cooperation driven by moral desire for human associational reciprocity and mutuality. "Desire for free and uncoerced agreement" strongly suggests the kind of motivation by which T. M. Scanlon would explain why anyone should care about morality at all: that is, a "basic desire" that we have "to justify our actions to others on grounds they could not reasonably reject . . . given the desire to find principles which others similarly motivated could not reasonably reject."[35] Scanlon thinks "most people" have this motivation, and Rawls suggests that history shows people capable of having it. It seems, though, that both also hold that we must regard ourselves as having it, or the capability for it, in order to explain what wants explaining, or to defend what we have to defend.[36]

To ask whether the motivation to fairness might be a transcendent element in the Rawlsian construction of political justice is not to question that the idea of it may come, as a kind of discovery, in the course of an effort of reflection on the empirical practice of democratic constitutionalism. One might think that although the idea may *arrive* in the course of such reflection, it nevertheless *comes from* somewhere beyond the practice construed, perhaps from the interpreter's own experience of the moral "ought" which he presumes his interlocutors to share.

B. Moral Motivation and Transcendence

None of this, however, allows us yet to conclude that there is anything not drawn from practice in Rawls's interpretation of constitutional democracy. One reason why not is that we have yet to get clear precisely what we want to mean by the notion of a regulative idea being drawn from an empirical practice. How

strong a set of necessary conditions do we want to impose on
this notion?

At the outside, we should take care not to make the conditions so strong as to swamp the distinction between elements in
a theorization of practice that are utopian—consciously counterfactual—and elements that are drawn from outside the practice. Consider the following brace of propositions:

> (1) No social philosophy, liberalism included, can wholly rest its
> case on social agreement. Each must ultimately advert to
> truth-claims that are bound to prove controversial.[37]
>
> (2) This very understanding is endemic in a public culture that
> begins by declaring: "We hold these truths to be self-ev-
> ident."[38]

The first proposition may seem at first to say that any regulatively ambitious theory of justice must appeal beyond empirical
practice to something that transcends it. The second, though,
forces a different reading. For plainly we are to understand that
(1) and (2) respectively refer to extensionally equivalent sets
of "truth-claims" and "truths." (The "truth-claims" of the first
proposition become the "truths-held-to-be-self-evident" of the
second.) The first says that liberal premises—even and especially those resulting in doctrines of neutrality and toleration—
are actually controversial. The second says that empirical liberal
public culture is marked by insistence on placing those very
same controversial premises beyond question in political argument.

Moreover, (2) evidently means to couple the public culture of
which it speaks with a certain spatially and temporally identifiable human society, as *the* political-cultural practice *of* that society. So what (1) and (2) together say is that the *holding-to-be*-self-
evident of certain premises (that are actually controversial) is a
cognizable element in a certain empirically identifiable practice
of political liberalism. This discovery may reveal political liberalism to be an utopian doctrine. If so, that still is not yet to locate
outside the empirical practice the sources and inspirations of its
distinguishing regulative ideas.

We can distinguish two different attitudes towards this discovery, that might be taken by a law-abiding resident of the

United States, say, who willingly accepts the benefits and burdens of a liberal constitutionalist order. Consider, first, those who understand themselves without reservation as full participants in the political practice of which this holding-to-be-self-evident-certain-actually-controversial-premises is agreed to be a feature. If Rawls is correct, reflection by these people on their practice (and this feature of it in particular) brings them to cognize in the practice, and hence to cognize as their own, an ideal of fair social cooperation joined with a conception of persons, politically speaking, as free and equal, constituted by the two moral powers and corresponding higher-order interests. *Via* this cognition (by Rawls's argument), these people come to recognize justice as fairness as "the most reasonable doctrine for [them]." Nothing trans-empirical there.

Almost certainly, though, there are also those for whom the case is as follows: (1) they agree that the holding-to-be-etc. is a feature in the political practice of the society in which they non-rebelliously live; (2) they further agree that this feature does imply the Rawlsian political conception of the person; but nevertheless (3) they do not accept as their own this conception of the person; and hence (4) they cannot accept that a political doctrine tailored to the conception is the most reasonable one for them. If that is where their story must end, then these people are locked outside the overlapping consensus. For them, the liberal injunctions of tolerance and secularism in public life, for example, gain no normative pull from any cognizability, in the surrounding society's practice, of a conception of the person to which those injunctions are tailored. For them, the regime is a *modus vivendi.* Its utopia is not theirs. They are not "us."[39]

Regarding this second case, two remarks come to mind. First, the second case does not hurt the argument that for whoever is within the first case, justice as fairness is non-transcendently regulative. Second, Rawls would not be content to let the second case story end just yet. The second-case people, after all, know they are living non-rebelliously in liberalism, accepting (albeit with reservations) its benefits and burdens, even as (as they now see matters) they do not accept liberal premises. Their case is in this respect intriguing, sufficiently so that we may expect them to reflect on it. Rawls suggests that as they do so they will learn that liberal premises are not so foreign as they had thought to themselves as they actually are—to themselves, that is, as *(inter alia)* willing cooperators in liberalism. We cannot in this space undertake to pass judgment on this suggestion. If sound, it leaves us not yet having nailed down any trans-empirical element in justice as fairness.

C. *(Il)logic of Immanent Critique*

What about the claim that there logically must be such an element there?

Interpretative theories—including justice as fairness as one of them—have a dual aspiration. They want to be accredited as valid theories *of* the particular empirical practices they claim to theorize, *because* they want at the same time to exert a normative or corrective pull *on* those same correspondent practices. They want, as Rawls says, to provide effective guidance when dispute breaks out about how some part of the object-practice is to be conducted. Their dual aspiration makes interpretative theories Janus-faced. Looking backward (so to speak), an interpretative theory seeks accreditation by pointing to its *correspondence* with its object-practice. Looking forward, the theory wants to be able to exert regulative force by pointing to *deviation* of the empirical practice from itself. The consequent tension is apparent, and well-known.

Consider an example. Suppose we try to think about two empirical practices of democratic constitutionalism, one called judicial constitutionalism *(JC)* and the other parliamentary constitutionalism *(PC)*. To the naked eye, *JC* and *PC* look very similar. All that separates the two is some measure of judicial supremacy: some provision for granting away from parliamentary authorities, to unelected judges, a superior power to decide the meanings-in-application of the country's highest-ranking political laws. *JC* allows for some measure of judicial supremacy, whereas *PC* does not. Although there is only this one apparent difference between the two practices, it does look like a quite significant difference. It would seem, therefore, that if some interpretative theory wants to exert a *correspondence-based* normative pull on disputes that break out within the practice of *JC*, then it had better qualify as a good theory *of that practice*, not to be confused with a theory of the similar-looking but (it seems) significantly different practice of *PC*.

But then what happens if the disputed matter of immediate practical concern to us—the matter in regard to which we might look to interpretative theory for guidance—is the very feature that differentiates *JC* from *PC*, that is, judicial supremacy? We (let us say) are judicial constitutionalists. As such (let us say), we experience judicial supremacy as a main fixture in our practice. Below, I contend that justice as fairness pulls strongly toward a conclusion that judicial supremacy is unjust. Suppose I am right and it does. In that case, it looks as though the practice for which justice as fairness is a good theory is not *JC* but *PC*. But if, then, the case is that *PC* and not *JC* is the practice for which justice as fairness is a good theory, and this is the case in virtue of the fact that *PC* differs from *JC* in just the respect that now concerns us, and we know ourselves in that precise respect to be not parliamentary but judicial constitutionalists, then what can justice as fairness (*qua* interpretative theory) possibly have to say to us?

Reflection on such puzzles leads some to infer that all regulatively ambitious interpretative theories of practices logically must contain normative elements external to the practices they profess to theorize. Others hold this inference to be unwarranted, for the following reason. It is possible, say these defenders of "immanent" or "internal critique," that a major structural issue (judicial supremacy, e.g.) is contestable *within* an identifiable practice (political liberalism, e.g.). That is, the practice will remain identifiable as itself whichever way the issue is resolved. As long as *some* critical mass of family features remains present, it is still political liberalism, with or without judicial supremacy. Moreover (continue the defenders of immanent critique), it may well be possible to make cogent arguments of the form: *I* militates for *C*, where *I* is some normative idea said to knit and hold the family features together as a family, and *C* is thumbs-up or thumbs-down on (say) judicial supremacy. "Cogent" here does not mean not-reasonably-disputable; it means not-reasonably-dismissable-as-unreasonable.

The familiar short way of saying all this is: for political liberalism, the question of judicial supremacy is a matter of interpretation. That there may well be more than one contestably valid—cogent, not-unreasonable—interpretation does not defeat the possibility of immanent critique. To which some skeptic will always retort, suppose you are faced with two contesting interpretations of your practice, leading to opposite answers to important practical questions, and you honestly and truly see each contestant as a defensible interpretation of your practice. How, then, you can possibly judge what to do without reaching for some reason that comes from outside the practice? The skeptic's point is clear: to judge what to do is to resolve decisively (for this case, at least) the contest between the two interpretations. To say that you decide between the two is surely to say that you have a reason for judging one superior to the other. Whence do you take the decisive reason? If you don't draw it from outside the practice (which is what the skeptic is saying you must do) then you find it inside it. But once you find the decisive reason inside the practice, then how can you (any longer) regard as a valid interpretation of the practice the contestant whose practical implications stand at odds with that reason?

In what follows, we examine this controversy further without trying finally to resolve it. Using justice as fairness as the case in point, the strategy is to locate a place where the theory could plausibly be said to pull strongly and surprisingly away from some ostensibly salient feature of a supposedly correspondent empirical practice. Such a point of strain is where any transcendent elements in the theory should be most visible.

I will propose that the question of judicial supremacy marks just such a point of strain between the apparent implications of the theory of justice as fairness and a widespread empirical understanding of American constitutional democracy. We can locate within the theory both precise sources of the strain and resources for managing it. Close inspection of both the sources and the resources will suggest an utopian spirit in justice as fairness quite different from any we've considered so far— except, again, in the respect that suspicions of its trans-empirical origins prove hard to nail down.

III. (IN)JUSTICE OF JUDICIAL SUPREMACY

A. Judicial Supremacy Defined

Commonly found in constitutional-democratic orders are the following features: the state's powers are considered to be bounded by (some) legal limits; people are considered to have (some) legal rights; (some of) these limits and rights are considered to be set forth in a body of constitutional law considered to outrank any ordinary parliamentary enactment; and when concrete claims of violations of limits and rights are submitted to judges for resolution, judges are expected to resolve the claims. It is a logical consequence of these features in combination—a commonplace of constitutionalism—that judges may be called upon to rule on the legal validity of ordinary parliamentary enactments, and hence on the meanings-in-application of constitutional rights and limits. Let us call this consequence "judicial review." Judicial review *simpliciter* is certainly not contrary to justice as fairness. "Judicial supremacy" names a *subset* of judicial review that *is*, as I shall argue, *prima facie* contrary to justice as fairness.[40]

Judicial renditions of constitutional meanings may be comparatively weak or strong along each of four dimensions: freedom, independence, authority, and finality. Judicial supremacy is a judicial review practice in which the renditions rank as comparatively strong on all four dimensions.

Freedom. Judicial renditions of constitutional meanings are *free* insofar as disagreement about such meanings is considered to be normal, even after full debate among informed persons striving to exercise disciplined judgments in good faith; that is, the issues are regarded as reasonably contested. The contested issues may be issues of both method (e.g., does the constitution mean all and only what its historical authors specifically and consciously intended?) and application.

Independence. Assuming that parliamentarians intend to abide by the constitution, every parliamentary enactment implies a corollary proposition about constitutional meaning, that is, that the constitution (relevantly) means whatever it logically must in order for the enactment to be proper. Judicial renditions are *independent* insofar as the judges do not simply defer to the attributions of constitutional meanings always thus implicit in parliamentary enactments under review. A non-independent practice of judicial review is one in which judges do defer to these implicit corollary propositions, except perhaps in rare cases of flagrant parliamentary misconduct.

Authority. A judicial rendition is *authoritative* insofar as, once uttered in the course of deciding a particular concrete case, it is considered to become a somewhat general proposition of "constitutional law" binding (until reversed or overruled) for all future cases coming before the same or any subordinate court, and (by implication) for all future parliamentary and executive actions that might be tested in any such court.

Finality. Judicial renditions are *final* insofar as they cannot be overridden by ordinary parliamentary-majoritarian or popu-lar-majoritarian political action, but only (if at all) by a con-stitutional amendment procedure so designed as to make amendment accomplishable only on extraordinary occasions of national consensus.

I would call the American practice of judicial review one of judicial supremacy. In our constitutional culture, a considerable degree of freedom-in-fact is widely conceded to judicial rendi-tions of constitutional meaning. Yet such renditions are also widely, and with little objection, perceived to be strongly inde-pendent and authoritative. As for finality, it is obvious that a high-court determination of the unconstitutionality of a given type of government action can drastically damage the political prospects of those who favor such action and believe it constitu-tional. All told, it seems appropriate to speak, as I do below, of high-court judges having extra helpings of franchise. Nor is this superfranchise at all required for performance by judges of their function of resolving legal disputes. Efficacious judicial dispute-resolution would be in no way hindered by a firm ex-pectation that courts abide unquestioningly by the most recent, applicable, duly enacted majoritarian (parliamentary or popular) determinations of constitutional-legal contents and meanings, express or plainly implied.

B. *The Prima Facie Case against Judicial Supremacy*

Judicial supremacy is obviously a part of a regime's basic structure. According to the political conception of justice as fairness, the first principle of justice for the basic structure posits the equal right of each person to a fully adequate scheme of equal basic liberties which is compatible with a like scheme for all.[41]

Consider now a certain general fact (as Rawls might call it) that we can name the fact of interpretation. The kinds of commands written—and likely to be written—in liberal constitutional bills of rights require interpretation. Even with our enacted bill of rights, we cannot, in a plural society like ours, regularly expect publicly certifiable, objective certainty about exactly what our constitutional rights are. (Consider recent controversies over hate speech, affirmative action, school prayers, and personal privacy rights.) The fact of interpretation accompanies what Rawls calls the fact of reasonable pluralism. It helps explain the dimension of "freedom" in judicial review.

Accepting this fact of good-faith irreducible uncertainty about constitutional meanings, democracy requires, as Jeremy Waldron has argued, institutional structures that will respect the ability of ordinary men and women to deliberate upon and grapple with these issues.[42] As Waldron further argues, this means letting these interpretive issues be resolved by the people and their elected representatives.

Let it be clear that more is involved here than Aristotelian or Arendtian regard for political action as a mode of human flourishing. Evidently at stake are moral entitlements to equal participation in determinations of the fundamental laws of one's country, unrenounceable by Rawlsians whose political conception of persons as free and equal centers on the two moral powers and higher-order interests in their exercise. Institutions deny equal political liberty if they fail to accredit (as Waldron writes) each man or woman as an agent entitled to participate on equal terms in the framing of laws with others who live beside her in society (including, Waldron pointedly means, the judges).[43]

People, writes Waldron, "fought long and hard for the . . . right to govern themselves, not just on mundane issues of policy, but also on high matters of principle" (including, Waldron pointedly means, at the point not just of initially formulating rights but of interpreting them as well).[44]

Waldron holds it entirely possible that, if asked, members of the voting community would turn their minds in good faith to pending interpretive questions about what are our constitutional rights. Good faith here means decision according to one's best, free judgment of the pertinent constitutional truth. Let us call a "people's court" any parliamentary-majoritarian or popular-majoritarian forum for resolving constitutional-interpretive questions. Assuming good faith, Waldron cogently points out, there is nothing particularly arbitrary or tyrannical about a people's court, any more than when a majority of high court judges resolves such questions over the good-faith dissent of a judicial minority. No more (assuming good faith) is interpretation by a people's court antithetical to constitutional entrenchment of certain rights and limits against preference-driven majoritarian political action. Perhaps it is true, as often urged, that various such entrenchments are required for the support of democracy, on the most compelling view of what is democracy.[45] This does not obviate good faith interpretive differences over the meanings of the entrenchments (do political campaign contribution limits violate constitutional freedom of political expression?), and no more can it resolve the question of who— as between a high court in the one hand and ordinary parliaments or plebiscites on the other—ought to have the last word in resolving the differences.

Needless to say, good faith in Waldron's sense is utopian, an ideal from which everyday popular and parliamentary politics as we know them fall well short. However, Rawlsian ideal theory cannot by this observation turn aside Waldron's case against judicial supremacy. In ideal theory, principles of justice are selected and applied on the assumption that all concerned will thereafter strive conscientiously to comply to the best of their abilities.[46] A regulative idea of good faith is already contained in the moralistic (political) conception of *persons* built into the Rawlsian construction of a conception of *justice*. As we have already seen, this personal ideal provides the construction with a part (at least) of its motivating theory of value and human worth. It would be worse than idle to philosophize a regulative public conception of justice tailored to people conceived in ways that real people cannot be or have no basic interest in getting to be.[47]

Especially in light of such considerations, there must be at least an initial presumption that judicial supremacy violates the first principle of justice. Rights of political liberty, of course including the right to vote, are emphatically among the basic liberties covered by the first principle—so much so, indeed, that their so-called fair value is exceptionally protected by the first principle.[48] Surely these rights encompass a *prima facie* right to have one's judgment counted along with the judgments of others, whenever the import of the country's highest laws undergoes significant redetermination by persons casting judgments on the question. The fact of interpretation says that precisely this goes on when high court judges resolve contested issues of constitutional meaning.

C. *Justification: Office and the Interest in Good Answers*

Judgeship is an office. Accordingly, any attribution of special decisional powers to the judicial office may be covered by something like the Rawlsian second principle of justice. The second principle says that *social and economic* inequalities are just if, first, they are attached to offices fairly open to all and, second, they work to the greatest benefit of the least advantaged members of society.[49] True, this does not directly reach our case of a schematically unequal attribution of *basic liberties* (to judges and non-judges respectively). However, the first principle of justice itself incorporates an analogue to the second. As applied to cases of public office, the first principle's requirement of equality (and fair value) of political liberty can sometimes be satisfied if "everyone has a fair opportunity to hold public office and [thereby] to influence the outcome of public decisions."[50] There is room to argue that judicial supremacy is just (assuming judgeships are meritocratically awarded) because judicial supremacy works to the greatest benefit of the non-judges—meaning, pre-

sumably (since we deal here with a refinement of the first principle of justice), in regard to the kinds of interests people have in
the fullness and adequacy of the liberties attributed to them.

Plainly, we must not open the door too wide to this sort of
argument. Letting strict equality of basic political rights be
freely defeated by the device of rigging offices with extra helpings of franchise could rip a big loophole through the first
principle. Still, Rawls's texts do provide plain support for sometimes allowing this to be done for the sake of strengthening the
total system of equal basic liberties shared by all.[51] Overall, the
correct reading must be that attaching extra helpings of franchise to offices remains a *prima facie* but not absolutely unjusti-
fiable deviation from the first principle. Any such arrangement
is presumptively unjust, pending demonstration that the arrangement does indeed strengthen the total system of liberties
shared by all. Defenders of judicial supremacy must show convincingly, by publicly reasonable arguments, that there is likely
to be less injustice all-round, relative to the standards of the
first principle of justice as fairness, with judicial supremacy
than without.

D. Other Justifications Rejected

What could possibly make be true a claim of that general type?
Two premises seem requisite: (1) There are better and worse
answers—answers more and less consonant with justice—to
contested questions of constitutional meaning, and (2) assuming
good faith all-round, a well-designed judicial establishment is
more likely to reach better answers than is a well-designed people's court. Now suppose this charts the only available Rawlsian
line of defense for judicial supremacy. Suppose further that
such a premise as (2) cannot be firmly established within the
terms of Rawlsian argument. Then Rawlsians would have to
conclude that judicial supremacy is unjust. I suggest below that
Rawlsian argument does indeed run into trouble sustaining the
proposition that a judiciary is more likely than a people's court
to find the more-consonant-with-justice answers to questions of
constitutional meaning. Here, we consider whether there is

likely to be any good (Rawlsian) argument in defense of judicial supremacy that avoids reliance on such a proposition.

1. Institutional Design Considerations. Suppose that both parliamentarians enacting laws and an independent judiciary reviewing the laws are always striving in good faith to ascertain the pertinent constitutional meanings in a manner consonant with justice. Then (it may be said) judicial supremacy improves our chances of having the work well done, quite aside from any supposition that a judiciary is better at it than a parliament is. It is simply a matter of two heads being better than one, or of two checks being better than one.

To see what is wrong with this familiar sort of argument, let us recast it into an alternative equivalent form, also somewhat familiar. Although (it is said) judicial supremacy may infringe on *political* liberties, it can only result in augmentation, not diminution, of primary *substantive* liberties. The unstated premise here is that a court setting aside an ordinary legislative act cannot thereby be imposing, but may very well be lifting, a restraint on substantive liberty. In a somewhat stronger form, the premise is that legislative action is presumptively inimical to the net balance of substantive liberty. However, nothing in the general conception of justice as fairness requires or warrants such a presumption. In any given case, a legislature enacting a law may be engaged in protecting substantive liberties or mediating conflicts among them. Consider, for example, the questions of precisely how far our Constitution, justly construed, permits restriction of political campaign contributions or of the activities of Operation Rescue. Unless we assume the judiciary knows best, there is no net systemic advantage to justice in having the judiciary "go last" on such questions or in giving the judiciary's answers a privileged status.

Just how general is this phenomenon of conflict-of-primary-liberties, amenable to legislative mediation? The answer depends on how far we extend the class of primary liberties beyond freedoms of thought and conscience. If the class includes rights of expression and personal autonomy ("privacy") and also rights against class-based discrimination and status hierarchies, the phenomenon becomes quite common. It becomes overwhelmingly so if primary liberties further include libertarian *prima facie* property rights.[52]

2. Judicial Supremacy Suits Us. Perhaps judicial supremacy suits the sort of creature that we are (or that many of us are) and thereby serves our good. Virtually everyone has some central interests in life that lie apart from political participation. For many or most people in contemporary constitutional democracies, these other, private interests are the dominant ones in their lives. For them, it may be positively liberating to have the always necessary work of fundamental-law interpretation carried out independently by judicial agents. On this view, the libertarian good of judicial supremacy—its net-positive contribution to liberty—depends not at all on expecting an independent judiciary to reach substantively better interpretations than those to be expected from a people's court; all we need assume is that the judiciary will not make decisions that are substantially worse.

How much can this argument justify? Conceivably, it can justify a right to refuse participation in the work of a people's court. How, though, can it possibly justify *supplantation* of the people's court by a supremacist judiciary, in the teeth of complaints by some that the relative disfranchisement they suffer as a result (vis-à-vis the judges) violates the first principle of justice? The only way I can see is by subordinating the political to the "private" liberties. Whenever an important issue of fundamental-law interpretation is submitted to a people's court (the argument goes), many who find participation a loss of liberty feel impelled to incur this loss by dangers they perceive (to justice or to interest) in leaving the field clear for "activists"—meaning either people who care especially about the issue at hand or people who get their kicks from participation. Supplanting the people's court with a volunteer independent judiciary avoids this involuntary sacrifice of private liberty.

Arguing in this way plainly is tantamount to subordinating the political to the "private" liberties. Now, this cannot be a ranking of the intrinsic values of the two classes of liberties. No such intrinsic value-ordering is entertainable by a political conception of justice as fairness, because no such ordering is supported by an overlapping liberal consensus, nor can its opposite plausibly be called liberally unreasonable. In these circumstances, a liberal political conception of justice simply cannot incorporate such an intrinsic subordination of political to private liberties. Such a subordination, therefore, cannot be available to Rawlsian public reason as a ground for overriding the *prima facie* injustice of judicial supremacy.

It may well be that most citizens of modern constitutional democracies do as a matter of fact tend to hold the private liberties dearer.[53] It is hard to see, though, how such a cultural contingency can sustain a robust Rawlsian defense of judicial supremacy. Cultural contingency aside, Rawls never doubts that the political liberties are basic. (How could he?) But a schematic inequality in attributions of basic liberties cannot ever be justified, in justice as fairness, by the fact that most citizens would in consequence rate their total package of liberties as more valuable. In justice as fairness, such inequalities can be justified (to the "least advantaged," as required) only by showing that they strengthen the total system of equal basic liberties shared by all.

E. Specialization and Public Reason

It still appears, then, that a robust Rawlsian defense of judicial supremacy depends on showing that a judiciary is more likely than a people's court to find the better answers to questions of constitutional meaning, meaning answers more consonant with justice. But what—we may now ask once again—could possibly make such a claim be true?

Most straightforwardly, its truth would depend on the existence of an additional general fact to be placed alongside the fact of interpretation. This additional fact we may call the (alleged) fact of specialization. The fact of specialization would be a fact about the ways in which constitutional interpretative issues are hard, when they are. It would say that such issues tend to be hard in ways such that they are especially likely to be best resolved—in ways most favored by justice as fairness—by people selected for certain special abilities, or who work under specially favorable conditions of training, career commitment, peer expectation, and other aspects of professional and institutional situation such as cloistering or life tenure. Suppose some such fact as this is true. Then it would seem that a just constitutional order must be one that makes due provision for *both* the fact of interpretation *and* this additional fact of specialization. Some measure of judicial supremacy, the argument finishes, is meant to be that provision.[54]

The Rawlsian defense of judicial supremacy now rests squarely on the existence of the fact of specialization. But not, it must now be emphasized, just on the *existence* of this fact. The defense depends no less on the ascertainability of the fact's existence by public reason. And just there we run into trouble. The trouble stems from the obstinate doubts and reservations held by many people regarding the fact of specialization.

Very many citizens in constitutional-democratic societies have long deeply doubted the truth of this alleged fact. They doubt that there is a set of special criteria for judicial abilities and judicial institutional arrangements, such that a judiciary established according to those criteria is especially and highly likely to arrive at whatever most-consonant-with-justice solutions there conceivably may be to contested questions of constitutional meaning. They deny that public reason can presently claim knowledge of any such set of criteria and of its special justice-serving virtue. Accordingly, they deny that it can be publicly reasonable to conclude that any concrete judicial-supremacy arrangement materially advances justice, with force enough to override the plain *prima facie* violation of the first principle of justice wrought by judicial supremacy.

Unless this denial is itself unreasonable, and can (at least in principle) be shown to the deniers to be so, judicial supremacy must be held unjust by Rawlsians. This does not mean unjust bracketed or scare quoted, or unjust pending advancements in knowledge available to public reason. It means unjust. Period. In a Rawlsian view, the following is perfectly possible: If the truth were known, judicial supremacy would be just because it would be publicly justified as a component of the best constitutional system for securing justice over all; and yet current constitutional establishments of judicial supremacy are plain-out contrary to justice.

Now, you may think that what I just wrote must be wrong because it makes Rawls's political philosophy incoherent on its face. Not so. I wrote that, in a Rawlsian view, it can happen that an arrangement that would be just *if* some truth were known is unjust *given that* the said truth is not known. There is no incoherence here. To the contrary, there is an implication. The implication is that sometimes whether or not an arrangement is just depends on what truths are known. This implication may strike you as paradoxical, but paradox does not make the body of thought that carries it incoherent; it makes it interesting. In fact, it is quite clear that Rawls's political philosophy does make the justice-or-not of an arrangement sometimes depend on what truths are known, in that it makes it depend on what truths are ascertainable by public reason. As a conception of reason, justice (as fairness) has to shoulder and bend to the burdens of judgment, as Rawls calls certain ineluctable causes of reasonable disagreement among reasonable persons (given the fact of pluralism).[55]

As we are seeing, this feature of justice as fairness mightily affects the question of the justice of judicial supremacy. Doubtless, we hear a good deal of evidently sincere and even passionate insistence that the fact of specialization is true, and judges really do have their special ways of keeping in touch with justice. Doubtless, too, the leading sources are (some) judges and their academic vicars.[56] The fact of specialization is true, they keep telling us (or ought I say we keep telling ourselves?), in our special knowledge and experience. This does not help. It does not help because arcane knowledge is not public reason.

Neither justice as fairness nor public reason under its sponsorship may ask the constituency to take tendentiously loaded facts on faith. This restriction springs from the consensus-starting task of a political conception of justice given the fact of pluralism.[57] From the point of view of political liberalism, it is unacceptable to use coercive political power, the power of free and equal citizens as a corporate body, to enforce a view regarding the basic structure about which citizens laboring under the burdens of judgment reasonably differ.[58] Hence Rawls's formulation of the liberal ideal of political legitimacy: determinations of the basic structure must be such as "all citizens as free and equal may reasonably be expected to endorse in the light of principles and ideals acceptable to their common human reason."[59]

Public reason, therefore, may not pull rank. This does not mean that public reason's empirical grounds and modes of inference are restricted to whatever is apparent to ordinary common sense. Public reasoners may also sometimes appeal to the methods and conclusions of science. They may do so when these are uncontroversial among the scientists and their science is respected as authoritative in the public culture at large.[60] Shall we speak, then, of the science of jurisprudence? Does jurisprudence occupy a scientific-objective status in our society? Within whatever publicly recognized jurisprudential-scientific establishment you think there may be, does the particular jurisprudence of Judge Hercules—the particular jurisprudence of right answers—now reign as acknowledged normal science? Unless and until we can firmly say yes and yes to both those questions, justice as fairness cannot justify judicial supremacy. (And where does the story begin about how the myth of Hercules comes to be, if not right here?)

IV. Implications: Truth, Justice, Transcendence

The Rawlsian critique of judicial supremacy looks formidable. Lying near the root of the formidable critique is the possible gap between what would be just if the truth were known and what is just given what public reason can claim to know now.

We can imagine a super-ideal world in which public reason just does know what there is to be known. The case may very well be that, in such a world, judicial supremacy, in at least the measure in which we now have it, is just (that is, according to the conception of justice as fairness represented by the two principles); the case may be that replacing judicial supremacy, in any measure, with a people's court is unjust. There are among us many good, able, and sincere people who deeply believe that this is so. Yet justice (as fairness) may be deaf to their belief, not because it is not true but because it is not accessible by public reason.

Now this is not exactly a comfortable fix for us to be in. Because, as we now have it set up, it is a fix in which it may very well be that something supremely valuable has to give: either justice itself, or the truth about justice. Which, then, shall yield? The truth? Can that be what Rawls means? *Fiat iustitia, ruat veritas? Fiat iustitia, veritas perdita sit?* "[T]he absolute priority of freedom over truth?"[61]

It is just plain hard to swallow that Rawls's meaning can finally be that. Consider, therefore, a different reading: Rawls intends us to regard the knowledge gap—the possible gap between justice and the truth about justice—as transitional. He intends us to regard the burdens of reason as always in process of being overcome by the public striving after justice as fairness.

Maybe, when we get right down to it, what Rawls calls reasonable faith just means faith in judgment. Maybe reasonable faith in the possibility of a just constitutional regime means faith that knowledge of the truth about justice, once grasped by someone, is never finally, obstinately arcane. Implicit in the total conception of justice as fairness, then, would be faith that such knowledge is always on its way to being fully public. Reasonable faith in the possibility of justice would mean rejecting the postmodernist sense of the insuperable plurality of incommensurable discourses (and along with it, the postmodernist hope that justice and "the unknown" could ever co-constitute a social world.[62]) It would mean (one might say) barring the fact of pluralism from final conquest of the realm of reason. Modernist faith—Enlightenment—would, then, be an utopian element in justice as fairness. That would be one way in which justice as fairness retains its tie to Kant.

Again, however, that the faith may be utopian does not mean it is not drawn from practice. Confidence in the marketplace of ideas and the power of truth to drive out falsehood is endemic in the public culture of modern constitutional democracy. Although the grounds for such confidence are today hotly contested in academic and literary circles, "our" public constitutional culture remains—and so it must for as long as it may persist at all—a culture of faith in the power of free debate to establish the truth. Though the faith be ineluctable, a conception of justice reared on it may rightly claim (to that extent, at least) to be drawn from no source outside the empirical commonplace culture of democratic constitutionalism. Once again, it appears that if justice as fairness is not finally a case of regulatively potent rational reconstruction without transcendence, then it is one of close encounter with the logical limit.

NOTES

Thanks for helpful comments to Heidi Feldman, Kent Greenawalt, Lawrence Solum, and members of the Society for Ethical and Legal Philosophy.

1. See Donald Davidson, *Truth and Interpretation* (Oxford: Oxford University Press, 1984), 152–53.

2. This article was substantially completed prior to the publication of John Rawls, *Political Liberalism* (New York: Columbia University Press, 1993), hereinafter cited as *PL*. I relied on six writings of Rawls that have been substantially incorporated, in revised form, in *PL*. Wherever possible, I have now provided citations to relevant material in *PL* and dispensed with citations to the separate writings. In a few places, I have retained especially apt direct quotations from the earlier writings that are substantially confirmed by *PL*.

The six earlier writings are: John Rawls, "Kantian Constructivism in Moral Theory," *Journal of Philosophy* 9 (1980): 15, hereinafter cited as "Dewey Lectures"; John Rawls, "The Basic Liberties and Their Priority," in *The Tanner Lectures on Human Values,* vol. 3 (Salt Lake City: University of Utah Press, 1981), 3, hereinafter cited as *Tanner Lectures;* John Rawls, "Justice as Fairness: Political Not Metaphysical," *Philosophy and Public Affairs* 14 (1985): 223, hereinafter cited as "Political Not Metaphysical"; John Rawls, "The Idea of an Overlapping Consensus," *Oxford Journal of Legal Studies* 7 (1987): 1, hereinafter cited as "Overlapping Consensus"; John Rawls, "The Priority of the Right and Ideas of the Good," *Philosophy and Public Affairs* 17 (1988): 251, hereinafter cited as "Ideas of the Good"; and John Rawls, "The Domain of the Political and Overlapping Consensus," *New York University Law Review* 64 (1989): 233, hereinafter cited as "Domain of the Political."

3. See *PL*, 6. On the egalitarian content of justice as fairness, see Joshua Cohen, "Moral Pluralism and Political Consensus," in David Copp, Jean Hampton, and John E. Roemer, eds., *The Idea of Democracy,* 270 (Cambridge: Cambridge University Press, 1993).

4. See Cohen, "Moral Pluralism," 279.

5. "Political Not Metaphysical," 224–25, 228–29, 231–33; *Tanner Lectures*, 15; and see *PL,* 8–9, 13–15.

6. *PL,* 20–21.

7. See *PL,* 74, 106.

8. See *PL,* 72–81, 93–95, 103–4, 304–5.

9. See *PL,* 8–9, 48.

10. "Overlapping Consensus," 15; see *PL,* 45–46.

11. See "Ideas of the Good," 261–62; "Political Not Metaphysical," 229; and *PL,* 115, 192.

12. "Overlapping Consensus," 9; see *PL,* 4, 140, 171. For recent development of this view in the specific context of jurisprudence, see Cass Sunstein, "On Analogical Reasoning," *Harvard Law Review* 106 (1993): 741, 771–73.

13. See *PL,* 11, 13; Kurt Baier, "Justice and the Aims of Political Philosophy," *Ethics* 99 (1989): 771, 772. On justice as fairness as a body of restricted-range, mid-level principles, see Thomas E. Hill, Jr., "Kantian Constructivism in Ethics," *Ethics* 99 (1989): 752.

14. See "Overlapping Consensus," 5–6.

15. See *PL,* 36–37.

16. See *PL,* 10, 152.

17. See *PL,* 35, 156, 230. On simplicity, see Joshua Cohen, "Democratic Equality," *Ethics* 99 (1989): 727, 744–46.

18. See *PL,* 97, 100–1, 150–51, 192.

19. See *PL,* 39–40, 142–44.

20. See Jean Hampton, "Political Philosophy Without Metaphysics?," *Ethics* 99 (1989): 791, 802–7.

21. See *PL,* 147–48, 168, 208, 316–17; Cohen, "Democratic Equality," 748–49; Gerald Doppelt, "Is Rawls's Kantian Liberalism Coherent and Defensible?" *Ethics* 99 (1989): 815, 831; William Galston, "Pluralism and Social Unity," *Ethics* 99 (1989): 711, 715.

22. Doppelt, "Rawls's Kantian Liberalism," 823–24.

23. See *PL,* 83–85, 202–4.

24. See *PL,* 77–78, 305–6; compare Cohen, "Moral Pluralism," 275: "a consensus on norms of justice provides a way to reconcile the ideal of an association whose members are self-governing with an acknowledgment of the central role of social and political arrangements in shaping the self-conceptions [and choices] of citizens." Also compare, ibid.: "If . . . a moral consensus is attractive because it provides a way to make the ideal of free association consistent with the unavoidable chains of political connection, then the consensus must be a free moral consensus and not simply a form of enforced homogeneity."

25. See *PL*, 207. It is in this connection that Rawls sometimes speaks of the very great values (or virtues) of the political. See *PL*, 139, 157.

26. See Galston, "Pluralism and Social Unity," 714, 717.

27. Hampton, "Political Philosophy," 804.

28. Cohen, "Moral Pluralism," 273.

29. See Cohen, "Moral Pluralism," 281.

30. "Dewey Lectures," 519; see *PL*, 90–95.

31. "Dewey Lectures," 568–69; *PL*, 14. See also Galston, "Pluralism and Social Unity," 719; and Doppelt, "Rawls's Kantian Liberalism," 822, 835–36.

32. *PL*, 172.

33. See "Political Not Metaphysical," 231.

34. Ibid.

35. See Thomas M. Scanlon, "Contractualism and Utilitarianism," in Amartya Sen and Bernard Williams, *Utilitarianism and Beyond* (Cambridge: Cambridge University Press, 1982), 103, 116; and *PL*, 50–51.

36. See *PL*, 49–50 n. 2, 124.

37. Galston, "Pluralism and Social Unity," 712.

38. Galston, "Pluralism and Social Unity," 725.

39. Compare the situation the Old Order Amish in the United States, as related in Robert Cover, "Foreword: *Nomos* and Narrative," *Harvard Law Review* 97 (1983): 4.

40. For a careful defense of non-supremacist judicial review, see Carlos Nino, "A Philosophical Reconstruction of Judicial Review," *Cardozo Law Review* 14 (1993): 799.

41. See *PL*, 291.

42. Jeremy Waldron, "A Right-Based Critique of Constitutional Rights," *Oxford Journal of Legal Studies* 13 (1993): 18.

43. Waldron, "Critique," 36–38.

44. Ibid, 49.

45. See, e.g., Ronald Dworkin, "Equality, Democracy, and the Constitution: We The People in Court," *Alberta Law Review* 23 (1990): 324.

46. Compare "Domain of the Political," 236. For ambiguities of "ideal theory," see Henry Shue (this volume). For a proposed defense of judicial review as an outcome of non-ideal theory, see Frank I. Michelman, "In Pursuit of Constitutional Welfare Rights: One View of Rawls' Theory of Justice," *University of Pennsylvania Law Review* 121:962 (1973): 991–1019.

47. PL, 174. ("Just institutions and [allied political virtues] would not be institutions and virtues of a just and good society unless they . . . sustained ways of life fully worthy of citizens' devoted allegiance.")

48. See *PL*, 327–30.

49. See *PL*, 291.

50. *PL*, 327.

51. See, e.g., *Tanner Lectures*, n. 40 at 46 (referring to John Rawls, *A Theory of Justice* [Cambridge: Harvard University Press, 1971], 250).

52. See *Tanner Lectures*, 12; Jeremy Waldron, "Homelessness and the Issue of Freedom," *UCLA Law Review* 39 (1991); Frank I. Michelman, "Liberties, Fair Values, and Constitutional Method," *University of Chicago Law Review* 59 (1992): 91.

53. See *PL*, 299, 330.

54. Rawls acknowledges this line of argument in *PL*, 80. It remains unclear whether he is convinced by it. He expressly declines to go beyond saying that judicial "review" can "perhaps be defended given certain historical circumstances." *PL*, 240. This concession may itself depend on a flat characterization of judicial review as non-final (see ibid., 231, 237) that seems to me discordant with the realities of American practice.

55. See *PL*, 256–57. The causes are (1) difficulties of assessing conflicting, complex empirical evidence; (2) disagreement over relative weights to be accorded competing relevant considerations; (3) definitional ambiguities of moral and political concepts; (4) perspectival conflicts arising from different life experiences; (5) incommensurability of relevant competing considerations; and (6) impossibility of accommodating all recognized goods in any one system of institutions.

56. See, e.g., Ronald Dworkin, *Taking Rights Seriously* (Cambridge: Harvard University Press 1977), 81–130; Owen Fiss, "Foreword: The Forms of Justice," *Harvard Law Review* 93 (1979): 1; Charles Fried, "The Artificial Reason of the Law, Or What Lawyers Know," *Texas Law Review* 60 (1982): 35; and Frank Michelman, "Law's Republic," *Yale Law Journal* 97:1493 (1988): 1532–37.

57. See *PL*, 162.

58. See *PL*, 62, 138.

59. *PL*, 137, 139–40; see ibid., n. 2.

60. See *PL*, 67, 224–25.

61. Thus William Galston apparently concludes that this *is* what Rawls means. See Galston, "Pluralism and Social Unity," 725. See *PL* at 218–19 (discussing reasons why, in some cases, "we should not appeal to the whole truth as we see it, even when it might be readily available").

62. See Jean-Francois Lyotard, *The Postmodern Condition: A Report On Knowledge*, trans. Geoff Bennington and Brian Massumi (Minneapolis: University of Minnesota Press, 1984), 67.

PART V

THE PUBLIC IMPLICATIONS OF THEORY

12

PUBLIC PRACTICAL REASON:
POLITICAL PRACTICE

GERALD J. POSTEMA

In "Perpetual Peace," Kant argues that no law can lay claim to justice unless it can withstand full public scrutiny. "All actions affecting the rights of other human beings are wrong," he maintains, "if their maxim is not compatible with their being made public."[1] This condition of legitimacy has its roots in a broader conception of public reason. Reason's verdict, Kant insists, "is always simply the agreement of free citizens, of whom each one must be permitted to express, without let or hindrance, his objections or even his veto."[2] This notion, while it bears Kant's distinctive stamp, is one important legacy of the eighteenth century on which liberal democratic political theory has been built.

The notion of an essentially public exercise of practical reason—of public deliberation and justification—has become increasingly prominent in contemporary political philosophy, especially since Rawls's revival of Kantian political theory. It is frequently said to lie at the heart of liberalism, expressing a distinctively liberal conception of political order,[3] and even a distinctively liberal way of life.[4] It is also the centerpiece of a revival of democratic political theory that has focused attention on the conditions and institutional forms of "deliberative democracy."[5] My project is to articulate and defend this idea and ideal of public justification. I believe the notion is best under-

stood as an extension to the political context of a notion of
public practical reason that has roots in the demands of ordinary moral life. Thus, in a companion essay,[6] I explore the role
of public reasoning in the thought and practice of ordinary
moral life. In the first two sections of this essay I continue that
inquiry. In section 1, I summarize the results of the companion
essay; in section 2, I explore the core idea of consensus as a
regulative idea for public discussion. In the final section, I consider the special features and problems of public justification in
political life.

I. The Moral Point of View
and Public Justification

A. Transcendence to the Common

Moral judgments are *public* judgments (whether one utters them
publicly or not). They make an implicit claim to correctness
which we expect other moral judges to recognize and assent to.
As Hume observed, this fact about moral judgments is reflected
in our language.

> When a man denominates another his *enemy*, his *rival*, his *antago-
> nist*, his *adversary*, he is understood ... to express sentiments
> peculiar to himself, and arising from his particular circumstances
> and situation. But when he bestows on any man the epithets of
> *vicious* or *odious* or *depraved*, he then speaks another language.[7]

This is not merely an accident of language; language here signals a deep feature of moral life and its characteristic practical
discipline. Moral language and the commitments implicit in the
moral judgments we make demand of us a kind of *transcendence*.
As Hume observes, to engage in moral discourse one must
"depart from his private and particular situation, and must
choose a point of view, common to him with others" (ibid.).
The discipline of moral reasoning requires us to transcend our
immediate and singular responses and intuitions, and judge
matters from a *moral point of view*. As Hume sees it, this is not
the point of view of some ideally equipped observer; rather, it
is an essentially intersubjective perspective that emerges from
attempts of moral agents, engaged in actual social interaction,

to articulate the outlines of common moral world. The transcendence of moral judgments is *transcendence to a common* perspective on moral life. Justification of attitudes, judgments, and actions is made from this public perspective.

The Humean account of the moral point of view is noteworthy in several respects. First, on this account the moral point of view is a frame of reference or interpretive set. From within this frame we "adjust" or "correct" our immediate and singular sentiments, attitudes, and judgments. Just as participation in a common visual world forces us to regiment our sensory information to a common perspective, so, too, to judge from the moral point of view is not to purge from one's view all the "data" available from one's personal perspective, but rather to shift the framework of interpretation in which it is articulated and pursued.

Second, the analogy to visual perception also highlights the essentially *interactive* dimension of assessment of actions and norms from the moral point of view. An agent viewing experience from this perspective seeks to integrate into a coherent whole information about her common moral world gained from viewing that world through the eyes of other participants. The process is analogous to the process by which one judges the size or shape of a material object by interpreting the data of one's own viewpoint on the object in the context of what one knows from all the others of which one is aware.[8] The public moral world in which we live is a reflective projection from our individual and common experiences and sentiments. This moral point of view provides each of us with a perspective on our private experiences and judgments from which we can assess them and offer grounds to others for them. At the same time, the judgments individuals make from this common perspective are their own judgments, by virtue of the fact that they regard themselves as members of the community who participate in judging from this common perspective.

Third, the moral point of view supplies a criterion of the *legitimacy* of a person's commitment to a moral norm. A person may legitimately hold and act on a norm or judgment if and only if she, participating with others in the practice of public deliberation and argument shaped by the moral point of view, can marshal reasons for the norm which she in good faith regards as conclusive support for the norm, and other participants would at least recognize the reasons as relevant and appropriate when they view them from their common moral point of view.

Finally, while the moral point of view is common and public, it is *not* necessarily universal, *nor* is it necessarily restricted to any actual local community or tradition. In my moral judgments I claim to speak *for us,* but the "us" is *implicitly and defeasibly unlimited.* Thus, moral discourse and argument between agents who do not belong to the same local communities or traditions are possible, as are attempts to assess the criteria of membership of our local communities. We approach interaction and discourse with others whom we identify as moral agents with the *defeasible* assumption that there is available to us sufficient common moral ground between us to enable us to identify a common moral point of view. The assumption represents an *aspiration* or practical orientation, not a *pre-condition* of moral judgments. The defeat of this assumption with regard to some agents challenges one's title to speak for the "us" that implicitly encompasses these agents, but it does not thereby undermine the legitimacy of one's judgment as it bears on those who fall squarely within the pale of that implicit community.

B. Public Reasons in Moral Justification

Associated with this account of the moral point of view is a conception of the nature and point of moral justification. Moral justification, in Bentham's phrase, is essentially a matter of a "person addressing himself to the community."[9] However, this idea of public justification can be given different interpretations. I defend a robustly intersubjective interpretation. This conception of public justification rests on a concept of *public reasons.* We can best approach this idea of public reasons through the familiar distinction between agent-neutral and agent-relative reasons.

Regarded as marking *contraries,* the distinction between agent-neutral and agent-relative reasons leaves room for a middle case. On my understanding of them, agent-neutral reasons are characterized in terms of *universality*. They are considerations such that, if they count as reasons for any particular rational agent, they count equally as reasons for all rational agents (regardless of their more particular interests, values, commitments, relationships, and the like). Agent-relative reasons, then, are relative to particular agents, and, viewed as the contrary of agent-neutral reasons, they must be taken to be reasons for *some particular* agent *only*. Agent-relative reasons are *first-person singular reasons*. On this way of reading the distinction, these two classes of reasons are not exhaustive. They leave room for a third class of reasons that are, as it were, *trans-individual* but may fail to achieve full universality. These reasons are shared by *some* agents, but not necessarily by all.

Public reasons are a species of trans-individual reasons, distinguished from other species by their robustly intersubjective character. They are relativized to some group or "public," but, within that group, public reasons are not relativized to any of its members. Public reasons are *first-person plural* reasons—"reasons for us," as they would put it. There are two varieties of public reasons. First, *restricted* public reasons presuppose or implicitly include a restriction on the membership in the "us." They are regarded as reasons for *us qua X* (for some property *X*)—that is, "reasons for us *and not for them*." Contrast these potentially xenophobic reasons with *unrestricted* public reasons. While the latter appeal to some common group, they presuppose no criteria of membership in the group. In uttering such reasons, one's pragmatic focus may be on one's immediate audience, but this must not be taken to *exclude* others. In fact, at the limit, unrestricted public reasons may be universal. Even so, they would not thereby qualify as agent-neutral reasons, since they presuppose a context of interaction and a common point of view from which agents assess and embrace reasons and that seems incompatible with the logic of agent-neutral reasons.

Rational agents can be said to "share" reasons in several senses. Public reasons are "shared" in a strong sense. To fix a point of contrast, consider other ("weaker") senses in which reasons may be said to be "shared." First, the sharing may involve nothing more than the fact that the reason is simultaneously a reason for one person *and* it is a reason for the other (or

an end is both Jones's end and Smith's end). A reason shared in
a group in this weak sense is a reason *for each* member of
the group considered distributively. These reasons are "shared"
only by virtue of *convergence*. Second,[10] one may be said to share
the ends of another agent (and those ends may give reasons to
both agents) if one recognizes the other agent's commitment to
those ends and one finds reason in that fact to promote, or at
least not hinder, that agent's pursuit of it. One finds reason to
promote the other agent's pursuit of those ends because they
are her ends, even though they are not one's own ends (and so
do not directly give one reason to act). Such "shared" ends and
reasons are not intersubjective. Third, one might *adopt* another
person's ends as one's own *because they are hers*. This third kind
of sharing is intersubjective in a derivative and radically one-
sided way: one sees the end or reason as *one's own* because it is
hers, but *not* because it is *ours*. In contrast, public reasons are
shared in the robust sense that they are reasons *for each* in virtue
of being reasons *for all* of us. Reasons that I acknowledge as
public reasons are, as I see it, "reasons for me" because they are
"reasons *for us*" and I regard myself as "one of us."

Now that this notion of unrestricted public reasons is clarified, I can describe the robust kind of public justification that I
believe is involved in moral discourse. It contrasts with the
thinner conception familiar from Gauthier's work.[11] On his
conception, the aim of public practical reasoning is *agreement* of
all parties on a set of rules to structure their interaction. Public
justification is governed by a regulative ideal of *strategic bargaining* under conditions of full information. The exchange of
reasons and arguments takes the form of making conditional
offers of cooperation and forbearance and pointing out reasons
others have to accept these offers. Its stock in trade is agent-
relative reasons arising from the interests, aims, and preferences of individual participants. Public justification on this conception is strictly *ad hominem*. Participants offer reasons to each
other that the other parties can recognize as relevant and normative; however, the reasoning of each participant is at bottom
parametric. From their individual deliberative points of view, the
considerations they offer other parties are merely parameters
of the *environment* of their own deliberation and action. Partici-

pants need not regard the reasons they offer *others* as considerations normative *for themselves*. As far as they are concerned, reasons for others and reasons for themselves do (or need) not fall within the same horizon of practical concern.

In contrast, robust public justification is not merely *ad hominem*, it is essentially *inter homines*.[12] It involves reasoning addressed by persons to a public of which they consider themselves members. The reasons I offer you in the spirit of this form of practical reasoning are not merely reasons that *I* for my own part find persuasive, nor reasons I believe *you* do, but rather reasons I believe *we* do or would find persuasive. They are *public* reasons, offered with the implicit claim to be *reasons for us*. Moreover, public justification is directed not only to individual vindication, but also to common formation of judgment. The aim of robust public justification is not only mutual agreement, but evaluative common ground, not just coordinated behavior, but coordinated behavior rooted in common orientation in judgment. For this purpose, participants make use of all the familiar techniques of practical thought: deliberation, judgment *(phronesis)*, argument, and what I have called "evaluative articulation."[13]

Discourse *in public* plays a critical role in establishing the common orientation lying at the root of the moral point of view. First, and minimally, through conversational *exchange* (both talking and *listening*) we learn how to make matters intelligible to others. Second, uttering arguments or articulating concerns in public has the effect of bringing reasons and concerns within the horizon of the perspective that participants share. Even more importantly, public utterance and conversational exchange can have the effect of *forming*, or contributing to the formation of, this common horizon of attention and concern. Hume's remarkable account of the origins of justice rests on the premise that human beings, facing practical problems of social interaction demanding their cooperation, are capable of solving them not, as Hobbes would have it, by seeking some imposed solution from the outside, but by the formation of common intentions and by taking action on those intentions. Hume observes that, by uttering their assessments of the practical problem they face, people sometimes develop "a common sense of interest." [14] This provides them a new *perspective* on the practical problem they face in which it is seen as "a problem for us" rather than "a problem for me given that I must interact and deal somehow *with them*." This enables them to achieve a solution that, in the absence of conversation, was inaccessible to them.

Thus, robust practical discourse is a concretely public, essentially interactive affair. We cannot hope to achieve this common orientation in the abstract, or from some merely hypothetical point of view. Public practical reasoning is not just practical reasoning *about* matters that affect the public, or even practical reasoning utilizing "public" materials; it is essentially practical reasoning *in public,* carried on amongst, and through conversation with, others.

II. The Public Face of Practical Reason

A. *Conflict and Consensus in Public Practical Discourse*

It is time to address a serious challenge to the conception of public justification I have begun to sketch. Public practical reason appears to be forced to proceed from already accepted premises to explicit agreement about particular judgments. Yet, a realistic view of public debate leads one to conclude that it is perversely unsuited to this task. Modern moral communities are characterized at least as much by dissensus as consensus, and moral debate seems bent on undermining, rather than fostering, agreement, even when the debate is carried on by competent persons exercising their rational capacities under the best conditions of information we can humanly hope for. Consensus, it seems, must be both a *terminus a quo* and a *terminus ad quem* of public practical reason, yet the former is unavailable and the latter is unfeasible.

In this section, I hope to remove the sting from this challenge. But first I want to say a word about why we might find dissensus a *welcome* rather than a fearsome reality. We will then be in a better position to explore the roles of consensus and dissensus in a practice of public justification. While Hobbes traced our malaise to the radical subjectivity of value judgments and the perverse effects of the exercise of reason, Rawls explains it as the product of the "burdens of reason" we must bear.[15] Essential concepts or standards of morality are vague or indeterminate, allowing for hard cases which reasonable persons will decide in different ways, in part because the evidence on which we must base our decisions is often complex, conflicting, and hard to assess, and in part because we tend to give different weights to the same values reflecting our different courses of life experience. This goes some distance towards explaining why we face problems of dissensus in modern societies without embracing Hobbes's skepticism, but it does not explain why we might welcome dissensus. For that explanation we must appeal to two further considerations: the plurality of values and the importance of individual autonomy for essentially social beings.

Part of this explanation lies in the fact that Isaiah Berlin never tired of celebrating: the very rich plurality of values to which human appreciation is susceptible and towards which human life and imagination can be directed, a plurality so rich that it cannot be harmonized into any single, coherent scheme. "Some among the Great Goods cannot live together," he insisted. "We are doomed to choose, and every choice may entail an irreparable loss."[16] Commenting on Berlin's thesis, Bernard Williams adds: "we have no coherent conception of a world without loss . . . there can be no incontestable scheme for harmonizing them."[17] This choosing is done by communities and cultures which, through time and concrete experience, construct ways of life around a more or less ordered selection of human values. It is done also, though perhaps on a lesser scale, by individuals, ordering their lives and molding their characters around a selection of values available in their culture and experience. Thus, persons may find the fulcra of their moral worlds fixed on different values. Since every coherent scheme of values represents a selection and an ordering, it is not surprising that different individuals, not to mention different communities or cultures, will embrace different and potentially incompatible schemes.

Thus, the existence of moral dissensus is not simply the result of human failure or fallibility; rather, it is a tribute to the rich

palette of values available for human commitment. It is also a
tribute to the value of human autonomy, and a necessary condition of its development and exercise. Moral dissensus creates
the *space* and provides the model for the exercise of autonomous moral and practical judgment. This line is usually thought
to rest on an atomistic conception of human personality. The
autonomous agent is said to be one who succeeds in shaping her
plans, projects, and commitments outside of and in opposition
to the influences of society. But this conception of human moral
personality is highly suspect on both psychological and metaphysical grounds.[18] The same thesis can be defended, more
plausibly to my mind, on holistic grounds. The critical holistic
premise for this argument is that human beings become individuated selves only through *socialization* in the context of thick
social relations. As Habermas observes, "unless the subject ex-
ternalizes himself by participating in interpersonal relations
through language, he is unable to form that inner center that is
his personal identity. . . . The more the subject becomes individuated, the more he becomes entangled in a densely woven
fabric of [social relations]."[19] But social relations simultaneously
nurture the formation of individuated selves and threaten to
distort and cripple them. This process of human growth leaves
individual persons vulnerable at the core. If they are to develop
into autonomous selves, they need *social* and *cultural* resources
to enable and to model autonomy for them. Among these is
the *space* for individual persons to stand back from received
judgments, to reflect on them in the context of broader individual and social experience, and decide whether or not to make
them one's own. For this to be a real possibility, dissent and
disagreement within a moral community must be more than a
theoretical possibility. There must be a recognized practice of
loyal moral opposition, as it were, a practice that allows dissent
without penalty of alienation from the community. It appears,
then, that if we value individual autonomy, we will find reason
to welcome not only the possibility but the actual practice of
moral dissensus. Communities that have been able to develop
practices of loyal dissent appear to us, in this respect at least,
preferable to those in which such practices either have never
flourished or are currently being undermined. Practiced moral

dissent within a community is witness, not to self-defeating moral skepticism within that community, but to that community's commitment to the value of autonomy.

Return, now, to the challenge posed by the pervasive moral disagreement that seems characteristic of modern moral communities, and the apparent impotence of debate to achieve reconciliation. Are not the prospects for public practical reasoning hopeless? They are, we must admit, if the moral point of view is identified with a code of mutually accepted, determinate principles, and public practical reasoning is limited to applying this code. This is the way Hobbes thought of public reason, and he proposed Law (defined as the explicit command of a unitary sovereign) as its only feasible embodiment.[20] Rawls's notion of public justification also assumes fundamental agreement as a starting point, although the agreement focuses on a conception of justice rather than the authority of a sovereign's commands.[21] The account of the moral point of view that I have sketched, however, is not committed to this picture. The moral point of view does not presuppose an agreed-upon code, and practical reasoning is not just a matter of *demonstration*. While it is true that from the moral point of view we together attempt to construct a "common moral world," this need not be (and we have now seen that we have reason to make sure it is not) a monochrome world of uniform judgment and rigid conformity. Our practices of counting and measuring, perhaps, call for such lock-step conformity of action and judgment, but our moral practices do not, and, if we value autonomy, they *ought* not do so. Morality is not properly viewed as a code of rules *from which* we reason to particular judgments we expect others to concur in; rather, it provides a framework of thought and practice within which we deliberate and decide and *about which* we together reflect and argue. Justification within such a framework proceeds despite differing strategies of reasoning. It involves not only justifying particular judgments, but also justifying the way one has reached those judgments *to* others who may reason differently. As Tom Morawetz reminds us, the attempt to convince others of the correctness of one's actions or decisions may involve, not only getting them to assent to one's conclusions, but also bringing them around to deploy reasons in the way one does.[22]

B. Consensus as a Regulative Ideal

We must now try to incorporate into the robust conception of
the practice of public discourse this understanding of the moral
point of view and the place of conflict and dissensus in it. The
key is to define more precisely the nature and role of consensus
in that practice. It is my thesis that consensus is neither a *terminus a quo* nor a *terminus ad quem* of robust public practical reason; it is neither a postulate nor an immediate aim or condition
of success. It is, rather, a *regulative ideal*. Agreement among
members of the community is set as the *open-ended task* or *project*
of this exercise of practical reason and judgment. Practical
moral or political discourse is robustly public when reasonable
people, mutually committed to this project and submitting to
its discipline, engage together in articulation, deliberation, and
argument about the structure and direction of their common
life. This regulative ideal structures the mutually accepted understanding of the project of public practical reasoning and the
spirit in which it is pursued. Thus, participants propose policies
or judgments, bring relevant evidence to public attention, suggest ways of articulating the values at stake in the public choices
involved, and the like, all in the manifest spirit of contributing
to the joint reconstruction of their common moral world. The
policies or judgments, thus, are put forward as those *they together*
can endorse on the basis of reasons *they together* can recognize as
having force for them.

The Discipline of Consensus. Aristotle warned that public deliberation has a point only if participants submit in good faith to
its discipline:

> You ought not to discuss with everybody . . . for with some peo-
> ple argument is sure to deteriorate; for with a man who appears
> to try every means to escape from the right [conclusion] you
> are justified in trying everything to come to such a conclusion;
> however, this is not a seemly proceeding. . . . [It] can only result
> in a debased kind of discussion.[23]

Public practical reason is not merely an offering of arguments
in the presence of others. It rests essentially on the mutual

commitment of participants to the task defined by consensus as a regulative ideal. Consideration of the distinctive elements of the *discipline* imposed by this regulative ideal will give us a clearer idea of the nature of the process of public practical discourse.

First, since the aim of the regulative ideal is agreement of conviction on the basis of public reasons uttered and assessed in public discourse, each participant follows Kant's maxim: "Allow . . . your opponent to speak in the name of reason, and combat him only with weapons of reason."[24] Participants accept that there is no place in the practice for the exercise of coercion or the exploitation of bargaining position. In this realm, they acknowledge, as Habermas puts it, "nothing [is to] coerce anyone except the force of the better argument."[25] Governed by the regulative ideal, participants recognize that to reduce others to silence or mute compliance would defeat the purpose of engaging in the practice: only common conviction will fully satisfy their aims.

Second, the agenda of this public forum is *open* to all issues, proposals, and subject matter, subject only to the discipline of the regulative ideal. In "What Is Enlightenment?" Kant contrasts the public use of reason with what he calls the "private" use of it. Reason is in "private use," he says, when officers address their troops, when civil servants address taxpayers, and when clergy address the faithful.[26] The private use of reason is restricted, deprived, and confined within externally imposed limits. For Kant, the public use of reason is the polar opposite of this private use. Reason in its public use is reason restricted by nothing but its critical discipline, recognizing no unchallengeable authority but reason itself.[27] Robust public discourse is open in this sense: no restrictions are placed on the issues or proposals that may be brought to public attention, nor on the views, opinions, reasons, or arguments to which participants may appeal in their discussion of them, except those entailed by the discipline of public practical reason itself.[28]

The regulative aim of common conviction implies, third, that each participant is bound by a maxim of *sincerity*. This imposes a two-fold obligation on them. First, they expect themselves and others to participate in good faith. Anyone who approaches the

forum in the spirit of Aristotle's "casual person" is turned away
at the gates. Public practical reasoning is not *eristic* discourse. If
public deliberation is not to be understood as a form of strategic
bargaining, neither is it to be regarded as a contest, either of
wills or of words. No one is a "winner" in this form of discursive
engagement unless all are. Second, participants are expected
and themselves aim to present proposals, evidence, interpretations, and arguments which they fully endorse. This precludes
both opportunistic exploitation of argument, and the kind of
strategic bargaining characteristic of Gauthier's version of
"thin" public justification. It does not entail that participants
only present the reasons that actually *decide* or *motivate* them to
adopt the proposals they make.[29] It does require, however, that
participants *endorse* them, and that they sincerely hold that, in
the absence of other considerations, these reasons would figure
prominently amongst their reasons for the proposal. Note that
this maxim of sincerity does not rest on the view that offering
reasons one does not endorse is in some way manipulative,
disingenuous, or otherwise fails to respect other participants.[30]
Rather, the maxim is a direct implication of the regulative ideal
of public practical reason: each individual wants to participate
in the common venture of uncovering *public reasons,* reasons
that are *for us,* and so *for you* and *for me,* to preserve or reconstruct our common life in some way. Closely related is the
fourth constraint. Parties regard themselves bound by a maxim
of *integrity,* by which I mean a commitment to consistency of
principle. For participants who do not hold official positions,
this involves at the minimum the willingness to accept the implications of the principles they endorse and a willingness to act
on them or apply them to their own case (or to abandon the
principles if they cannot accept their implications).[31]

Fifth, the participants seek to address their judgments to the
public, and to utter the basis of their judgments so that, in
Nagel's words, others "have what [they] have, and can arrive at
a judgment on the same basis."[32] Their reasons are offered in
the good faith belief that they are intelligible to (i.e., both cognizable and normatively appreciable by) co-participants, if not
immediately, then after good faith efforts are made by all parties to articulate and understand them. They accept that their

proposals and the rationales for them must be both *accessible to* each member of the community and *assessable by* each member. This does not entail that everyone must accept the considerations as true by appeal to their own experience, or that the propositions expressing them are never disputable. Rather, it means that, in spite of dispute over the truth of the considerations, it is agreed that if the consideration is true, it is a reason for the conclusion drawn.[33]

Sixth, participants will regard their interpretations, reasons, arguments, and the claims they make on behalf of them, as *defeasible* by the evidence and arguments offered by other participants. Public justification requires that one be prepared "to submit one's reasons to the criticism of others, and to find that the exercise of a common critical rationality and consideration of evidence that can be shared will reveal that one is mistaken."[34] Participants weigh their judgments with those of other participants, and make an effort to locate their interpretations of value in the (potentially different) visions of good which others embrace, or try to relate as best they can their own visions to these competing visions. They shape their proposals, interpretations, and arguments in light of and subject to the correction of the articulations, interpretations, and arguments of others. Note that participants in the practice of robust public practical reasoning make claims of correctness on two levels: (1) as to the *substance* of their proposals, that is, as to their truth, soundness, or validity, and (2) as to their *being common,* that is, as to their claim to be *ours.*[35]

Seventh, they reject any rule of final *closure* of discussion. Since participants regard any genuinely public dispute to be a disagreement about that which is common to them, when they are faced with disagreement, they will persist in the commitment to continuing in good faith the process of discussion aimed at resolving the disagreement. Public discussion must remain open until common conviction is reached. At the same time, however, they recognize that the demands of daily life may force them to close off discussion despite lack of consensus. Thus, they accept *conditional, temporary,* pragmatic closure of debate.[36] Similarly, participants may adopt certain constraints on their discourse in the interest of achieving, in Gutmann's and Thompson's apt phrase, an "economy of moral disagreement."[37] Although they will not abandon their convictions without good reason, or fear to give them public voice, participants will seek to formulate their arguments or interpretations in terms which minimize rejection of the convictions of other participants.[38] They will seek common ground from which they can bring their different visions into common focus.

Finally, these pragmatic constraints on discourse, like every other condition imposed on it, must satisfy the maxim of *reflexivity:* any constraint on the practice of public practical reason must itself be able to survive critical scrutiny in this forum, and may be adopted only if participants are convinced that they can and do survive it.

The model of public practical discourse that I have just sketched is not meant merely as a heuristic device, like Rawls's "original position," describing the reasoning of a hypothetical congregation of abstract, representative, rational beings whose choice under restricted conditions is supposed to tell us in a vivid way something about the principles we have reason to endorse. Rather, it is intended as a model for real moral discourse in concrete, historical, social conditions. It is an idealization, to be sure, but it is an ideal to which we can demand real social and political institutions to approximate.

If so, then robust public discourse is possible only if it is *rooted in a public.* It can be practiced only in a company of persons marked by a degree of common or overlapping experience. This common experience provides a point of departure, and a publicly available point of reference, for articulation and argument. It is from this soil that the mutually acknowledged commitment to its regulative ideal springs. Note that public reasoning on the *thin conception* need not be rooted in common experience. People can negotiate the terms of coexistence and mutual forbearance, and can even negotiate the structure of a degree of cooperation, while interacting only at the margins of their lives. It is probably true, however, that as mutual forbearance ripens into cooperative interaction, and that interaction deepens and broadens, people begin to build a base of genuine interdependence and common experience.

This leads us to two further sets of questions. First, how might this model of robust public discourse be institutionalized in political society? How might it shape our politics? What values might be served by doing so? Second, what background social and political conditions must be in place for public discourse to have this value for us? I will pursue answers to these questions in the next section of this essay.

III. THE POLITICAL FACE OF PUBLIC PRACTICAL REASON

A. *Pluralism, Politics, and Autonomy*

What does the model of robust public discourse have to do with the practice of politics? Where might it fit into life in modern political society? The answer to these questions is relatively clear. An argument for politics organized around the model of robust public discourse is in effect an argument for a particular form of political constitution and culture of politics: the constitution and culture of *deliberative democracy*.[39] Deliberative democracy shapes the institutions and principles of liberal majoritarian politics by reference to the fundamental aim of enabling and enhancing collective and individual self-government. It gives expression to a vision of political society as a moral community writ large, a community in which robustly public deliberation is not merely an option but a responsibility and the community's organizing principle. However, you might respond at this point that, while the notion of robust public discourse has its attractions, regarded as a model of *moral* discourse it surely founders on the hard rock of modern politics. I regard this as a serious challenge. This section is devoted to assessing the feasibility and value of politics modeled after the robust conception of public justification I have sketched above. As a first step towards such an assessment, I want to make a brief inventory of features of modern political societies that distinguish them from informal communities of moral judgment.

1. Moral Points of View and Modern Politics. Perhaps the most immediately evident feature of political society is that it is pervasively non-voluntary, indeed, pervasively coercive. Membership is virtually beyond the control of all but a few individual citizens. More importantly, behavior, relationships, arrangements, and institutions are coercively enforced, or at least underwritten by coercive institutions. Politics, unlike morality, operates in an environment of power and is always concerned, explicitly or implicitly, with a struggle over the exercise of power. Second, life in political society is pervasively mediated through institutions. Relationships among citizens are distant, non-intimate, and typically unidimensional, or nearly so. Life in political society is, in Charles Williams's phrase, "unexclusive life."[40] Relations amongst citizens are largely relations among strangers. Common experience is overlapping rather than directly shared and it is mediated through participation in overlapping groups and highly organized institutions. Thus, in political life, the nuance of attitude and the texture of interpersonal relationships are less central than in moral life; more important are the structures of social interaction and mutual dealing, the coordination of the efforts of large social groups, the institutionalized constitution of power, and the modes and limits of its exercise. Third, the effect and influence of political institutions and arrangements on the lives of citizens is pervasive and often dramatically unequal. Their control over these influences is limited and mediated through participation in institutions and parties. Fourth, discourse in political society is less personal than in more intimate moral relationships. It is typically not face-to-face, but rather, again like most aspects of the lives of citizens, mediated by institutions. At the same time, the scope and scale of the practical issues of politics are much larger, involving more people and larger concerns. Politics seeks to coordinate collective action to achieve and secure public goods and minimize or ameliorate public evils. Fifth, the focus of political power, political action, and political discourse is trained predominantly, albeit not exclusively, on institutional centers of power and authority in society, especially the government.

Finally, modern political societies are characterized by what Rawls calls "the fact of pluralism."[41] Informal moral communities, we have seen, may display a wide diversity of evaluative focus and divergence of moral judgment. Politics, however, throws its net over a far wider area; hence, the range and heterogeneity of moral and evaluative experience in modern political societies is much greater. At the same time, the pluralism of moral views and visions of the good is congealed firmly in the practices of local communities and groups, often embedded in rich histories and traditions. Modern political societies tend to gather together a very wide array of communities and traditions that compete for standing, resources, space, and especially power. Because of the very broad range of life experiences and the divergent fundamental evaluative orientations of these subcommunities, conflict over moral and political issues can be deep and pervasive. Unlike smaller communities of judgment, political societies constantly face the challenge of "simultaneously trying to act and remain a community," as Wolin put it.[42] What most characterizes life in political society is "the problem of continually *creating* unity, a public, in a context of diversity, rival claims, unequal power, and conflicting interests."[43]

In view of these large and significant differences between political society and less formal, more intimate communities of moral judgment, sober realism may force us to reconsider the value and even the feasibility of politics organized around robust public discourse. Not only is such a politics costly to individuals and society at large, but it may also pose a serious threat to social stability. Tocqueville observed that public discussion frequently intensifies rather than resolves conflict. The heat of debate drives partisans beyond the civilized limits of the regulative ideal of public discourse and even beyond the limits of their own views. They lose sight of the aims they are pursuing.[44] This is a lesson well-learned by political theorists who, like Hobbes, plied their trade in the midst of the revolutions and religious wars of the seventeenth century.[45] Their response was not to institutionalize open public discourse, but rather to establish a regime of Law designed, in Hume's phrase, "to cut off all occasions for discord and contention" (*Treatise,* 502).

More seriously, it might be argued that the fundamental problem with the model of robust public discourse is that it fails to face squarely the radical pluralism of modern political societies, and so, for this reason, is impossible. Modern Western political societies embrace within their borders many communities of judgment, whose histories and practices yield fundamentally different and deeply conflicting conceptions of morality and visions of human good. Rawls even admits that for all practical purposes these conceptions are incommensurable, and yet not obviously irrational. Modern political societies are high-tech versions of the city of Babel, plagued by a confusion of moral tongues. Any one such moral language may provide for its native speakers a suitably public perspective for coherent moral judgment, yet no one of them has wide enough currency to define a public wide enough to encompass a modern "multi-lingual" political society.

However, I believe the skepticism of the previous paragraph overestimates the moral and political confusion characteristic of modern political societies, and in the process loses sight of the possibility of a form of politics that is essential to individual and collective autonomy in modern political society. It should be clear by now that it is not my intent to minimize either the fact of the diversity of moral views and visions of the good that can be found in our political societies, or its desirability. But I want to suggest that we should not so quickly conclude that a robust public discourse is unfeasible.

First, as we noted earlier, there is some reason to hope that the techniques of robust public discourse, especially when deployed *in public,* are able to establish a foothold for an emerging common sense of interest, or *common orientation,* among participants. It provides a way for private experience to take on public character and so to be added to the stock of common experience. We have no guarantee that it will succeed, but in view of the stakes, we must not ignore this avenue for building a political community.

Second, it must be emphasized that the "public" in which robust public discourse must be rooted must not be understood on the model of a family. It is, in the words of one author, "a company of strangers."[46] Its members are not necessarily on intimate terms with each other; they need not be bound by blood or affection. They are bound, rather, by complex and overlapping lines of interdependency and experience. Neither is such a "public" a homogeneous community; indeed, it may be characterized by a wide, even alarming, diversity of views about the common good and the meaning of human life. Public discourse is not a language of intimacy, neither is it the language in which we recite together a common and historic creed. The kind of public discourse I have sketched depends not on homogeneity, but only on the ability to uncover points of commonality across lines of difference. In fact, homogeneity may even prove an obstacle to developing a vigorous public discourse. In the Biblical story, the people of the earth gathered on the plain of Shinar. They all spoke a single language; and, we are told, they needed few words.[47] There is little use for public discourse where experience is uniform and moral imagination homogeneous. However, when we gather in the city of Babel, from the far corners of moral experience, in a confusion of tongues, the tools of public discourse become indispensable. With them, and the materials supplied by our interdependence and common experience, we can begin to build and refine a common moral language. This common language, of course, will be forever shaped and enriched by, and must always respect, the diversity of the languages from which it emerges.

Third, the moral diversity in modern political societies has been conceptualized in recent political theory in such a way as to make it appear far less tractable than it may in fact be. This happens, for example, when Rawls characterizes the social "fact of pluralism" in terms of competing and conflicting comprehensive *conceptions* or *theories* of human good or meaning to which subcommunities are loyal. These conceptions or theories are judged quite plausibly to be incommensurable on any common, rational basis. In consequence, the conflicts citizens face in modern pluralistic societies seem entirely intractable.

This way of viewing the fact of pluralism, however, stands the social reality on its theoretical head. The conflicts experienced by citizens in modern political societies are, first of all, conflicts in their *lives* and *conduct,* not in theories or congealed conceptions of the good. But increasingly, these people find themselves caught in webs of interdependency with people trying, as they are, to live out their visions of the good in their own historical communities. Also, people find they are forced to become morally multilingual because they find themselves members of different communities at the same time. Finally, the "conceptions of human good" actually *lived* by people are seldom fully articulated in a systematic fashion. They are to one degree or another incomplete and open-ended. If we take these features seriously, I think, we should be less inclined to see modern democratic societies as battlegrounds on which theoretical titans contend, and more inclined to see them as arenas in which individual citizens—as well as groups of citizens, and historic communities, with overlapping memberships—compete for social resources and struggle over the structure and direction of their common institutions. The views and commitments of these partisans tend to be informed by, rather than strictly identified with, the systematic conceptions and visions of human good taught in the historical communities loyal to them. Thus, when citizens engage in moral and political discourse, they are likely to feel themselves pulled in different directions, but also, perhaps, pulled toward finding some common point of reference. We should not mistake the theoretical incommensurability of different systematic conceptions of the good, for the practical impossibility of locating moral and political common ground through public discourse.

2. Deliberative Democracy and Collective Autonomy. All this granted, I do not deny that conflict and disagreement exist at a deep level in modern political societies. Yet, because so much is at stake, the only solution to this situation, in my view, is to widen the scope and increase the depth of public discourse. This is the only way in which we can create space for genuine individual autonomy in modern political societies. The fundamental value of a politics of robust public discourse, given institutional shape in a constitution and culture of deliberative democracy, lies in its enabling free and equal citizens to participate in collective control of common and collective aspects of their lives in the face of pervasive moral and political disagreement. Let me develop this argument a bit more fully.

To begin we must consider the fact that a large part of our lives is either directly involved in or significantly shaped by the basic institutions and practices of our political societies. Furthermore, these institutions and practices are not simply natural facts, but rather they are *social products,* the results either of our collective activity or of aggregated individual interactions over which we can hope to exercise collective control. These institutions and practices decisively influence the shape of the environment in which we identify, evaluate, and embrace our individual aims and commitments, and thus determine the conditions under which we become the persons we are and pursue our aims and commitments. Also, we depend on the cooperation of others in the society at large both to achieve our individual goals and to define and successfully pursue common goals. In a large part of our lives, then, we participate in institutions, practices, and activities which are public or collective in nature. We pursue projects and commitments which depend for their formulation, for their having value for us, or for their fulfillment, on the existence and integrity of social institutions and a public environment of cooperation. Political authority exercises the greatest (albeit not exclusive) control over these common and public aspects of our lives. To the extent that we are excluded from that political authority and to the extent that it is exercised by unaccountable elites, to that extent we, both collectively and severally, lack autonomy in our lives.[48] In virtue of the reach of political power, this lack of autonomy extends from our lives as citizens into our non-political lives.

Autonomy is a fundamental good, a "highest order interest" for us. We conceive ourselves as moral selves, free persons. As such we have a fundamental interest in how our lives go. We wish our lives to be good, but we also wish to be actively involved in them; we wish them to proceed subject to our control, according to our reflective, deliberative best judgment. Since our lives are pervasively subject to the forces and institutions of our social world, we also want to subject our social world to our reflective, rational control to the extent that this is possible. Since this world is a common product, reflective, rational control must take the form of participation in a process of *collective* rational determination of its structure and directions. The alternative to secure, institutionalized opportunity for full and meaningful participation in deliberative collective control of political authority is not greater scope and resources for the exercise of individual freedom, but rather the loss of all control of collective, and many individual, aspects of our lives to unaccountable elites and ungoverned centers of power.

Thus, decisions made for and in the name of citizens of a political society, are best and most properly made through robustly public political deliberation. All politics is concerned in one way or another with the exercise of power. In the context of politics, public discourse is also a form of power. But, as Gutmann argues, "it is the most defensible form of *political* power because it is the most consistent with respecting the autonomy of persons, their capacity for self-government."[49] Where there is equal opportunity for full participation in the deliberation leading to political decisions, we are provided a rich opportunity for active intervention in our own fate, an opportunity to take charge, along with others, of the direction of our common life, and, with that, to take control of a large part of our individual lives. Without such an opportunity, regardless of the amount of freedom secured to us to carry out our actual aims and projects without interference, a large part of our lives will be determined by drift and inadvertence, or, perhaps even worse, determined by others, without our active involvement.[50]

Autonomy is not the only human value, of course. Indeed, the thought that autonomy is the only value is unintelligible, for it *presupposes* for its intelligibility that there are other goods worthy of our pursuit, principles claiming our allegiance, and relationships demanding our loyalty. Autonomy as a moral ideal and deliberative democracy as its political manifestation are *structural, enabling* ideals. They are fundamental and intrinsic, yet they are realized most fully when they make way for the realization of other intrinsic goods and the enjoyment of other fundamentally human experiences. If politics is as pervasive as I have suggested above, then it may touch almost all aspects of life. If autonomous control of our lives is possible only if our politics is democratic, then deliberative democracy will play an important part in lives. But, as Ian Shapiro reminds us, "democracy should condition everything we do without ever displacing what we do."[51] Nevertheless, the value of autonomy, collective as well as individual, is sufficiently deep and pervasive to warrant our most serious efforts aimed at institutionalizing the ideal of robust public discourse in a politics of deliberative democracy.

B. The Institutional Shape of a Politics of Robust Public Discourse

Earlier I sketched an account of the *discipline* that the regulative ideal of consensus imposes on a practice of robust public discourse. The time has come to see how that account might be given institutional shape in political society. Since political societies differ in important ways from informal moral communities, a credible proposal for a practice of public discourse for modern political society must take these significant differences into account.

1. Deliberative Democracy. First, it might be helpful to recall the main components of the discipline of robust public justification I outlined earlier. (1) The discourse proceeds only by means of exercising the techniques of practical reasoning: articulation, argument, deliberation, and judgment. (2) The agenda for public discussion is in principle *open,* not only with regard to issues or questions, but also with regard to evidence and argument, with the sole proviso that all matters brought to public discussion are subject to the discipline of its regulative ideal. (3) Participants regard themselves as bound by a principle of *sincerity* to present proposals and evidence, arguments, and interpretations that they can fully endorse. (4) They are also committed by a principle of *integrity* to accept the implications of the principles they endorse. In the case of officials, this responsibility takes the form of a commitment to act only from a coherent theory which they can publicly articulate of the normative domain they are authorized to administer.[52] (5) They accept that the reasons they advance must be *accessible to* and *assessable by* all the other participants in the discourse. (6) Participants regard their own proposals, reasons, and arguments as *defeasible,* both with regard to their *substantive* claims and with regard to their claim to *speak for community,* and so accept the obligation to *integrate* the views of all other participants into their interpretations, reasons, and arguments. (7) They accept final *closure* of argument on an

issue only upon full and willing agreement of all the participants based on the strength of the arguments alone; but they
also accept the pragmatic necessity for *temporary conditional closure* of debate. (8) Finally, they accept the governing constraint
of *reflexivity*, that is, they recognize that any closure devices, and
any other constraints on full and open exercise of public practical reason by all capable participants, must themselves survive
critical scrutiny in a fully open public process of deliberation
and argument governed by the discipline of consensus as a
regulative ideal.

In politics this discipline is given shape in institutions governed by the ideal of deliberative democracy. I cannot discuss
these institutional features in detail here, but I do wish to briefly
discuss four salient features which, I hope, will illustrate the
direction in which further development of the ideas in this essay
are likely to proceed. The first two features I will mention start
from the observation that life and discourse in modern political
societies are carried on among strangers mediated through institutions and groups. Thus, first, we cannot plausibly conceive
of the *forums* in which public practical reasoning about common
and public matters must be carried on as simple, undifferenti-
ated public squares writ (very) large. Rather, public discourse
typically will be carried on in a host of subcommunities, associations, institutions, and corporate entities that form an inter-
locking and overlapping network in political society.[53] This is
important, not only because a polis-wide forum is radically unfeasible, but also because deliberative discourse is meaningful
only within a relatively small, local group of participants. Participation in a truly nationwide, but unmediated debate over a
given public issue would surely be reduced to insignificance for
any given participant. Participation takes on significance if one
can participate in genuine reasoned exchange with other citizens at a local level, and if this local exercise can plausibly be
seen by participants as contributing to the larger debate
through a properly functioning network of such local forums,
assisted by accountable media.

Second, while the practice of *public discourse* will be society-
wide and, as I shall argue presently, open equally to all, collective decision making reflecting this discourse is best delegated

to *representatives* in publicly accountable official positions (not only legislative, but also executive and judicial).[54] The justification for this division of labor should be clear from our earlier discussion. I defended the practice of robust public reasoning on the grounds that it was essential to collective, and consequently individual, *autonomy*. It assumes the fundamental intrinsic good of governing one's life in accord with deliberation and reflective judgment. It does not assume, however, that this is the *only* good to which we are committed; on the contrary, the value of autonomy presupposes that we are committed to *other* goods. Autonomy is a structuring and enabling value; it cannot by itself supply the focus of one's life. It must not *displace* our pursuit of other aims and goals. Thus, with the aim of husbanding our resources, we have good reason to delegate to others the task of exercising political authority concerning public concerns in our names. However, while we may be justified in *delegating* such authority, we must not completely *alienate* it. In the interest of maintaining real reflective control of our own lives in the face of the exercise of political authority by others, we must insist on the full *public accountability* of all public officials.[55] They must be fully accountable to the public deliberations carried on at local levels throughout the political society. Thus, institutional devices making political officials accountable are essential to deliberative democracy and to a politics of robust public discourse.

The institutions of deliberative democracy also give shape to the constraints we noted earlier on closure of debate. The ideal of closure of debate *only* upon full agreement amongst all participants based only on the arguments is, of course, as unfeasible in the real world of politics as it is in the real world of ordinary practical decision making. We are typically forced by circumstances to make decisions not only on the basis of incomplete information, but also on the basis of uncompleted deliberation.[56] Participants committed to the discipline of consensus as a regulative ideal are not rendered impotent by this fact of life, rather they accept the pragmatic necessity of premature closure of debate, but they regard premature closure as legitimate only as a temporary measure. Since they regard closure devices as temporary expedients, they will interpret the results of such closure narrowly and will regard it as entirely legitimate to reopen temporarily closed issues in a timely and orderly fashion.

This general approach to closure rules is given shape in two principles governing the structure of deliberative democratic institutions. First, when debate must be brought to closure, the only fair procedure that recognizes both the paramount importance to each citizen of reasoned deliberative determination of public issues and the right of individual citizens to participate in deliberative determination of their lives is a *majority decision rule* implemented only after extensive and exhaustive (if not conclusive) reasoned deliberations and interpreted as a fair pooling of their tentative deliberative judgments, given the constraints of time and feasibility.[57] Any decision rule that departs from the majority principle in the direction of unanimity— favoring either maintaining or changing the status quo—represents a judgment *either* on the substantive merits of the arguments, which we are not entitled to make outside the deliberative process itself, *or* on some basis apart from the merits of their arguments, which gives greater weight to the views of some participants than others. But arguments and proposals (including the merits of maintaining or altering the status quo) are to be judged *only* on their merits through public discourse. If closure is pragmatically necessary, then we must base the temporary closure rule on considerations other than the merits of the arguments themselves. Viewed apart from the merits of the arguments and proposals they submit for common discursive consideration, each participant must be treated as an equal. The majority decision rule most closely approximates this requirement of treatment of each participant as an equal. Moreover, because the vote governed by the majority decision rule must be interpreted as a device for pooling deliberative judgments of participants, the device of voting must be used only after thorough public deliberation, *and* participants are bound to cast their votes not as expression of their *preferences* but of their best *judgments* on the evidence and arguments presented in the debate.

Second, we must resist the Rousseauean temptation to represent the outcome of the vote as either the expression of, or best evidence for, the *general will*. The decision represents the best device we have, consistent with recognizing the autonomy and equal status of each participant, for temporary closure of debate. Yet, the outcome represents *the majority's* judgment. The decision does not *absorb* the minority into the majority will.[58] The minority judgment still stands in opposition to that of the majority, possibly only temporarily. Viewed in this way, the minority judgment is given *standing*. In political discourse we do not realistically expect to eliminate dissensus, and, in view of the importance of a space for dissensus for the development and exercise of individual autonomy, we do not even wish for its eradication. Rather, we hope effectively to *contain* it within the political society.[59] Effective containment of dissent and adequate public recognition of the standing of minority judgment require democratic institutions that define a space within politics for *meaningful opposition* before, during, *and after* decisions are made by political authorities.[60] Civil disobedience, of course, will be recognized as legitimate, but dissent must also be more formally institutionalized. The legislative process must recognize the legitimacy of opposing political parties, and the judicial process must allow for the regular challenge and review of the exercise of legislative and executive authority. Moreover, the institution of judicial review must be structured in such a way that access to it and participation in it are available broadly in the community and must engage the responsible public discourse carried on in the political community at large.[61]

2. Equality and Openness: Two Principles of Deliberative Democratic Design. Two fundamental principles of institutional design are implicit in the above remarks and I will close my defense of a practice of robust public discourse with a brief discussion of these two principles. First, *equality*. Because the only coin of this realm of public discourse is that of practical reason, all other factors which may influence deliberations must be neutralized so far as feasible. A consequence is that each participant must be assured of formally and substantively equal opportunity of full participation.[62] Parties are formally equal only if each has an equal and substantial voice in all collective deliberations and equal representation by publicly accountable officials authorized to make political decisions. They are substantively equal if social and economic conditions do not distort their chances to contribute to the public discourse.[63] Note that equality does not require equality of political power, nor equality of political influence, nor equal representation in the outcomes of political decisions. Rather, it requires equal opportunity to participate in full and meaningful public deliberations, to which all public officials and their decisions are fully accountable. This is a tall order. For it requires not only formal, legal support, but a substantial degree of material support for a public *culture,* as well as political institutions, which give the fullest and widest possible opportunity to all citizens to participate on an equal basis.

Second, the *public* in which robustly public practical discourse must be rooted is characterized by radical *openness.* Note three important dimensions of this openness. First, we noted earlier that it is an essential feature of robust public discourse that it be carried on amongst others. Public discourse takes place out in the open, *in public,* in open conversation and debate with others. Second, this public is characterized by *open access:* everyone who is capable is entitled to participate.[64] Their only qualifications are a stake in the common enterprise and a willingness to submit to the discipline of the regulative ideal on condition that other co-members of the public do likewise.

Finally, as we noted above, robust public discourse, not only in its moral practice, but also in its political practice, must be *radically open* in the following sense: no restrictions are placed on the issues or proposals that may be brought to public attention, nor on the views, opinions, reasons, or arguments to which participants may appeal in their discussion of them, except those entailed by the discipline of public practical reason itself. This discipline requires only that issues and questions brought to the public deal with matters of the public's common life,[65] and that all articulation, deliberation, and argument be governed by its regulative ideal. Thus, participants are not required to check their most deeply held convictions at the forum gate; they are required only to agree along with all other participants to subject them to the discipline of the public practical discourse.

Several contemporary political theorists'[66] in effect embrace for the political practice of public justification the old Baconian maxim that we must "set aside [our] staunchly held views and presuppositions and discuss [our mutual problems] together." [67] They recommend that, in the face of fundamental disagreement on political issues rooted in deeper conflicts of moral principle and comprehensive visions of the good, we should seek common judgment by *prescinding* from all disagreement, in effect "gagging" the expression of disagreements that have their roots in values that are not already widely shared.

We must reject this "gag strategy" for dealing with "the fact of pluralism." First, in view of the breadth as well as the depth of disagreement in modern political societies, we have good reason to expect citizens may *bring to* the public forum very little that is already shared. To permit appeal only to considerations *already shared* may limit public discussion to very little, if anything, of moral importance to those who wish to participate. Second, this strategy ignores the potential within the practice of robust public discourse of *making public for* the participants matters they did not share, prior to their participation. Third, attempts at suppression of deeply held convictions are very likely to fail. The effect of containing the pressure of such deeper disagreements is that it will erupt elsewhere or later, probably with far more destructive force. [68]

Moreover, the principled argument most often given for the gag strategy seems misguided. It is often argued that to put forward an argument with which we know others will disagree is to fail to respect them as rational, autonomous agents. But this is just a mistake. There is nothing demeaning in being put in a position of having to respond to reasonable public challenges to one's moral beliefs. To revise one's moral beliefs, even very deep ones, in response to honest reasonable challenges is not to be *forced to renounce* those beliefs, but rather to respond to precisely the kind of pressures to which beliefs held in this way are thought to be vulnerable. We wish to govern our lives not merely by *our own* beliefs, but rather by beliefs we can endorse *as true, sound, or valid.* Thus, for us to treat the moral beliefs of other persons merely as preferences, or matters that are not of any concern to any other person, is to fail to recognize the role such beliefs play in their practical perspectives.

Respect *requires us* to assume until we have good evidence to the contrary that our interlocutor wishes to claim public status for her or his evaluative beliefs.

In view of its regulative aim, the discipline of public practical discourse cannot require participants to abstract from or set aside their convictions when they engage in public discourse; neither can it require them to remove from the public agenda those issues which bring these convictions into play. The regulative aim is *common conviction:* only if citizens attempt to give voice to their deepest convictions (when they bear on matters under public scrutiny), in language which others can find intelligible, can they hope to bring different visions into focus for common purposes. If this expression is *gagged,* if co-members of a public are denied the opportunity to articulate their convictions subject to the discipline of public discourse, they will never be able to explore the territory that still separates them. Again we see that the notion of robust public practical discourse does not assume or enforce *uniformity;* on the contrary, it recognizes, welcomes, and seeks to give constructive shape to *difference* and *disagreement.*[69] The aim of robust public discourse is to enable people to carry on deliberations even when they disagree deeply. To purge political discourse of all but superficial disagreement is not to advance this project but rather to abandon it. Dissensus within the practice of robust public discourse is a sign of moral and social health, not of moral or social dysfunction.

One important consequence of the *openness* of public practical discourse is that the practice is in a certain respect self-policing. A scene in Brecht's little play, "The Exception and the Rule," teaches a useful lesson about the pretenses of public discourse and the powers of publicity to expose them. The merchant, driven by greed, loads his coolie high with drilling equipment and sets off across the desert to Urga. Exhausted by the arduous journey and the merchant's abuse, the coolie finally reaches the end of his patience and energy and refuses to cross a deep, rushing river at great risk to his life. Urging him on, the merchant explains the necessity of the journey: "Are you too much of a fool to understand it's doing mankind a service to extract oil from the earth?" he asks. "When the oil is extracted, there'll be railways here and prosperity will spread. ... And who will bring this about? *We* shall. It all depends on *our* journey." To this the coolie responds: "WE and YOU AND I/Are not the same. WE defeat the foe/But YOU defeat ME." [70] Moral and political judgments purport to be public judgments based on reasons that are public (for us). Brecht's coolie makes clear that this pretense of public justification can be egregiously false. But, precisely because public justification is necessarily justification *in a radically open public,* the pretenses of public justification are publicly put to the test. Among the most important things one learns through participation in truly public discourse is the scope and validity of the claim one implicitly makes in saying "we." One learns precisely who turns out to be willing and able to endorse that claim. [71]

3. Conclusion: Legitimacy, Truth, and Public Justification. This completes my attempt to articulate and defend the political practice of public practical reason. I conclude with a word about the moral force of decisions and actions that flow from institutions that meet the conditions of this account of the practice. This account of public practical reason, and its embodiment in institutions of deliberative democracy, provide us with an account of the moral/political *legitimacy* of decisions and actions of political authority. I do not regard them as defining conditions of justice (or moral-political truth). Decisions and actions of political authority are legitimate not merely by virtue of the fact that they *could* (hypothetically) be defended publicly, but only if they are the products of actual public deliberation that meets the conditions laid out above. Where decisions and actions of political authority are legitimate, citizens have an obligation to comply with, or in other appropriate ways respect, those decisions and actions. From this it does not follow, however, that those decisions or actions are *just* or fully *justified,* or that those who are bound by them have no grounds for complaint. Indeed, decisions and actions that are the product of fully public deliberation as I have defined it are likely still to draw critical fire on substantive moral grounds from reasonable persons. This is obvious from our discussion of the possibility of dissensus and opposition within the context of exercises of political authority governed by majority rule. Politics in a deliberative democracy is a constant struggle for justice (and other fundamental common and public goods) according to the rules and discipline of public practical reason. Public practical reason issues no guarantee of truth, but only a warranty of reasonableness; a guarantee not of justice, but only of legitimacy. However, we must not regard this as settling for second best. For to insist on anything *more,* is in effect to settle for something far *less;* for it is to accept that the struggle for justice can better be waged through non-democratic means by those who have some greater claim than the rest of us to insight into moral and political truth. The legitimacy promised by deliberative democracy is no guarantee of truth or justice, but it does seem to be the only appropriate way to carry on the struggle that adequately respects the autonomy and dignity of each citizen.

NOTES

This is the second part of a two-part exploration of the idea of public practical reason. The first essay, "Public Practical Reason: An Archeology," is forthcoming in *Social Philosophy and Policy.* In March 1990, I had the very great pleasure of presenting ancestors of the ideas developed in these essays in a series of seminars for the Faculty of Law at McGill University. I wish to express my gratitude to Stephen Perry, and the Faculty of Law at McGill, for providing me with this opportunity and offering me many helpful suggestions and criticisms. Over the intervening years, versions of these essays have been presented to several audiences: the Legal Theory Workshop of the Faculty of Law at the University of Toronto, the Political Theory Workshop at Yale University, and The Ethics Discussion Group at Chapel Hill. I am grateful for searching discussions of these ideas with each of these audiences. Special thanks for discussion of ideas in this second essay in the series are due to Stephen Perry, Leslie Green, Brian Langille, Ernest Weinrib, Arthur Ripstein, Joseph Carens, Bruce Ackerman, and Ian Shapiro.

1. I. Kant, "Perpetual Peace," in *Kant's Political Writings* ed. H. Reiss, trans. H. B. Nisbet (Cambridge: Cambridge University Press, 1970), 126.

2. I. Kant, *Critique of Pure Reason,* trans. N. Kemp Smith (New York: St. Martin's Press, 1965), 593 (A737–8/B767–8).

3. B. Ackerman, "Why Dialogue?" *Journal of Philosophy* 86 (1989): 8.

4. S. Macedo, *Liberal Virtues* (Oxford: Clarendon Press, 1991), 59.

5. See, for example, J. Cohen, "Deliberation and Democratic Legitimacy," in *The Good Polity,* ed. A. Hamlin and P. Pettit (London: Basil Blackwell, 1989), and "The Economic Basis of Deliberative Democracy," *Social Philosophy and Policy* 6 (1989): 25–50; also A. Gutmann, "The Disharmony of Democracy," in *Democratic Community: NOMOS XXXV,* ed. J. W. Chapman and I. Shapiro (New York: New York University Press, 1993).

6. "Public Practical Reason: An Archeology," *Social Philosophy and Policy* 12 (1995): 43–86.

7. D. Hume, *Enquiry Concerning the Principles of Morals,* 3rd edition, ed. P. H. Nidditch (Oxford: Clarendon Press, 1975), 272.

8. Note that the *shape* of an object cannot be construed as the shape that appears to a single observer under ideal conditions, since there is no *single* perspective that can convey to us the shape of the object. That is, as it were, a construct from the reports of an indefinite number of observers viewing the object's profile from an indefinite number of perspectives, or of the profiles one observer perceives while traveling around the object.

9. J. Bentham, *Introduction to the Principles of Morals and Legislation,* ed. J. H. Burns and H. L. A. Hart (London: Athlone Press, 1970), 28.

10. This sense of sharing and the next are suggested by Christine Korsgaard in her essay, "The Reasons We Can Share," *Social Philosophy and Policy* 10 (1993): 40–41.

11. David Gauthier defends a conception along these lines in "Constituting Democracy," Lindley Lecture, University of Kansas, 1989; see especially 10–11, which draws on his *Morals by Agreement* (Oxford: Clarendon Press, 1986), chapter 5.

12. I borrow the term from Michael Oakeshott, *Of Human Conduct* (Oxford: Clarendon Press, 1975), 35–36, but I use it in a different sense. See also M. Nussbaum, *Love's Knowledge* (New York: Oxford University Press, 1990), 234.

13. Evaluative articulation involves bringing to *public attention* relevant evidence or experience which may be known only to some or known only privately. More importantly, it involves giving articulate *public shape* to concerns, needs, aims, values, and projects, thereby making them eligible for adoption by the group in question. By uttering and articulating them in public, they are no longer matters for

the participants severally, but they become matters *for them together.*
They become matters of *common* (that is, mutual, public) *knowledge,* and
thus take shape as matters for their common attention. See C. Taylor,
Human Agency and Language I (Cambridge: Cambridge University
Press), 259–60.

14. D. Hume, *A Treatise of Human Nature,* 2nd edition, ed. P. H.
Nidditch (Oxford: Clarendon Press, 1978), 490, 498. Recent work in
experimental game theory seems to support Hume's premise. Researchers have found that parties who are placed in prisoners' dilemma
situations and given an opportunity to discuss their situation among
themselves are far more likely to cooperate than parties who were not
given such an opportunity. Discussion typically moved from consequences of cooperation or defection for each party individually to
consideration of what "we" should do. Researchers speculate that a
sense of "group identity" often emerges from such conversation, which
sustains a resolve to do one's part in a cooperative scheme despite
strong incentives to defect. See J. M. Orbell, R. M. Dawes, and A. J. C.
van de Kragt, "Explaining Discussion-Induced Cooperation," *Journal
of Personality and Social Psychology* 54 (1988): 811–19, "The Limits of
Multilateral Promising," *Ethics* 100 (1990): 616–27, and "Cooperation
for the Benefit of Us—Not Me, or My Conscience," in *Beyond Self-
Interest,* ed. J. Mansbridge (Chicago: University of Chicago Press,
1990), 97–110. I discuss Hume's notion of a "common sense of interest," and the relevance of this experimental evidence to it in "Morality
in the First-Person Plural," *Law & Philosophy* (forthcoming).

15. J. Rawls, "The Domain of the Political and Overlapping Consensus," *New York University Law Review* 64 (1989): 237.

16. I. Berlin, *The Crooked Timber of Humanity,* ed. H. Hardy (New
York: Knopf, 1990), 13.

17. B. Williams, introduction to I. Berlin, *Concepts and Categories,*
ed. H. Hardy (London: Hogarth Press, 1978), xvi.

18. I cannot supply reasons for this suspicion here. Philip Pettit
does an especially good job of arguing the case for holism (while
defending individualism against collectivism) in *The Common Mind*
(New York: Oxford University Press, 1993), chapters 3 and 4.

19. J. Habermas, *Moral Consciousness and Communicative Action,*
trans. C. Lenhardt and S. W. Nicholsen (Cambridge, Mass.: MIT Press,
1991), 199.

20. T. Hobbes, *A Dialogue between a Philosopher and a Student of the
Common Laws,* ed. J. Cropsey (Chicago: University of Chicago Press,
1971), 67; *The English Works of Thomas Hobbes* 5, ed. W. Molesworth
(London: 1839–45), 176. For a discussion of Hobbes's attempt to estab-

lish a firm basis for public "Right Reason," see Postema, *Bentham and the Common Law Tradition* (Oxford: Clarendon Press, 1986, revised edition 1989), ch. 2, sect. 2.

21. Rawls, "The Idea of Overlapping Consensus," *Oxford Journal of Legal Studies* 7 (1987): 5–6; "Justice as Fairness: Political Not Metaphysical," *Philosophy and Public Affairs* 14 (1985): 229.

22. T. Morawetz, "The Epistemology of Judging: Wittgenstein and Deliberative Practices," *The Canadian Journal of Law and Jurisprudence* 3 (1990): 42.

23. Aristotle, *Topics,* Loeb Classical Library, trans. E. S. Forster (Cambridge, Mass.: Harvard University Press, 1966), 739 (164b8–14). I have altered Forster's translation slightly.

24. I. Kant, *Critique of Pure Reason,* 597 (A744/B772). The "weapons of reason" include articulation, argument, deliberation, and judgment *(phronesis).*

25. J. Habermas, *Moral Consciousness,* 198.

26. Kant, "What Is Enlightenment?" in *Kant's Political Writings,* 55–57. O'Neill brought this passage to my attention, see *Constructions of Reason,* 17.

27. "[A]rguments are to be accepted by authority of the speaker's reasons, not by reason of the speaker's authority." See N. MacCormick, "Legal Reasoning and Practical Reason," in *Midwest Studies in Philosophy VII,* ed. P. A. French, T. E. Uehling, Jr., H. K. Wettstein (Minneapolis: University of Minnesota Press, 1982), 274. Note that appeals to authority are not excluded, but only claims that are regarded as not themselves subject to the reflexivity maxim mentioned below—that is, claims put forward as beyond challenge and critical assessment in the same forum of public discourse as all other, both empirical and normative, claims. Thus, the clergy's address is "private" not because it regards matters of religion, but because it allows no open challenge to its authority.

28. Regarded as an ideal of politics, this, of course, is a highly controversial claim. I will address objections to this political ideal near the end of this essay.

29. R. Audi seems to make this a condition of participation in public debate in "The Separation of Church and State and the Obligations of Citizenship," *Philosophy and Public Affairs* 18 (1989): 284–86. But this is too strong.

30. This is one of Audi's arguments for the maxim (in his stronger version). See Audi, "The Separation of Church and State," 282. See also J. Hampton, "Should Political Philosophy Be Done Without Metaphysics?" *Ethics* 99 (1989): 807.

31. A. Gutmann and D. Thompson, "Moral Conflict and Political Consensus," *Ethics* 101 (1990): 78.

32. T. Nagel, "Moral Conflict and Political Legitimacy," *Philosophy and Public Affairs* 16 (1987): 232.

33. J. Raz, "Facing Diversity: The Case of Epistemic Abstinence," *Philosophy and Public Affairs* 19 (1990): 39.

34. Nagel, "Moral Conflict and Political Legitimacy," 232.

35. I will return to this important point below, 376–77.

36. J. Cohen, "Deliberation and Democratic Legitimacy," 23. I will discuss below the political forms such closure may take; see 371–73.

37. A. Gutmann and D. Thompson, "Moral Conflict and Political Consensus," 82.

38. However, it is important to remain cognizant of the danger that rules of "civility" can pose for genuine public discourse. These dangers are compellingly chronicled by William Chafe in his account of the civil rights struggles of the 1950s and 1960s in North Carolina. See W. Chafe, *Civilities and Civil Rights* (New York: Oxford University Press, 1980). Concern for civility in the racist environment of that time blocked understanding, blinded people to the depth of black resentment, forced into silence deep grievances and challenges to the rules of power, and generally provided a cover for subtle but firm control of oppressed people by the dominant culture.

39. See references in note 5.

40. C. Williams, *The Image of the City and Other Essays*, selected by A. Ridler (New York: Oxford University Press, 1958), 107.

41. Rawls, "Overlapping Consensus," 4 n. 7; "The Domain of the Political," 234–35.

42. S. Wolin, *Politics and Vision* (Boston: Little, Brown, 1960), 62; quoted by H. Pitkin, *Wittgenstein and Justice* (Berkeley: University of California Press, 1972), 216.

43. H. Pitkin, *Wittgenstein and Justice*, 215.

44. S. Holmes, "Tocqueville and Democracy," in *The Idea of Democracy*, ed. D. Copp, J. Hampton, and J. Roemer (Cambridge: Cambridge University Press, 1993), 28.

45. Equally, Hume, writing a century later, was keenly aware of the power of political factions to divide and destroy a nation, and this awareness deeply influenced his political theory. See D. Hume, "Of Parties in General," in *Essays: Moral, Political, and Literary*, ed. E. Miller (Indianapolis: Liberty*Classics*, 1985), 54–63; and *History of England* (Indianapolis: Liberty*Classics*, 1983–5), III, 210–12; IV, 354–55.

46. Parker J. Palmer, *The Company of Strangers: Christians and the Renewal of America's Public Life* (New York: Crossroads, 1981).

47. Genesis 11:1–9.

48. A. Gutmann, "Disharmony," 142–43.

49. A. Gutmann, "Disharmony," 141.

50. On this point see H. Pitkin, "Justice: On Relating Private and Public," *Political Theory* 9 (1981): 344.

51. I. Shapiro, *Democratic Justice*, chapter 2 (manuscript). I am grateful to Ian Shapiro for bringing to my attention the points made in this paragraph and for permission to quote him here.

52. See R. Dworkin, *Taking Rights Seriously* (Cambridge: Harvard University Press, 1978), 160–61; and *Law's Empire* (Cambridge: Harvard University Press, 1986), chapter 6.

53. Seyla Benhabib suggested this way of conceiving of the public forum in her contribution to the ASPLP Meeting on the topic of Theory and Practice, Washington, D.C., December, 1992.

54. Here I follow Amy Gutmann's proposal; see "Disharmony," 141–44.

55. Ibid.

56. Some of these problems are outlined by Thomas Christiano in his "Freedom, Consensus, and Equality in Collective Decision Making," *Ethics* 101 (1990): 166–68.

57. I should note that my proposal shares with the so-called "epistemic conception of democracy" the view that votes are to be interpreted not as expressions of *preferences exogenous* to the process of public deliberation and decision making, but as expressions of *judgments formulated in the course of participation in that process*. (On this view, see J. Cohen, "An Epistemic Conception of Democracy," 26–38 and D. Estlund, "Democracy Without Preference," *Philosophical Review* 99 [1990]: 397–423.) But I do not accept the implausible thesis of epistemic democracy that the majority outcome is to be taken as conclusive evidence of the *truth* of the proposal or judgment it supports. (For a discussion of this thesis see J. Coleman and J. Ferejohn, "Democracy and Social Choice," *Ethics* 97 [1986]: 16–17; Cohen, "Epistemic Democracy," 34; Christiano, "Collective Decision Making," 165). My view is that majority rule is preferred when closure must be achieved because it meets conditions of equality when there is no neutral, non-controversial basis distinguishing the relative merits of the judgments of the participants. Because any voting mechanism is a second-best substitute for the process of achieving agreement by unlimited reasoned discourse, the outcome must be regarded as legitimate conditional upon the possibility of further public deliberation, which deliberation may be initiated by a challenge to the truth or soundness of the majority judgment.

58. See B. Manin, "On Legitimacy and Political Deliberation," *Political Theory* 15 (1987): 360.

59. H. Pitkin, *Wittgenstein and Justice*, 208.

60. Ian Shapiro makes much of this point in his *Democratic Justice*, chapter 3 (manuscript).

61. This, of course, only hints at the direction that I believe the institutionalization of opposition and democratic accountability should go. Much more needs to be said about the forms such institutionalization should take and the safeguards that must be put in place to protect the fundamental aims of deliberative democracy. But I want to stress here that we must not limit the scope of robust public practical discourse to either elective or legislative politics. A vigorous institution of judicial review is not a challenge to democracy properly understood, but an essential component of it.

62. J. Cohen, "Deliberation and Democratic Legitimacy," 22–23; R. Alexy, *A Theory of Legal Argumentation*, trans. R. Adler and N. MacCormick (Oxford: Clarendon Press, 1989), 119–20, 130.

63. J. Cohen, ibid., 23.

64. See R. Alexy, *Legal Argumentation*, 130–31, 193; Habermas, *Moral Consciousness*, 89.

65. I have argued for the importance of this substantive constraint on public discourse in "Public Faces—Private Places: Liberalism and the Enforcement of Morality," in *Morality, Worldview, and Law*, ed. A. W. Musschenga, B. Voorzanger, and A. Soeteman (Assen: Van Gorcum, 1992), 167–69.

66. For example, Rawls, "Overlapping Consensus," 8, 13–14, 17; B. Ackerman, "Why Dialogue?" *Journal of Philosophy* 86 (1989), 16–17; S. Holmes, "Gag Rules or the Politics of Omission," in *Constitutionalism and Democracy*, ed. J. Elster and R. Slagstad (Cambridge: Cambridge University Press, 1988), 19–58.

67. F. Bacon, *Instauratio Magna* (1323) in *The Works of Francis Bacon I*, ed. J. Spedding, R. L. Ellis, and D. D. Heath (London: Longman, 1858; facs. reprint, Stuttgart: Friedrich Fromann Verlag, 1963), 132–33. Kant uses this passage as the motto for his *Critique of Pure Reason*. See O. O'Neill, *Constructions of Reason*, 6–7.

68. See here Stephen Holmes' discussion of the constitutional attempt to contain anti-slavery sentiment in the late-eighteenth-century and early-nineteenth-century United States: "Gag Rules," 31–43.

69. Note, however, that the argument does not depend in any way on the value of *expressing* one's convictions in public, except insofar as doing so is essential to participation in, and in fact advances, public deliberation about and collective determination of important elements

of common life. To the extent that such expression takes on the character of eristic argument—that is, argument aimed at goals other than those sanctioned by the regulative ideal of consensus—such expression is ruled out of the public forum. Expressivist arguments play no important role in my account of deliberative democracy or the ideal of robust public discourse to which it gives political shape.

70. B. Brecht, "The Exception and the Rule," scene 5, in Brecht, *The Jewish Wife and Other Short Plays*, trans. E. Bently (New York: Grove Press, 1965), 125.

71. H. Pitkin, *Wittgenstein and Justice*, 208.

13

"TRUTH" OR CONSEQUENCES

KENT GREENAWALT

I. Introduction

The papers and comments at the Society's meeting on Theory and Practice reminded me of a disquieting problem about scholarly sincerity. The problem concerns the responsibilities of theorists who believe that stating factual or normative "truths," as they understand them, will probably have harmful effects. I outline the problem, focusing on one of its aspects, and comment briefly on possible resolutions. Finally, I suggest a connection between favored resolutions and the perceived status of normative judgments: namely, that people who believe normative judgments have some kind of objective status may in general be more likely than those who do not have that belief to opt for sincerity at the risk of harmful effects.

The issue about sincerity can arise over ordinary factual or normative assertions. I concentrate on normative assertions, but it is well to begin with the simpler and more commonly noticed worry about factual statements. Suppose a theorist believes that the data, on balance, support the claim that the average level of intelligence is slightly higher among the members of some race(s) than the members of some other(s). (A serious claim of this sort would require a refined account of various intellectual abilities and of who count as members of particular races, but the cruder formulation conveys the basic idea adequately for our purposes.) The theorist might conclude that a proper understanding of the data has no, or virtually no, implications for public policy. If the difference in intelligence is an average one and relatively slight, it should have little bearing on what individuals should occupy what positions, or on other matters for which distribution according to race might seem important.[1] The theorist realizes, however, that her subject is explosive, that a wide public is interested in claims of this variety, that reports by the public press of her findings may seriously distort them, that listeners and readers may distort them still further, and that her modest claim may end up supporting unwarranted policy conclusions.

The possibility of a rather different kind of harm has been raised in response to the present research project of Elaine Pagels, who is exploring, among other things, the way that Jews are portrayed in the New Testament. Some friends have expressed concern that an account of what she learns may stir up emnities between Christians and Jews.

In short, theorists may worry that candid descriptive accounts will have untoward practical effects. They may face a choice between asserting the truth in which they believe or remaining silent, or perhaps even denying what they believe.[2] The reality of such dilemmas, if not their resolutions, is clear.

II. Normative Assertions that May Have Harmful Effects

A similar but more complex problem arises when the theorist believes that a sound normative assertion will probably have harmful practical effects. By harmful practical effects, I do not, of course, mean *any* harmful effects, but effects that, on balance, are worse than if the theorist remained silent or asserted something other than what he or she believes to be sound.[3]

I shall offer examples of normative assertion that are at a deep and very abstract level and at what we might call a middle range. My abstract illustrations are tied to issues concerning consequentialism and its variations or alternatives.

In the theory of criminal punishment, a basic distinction is drawn between retributive and utilitarian rationales for punishment. Simply put, retributivists assert that punishment is intrinsically deserved, that its appropriateness does not depend on good consequences. Utilitarians (here encompassing consequentialists of all sorts) say the value of punishment rests on a favorable balance of effects. One intermediate point of view is that the *real* philosophic justification for punishment lies in consequences, but that consequences will actually be best if people believe in retributive justifications. This view is not implausible. Chances for reform of criminals, for example, may be greatest if they and others believe their punishment is intrinsically deserved, not just a means to a greater end. This theoretical possibility concerning punishment may be generalized to the wider competition between consequentialism and deontology. Perhaps human welfare (good consequences) will best be served if people generally believe in a morality that accords a substantial place to duties and rights that do not rest directly on consequential analysis.[4]

Whether considering punishment or moral behavior more broadly, a theorist might be concerned that revealing the necessity for deep consequential justifications would undermine or weaken to some extent desirable nonconsequential moral attitudes. At this level of abstraction, however, the connection between theoretical assertion and ordinary moral attitudes seems so tenuous and uncertain that the theorist's conceivable dilemma takes on little urgency. Her practical worry may seem more pressing if we turn to the middle range of normative assertion.

Here, I shall use two examples of criticisms of positions I have taken in recent years. To oversimplify a lot, I claimed in a series of lectures that moderate use of religious convictions was appropriate for citizens and officials trying to resolve political issues in liberal democracies.[5] Some listeners put roughly the following challenge: "Religious citizens will inevitably use religious convictions to some extent, and their modest use is all right. But if modest use is recommended, actual use will be excessive. A recommended principle of no use will bring about a more appropriate degree of use."[6]

In a paper reviewing Bruce Ackerman's *We the People: Foundations,*[7] I assert that judges should not, as Ackerman recommends, decide whether or not popular support for constitutional changes amounts to "higher lawmaking"; but I also say that judges appropriately give *some* weight to popular support for claimed constitutional principles.[8] At a faculty lunch discussing the paper, my colleague Richard Pierce urged that, of course, judges inevitably will give some weight to popular views—"The Supreme Court follows the election returns"—but that the appropriate principle for decision was that they should give no weight. I inquired whether he thought *giving no weight* was actually the best practice or whether he thought *giving modest weight* was the best practice but that it would come closest to realization if a principle of *giving no weight* was recommended. He responded that he was inclined to the latter position. That position presents the following issue for the theorist. Should she recommend modest weight despite worries that excess weight may follow? Should she recommend a principle of "no weight"? If so, should she reveal that she is recommending the principle because she thinks judges aiming at that (or perhaps self-consciously evading it to some degree) will actually come closest to the desirable consequence of modest weight? Needless to say, if judges and others understand that the real value of a principle of "no weight" is to produce a desirable result of modest weight, they may approach the stated principle of "no weight" differently than if they believe what it recommends is really the most desirable outcome. The theorist who adopts Dick Pierce's view of the situation faces a difficult question what she should say and not say.

This question, of course, reflects tensions between ideal theory and a full theory that takes into account human inadequacies. The difficulty for practice arises from imperfections in people who will receive the theory. They may not grasp the nuances of the normative claim and thus may fail to understand its significance. Even if their conceptual understanding is fine and they conscientiously try to apply the normative principles, they may be unable to do so accurately enough; citizens aiming to give modest effect to religious convictions or judges aiming to give modest effect to popular support of proposed constitutional norms may tend to give more weight than the principles call for. Further, the best principle for ideal people need not be framed to foreclose intentional avoidance; a more absolute alternative that forcefully combats avoidance may seem needed for real people. A judge told to give only modest weight to popular support of proposed constitutional norms may feel much more comfortable giving very great weight—after all, how important is a matter of degree?—than a judge told that *any* intentional weight is impermissible.

III. POSSIBLE RESOLUTIONS

The distinguishing feature of the problem about ideal and full theory that I am considering is its concern with the choice for theorists how and when to express their views once they reach the most compete understanding they can achieve. What should the theorist do if she believes that what is in some sense a sound normative position will be misunderstood or misapplied by enough people so her very statement of the position may be harmful in practice? One can imagine various ways the theorist might resolve such a conflict. She might decide either that an apparent conflict dissolves in some manner or that some absolute or near absolute ordering is possible.

Suppose someone put no intrinsic value on telling the truth. For him, the question what to say might always reduce to what will produce good effects, since the value of stating sound normative insights lies in their typically yielding beneficial consequences. He recognizes that sometimes actions that will produce long-term desirable consequences will have short-term negative ones; but all he has to do is to calculate overall consequences as carefully as possible. Such a position would be embraced by a "greatest happiness act-utilitarian"; he would treat silence or insincerity according to likely effects. For him, there might be an opposition between truth and consequences, but the "conflict" would have no normative significance.

Another way in which an apparent conflict could be dissolved is by a conviction that telling the truth will never have overall harmful effects. Such a belief would be difficult to sustain from ordinary human experience. Almost all people find occasions in personal life when they believe they should withhold facts or sincere normative judgments, at least for the time being. Most of us have lived through instances when untempered candid expression at the wrong moment seems to have gone awry. Of course, much of the difficulty is that at certain moments people are too upset emotionally to cope with unvarnished truth about their lives. That difficulty is *less crucial* for theoretical expression directed at many people, but ordinary experience does not rule out the possibility that honest theoretical judgment can be harmful. However, a person might believe, perhaps on some religious basis, that honest, accurate, theoretical opinions will never do harm that could be avoided by silence or insincerity.[9] He might acknowledge that temporarily withholding normative judgment may be desirable in personal conversation when the person to whom one speaks is angry or disturbed; but he might maintain that God has created human beings so that truth and good effects will coincide, so that revealing and publicizing general normative judgments that are true in some sense will not have adverse consequences. On this view, withholding the truth from people, at least over time, will never achieve desirable effects. If someone believes that the apparent conflict dissolves in one of these two ways, he will give absolute priority to what appear to be desirable effects or truth, according to the standpoint he takes.

We can imagine some positions that accord absolute priority to truth or likely effect, short of an assumption that an apparent conflict dissolves in one of the ways I have just discussed. With modest variations these positions can be turned into ones according near absolute priority; in that event, the ordinary priority could be outweighed, but only by something extremely powerful on the other side.

If someone believed that normative judgments are so unreliable that we can place little confidence in them and that harmful consequences of various sorts are usually much easier to ascertain, he might suppose estimates of effects should largely guide the decision of whether one speaks what one believes. A contrary position seems more plausible for a theorist, and I shall say a bit more about that. Suppose the theorist believes that human culture benefits in general from sincere normative statement, because sincerity has an intrinsic value, or because it promotes trust, or because it generates advances in understanding, and the desirable consequences they usually bring. If theorists strenuously censored themselves to produce desirable effects, knowing what to make of what they say would be much more complicated. What confidence could a libertarian student put in the philosophic arguments of a socialist professor, if he thought the professor would say anything to promote the rise of socialism? It might be responded that this worry is less significant for normative claims than for factual assertions. After all, the student can evaluate a normative claim on its merits, in a manner often not possible for statements of fact. Nevertheless, all of us, and beginners especially, would have increased difficulty sifting out normative positions if we could not believe they were put forward with sincerity by those who stake them out.[10] Substantial skepticism about the capacity of theorists to gauge the overall effects of fairly abstract normative claims may accompany belief in the values of sincere normative assertion. Given the uncertainty of effects in particular situations, the theorist might conclude that she should always speak the truth as she understands it, even though this might occasionally work out badly in ways she could not predict.

If this position is limited to theorists, rather than applied to all apparent conflicts between normative sincerity and good consequences, it has considerable affinity with some of the major views expressed in Jeremy Waldron's paper. Waldron suggests that theorists often make more substantial contributions when they do not concentrate on highly specific practical implications of their abstract theories. It is a short step from Waldron's own skepticism, about the ability of theorists to apply normative insights to complex social situations, to skepticism about the ability of theorists to judge the likely consequences of their theoretical expressions. The notion that theorists should attend to sound normative understanding and not worry too much about practical effects is one that joins this position and Waldron's.

In reflecting on this position, we should distinguish the role of the theorist from that of the politician, who is acutely concerned with practical consequences. For the theorist, consequences are often highly unpredictable. She does not know who will read her work, or how they will take it. As I have said, sincerity is important for intellectual interchange. And people expect sincerity *and* relatively full disclosure from the theorist.[11] A final reason, one suggested by Waldron, is that great attention to immediate consequences may blur the theorist's judgment and impede deep thought about fundamental subjects.

Politicians and judges are different. Politicians—Lincoln's views on slavery are a notable example—are rightly attentive to what the consequences will be if they assert particular normative principles at any particular time. There is an important distinction as well between judges and academics. Consider the question whether judges should give modest weight to popular support for proposed constitutional principles. In our system, what a law professor says has a radically different significance from what a high court says. (Matters are somewhat different in civil law countries.) If a highest court announces in an opinion that judges should give weight to forms of popular support when novel constitutional principles are argued before them, the court must expect that lower court judges will follow its direction, and that judges of the highest court in future cases will also do so (unless persuaded that another method of interpretation would be preferable). The judges in the initial case need to think fairly hard about whether announcement of such a position will have the desired effect, or whether, no matter how they state the amount of weight judges should give, the result will be that judges will give more weight to popular support than is warranted. If that is what they conclude, they may do well to follow Dick Pierce, remaining silent or announcing that popular support is irrelevant, expecting that it will inevitably be given effect anyway.

The saying that, when law professors write on particular legal topics, they adopt the standpoint of a judge is often accurate; but here some division of responsibility is appropriate. The theorist may analyze thoughtfully the kind of weight for various factors that should be given. Unless she is an expert on judicial psychology, she may be less well suited to estimate how judges will actually react to various stated principles of decisions. By itself, the theorist's proposal of an appropriate approach to decision may have little effect if it is not accepted by a court. (It is, of course, *possible* that present judges, or present students or

colleagues who become judges in the future, will be influenced
by the theorist's approach even if no court ever explicitly endorses it.) The theorist is warranted in saying what judges
should do, even if she doubts that a judicial principle stated in
those terms is actually the best way to get the judges to do what
would be best.[12]

For the theorist who finds no basis for dissolving conflicts of
truth and consequences or for according absolute or very great
priority to one or the other, the dilemma of choosing in particular instances will remain. Of course, various factors I have mentioned may figure in her approach to the problem, but the
decision may seem to come down to one between incommensurable values. So far, I have tended to slide over differences in
the sacrifice of truth, and these may emerge as extremely important in actual situations of choice. Remaining silent sacrifices
truth less than speaking falsely; waiting for an appropriate time
to speak sacrifices truth less than remaining silent forever;
avoiding inquiry about subjects that might yield potentially
harmful answers probably sacrifices the value of truth less than
withholding conclusions reached after diligent examination.[13]

IV. THE RELEVANCE OF BELIEF ABOUT THE STATUS
OF VALUE JUDGMENTS

What difference will it make to the theorist whether, to put it
crudely, she believes that value judgments can be objectively
true or false or, instead, are subjective and relative? On this
complex topic, my broad suggestion is that, in general, believers
in objective value judgments will be somewhat more likely than
others to opt for truth rather than practical effects; that, in
short, some very loose connection exists between one's position
on the conflict discussed here and one's deeply held metaethical
views.[14] I reject in this context the position occasionally taken
that metaethical views have nothing or little to do with how one
reasons about particular moral and political questions. I think
that in many instances involving this sort of conflict, differences
in understanding of the status of normative judgments do
matter.

Among objectivists, a common view is that truth and sincerity are intrinsically valuable. Normative judgments represent an attempt to determine some larger truth. Stating those judgments is one form of sincerity or honesty, the truthful disclosure of what one thinks. This places some substantial weight on the side of speaking truly. Further, common religious views, and some other objectivist positions, assume a basic compatibility between normative truth of various kinds and good consequences. A holder of one of these views, having reached some perceived insight into normative truth, will tend to discount worries that proclaiming the insight will generate a balance of harmful effects.[15]

The position of a subjectivist (especially one who does not revert to objectivist feelings when making moral judgments) differs in important respects. As far as normative judgments are concerned, there is no objective truth for this person, only one's attitudes or feelings about what is right. Indeed, from a thoroughgoing subjectivist perspective, one would have to reformulate the whole vocabulary of the tension I have posed, recasting the conflict as between full, sincere expression of one's point of view and likely harmful effects. Altering the vocabulary in this way seems to lower the value of honest statement somewhat. Further, given the strange ways in which people react to various assertions, this subjectivist view of the moral universe seems to eliminate or reduce any broad confidence that honest theoretical expressions will actually have good effects. As a consequence, the serious subjectivist may tend to give somewhat less importance to the "truth" or sincerity value.

It might rightly be objected at this point that I have omitted something very important. For the subjectivist, his own estimation of good consequences is not more objective than the importance he attaches to sincerity. In contrast to the objectivist who thinks some consequences are truly better than others, the subjectivist takes his estimation of good consequences as representing only his attitude or feelings about what consequences are desirable. The strength of the value of good effects may be reduced for the subjectivist as much as the truth value; thus, the practical resolution of these conflicts may be accomplished by weighing the two values in a roughly proportional manner as that of the objectivist.[16]

This point is significant, but it does not undermine my thesis. Importantly, it does not touch the possibility that the objectivist (or some kinds of objectivists) will be somewhat more likely to assume a compatibility of truth (or honest expression of view) and good consequences (or one's opinion about good consequences). That confidence pushes one toward speaking the truth as one understands it.

A more subtle relation may also matter a good deal. In the subjectivist position *per se*, no basis exists for preferring good consequences to stating one's sincere view of normative principles. However, if these principles are not true or valid by any objective standard (because no principles are true or valid by such a standard), what exactly is the point of stating them when one believes doing so is likely to have bad effects? One might adopt a kind of existentialist stance that emphasizes sincerity and authenticity, the importance of saying what one thinks and feels; but doing so may seem more than a little self-indulgent, if other people are going to suffer as a result. If one focuses, instead, on harms and benefits, one commits oneself to a larger cause, albeit one is evaluating effects subjectively. Thus, one can tie one's activities to the promotion of the poor or oppressed, or to attacks on exploitation, or to achieving justice, as one sees these things. One can also find reassurance in the solidarity one feels with others similarly situated who make similar evaluations of good consequences.

Modern American law schools provide some confirmation for my claim that those who reject the notion of objective truth in normative judgments are more likely to focus on effects than sincerity. Many, though not all, critical scholars, that is, adherents to critical legal studies, critical feminists, and critical race theorists, challenge ideas of objective normative truth. By and large, they see much less distinction between scholarship and activism, between supposedly detached reflection and advocacy, than do people who cling to various ideas of objective value. Their explanation often is that the concept of objectivity is a cover for the interests of dominant people in power. Whether they are right about this, their emphasis on effects seems to bear some affinity with their value skepticism. The objectivist may bemoan their failure to accept the value of detached scholarship. Lying near the heart of the disagreement may be divergence over the status of normative claims.

Of course, one should be wary indeed of generalizing far from this limited data, interpreted in such a summary manner. Even if the present scene does reveal some loose connection between anti-objectivism and an emphasis on consequences (as contrasted with full disclosure of all one thinks about normative issues), that connection may be historically contingent. A serious comparative and historical study would be needed to render solid support for the thesis I suspect is true: that, by and large, objectivists are somewhat more likely to value honest revelation of what one thinks than are their opponents.

NOTES

1. Some finding of slight average differences might lead one to conclude that slight correlated average differences in positions and incomes were the result of differences in intelligence rather than discrimination. This, in turn, could possibly affect one's belief about the need for corrective social action. Of course, if one thought the levels of intelligence or their measures were affected by discrimination, one might think the reported differences were themselves a product of discrimination.

2. If the theorist is a person of some foresight, she may have the prudence not to get involved in research whose outcome may produce such a dilemma. Those friends concerned about Pagels's findings may be implicitly suggesting that she turn her research attention elsewhere.

3. A slight variant on this problem would be if one thought that overall consequences would be positive but that effects on some group to which one owed special loyalty would be negative. Such a problem is discussed by George Fletcher in *Loyalty: An Essay on the Morality of Relationships* (New York: Oxford University Press, 1993), 156–61.

4. One might initially suppose that "rule utilitarianism" provides a way out of this paradox, but if people understand that the justification for following moral rules lies in good consequences and they are confident that on particular occasions breaking the rules may lead to good consequences, *mis*judgments that lead them to break the rules might result in worse consequences than would have occurred if they had

believed the rules had an underpinning that did not depend on consequences at all.

5. Kent Greenawalt, *Religious Convictions and Political Choice* (New York: Oxford University Press, 1988). My position has altered somewhat, as explained in *Private Consciences and Public Reasons* (to be published by Oxford University Press).

6. This challenge was sharply put by members of the University of Michigan Law faculty after the lectures. A somewhat more complicated version of the same position is raised in respect to officials in Frederick Schauer, "May Officials Think Religiously?" *William and Mary Law Review* 27 (1986): 1075.

7. Bruce Ackerman, *We The People: Foundations* (Cambridge: Harvard University Press, 1991).

8. *Dualism and Its Status*, 104 *Ethics* (1994), 480.

9. I am avoiding a subtle distinction. One might think the assurance that effects overall will not be negative attaches only to correct substantive positions, or one might think the assurance attaches to one's honest affirmations even if they are of faulty substantive views.

10. I recognize that the assertion in the text might be contested, and I have not provided supporting argumentation for it. Further, in law school classes and other disciplines, professors often advance positions in which they do not believe in order to prod students to careful thought on their own. I find this practice unobjectionable in principle, but I do believe, again without supporting argument, that it is not helpful for students if they are generally confused about whether a professor is speaking "for himself."

11. Of course, an expectations argument, taken by itself, is circular. If theorists commonly lied or withheld their opinions, others would come not to expect full disclosure.

12. I do not mean to suggest that legal academics should be indifferent to considerations of "administrability" of proposed principles; indeed, that is part of my criticism of Bruce Ackerman's position. I will not try here to sort out which aspects of administrability most legal academics are especially well or ill suited to evaluate. I *am* asserting that administrability should be *less central* to most theoretical writing than to judges writing opinions and to professors and others drafting practical guides (such as Restatements).

13. This last judgment is certainly debatable. It might be said that it is better for one person to know the truth than none, especially if that person will eventually make some indirect use of what she has learned. On the other hand, if the theorist had chosen some other area to investigate, she would end up with fuller disclosure. More broadly,

there is something disturbing to the idea of intellectual inquiry for people to engage in scholarship then to remain tight-lipped about what they believe they have learned.

14. I do not claim any logical entailment or tight connection. A person who believes that act-utilitarianism is objectively true will give overwhelming weight to likely consequences. Even a person who believes truth has some objective intrinsic value may think the truth of most normative assertions is so uncertain that one should remain silent (or even tell falsehoods about one's state of mind) rather than risk foreseen bad effects. A person, on the other hand, who thinks that value judgments are subjective might happen to place a very high value on "truth" and open sincerity. And two people, one an objectivist and one not, might well give roughly equal importance to truth and effects, resolving concrete conflicts in exactly the same way. (Similarly, one whose metaethical position shifts might well not alter his manner of making ethical judgments.) Thus, some objectivists may resolve these conflicts between honest statement and foreseen consequences like many anti-objectivists. Plainly, no straightforward connection can be drawn between choices of resolution and metaethical positions that are categorized in this gross way.

15. I am putting aside here an important class of objectivist views, those that hold that certain people have special authority to discern normative truth. Such views have dominated for much of human history. The predominance of such a view will discourage those who lack authority from stating views in opposition to those taken by those with authority. Religious inquisitions are only one, striking and extreme, example. This combination of views (objective truth and special authority) generates doubt about his insight for the person who accepts authority but arrives at a view in opposition to views authoritatively announced; and a general public confidence in authority enhances the likelihood of a hostile reaction to heretical positions. I am focusing in the text on circumstances when a person has confidence in the truth of his insight and is not inordinately concerned about hostility *towards him* if he discloses it.

16. If all values ended up have the same proportional importance, the idea of "reduction" might itself be misleading.

PART VI

PRACTITIONERS AS THEORISTS

14

THE END OF MORALITY?
THEORY, PRACTICE, AND THE
"REALISTIC OUTLOOK" OF
KARL MARX

JOHN KANE

With communism officially dead, whither Marxism? Must the legions of Marxist scholars now reclassify themselves as historians of ideas, or maybe hang up their stetsons and take to whittling on the porch? Or is there mileage left in the old warhorse yet, despite the sudden demise of its misbegotten progeny? It is quite likely that Marxist thought has penetrated intellectual discourse too deeply and too widely to be imagined as simply withering away, and in the field of political theory, particularly, there are reasons for thinking it may still have some relevance. Many of the questions which Marxism sought to answer are with us still and, if anything, more urgently pressing at the close of the twentieth century. The forward movement of the global capitalist economy is beyond the sensible control of any firm, cartel, or national government, and continues to throw up hard challenges—of technological change, social dislocation, environmental degradation, and resource depletion, not to mention the old, perennial potential for conflict between capital and labor. Marx sought to transform the great, productive beast from humanity's master to its servant, and it is just possible that this remains for us, his legatees, the challenge of challenges.[1] The problem is one of both theory—adequately understanding the beast's nature—and practice—how to intervene politically to make the most of productive opportunities and to avoid the worst of possible disasters. The question of ethics also figures. It is easy enough ethically to identify particular ills and evils, much harder to know how to gain a remedial purchase on them. One does not have to be a Marxist to be skeptical of the capacity of moral persuasion, divorced from political or economic power, to influence events and alter social structures.

For these reasons, if no others, I believe there is still some value to be had in pondering Marx's comprehensive approach to the problem, and the distinctive answer he gave to it. This answer was implied in a certain Marxian political attitude, termed the "realistic outlook" at whose heart lay the well-known (or notorious) doctrine of the unity of theory and practice. Incorporated within this doctrine was the theory of ideology, whose influence has extended far beyond the bounds of traditional Marxism and whose importance as a potent critical conceptual apparatus is likely to persist, whatever the fate of the politico-economics. In the realistic outlook (whose full import has seldom been adequately understood), the problems of theoretical understanding, effective political action and revolutionary motivation were simultaneously solved in a unique way. In trying to instil this outlook in his revolutionary compatriots, Marx sought to displace a discredited attitude that he labeled "utopian socialist." One might view Marx's disparagement of this attitude with some irony given the radically utopian aim of his own endeavor, but it was not the end of the game that was in question, rather the means to its realization. The utopian socialists were misguided in wishing to make the world conform to certain externally imposed ideals; in Marx's view, this was just fruitless moralizing. In adopting the Marxian realistic outlook, the true revolutionary eschewed moralizing altogether, typically with an attitude of impatience and loathing. Morality as a form was, according to Marxian theory, hopelessly compromised because inherently ideological and "illusory."

Of course, the Marxist stance here has seemed to many to be tinged with a fatal ambivalence. The rejection of morality sits oddly with the undoubtedly ethical thrust of Marxist theory, which embodies, in the words of Alan Gilbert, "a moral vision of great stature."[2] The paradox was neatly stated and textually illustrated by Steven Lukes in his book *Marxism and Morality*.[3] I will be discussing Lukes's resolution of the paradox later; and also his solution to another puzzle which has received scholarly attention in recent years, this one concerning Marx's opinions about the supposed justice or injustice of capitalism. These issues come naturally into focus when viewed through the lens of the realistic outlook, as do other important topics underemphasized by Lukes—for example, the historical conditions for effective action and the question of revolutionary motivation.

The passage in which Marx explicitly avows his outlook is to be found in the *Critique of the Gotha Programme*. There he has been forced to spend some time expounding the distributive principles which will characterize the lower, imperfect stage of communism, and to speak of "equal right" and "fair distribution," though his distaste is clear. He has only dealt with these matters at length, he says,

> in order to show what a crime it is to attempt, on the one hand, to force on our Party again, as dogmas, ideas which in a certain period had some meaning but have now become obsolete verbal rubbish, while again perverting, on the other hand, the realistic outlook, which it cost so much effort to instil into the Party but which has now taken root in it, by means of ideological nonsense about right *(Recht)* and other trash so common among the democrats and French socialists.[4]

I believe this passage accurately depicts Marx's deepest feelings and opinions about morality, and about the value of his own brand of realism as a more than adequate substitute. But what did this realism imply? According to one latter-day Marxist, it expressed a criticism of the tendency of ethical discussions about socialism to become *substitutes* for explanatory accounts of history, thus denoting "the vain intrusion of moral judgements in lieu of causal understanding."[5] But there was much more to it than that. Marx's realism certainly implied the need for a correct understanding of society, an understanding which explained the limited potency of the moral outlook and also instructed when times were ripe for effective political action. But further, it claimed that such understanding was not merely a *precondition* of effective political action—such an instrumental interpretation would hardly have been controversial—but was *in itself* effective practice. Theoretically dispelling ideological illusions about reality (including illusions about morality) was held, in the very act, to change that political reality in a significant way. It was because of its efficacy in this respect that the realistic outlook could be held to displace vain moralizing altogether from the field of political practice.

The realistic outlook was both hard-headed and eternally optimistic. Realistic revolutionaries were concerned, on the one hand, to understand the real forces operating in society, to discover the opportunites and obstacles presented to revolutionary action, to unmask deceptions and to avoid being deceived; on the other hand, they proceeded in the certain hope, or faith (called "knowledge"), that history was working inexorably on their behalf. They themselves, in fact, were but a (necessary) moment in the real workings of the forces of historical progress. On the hard-headed side, their realism expressed the futility of opposing a complex, historical socio-economic structure with an external ideal to which it *ought* to conform; on the optimistic side, it expressed their identification with the real, ideal society they thought to observe coming into being within the body of the old.

This chapter will describe this outlook in some detail, and examine the merits and limitations of the critique of morality and justice that it implied. I will try to show that some sense can be made of the theory-practice fusion, even independently of Marxist epistemology, and that the Marxist ethical attitude, while not contradictory, was ultimately unsound. The failure to clarify this ethical position, moreover, sowed confusion among Marxists, with disastrous consequences. I begin with a look at the importance, for Marx's realism, of the historically developing conditions of effective political practice.

The Developing Conditions for Action

Marx was, famously, not a dispassionate social scientist on a disinterested quest for objective truth. He was passionately *en-*

gaged, and his politico-economic theory was forged primarily as a political weapon in the class war. Material force could only be overthrown by material force, and the instrument embodying the necessary material force he had discovered in the masses of the rising proletariat.[6] But these masses inhabited a purely "sensuous" realm, and needed theoretical vision to guide them. Marx's calling was to produce a work that would fulfill this need, a theoretical work that would also be profoundly practical. Other "critical" German philosophers of the day suffered, in Marx's eyes, from a surfeit of theory, while activist French socialists suffered from a deficiency of it, and if theory without action was impotent, then action without theory was blind. His great work of analysis and education would bring together pure theory and blind practice, giving sight to the revolutionary masses and point to their activities.

The fact that theory was thus intended as a political instrument was not held to disqualify it as genuine science, or in any way to compromise its truth value. Indeed the connection between the theory and its validation was held to depend precisely on its political efficacy (see later). At the heart of the matter lay the theory of historical materialism, which purported to explain how the development of the material forces of production brought into being the conditions for effective political action.

Ironically, however, the teleological character of this theory seemed to be in tension with its insistence on voluntaristic political action by a class to create a social revolution. The teleological component, inherited from Hegelian philosophy, tended to portray the historical movement as inexorable and inevitable,[7] thus leaving the role of the political activist in some doubt. If one compares Marx in this respect with another great theorist of political action and the conditions for its success, one might note that Machiavelli at least gave equal weight to each of his causal categories, *fortuna*—the fortuitous conditions for effective action—and *virtú*—the abilities which enabled individuals to grasp fortune by the forelocks and turn it to their advantage.[8] The teleological Marx lets the burden fall most heavily on his equivalent of *fortuna,* the historically developing conditions of social change.

Associated with the teleological element was the view of mind or "consciousness" as essentially dependent, even passive, determined ultimately by the forces and relations of production. Against Hegel, Marx argued that ideas did not exist independently of the beings whose ideas they were—they were not an independent causal reality. None of this implied that people's ideas were unreal or inefficacious (Marx's was not a *philosophical* materialism), though a technological determinist reading of the theory seemed to relegate them to a problematic and pathetic dependency so far as the content of those ideas was concerned.[9] Marx was perfectly aware, however, that what makes human action and production unique is that it is *intelligent,* and therefore quite distinct from the purposive behavior of animals.[10] He insists (again contra Hegel) that human beings via their intelligent productive activity make their own history (though not, of course, under circumstances chosen by themselves). When the socio-political actions of actual human beings are closely examined, moreover, the developmental story is not as straightforwardly predictable as the bare bones of materialist theory sometimes make it seem. In Marx's writings on contemporary affairs, especially after 1850,[11] a much more nuanced political, less resolutely determinist picture is presented (though class conflict is never lost sight of as the most salient feature of social existence).

Marx insists, however, that ideas or ideals on their own can have little effect on social reality. On the broadest reading, his view seems to be not that ideas are necessarily crudely determined by productive relations, but that ideas, however and wherever they arise, are *politically ineffectual* unless backed by power. In his attack on the left-Hegelians for their belief that social problems could be solved by mere intellectual abstraction, he wrote that mere ideas could not carry out anything at all; ideas could only be carried out by men who disposed of "a certain practical force." [12] The "practical force" that matters for Marx, at least in the long run, is class power as determined by the state of development of the forces and relations of production.[13] The limited efficacy of ideas divorced from class power is clearly revealed in his attack on Karl Heinzen, who had called for a socialist republic based on an appeal to "humanity."

Though it might be possible, Marx admits, that the attitudes of particular individuals might not be influenced by the class to which they belong, this could have little effect on the class struggle. What was possible for some individuals was not possible for entire classes locked together in relations of mutual antagonism based on real economic conditions. Classes would not melt away before the solemn idea of "humanity."[14]

The limits of ideas are, in another typical Marxian formulation, the limits of the political will. Political will alone, in the absence of suitable socio-economic conditions, can achieve nothing lasting. In *The Communist Manifesto* Marx notes that the proletariat's first attempts to attain its ends, in the flush of bourgeois revolution, *necessarily* failed both because the political class itself was undeveloped and because the economic conditions of its emancipation "had yet to be produced, and could be produced by the impending bourgeois epoch alone."[15] In *The German Ideology* he had written that the development of the productive forces "is an absolutely necessary premise [of communism], because without it privation, *want* is merely made general and with *want* the struggle for necessities would begin again, and the old filthy business would necessarily be restored."[16] In 1850, Marx warned his fellow communists that they were not yet ready for power, that if they attained power prematurely they would end up introducing petty bourgeois, not proletarian measures. "Our party," he declared, "can only come to power when the conditions allow it to put its own views into practice."[17]

Though Marx is stressing here, as he always stressed, the conditions that must exist to make ideas and political action effective, it is nevertheless clear that he also presumes an active category corresponding to Machiavelli's *virtú*, and that successful political action requires the confluence of *both fortuna*—the historically developed conditions—*and* the *virtú* of an organized revolutionary class. Indeed the Marxist schema begins to look like the Machiavellian one transposed from the confined arena of the Italian city state onto the world-historical stage—or would do, stripped (as it never was) of its teleology. The analogy appears even more apt when one considers Marx's remarks on contingency in revolution (made after the fall of the Paris

Commune). "World history," he writes, "would indeed be an easy affair if the fight were taken up only under conditions of infallibly favourable chances," and he notes that part of the contingency which makes or breaks each revolutionary attempt is *the individual character of the leaders*.[18] Furthermore, the *virtù* of the proletariat was presumed to be concentrated in the organised communist parties. In an address to the General Council of his International Working Men's Association (IWA—the so-called First International) in 1870, Marx defended locating the Council in England rather than in France on the grounds that England had the "material necessary for social revolution" and the General Council would invest it with "the spirit of revolutionary fervour."[19] The material conditions may give rise to ideas and aspirations among the working class, but these would not necessarily be coherent or theoretically developed. In a letter warning against sectarianism within the communist movement, Marx remarks that the while the "real conditions" of society produced common aspirations in the working class, these were reflected in their heads "in the most diversified forms, more or less phantastical, more or less adequate," and those best able to interpret the hidden sense of the class struggle were the communists.[20]

There thus emerges a more complex, political view of the interaction between historical opportunity and class action than can be gained from a reading of the theory as a matter of mechanistic determination. Revolutionary action requires effective leadership and a united party as well as a willing proletariat. However, the historical grounds for such action remain crucial to its chances of success; the ideas and ideals that inform the political will of revolutionaries will be ineffectual unless the time is ripe for them, and the power to carry through such ideas is in the possession of the revolutionary class.

The Unity of Theory and Practice

There was more, however, to the realistic outlook than the fairly straightforward instrumentalism that the Machiavellian analogy allows. Indeed, it is not possible to describe Marx's theory in such simple terms (though Engels, notoriously, tended that way). If this were the whole story, revolutionaries who correctly divined that historical conditions were *not* ripe for action (as must be the case throughout most of history, since the material forces of production take time to mature) would have little to do but sit stoically on their hands and wait. That this was, to some extent, a real possibility we have seen in Marx's warning that the proletariat must not take power before both they and the material conditions are ripe. However, Marx did not believe that the wait could be very long, for the conditions which made possible a correct understanding of social reality (which is to say, Marx's theory) were the same conditions which made imminent the proletarian revolution. Theories may be advanced prior to this moment, and some may harbor valuable insights,[21] but until material and social development have reached a certain stage these can be nothing more than ideological apologies for the dominant class or utopian consolations for the oppressed. It was impossible to make society conform to some theoretical ideal when conditions were antithetical to its realization. However, as history moves forward and the struggle of the proletariat assumes clearer outlines, social theorists need no longer *imagine* utopias, but have only to note what is going on before their eyes and become its mouthpiece. As soon as the revolutionary potential in the poverty of the masses is realized, then "science, which is produced by the historical movement and associating itself consciously with it, has ceased to be doctrinaire and has become revolutionary."[22]

We may thus state three beliefs central to Marx's conception of realism. First, there is the belief in the futility of utopian theorizing which specifies ideals external to reality to which it wishes reality to conform; this wish is unrealistic when social conditions are not sufficiently developed to permit a genuine reformation. Second, is the belief that true science is the discovery of human emancipation as an observable process at work within reality, such observation being only possible when social production and social relations have reached a certain stage of development; so the possibility of social transformation and the possibility of genuine understanding are necessarily coincident in time—science is itself "produced by the historical movement." Third, this science is necessarily revolutionary, associating itself consciously with the movement and helping further it; indeed, the theory is itself one (possibly necessary) moment of the phenomenon it describes, an act of self-understanding without which the predictions of the theory would not (or at least may not) be realized.

That adequate theory is held to be *necessarily* revolutionary is one expression of the Marxian doctrine of the unity of theory and practice, and I will come to this shortly. First I want to address a comment by Lukes concerning Marx's claim that theory can express only knowledge of a self-transforming present, and not of an ideal future. Lukes criticizes Marx's "refusal to specify possible futures as closely as possible, indicating which are more or less probable, and to set the grounds for supporting the struggle for one of them," [23] a failure which led to an enduring "intellectual scandal" of socialist theory, namely, its paucity of thought concerning the workings of socialist society. This failure is real, and indeed scandalous, but Lukes founds his criticism on the objection that it cannot be possible to have knowledge that present society is transforming itself in an emancipatory direction without also having knowledge of the shape of future society. This is surely wrong. If human unfreedom is an observable fact of society (as it is), then it should be possible to observe moves towards greater freedom without knowing precisely where, ultimately, such transformations will lead. Consider the situation in South Africa at the present time, for example. Marx's failure was to be too sanguine about the possible directions such a future might take, partly for the reasons Lukes advances, [24] and partly because he held class division and oppression, created by scarcity, to be the sole significant source of all human evils (Marxism's greatest illusion, perhaps). If the end of class division were in sight, then the future could be nothing else but emancipatory, whatever the precise form it took.

However, Marx also had another reason for wanting to tie theory strictly to present, empirical reality, and this had to do with his critique of ideologies, and how such a critique could be successfully grounded. The theory of ideology forms the core of all Marx's work, and is the locus at which his doctrine of the unity of theory and practice finds its most plausible justification.

Harold Mah, in a fascinating book,[25] has shed light on the history of its development. He argues that the Young Hegelians, distraught when their hopes for a more rational society in Germany crumbled in the Prussian reaction of the 1840s, had cast about for a theoretical explanation of the failure of Hegelianism and of their own gullibility in believing in it. Their answer was that Hegel's extravagant claim for philosophy's sovereignty over the world was an inversion of the truth, a compensation for and justification of social and political reality. That they and others had been seduced by this philosophy was explained in the same way, as an unconscious transformation of a sense of powerlessness into a fantasy of power, thereby paradoxically strengthening the reality from which they sought to escape by giving it an intellectual legitimacy.[26] Thus the socio-political situation had shaped philosophy, not vice versa. The problem with such a critique was how or where to ground it so that it might itself escape the charge of being "ideological," that is, socially determined, a problem that caused great anxiety amongst the young intellectuals. Marx's answer, given in *The German Ideology,* was to reject philosophical abstraction altogether and to immerse himself in "sensuous reality," that is, in the mundane empirical world of human beings and their material needs, interests, and productive activities. Thus was born the theory of historical materialism, whose validity would only be verified *pragmatically,* which is to say only if it helped change the world according to its own form. Marx's antiphilosophical understanding of the world would be vindicated by the profoundly antiphilosophical proletariat, who were moved by nothing but "sensuous necessity." In other words, Marx's theory would be proved true to the extent that it contributed to proletarian revolution.[27]

We now see the intimacy of the link between theory and practice in Marxism. Theory, says Marx, will become material force as soon as it grips the masses.[28] On Marx's understanding, philosophy, though related to reality, had severed its links with it and become "objectless." Reflective contemplation must *realize* itself (a typically Hegelian aim) by a return to objective reality, to the world of human *praxis.* Theory, which hitherto has been separated from the world, must now rejoin it and, in so doing,

alter it. Marx is operating here from a particular epistemologi-
cal standpoint, one which deems it necessary to "overcome" the
classical distinctions between subject and object, knower and
known, idealism and materialism, theory and practice (for, despite his up-ending of Hegel, Marx remained as committed as
the master to the final synthetic annihilation of all so-called
oppositions or contradictions).[29] In this view, both the object of
understanding and the subject who understands are changed in
the process of that understanding. We need not ascribe to this
epistemology, however, to appreciate the sense of how an understanding of an ideology to which one has been unwittingly
subject may, by that very fact, alter one portion of reality. A
change in one's beliefs *is* a real change, and one which, given
the centrality of belief to selves and social structures, may lead
to wider changes in the world.

The principal way in which theory was to "grip" the proletariat was by revealing to it the true nature of its socio-economic
position. This meant exposing the reality that underlay the
illusory appearances of capitalist production and exchange, and
showing, as well, how these appearances were necessary to the
legitimation of the whole system, and existed precisely for that
purpose. We might note with respect to Marx's epistemology
here, that though the proof of the analysis might be held to
rest in its effect on workers, their enlightenment presumably
depended on their identifying the analysis as independently
true. At any rate, in coming to appreciate that the free exchange
of commodities conceals the reality of labor exploitation, that
the free selling of labor power for wages masks a condition of
semi-slavery, that the eternal truths of morality and the rational
commands of law conceal the coercive hand of the dominant
class, workers come to a new consciousness of themselves as
having being degraded to the status of objects or commodities,
and in this very act of understanding they constitute themselves
as active subjects who in their practice may abolish the system
that degrades them.

This model of what has come to be called "critical theory"
has, of course, proved one of the most influential parts of
Marx's work, and extended its range far beyond the bounds of
traditional Marxism.[30] One might point out, of course, that *all*

theory is, by its nature, critical, and therefore, on this reading, practical, whether it be about the natural world, the cosmos or human society itself.[31] All theory, that is to say, is practice not just in the trivial sense that it is something people make, but in the sense that it may have real and direct repercussions on our lives and beliefs. No theory, whatever it is about, is ever "neutral" so far as our beliefs are concerned. Well-supported theories may and frequently do undermine or overthrow widely held beliefs, or at least threaten to do so unless defensive action is taken—witness the resurgence of creationism in Western Christian countries today. (Even poorly supported theories can have this effect—for example, the supply-side economics of the Reagan era.[32]) The consequences of this for human action and behavior, given that factual beliefs are a central component of our actions and attitudes, can be profound depending upon the cultural importance of the beliefs being questioned.

Of course, there is a crucial difference in critical social theory in that the errors of belief it purports to expose are not merely the result of natural ignorance, but functional falsehoods promulgated (though not necessarily consciously) for the preservation of certain social relations. And if it can be shown, as Marx tried to show, that certain common beliefs about social relations are false, and further that these false beliefs are required to support a particular invidious structure of relations and exist precisely to serve this end, then it can hardly be denied that a blow has been struck at the relations themselves.

The unity of theory and practice figured here is reminiscent of the analogous processes in Freudian psychotherapy, wherein the *analysis* of a patient's symptoms is, simultaneously, the *treatment* of those symptoms. The dynamic explanatory model is, in fact, very similar in each. In each there exists a realm of consciousness which is a realm of symptomatic illusion (of "false consciousness" or "alienation" in Marxian terms), whose self-deceptions are explained as functional for the maintenance of the system as it exists, and whose causes must be sought in certain unresolved conflicts within a determining realm below consciousness and largely inaccessible to it. We have only to substitute "id" for "forces of production," "ego" for "social relations" and "superego" for "superstructure" to see how closely analogous the models appear. (It was indeed the contention of Wilhelm Reich that Freudian repression was the mechanism by which the class cleavages of society and the ideologies supporting them were individually internalized.[33])

Lukes claims that Marx fails to ask the question whether alienation is subjective (experienced as such by the alienated person) or objective (an observer's category applied to the situation and self-understanding of the alienated).[34] But on the Freudian analogy, alienation, like neurosis, would be a dysfunctional experiential category, though the dysfunction may not be clearly cognized by the subject and, certainly, its causes will be opaque to him or her. Only during analysis (psychotherapeutic or ideological) does the meaning of one's hitherto mysterious distress become clear. The effect of discovering the real source of one's dissatisfactions is, in either case, held to be a genuine liberation. As Marx says in a passage from the *Grundrisse* to which Jon Elster has drawn attention, labor's recognition of its real position is

> an enormous awareness *(enormes Bewusststein)*, itself the product of the mode of production resting on capital, and as such the knell of its doom as, with the slave's awareness that *he cannot be the property of another*, with his consciousness of himself as a person, the existence of slavery becomes a merely artificial vegetative existence and ceases to be able to prevail as the basis of production.[35]

This is a strong statement of the importance of the subjective element in the revolutionary process, and not, it must be said, typical. It might also seem wildly implausible that a slave's recognition of the impropriety of slavery could so readily signal the death knell of the institution (it should perhaps be remembered that Spartacus was one of Marx's great heroes). The causal story that seems to be indicated, however, by the phrase "itself the product of the mode of production," is that such awareness will only happen to any significant extent when the mode of production has reached a stage of such contradiction with the relations of production that social cleavages can no longer be contained by the justificatory strategies hitherto in force. This fits with the view of Marx's own theory as simply a moment in the development of capitalism's contradictions, one which would in turn feed back into worker's consciousness to further the process of revolution.

Whether or not one accepts this deterministically dialectical picture should have no bearing on the general proposition that dramatic alterations in one's consciousness of oneself and the nature of one's social relations can have potentially far-reaching personal and social consequences. Such changes may indeed mean the difference between acquiescence and rebellion. (The feminist movement has made extensive use of this model of ideology for the purposes of "consciousness-raising" and emancipation.) Such a conversion, of course, involves profoundly ethical judgments about humanity in general and the ills with which it is burdened. Marx, with his ethic of human emancipation, presumed that when the scales fell from the eyes of laborers, when they realized the truth of capital's dominion over them, they could no longer behave as acquiescent wage slaves but would be moved naturally to work for their own liberation, which would only be achieved in concert with their fellows. For who would live as a slave when with an effort of political will they might be free? A natural human desire for freedom would be all that was required to move this will, along with an assurance, based in theory, that the times were ripe for such a will to succeed in its goals.

Such then was the realistic outlook that Marx advocated. It was essentially an appeal for the adoption of a "correct" understanding of society. At one level, this understanding informed the activist of the possibilities and potentialities (or absence of them) for revolutionary action in a society at any time, and ensured that all efforts were directed appropriately so that wasteful tilting at windmills could be avoided. At a deeper level, such understanding was itself a moment of revolutionary *praxis*, a liberating opening of the eyes to the real nature of society and one's degraded place within it, from which awareness there could be no going back. Subjective liberation fed naturally into political practice aimed at objective emancipation, for a realistic assessment of the state of social development informed that times were ripe (or very shortly would be) for the dissolution of class and class oppression. So it was that Marx felt he could afford to dispense with the moral whip to encourage militant action—such action was naturally motivated by liberating awareness of oneself as an active subject of the coming society rather than a degraded object of capitalism. The moral attitude was one whose time had passed, and to cling to it further would be to invite corruption.

ANTI-MORALITY

But what are we to make of a theory driven by a powerful ethic of liberation which nevertheless condemns morality as ideological? Lukes solves the paradox by observing that Marx and Engels rejected the morality of *Recht* while embracing a morality of emancipation.[36] (*Recht* is a continental juristic term denoting, broadly, the morality of law, and covering such concepts as justice, rights, and obligations.) The rules of *Recht*, because inherently ideological and coercively constraining, were something from which humanity had to be freed in its general emancipation from the very conditions that make these rules necessary.[37]

I believe this captures the sense of the Marxist attitude, but I doubt that Marx would have approved the term "morality" being applied to his own position. Though much of his critique of morality focuses on the rules and principles of *Recht*, it seems pretty clear that Marx would have no truck with morality of any kind. Lukes quotes the passage from *The German Ideology* which declares that communists "do not preach *morality* at all. . . . They do not put to people the moral demand: love one another, do not be egoists, etc."[38] Later, Lukes also cites the passage stating that the possibility of criticizing the material conditions of production and intercourse which arose with the developing contradictions between bourgeoisie and proletariat "shattered the basis of all morality, whether the morality of asceticism or of enjoyment."[39] This obviously goes beyond the bounds of *Recht*, and into the traditional areas of normative moral theory. In fact, according to Kamenka, Marx regarded traditional moral problems of how to derive normative rules of right and wrong action as an accommodation to the evil of an irrational society.[40]

It might be better, then, to pose a distinction, as Kamenka does, between Marx's *ethical objectivism* and his *anti-moralism*.

As an ethical objectivist, Marx held that good and evil were real and observable phenomena in the human world. His most profound ethical concern in his life was indeed, as Lukes asserts, with human freedom, which, according to Kamenka, came down to a belief that free action was action characterized by harmony and cooperation, unfree or coerced action by disharmony and conflict. He did not, however, believe that such ethical identifications either did or could found normative rules of behavior or moral goals to be fulfilled—not a common position in ethics but not unique either.[41]

Marx had both theoretical and ethical reasons for this rejection of normative morality, though distinguishing them thus is slightly artificial, since the ethical identification of human unfreedom forms the very heart of his theory. However, the distinction is useful for making the point that from a theoretical standpoint we are shown both the illusoriness and limited efficacy of the moral mode, while from the ethical standpoint we are made aware of the ill effects of its application. I will deal first with the theoretical.

(1) *Theoretical objections.* Marx's materialist theory purports to explain three interrelated features of morality, namely its function, its content, and its limited potency. Morality *functions* to constrain the conflicts of class-divided society, and it does this by offering general justifications for existing or developing relations of production. Its *content* is thus explained by its function. The justifications of morality are presented in terms of universal and eternal truths, as they must be if they are to be acceptable to those oppressed by them and gratifying to those whose interests they serve, for analysis will reveal that moral codes are always tailored to the interests of particular classes in particular historical circumstances. Morality is thus the realm of determination in that its principles are not freely chosen but the result of determining interests. The *potency* of morality is real but limited: morality fulfills its function insofar as it succeeds in confirming a class in the rightness of its position, both in its own eyes and in the eyes of other classes whose acquiescence it

desires; however, this success is based not on the rational merits of the moral arguments, but on the extent to which the arguments are backed by effective economic power. Once this power begins to crumble, as the productive forces develop beyond the limits of control of existing social relations, so also does the moral code designed to justify it.

So it is that people in society may perceive moral rules as issuing from a universalizing, rational will, but in this they are deceived. This deception is held to be a necessary part of all juridical forms (for what is true of morality is also true, *mutatis mutandis*, of law), since their function is precisely to act as a veil upon the real relations of production and the operation of class power within them. All is determination in this picture. Moral and legal norms are, in reality, the expression of the will of the ruling class, which is itself determined by class interest, which is in turn determined by the relations and ultimately by the forces of production.[42] Morality is always class morality, either justifying the domination and interests of the ruling class or expressing the indignation and future interest of the oppressed class.[43]

Occasionally a utopian theorist might take the illusory harmony and eternal justice proclaimed by the bourgeoisie as characterizing their system, and try to transform it into an *ideal* to be realized. But this was hopeless. To take, for example, the bourgeois *illusion* of equal exchange and turn it into a corrective ideal for the reconstitution of society would only result in the reestablishment of existing society, for "it is totally impossible to reconstitute society on the basis of what is merely an embellished shadow of it."[44] So long as the mode of production was capitalist (as in the bourgeois epoch it had to be), just so long must the exchange of products take the form it does, a form that necessarily implied class antagonism.

The principal illusion of the juridical mode is its appearance as the realm of freedom—of freely chosen principles and actions—when it is in fact the mode of determination and class coercion. This illusion was a *necessary,* not a contingent feature of morality, for only by adopting this mask of freedom could morality perform its justificatory and stabilizing functions. The fact of coercion beneath the mask was the one of the bases of Marx's ethical objections to this mode of discourse.

(2) *Ethical objections.* There are in fact two objections here. The first relates to the coerciveness of morality just mentioned. For Marx, morality was an attempt to bind evils (that is, relations of conflict and disharmony) with evil. Morality was thus inimical to the human freedom that Marx valued above all else. It aimed at restraining human action with bonds of obligation and duty, and was thus a servile, undignified notion, incompatible with an ideal of the unconstrained, self-actualizing individual who would emerge in the absence of external necessities and extrinsic determinations (that is, under the conditions of communism).

This ethical belief in the evil of coercion was at the foundation of Marx's whole critique of capitalism. He took the "abstract" categories of the classical economists—rents, land, labor, capital, commodities, etc.—and tried to show the human reality that underlay them, a reality in which workers were alienated from the products of their labor and from each other, their activity wholly dominated by an extrinsic motive, necessity. Instead of a community of people organizing themselves for productive purposes, there existed a means of production which enforced on people its own principles of organization. The bourgeois revolution had brought political freedom, but the true situation of laborers was hardly better than that of slaves. In communist society all this would change. Legal and moral rules, in particular, would lose all point insofar as their function is seen as the constraint of conflict and competition, for these were evils that would not exist in non-class society. People there would be associated in a higher social bond from which such coercive constraints are wholly absent.[45]

Marx's second objection to moral rules concerned their "abstract" character (in the Hegelian sense of "abstract," meaning one-sided). Part of this objection, no doubt, was still concerned with the constraining nature of rules. Certainly the all-round, self-realizing individual who would apparently be typical of communism would tolerate no external constraint, to the extent of dispensing with rules of any kind.[46] The main focus of this objection, however, was not on freedom but on the issue of true equality. Any system of rules was deemed to be unsatisfactory insofar as it brought people under common standards, and thus denied their multi-faceted individuality. Abstract rules, by their nature, must treat people equally, but since people are all different, this treatment is in fact a recipe for inequality. Such rules would remain a necessity during the lower phase of communism, but when the last vestiges of bourgeois rule were swept away and production was fully socialized, they would be at last abolished.[47]

There is something we should note about this objection to moral rules. Although it portrays them as a necessary evil (because constraining and abstract), it does not claim them to be illusory. Indeed there is no reason why it should. In the lower phase of communism there will surely be no need for such illusions, for social relations will no longer be clouded by class antagonisms, the proletariat (the "universal class") being now in control. Such rules as may be necessary will presumably be accepted by the majority in patient good faith. This majority will not need illusions to sustain it. This fact then, gives the lie to morality as *inherently* and *necessarily* illusory, a point I will return to later. First, I want to look at the much-debated question of Marxism and justice, because this is something of a test cast for Marx's claim to have rejected morality altogether. If, as some have argued, Marx held capitalism to be unjust, then there is an obvious inconsistency with what has been said above.

THE QUESTION OF JUSTICE

Lukes lists four positions that have been convincingly argued concerning Marx's feelings about the justice or otherwise of the capitalist-worker wage relation. It has been variously claimed that Marx held this relation to be: (1) just; (2) unjust; (3) both just and unjust; (4) neither just nor unjust. Apparently contradictory, or at least ambiguous, remarks by Marx on the subject seem to justify any or each of these positions. Lukes's solution is to argue that Marx's view of capitalism's justice was "both internally complex and hierarchically organized."[48] First, says Lukes, he offered a functional-relativist account of the norms governing capitalist exchange relations; these norms prevail because they sanction and stabilize capitalist exploitation and thus the whole capitalist system (the truth of position [1]). Second, he offered an "internal" critique of these norms as registering the mere *appearance* of equivalence, while beneath this surface of appearance lay the reality of worker unfreedom/capitalist domination (the truth of position [3]). Third, he offered an "external" critique whereby the inequitable capitalist exchange is judged from the perspective of the principle that will govern lower communism, "To each according to his labor contribution." (This explains Marx's frequent characterization of these exchanges as "robbery," "plunder," "embezzlement," etc., and is the truth of position [2].) Finally, he offered a radical critique of all of the above from the perspective of communism's higher phase, from which standpoint, the very attribution of justice and injustice is a sign that society is still in a "prehistorical" phase, an archaism eventually to be transcended—the truth in position (4).[49]

I believe Lukes fairly captures the complexity of Marx's attitude on the question of the justice of capitalism, though I would quarrel with the third, "external," critique which has him judging capitalist exchange from the perspective of lower communism. This is after Husami, who argued that Marx, far from adopting capitalism's self-evaluation, "regarded capitalism as unjust precisely because, as an exploitative system, it does not proportion reward to labour contribution, and because it is not oriented to satisfy human needs."[50] It is true that Marx did not accept capitalism's self-evaluation—all his work was aimed at showing the inequitable, coercive reality beneath the appearance of equity and freedom, that was the whole point of it— and it is true that this appraisal is fundamentally ethical. But Marx would never, I believe, have concurred in describing these relations as "unjust." (It is notable how often Marx, when using moral words like "right" or "justice," or such morally loaded ones as "rob," etc., places them within scare quotes, thus distancing himself from any personal moral judgment that may otherwise seem implied.) When Marx rails satirically against the apparently equivalent exchanges between capitalist and worker as "embezzlement,"[51] or describes it as "the old dodge of every conqueror who buys commodities from the conquered with the money he has robbed them of,"[52] he is certainly pointing to the unequal reality underlying appearance, but one should not be misled by his typically colorful language into thinking he was thereby condemning capitalism for its injustice. To do so would have been inconsistent with his own theory and with its determinedly anti-moralist position.

Marx's preferred perspective, I believe, was position (4). That is, he did not regard justice as "a fit category either for political recommendations or for scientific analysis."[53] It was necessarily illusory—the creation of an illusion was its function—and its content at any time was determined by the existing conditions and relations of production, the exploitative nature of which it sought to veil in a cloak of eternal right. Once the illusions were dispelled, the whole category evaporated like a mist. Marx offered a relativist-functionalist account of justice which matched moral beliefs to prevailing productive relations—"slavery on the basis of capitalist production is unjust; likewise fraud in the quality of commodities"[54]—but this was a theory *about* morality, not *of* it.[55] To deal directly in moral concepts was, for Marx, to deal in the language of mystification and ideological illusion, and he saw his own work as precisely the attempt to dispel mystifications and expose illusions.

It is curious to note that, even had Marx allowed the validity of the moral category, he would still have been unable, on his theory of history, to condemn capitalism for its injustice. This is because, on any ordinary moral theory, "ought" implies "can," which is to say that what is impossible cannot be morally required. If, as Marx argued, exploitative relations were unavoidable in history, if, that is, they could not have been otherwise, then there can be no grounds for arguing the transhistorical injustice of them.[56] Exploitation is certainly depicted by Marx as an out-and-out evil, one whose final abolition he clearly desires, but it is not one that can be affected by moral condemnation or even that it makes sense morally to condemn. Capitalism was not only unavoidable, according to Marx, but *necessary,* necessary, that is, for forcing the material accumulation upon which, alone, a genuine socialism would be founded. The development of the productive forces was, he said, "the historical task" of capitalism.[57] Given this alleged necessity, Marx was in no position to issue a moral condemnation of capitalism on the grounds of its injustice (which would imply that such exploitation *ought not* to occur) even had he felt so inclined, which I would argue he never did. He did not think he needed to.

There were, however, even on Marx's own theory, certain conditions in which a condemnation of capitalism on grounds of its injustice was licensed. Remember that the Marxist argument is that morality has always been class morality, either justifying the domination of the ruling class or representing the interests of the rising, oppressed class in their struggle against that domination. The question might then be asked, even if we grant that morality as a category is suspect, can we realistically regard it as dispensable, at least until the higher stage of communism is reached? If it be supposed that the contradictions of capitalism have developed to such an extent that socialism has become a genuine possibility (as Marx believed was the case in England around 1870), what role might then be allowed to arguments of justice and injustice in working class political practice? On the face of it, the answer is perfectly simple. If conditions *are* ripe, and the bourgeoisie no longer necessary to force production, and freedom and equality for the mass of people is now a genuine possibility, then the exploitation that continues is no longer necessary or unavoidable. Under such conditions (it could be morally argued) the products of workers' labor should be their own. It would appear that an argument that this avoidable evil represents an injustice to workers and should thus be corrected could be unproblematically added to the polemical arsenal of the proletarian parties.

Some such judgment by Marx may explain the passage in the *Grundrisse*, previously referred to, which Elster uses to try to prove Marx held an absolute notion of justice. This claims that the "recognition [by labor] of the products as its own, and the judgment that its separation from the conditions of its realization is improper *(ungehörig)*—forcibly imposed—is an enormous awareness."[58] That the word "*ungehörig*" is ambiguous and may not mean "unjust," Elster takes as disproved by the fact that Marx repeats the passage almost verbatim some years later,[59] except that "*ungehörig*" is replaced by "*ein Unrecht*" ("an injustice"). Perhaps not too much should be read into this passage, however, particularly in view of the fact that Marx follows the word in question with the definitional "forcibly imposed," and it was with *this* recognition (of apparent freedom masking coercion) with which Marx was always principally concerned. It cannot be taken to license, at any rate, a judgment of capitalist exploitation as transhistorically unjust, though there is no theoretical reason why it should not be judged as *historically* unjust when capitalist relations are at last in contradiction with the forces of production.

The very uniqueness of such a passage, however, is evidence of the odium in which Marx held moral discourse, even if its use was sometimes theoretically warranted. Moral usage was, as I have noted, out of key with his own "realistic outlook," the same outlook he hoped to instil in his fellow communists and their proletarian allies. Marx's impatience with the idiom of rights and justice was almost absolute. *Everything,* he once told the General Council of the IWA, every possible form of oppression has been justified by appeals to abstract rights, and it was high time to abandon this mode of agitation.[60] It is true that in an address on the Franco-Prussian war of 1870, he began with an approving reference to the founding principles of the IWA which desired to see the "simple laws of justice and morality" reign between nations.[61] Such an utterance was, however, merely politic. Indeed, Marx had himself drawn up these principles, and had complained in a letter to Engels at the time that it was difficult to express himself "in a form which made our views acceptable at the present stage of the labour movement."[62] Lukes also points to a passage in *The German Ideology* in which the appeal to the rights of the workers is plainly stated as politically expedient for their revolutionary development as a class.[63] Nevertheless, it is clear that a certain ambivalence towards the moral was unavoidable in Marx's outlook. Much as he might have liked to ban such discourse altogether, his own materialist theory allowed it a certain, perhaps even indispensible, role in revolutionary movements. Only at the stage of full communism could morality, along with the state and all other superstructural forms and institutions, be expected to be finally "overcome." Till then it would presumably have to be tolerated, however grudgingly, at least to some extent.

Is Morality Dispensible?

Marx's realistic outlook, I have argued, is centered on a correct understanding of the state of societal development and of the real nature of one's position within society. It is in part an instrumental outlook, in part a revelatory one. In its instrumental mode, it counsels a thorough analysis of social forces and situations and of the opportunities and obstacles for practice presented by them; this is realism in the traditional sense of the word (and the only sense in which, too often, it has been interpreted by followers of Marx). In its revelatory mode, it reveals to the analytical eye the ethical reality of inequity and coercion beneath the ideological appearances that enfold class society, and by that action provides the motivational impulse toward emancipation. This was the outlook Marx wished to instil in his contemporaries in place of the old, outmoded moralistic one. But, we must ask, how realistic was Marx's realistic outlook in hoping to displace morality in this way?

It no doubt galled Marx terribly, given his straightforward nature, to have to stain his tongue with a usage he regarded as inherently corrupt, even if his own theory warranted such usage. A certain cynicism would seem unavoidable—though it has to be said that the cynicism involved need not have been very profound, given that the proletariat, uniquely among historical classes, was in a position to argue that its own interests were precisely coincidental with those of the mass of humankind. Where, indeed, is the necessity for illusion in the case of the proletariat? I argued previously that Marx's admission of the utility of *Recht* in the lower phase of communism, anyway, gave the lie to his claim of the *essential* illusoriness of morality, and in fact this was a claim Marx could never successfully establish.

The model on which the Marxist theory of ideological illusion was ultimately based was Ludwig Feuerbach's analysis of religion, wherein the religious mode was interpreted as a projection of human consciousness onto an otherworldly realm.

Marx took this further, seeking the causes of the projection in the real conflicts, cleavages, and dissatisfactions of the social world, which led to a longing for consolation in an ideal other-world; religion was a way of interpreting the world which in fact threw a mystical veil over it and over people's real relations with one another and with nature, and only in a world where these relations were "perfectly intelligible and reasonable" would the need for that veil, and thus for religion, disappear.[64] On this model, the juridical mode (which includes *Recht*) must also be a product of unintelligible relations which create a mysti-fying veil through which people can (mis)interpret their rela-tions as justified products of their pure unconditioned wills. Morality, like religion, must be held to be ultimately dissoluble as a *form* when, in the conditions that will characterize commu-nism, such illusions are no longer necessary to make life tolera-ble; that is to say, morality must be in its *essence* ideological and illusory. But neither law nor morality can plausibly be regarded as, primarily, ways of *interpreting* the world: in the case of law, most obviously, it is a way of *regulating* it. Nothing Marx says convinces otherwise. Most of both his and Engels's remarks on the matter point merely to a causal story about the *content* of law and morality. The only illusion here seems to be that people believe their principles and rules are freely and rationally cho-sen, whereas in reality they are determined by class interests and ultimately by material necessity. Such an illusion may be dispelled, however, without destroying the form of, or indeed the need for, moral and legal reasoning, as Marx admits, when he accepts the necessity for such rules during the initial, imper-fect stages of communism when, whatever else may be the case, the need for an illusory veil over human relations will surely have passed away. Of course Marx, as we have seen, had other, ethical objections to rules as such, but these were based on their coerciveness and "abstractness" and not on their "illusoriness."

This brings me to a second problem: even if we reject Marx's theoretical analysis of morality, what are we to make of his ethical objection, which sees morality as intrinsically evil because coercive of behavior? A full response to this would require taking up the arguments not only of Marx himself but of the modern anti-moralists, whose arguments indeed contain a great deal which is attractive to anyone who believes that the true subject matter of ethics is the identification and encouragement of real goods in the world and the avoidance of evil. I can here only indicate a reply which would doubt the sense or possibility that normative morality could ever be expunged from human discourse, and question the anti-moralists' identification of moral reasoning with coercion. The aspect of normative morality which bothers them most is its apparently mysterious, authoritatively commanding nature, a mode meant to enforce unconditional obedience and discourage questioning. But such blind, oppressive moralism can be opposed without the necessity of discarding the moral form altogether. As for the supposed dispensibility of societal rules of *Recht*, convincing arguments have been offered to make one doubt this possibility even in a society of angels.[65]

A proper defense of morality to show that it may be rescued from moralism, that is, from the absurd exaltation of pure Duty, cannot be attempted here. Suffice it to say that I believe the moral mode to be a natural, ineradicable, and ultimately defensible form of human reasoning. It is implicit, I think, in Marx's acceptance of legal regulation during early communism, for even an argument for the acceptance of a necessary evil is a moral argument. Indeed, Marx's entire position was based on a view of capitalism itself as a necessary evil which must, to a large extent, simply be tolerated until such time as objective conditions permit its overthrow. Again, it is difficult to imagine that the principle that will govern distribution in higher communism—"From each according to his ability, to each according to his needs"[66]—would not be, at some level, a principle of justice. After all, it treats all persons equally as individuals with potentially unlimited needs, and implies that, in conditions of material abundance, there is no reason to deny each the means to pursuing or fulfilling their needs. In short, each must have a *right* to all necessary means under these conditions—so the argument must be. Even if it were true that in communist society no one would be inclined to deny another such means, it would not follow that denial, should it ever occur, would not be wrong. The fact that rights are never infringed does not mean that rights do not exist. In fact, it is exceedingly difficult to avoid the necessity for moral reasoning. Suppose it were true that under certain conditions rules of *Recht* are no longer necessary for ordering society, and that one accepted that such rule-ordering was inherently ethically deficient; it would surely follow that the abolition of such rules would be the morally *right* thing to do.

None of this is to deny the power and appeal of the ethic of human beings as uncoerced, self-actualizing individuals which underlay Marx's work. Marx himself was an exemplar of this ethic, and, certainly, he hoped to see it develop in the proletariat upon whom he had placed all his historical bets. As early as 1845, he was writing admiringly that one had to see the moral energy and urge for self-development of the French and English workers "in order to imagine the *human* nobleness of this movement."[67] The struggle for socialism was precisely, for Marx, an enterprise to inspire nobility and heroism, and he rejoiced when he observed these qualities in the working class movement. He praised the "heroism" of English workers who, even against their own immediate interests, strongly supported abolitionism during the American Civil War.[68] Later, in 1869, when war threatened between England and America, Marx appealed to the working men of America to avoid a war not hallowed by "sublime purpose and a great social necessity," for it was now the task of the working class to prove that it was conscious of its own social responsibility and "able to command peace where their would-be masters shout war."[69]

Yet, there was a tension between the vision of a noble, dignified working class animated by the spirit of true freedom and the role apparently allotted to the proletariat by materialist theory. Marx's reasons for settling on the proletariat as the vehicle of history in the first place was its very wretchedness, its lack of any real stake in the system by which it was oppressed. Only those with nothing to lose would have anything to gain by a thoroughgoing revolution. But if workers did make material gains under capitalism, the picture suddenly changed. The gamble on revolution and emancipation had now to be measured against real losses, and the problem of revolutionary motivation came to the fore.

Buchanan[70] has cast doubt on the proposition that individual proletarian rational self-interest, absent of any moral appeal, could plausibly be depended on by Marx to secure revolutionary action, even if workers know this to be in their best interests. Shaw[71] has replied that Buchanan portrays workers' "self-interest" too narrowly, that a broader reading can accommodate selflessness and sacrifice (Shaw, curiously, even permits a moral/ utilitarian motivation). A straightforward interpretation of the materialist theory, however, supports the narrower view. In historical materialism, all is determination. Class will is determined by class interest, and ultimately by the forces of production. The class interest which decisively determines the will is self-interest, albeit clothed in the garments of universalizing morality. All classes may present their own interest as the general interest, but in reality the interest served is as narrow as their own class boundaries—save in one ironic sense. Since the materialist theory is in essence a teleological one, each revolutionary stage is a necessary step toward the creation of conditions in which class and class antagonism are no longer necessary. Thus, the pursuit of narrow self-interest by a class is also a contribution to the general interest of humankind *in the long run*. Indeed, with the rise of the proletariat (the "universal class") self-interest becomes identical with the general interest in the grand foundation of socialism/communism. Thus, if capitalism should eventually give birth to a classless society that is better and more humane than anything that has gone before, this will be the result not of the moral pursuit of such an ideal but simply of the coincidence of a victorious proletarian class interest with the general interests of humanity. Marx's theory proposes something very like Adam Smith's "invisible hand" (whereby the unregulated self-interested economic actions of individuals lead providentially to an increase in wealth and welfare for the whole society) operating across historical time.

It should be remembered that Marx turned to the proletariat because he saw in it a class wholly moved by "sensuous necessity." However much he might, in practice, have desired nobility, heroism, and a positive emancipatory ethic to arise within its ranks, the fact was that in his theory the proletariat was characterised by negatives, by its misery, oppression, and alienation rather than by its positive virtues. But a free world, as

Kamenka argues, can only be brought about by a people who embody the true spirit of freedom and enterprise, and Marx, in the end, was not prepared to stake much on this idea, preferring history as a more powerful ally.[72] History did not, of course, proceed as Marx had foreseen. Workers gained a stake, and an increasing stake, in capitalism, a stake which had now to be thrown into the balance as something to lose against whatever might be hoped to be gained by social revolution. It is just this which gives point, and some poignancy, to the debate about the rational self-interest that was supposed to motivate revolution, and which manifestly failed to do so (at least within the heart of capitalism).

THE ETHICAL FAILURE OF MARXISM

Would a broader account of proletarian motivation, one that emphasized the positive ethical qualities which Marx undoubtedly hoped to see emerge, have made a difference? Marx failed, at any rate, to elaborate such an ethic in his theory, however much he may have tried to encourage it in practice. The ethic underlying Marxism remained largely unexplicated, and this fact, in combination with the theory's well-known debunking attitude toward morality, produced a confusion in the minds of adherents concerning their own motivation and the motives they might expect from working-class activists in general. The ambivalence could be acutely personal. The true Marxist's commitment to the cause (as anyone who has ever encountered a sincere Marxist will affirm) was typically deeply moral, a fact that most were unable satisfactorily either to acknowledge or to accommodate within the theoretical framework they had embraced. Most tended to ignore the matter, taking motivation for granted and immersing themselves in hard-headed analysis and practice, priding themselves on their grasp of real social forces and structures and contrasting their attitude to that of woolly minded reformers whose thoughts were for the ideal ought-to-be.

This avoidance, on a broader scale, permitted the theory to be transformed into a scientistic, instrumentalist justificatory device for ruthless and dedicated people, whether high- or low-minded. Much has been written about how far Marx can be held responsible for the later use to which his theories were put, particularly in the case of the doctrine of "the dictatorship of the proletariat,"[73] though there can be little doubt that he would have been appalled at most of the results that have been produced during this century in his name.

Nevertheless, it can hardly be doubted that his discrediting of morality and his failure clearly to expound his guiding ethic played a part in what was to follow. The "realistic outlook," narrowly and instrumentally interpreted, produced a void at the heart of Marxism, or rather a "contradiction," with a tendency to deny rather than to genuinely overcome the problem. Refuge was sought in hard-nosed economic and class analysis, in theoretical correctness, inevitably in schism reminiscent of the histories of rising religious movements, in which varying interpretations of foundational texts gave birth to multiple claimants to the office of keeper of the true flame. For the dethronement of morality and the enthronement of a narrow realism had done nothing to diminish the appeal of faith, had possibly enlarged it. In the world of morality there are goods to be done and evils to be averted, and the outcome depends upon whether morally motivated people take appropriate action. But in the realm of faith, the ultimate victory is assured, for the truth has been revealed once and for all and must in the end prove irresistible. Marxists, then, though having to eschew morality, could at least revel in the sense of having hitched their wagons to the star of history, and problems about ethical commitment could be washed away in the immersion of the convert.

On the broader political level there were also consequences. If Marxism had shown morality to be a sham and its true basis to be not reason but power, then only the language of power was pertinent to the achievement of revolutionary goals, and cynical pseudo-ethical principles of ends justifying means could be advanced to justify tyrannies great and small, and monstrous actions could be sanctified by Necessity.[74] (Curiously, the young Marx had himself condemned the idea that ends could justify means with the words, "an end which necessitates unholy means is not a holy end."[75]) In a world where moral right and wrong were meaningless, the concepts of theoretical correctness and incorrectness held sway, and could be manipulated by the unscrupulous to convict and condemn those whose opposition might impede the path to power. For the failure of Marxism to elaborate its ethical perspective left theoretical disagreement as the only possible avenue for reasoned opposition; yet theoretical disagreement in the realm of faith and in the absence of an overarching and constraining moral constitution can be readily interpreted as heresy, and the heretics cast to the flames. The petty, the cunning, and the duplicitous are the natural victors in this situation, and the most sincere and best intentioned among the earliest victims, the latter without the resources ultimately to mount even a token defence on their own behalf, voluntarily confessing to nonexistent crimes, pathetically sacrificing even their own integrity, and allowing themselves to be ground under the great wheel of history.

It would be absurd, of course, to blame all the abuses of communist regimes on the debasement of the moral point of view in Marxism. It would be foolish to imagine that Pol Pot's French Marxist training was solely to answer for the excesses of the Year Zero program in Cambodia, rather than the long, bitter, and peculiarly Cambodian struggles for regional and national independence. Nor, however, can we discount the effect of the lack of a base from which the decency and concern characteristic of the best kind of moral argumentation may exert its moderating influence. Of course, it is also true that people bent on doing ill to other people will find one or another moral justification for their actions, and great crimes, as Marx said, have been done—are being done this very day—in the name of moral right. However, distinctions must be drawn. Certain doctrines, from Nazism to ethnic cleansing, are moral perversions in which evil is redefined as morally good, and they naturally arouse horror and disgust in anyone not held in their thrall by temperament, partisanship, or the passion of conflict. There is an extra dimension of tragedy, however, when a doctrine sincerely seeks the betterment of all humankind, yet ends in terror, murder, entrenched corruption, and systematic falsehood. The tragedy is compounded when the good intentions at the core of the doctrine effectively silence the criticism of sincere and well-intentioned observers, who hope against hope that present, even persistent, evils may be temporary aberrations that will be corrected further on along the road to utopia, or who are tempted to condone such evils for the sake of that future and uncertain hope.[76] They bow to evil because Marxist ideology, in the gross immodesty of its long-range consequentialism, assures them that there will exist a future good which justifies any action and any sacrifice of others in the present. The very tawdriness of the societies that in fact emerged from the cauldron of communist revolutions was a sardonic testament to this ethical lie that lay at the heart of them.

CONCLUSION

Marx's realistic outlook implied an answer to a genuine and enduring problem of political theory: given a particular ethical assessment of social structures, how may one proceed, politically speaking, effectively to alter those structures so that perceived evils are eliminated and human satisfactions enabled? The realistic outlook's rejection of moral idealism was a recognition of the deep intransigence of social structures, of their resistance to change through mere moral exhortation. Marxian hard-headedness gave existent reality its due, and counseled the futility of denouncing and lamenting the world as it was in terms of its moral wrongness. Yet its own ethical drive toward change was profound. In its unique way it sought to square the circle, to show the necessity of accepting and understanding the world as it was, as it inevitably *had* to be, and yet to show also how people may act to alter it once and for all for the human good. For in its understanding, it discerned that the domination of human beings by others, and by their own creations, was bolstered and buttressed by seemings and justifications that encouraged the miserable acquiescence of the oppressed. Marxian realism claimed to look *through* appearances to the truths of coercion, necessity, and inequality, and by revealing these truths to undermine their justifications, emancipating the minds of the oppressed from the prison of false consciousness, thereby altering the reality so described and enabling its further alteration via the political action of the mentally liberated.

It was at this point that Marxian realism took a decidedly

hopeful turn. It instructed that present imperfect reality was not only unavoidable as a matter of fact, but *necessary* for the foundation of the ethically sound and rational society which was its political goal. It also argued that the emancipatory impulses of the mentally liberated and socially organized were assured of ultimate success by the inevitable development of the conditions for effective action. Marxism's ethical failure proved most profound here. For it is one thing to show that in present society certain opportunities exist for human betterment which, as it happens, have never existed in history before, and another to argue teleologically that such possible futures are in fact inevitably emerging from society's womb. This dichotomy embodies the essential difference between a political ethic and a political faith. In the former, possibilities may be realized by the actions of ethically motivated and politically able people but can never be assured; in the latter, it is assumed not only that people *will* act to realize an emancipatory future but that their success is guaranteed by History.

The realistic outlook proved unrealistic in the end because of this fideistic teleology, and because of its failure to clearly elaborate its ethic of human emancipation. The confusion generated by the rejection of moralism was aggravated by the historical guarantee of a future good, and led paradoxically to the perverting of all emancipatory hopes. In the absence of any clear guidance from its central ethic, the realistic outlook was easily transformed into a narrow instrumental tool, and became itself a perversion.

NOTES

Works in collection by Marx and Engels abbreviated as follows:

MECW: Karl Marx and Friedrich Engels, *Collected Works.* (London: Lawrence and Wishart, 1975–82).

MESW: Karl Marx and Friedrich Engels, *Selected Works.* (Moscow: Progress Publishers, 1973).

MESC: Karl Marx, *Selected Correspondence.* (Moscow: Foreign Language Publishing House, 1962).

1. For a recent economic approach to this problem, see Paul Ekins, ed., *The Living Economy: A New Economics in the Making* (London and New York: Routledge and Kegan Paul, 1986).

2. A. Gilbert, "Marx's Moral Realism: Eudaimonism and Moral Progress," in T. Ball and J. Farr, eds., *After Marx* (Cambridge: Cambridge University Press, 1984), 154.

3. S. Lukes, *Marxism and Morality* (Oxford: Clarendon Press, 1985), Chs. 1 and 2.

4. *MESW*, Vol. 2, 19.

5. Perry Anderson, *Arguments within English Marxism.* (London: New Left Books, 1980). 97–98

6. *Towards the Critique of Hegel's* Philosophy of Right: *Introduction, MECW*, 67.

7. See, for example, K. Marx and F. Engels, *The German Ideology.* (Moscow: Progress Publishers, 1976), 57, where the advance to communism is portrayed as virtually a logical movement from given premises to inevitable conclusion.

8. Nicolo Machiavelli, *The Prince.* (London: Penguin, 1975). 49–50.

9. See *Towards the Critique of Political Economy, MESW*, Vol. 1, 363.

10. K. Marx, *Capital*, Vol. 1. (Moscow: Progress Publishers, 1974), 173–74.

11. See H. Draper, *Karl Marx's Theory of Revolution*, Vol. 2 (New York: Monthly Review Press, 1978).

12. *MECW*, Vol. 4, 119.

13. *The German Ideology*, 366.

14, *MECW*, Vol. 6, 330.

15. *MESW*, Vol. 1, 134.

16. *The German Ideology*, 54. Author's emphasis.

17. *MECW*, Vol. 10, 628.

18. *MESW*, Vol. 2, 421.

19. Cited in M. Rubel and M. Manale, *Marx Without Myth: A Chronological Study of His Life and Work.* (Oxford: Basil Blackwell, 1975), 251.

20. Ibid., 255.

21. See Lukes, 38–40.

22. *MECW*, Vol. 6, 177–78.

23. Lukes, 42.

24. Ibid., 43–45.

25. H. Mah, *The End of Philosophy, the Origin of Ideology.* (Berkeley and Los Angeles: University of California Press, 1987).

26. Ibid., 222.

27. Ibid., 225–26.

28. *MECW,* Vol. 4, 182.

29. On Marx's epistemology, see Shlomo Avineri, *The Social and Political Thought of Karl Marx.* (Cambridge: Cambridge University Press, 1968), 69.

30. For a defence of its scientificity, see R. Bhaskar, *The Possibility of Naturalism* (Brighton, England: Harvester, 1979).

31. This point was made, contra the modern "critical theorists," by John Gunnell, "Political Science and the Theory of Action: Prologomena," *Political Theory* (February, 1979): 98.

32. I am indebted to Ian Shapiro for pointing this out.

33. See, for example, *The Mass Psychology of Fascism.* (New York: Simon & Schuster, 1976).

34. Ibid., 82.

35. K. Marx, *Grundrisse: Foundations of the Critique of Political Economy.* (New York: Vintage Books, 1973), 463; J. Elster, *Making Sense of Marx.* (Cambridge: Cambridge University Press, 1986), 106.

36. Lukes, 28–30.

37. Ibid., 29.

38. *The German Ideology,* 247; Lukes, 5.

39. *The German Ideology,* 419; Lukes, 6.

40. Eugene Kamenka, *The Ethical Foundations of Marxism.* (London and Boston: Routledge and Kegan Paul, 1972), 37.

41. See, for example, L. M. Loring, *Two Kinds of Values.* (London: Macmillan, 1974); D. R. Koehn, "Normative Ethics that Are Neither Teleological nor Deontological," *Metaphilosophy* 5:3; and Kamenka, ibid., 89ff.

42. See *The German Ideology,* 348–49.

43. See F. Engels, *Anti-Dühring* (Moscow: Foreign Language Publishing House, 1959), 131.

44. *The Poverty of Philosophy, MECW,* Vol. 6, 144.

45. See Lukes, 57.

46. Ibid., 55–57.

47. *MESW,* Vol. 3, 9ff.

48. Lukes, 58.

49. Ibid.

50. Z. I. Husami, "Marx on Distributive Justice," *Philosophy and Public Affairs* 8:1:52.

51. *Grundrisse,* 611.

52. *Capital,* Vol. I, 582.

53. R. Miller, *Analyzing Marx.* (Princeton: Princeton University Press, 1984), 80.

54. K. Marx, *Capital,* Vol. III (Moscow: Progress Publishers, 1974), 339–40.

55. Allen Wood, in *Karl Marx* (London: Routledge and Kegan Paul, 1981), puts the relativist case clearly but with apparent equivocation on this point (132). Marx was not himself a moral relativist, but an *anti*-moralist.

56. G. A. Cohen, in "Freedom, Justice and Capitalism," *New Left Review,* No. 126 (1981) has recognized the force of this, though he acknowledges it sits uneasily with his own claim that Marx condemned capitalism for its injustice.

57. *Capital,* Vol. III, 250.

58. Marx, ibid.; Elster, ibid.

59. Ibid.

60. Cited in Rubel and Manale, 245.

61. *MESW,* Vol. 2, 190.

62. *MESC,* Nov. 4, 1864, 182; Lukes, 6–7.

63. Lukes, ibid.

64. See *Capital.* Vol. I, 84.

65. See J. Raz, *Practical Reasons and Norms.* (London: Hutchinson, 1975), 159; Lukes, 94–99.

66. *MESW,* Vol. 3, 3, 24.

67. Cited in Rubel and Manale, 53. Author's emphasis.

68. *MESW,* Vol. 2, 22–23; Gilbert, 164.

69. Cited in Rubel and Manale, 244–45.

70. A. E. Buchanan, "Revolutionary Motivation and Rationality," *Philosophy and Public Affairs* 9:1 (1979).

71. W. H. Shaw, "Marxism, Revolution and Rationality," in T. Ball and J. Farr, ibid.

72. See Kamenka, 160.

73. See, for example, D. W. Lovell, *From Marx to Lenin.* (Cambridge: Cambridge University Press, 1984).

74. See Lukes, Ch. 6.

75. Cited in Kamenka, 26.

76. See Lukes, ibid.

15

HEIDEGGER AND POLITICAL PHILOSOPHY: THE THEORY OF HIS PRACTICE

STEVEN B. SMITH

Et humiliter serviebant et superbe diminabantur.
—Livy

The study of the relation between theory and practice ceases to be a sterile academic enterprise and gains color when one examines a thinker's ideas against his or her own political practice. When the thinker in question is, like Martin Heidegger, generally acknowledged as both one of the greatest philosophical minds of our age and a member of a political party responsible for some of the grossest barbarisms ever committed, the question gains not only life but a sense of real importance. That one of the greatest and most compelling philosophic minds of this century was also a Nazi raises the most fundamental problem concerning the relation between theory and practice.[1]

The facts of the case are by now fairly well known. In the early 1930s, Heidegger became a dues-paying member of the Nazi Party and was later to become Rector of the University of Freiburg. In 1933, he gave a famous (or rather infamous) rectoral address *(Rektoratsrede)* under the title, "The Self-Assertion of the German University."[2] The speech shocked and discom-

440

fited many of Heidegger's contemporaries in its attempt to connect the mission of the university to the service of the Reich. In one of the most alarming passages from the address, Heidegger wrote:

> The much celebrated "academic freedom" is being banished from the German university; for this freedom was not genuine, since it was only negative. It meant primarily freedom fron concern, arbitrariness of intentions and inclinations, lack of restraint in what was done and left undone.[3]

Rather than using his position to preserve academic freedom from the intrusive power of the Nazi state, Heidegger argued that this state was the fate and destiny of the German people. The university, rather than obstructing, should serve or minister to that fate.

It would be a great, even a fatal, error to see in Heidegger's speech a mere aberration or political mistake. In 1935, he gave a series of lectures in which he spoke of "the inner truth and greatness" of the Nazi movement. And when these lectures were published after the war in 1953 under the title, *An Introduction to Metaphysics,* he saw fit to let the statement stand as is, adding parenthetically that it referred to "the encounter between global technology and modern man."[4] Added to this was Heidegger's stunning silence about the Holocaust even after the Nazi atrocities were evident for all with eyes to see.

Heidegger's association with the Nazis has been a profound embarrassment to the legions of his admirers. Consequently, several strategies have been adopted to explain or explain away the offending evidence. The first strategy that his most pious defenders have adopted is to argue that Heidegger's philosophy is something entirely separate from his politics and that it is a mistake to confuse philosophic inquiry with political action. This strategy not only fails to make sense of Heidegger's politics, but is inconsistent with the basic premises of his existentialism. Any attempt to inquire into the fundamental grounds of Being that does not take into account the political situation of the inquirer can only result in self-deception and inauthenticity.[5]

A second strategy calculated to exonerate Heidegger has

been to admit his execrable politics but to argue that his association with the Nazis was relatively brief, after which he retired
from active support of the party.[6] During his time as Rector of
the university, it is claimed that Heidegger used his position to
protect Jewish faculty members and to defend the university
from political manipulation. This is more or less the account
that Heidegger has given in his own defense, but the recent
research of Hugo Ott, Farias, and others has shown conclusively
that it is largely fabricated, a tale of convenience.[7] Biographical
information provided by students and contemporaries alike
shows without a doubt that Heidegger's associations with National Socialism were longer and deeper than he wanted publicly to admit.[8]

A third and more sophisticated defense has been to argue
that Heidegger's later writings (about which I shall comment
later) represent an implicit, if not outspoken, critique of his
earlier views that led to his extreme right-wing politics. His most
recent defenders have argued that Heidegger's politics during
the 1930s were the outcome of an as yet incomplete emancipation from the metaphysical tradition. Thus the attempt of his
later years to work out a new form of "poetic" thinking was a
way of settling accounts with his erstwhile philosophical politics.
The purpose of this strategy has been to make possible an
appropriation of Heidegger's thought by the academic and even
political Left by showing that his later philosophy suggests a
self-criticism of his earlier positions.[9]

None of these views is adequate in my opinion. An interpretation of a thinker's ideas that cannot confront the relation
between theory and practice is not an interpretation at all. Heidegger was a Nazi and an unrepentant one at that. He should
at least be credited for consistency. It is the relation between
Heidegger's theory and politics which remains *the* problem
which any interpretation of his thought needs to honestly and
forthrightly confront.

Heidegger's thought is related to Nazism in two distinct but
related ways which I intend to explore. In the first place, Nazism functioned in his writings of the 1930s as a distinctly German alternative to Anglo-American democracy and Soviet-style
communism. Nazism was invested with the spiritual task of res-

cuing Germany from an increasingly nihilistic modernity that Heidegger believed had overtaken the rest of the earth. The language of "authenticity" and "resolve" *(Entschlossenheit)* played the same role for Heidegger as Carl Schmitt's supreme moment of "decision" did for his jurisprudence.[10] Second, Nazism came to function less as an alternative to, but rather as the fulfillment of the age of technology that came to dominate Heidegger's thought in his post-war writings. Nazism would, along with democracy and communism, help to bring modernity to a kind of completion, after which a new revelation or dispensation of Being would become possible. In fact, Hitler's Reich, with its death camps and routinized brutality, became the purest expression of the age of technology.

This is not to say that Heidegger's thought is exhausted by its relation to Hitlerism. Heidegger saw deeply and, if I may say so, profoundly into many of the deepest problems of modernity. His influence can be detected in virtually every contemporary movement of thought and practice. His emphasis on "authentic" existence against the alienating demands of mass society is at the basis of modern existentialism. His emphasis on such terms as "rootedness," "fate," and "being-in-the-world" prepares the ground for modern communitarianism; his critique of global technology as the outgrowth of Western metaphysics is at the root of the critical theory of society from Horkheimer and Adorno to Habermas; his conception of language as the "house of Being" which is best revealed not through reasoned speech but through poetry is at the core of the academic theories of hermeneutics and deconstruction; and his idea of *Gelassenheit* or "letting be" seems to open up the door to Zen and the religions of the East. Heidegger's influence has touched and transformed not only movements of thought but of practice as well. His followers range from Werner Earhardt, the founder of EST training, to current leaders of "green" politics and the deep ecology movement.[11]

As with any thinker of note, it is often difficult to account for one's prominence on the basis of books alone (although Heidegger's works will eventually fill over eighty volumes in the posthumously edited *Gesamtausgabe*).[12] Heidegger was born in

1889 in a rural area of southern Germany. His roots in a peasant region not far from the Black Forest were to exert a decisive
pull over how he saw the world and evaluated its dominant
trends. He attended university at Freiburg and later became a
teaching assistant to the phenomenological philosopher Ed-
mund Husserl. He was appointed to the position of *Privatdozent*
at Freiburg in 1919. Even before his first and still most important book *Being and Time* was published, rumors began to
circulate about the *Wunderkind* who had established himself as
Husserl's successor.

I can give some indication of the excitement generated by
Heidegger's lectures by quoting at some length the recollections
of one of his students who experienced them at first hand, the
young political theorist Leo Strauss:

> I remember the impression he [Heidegger] made on me when I
> heard him first as a young Ph.D. in 1922. Up to that time I had
> been particularly impressed, as many of my contemporaries
> were, by Max Weber: by his intransigent devotion to intellectual
> honesty, by his passionate devotion to the idea of science—a
> devotion that was combined with a profound uneasiness regard-
> ing the meaning of science. On my way north from Freiburg,
> where Heidegger then taught, I saw in Frankfurt-am-Main,
> Franz Rosenzweig, whose name will always be remembered when
> informed people speak about existentialism, and I told him of
> Heidegger. I said to him that in comparison with Heidegger,
> Weber appeared to me as an "orphan child" in regard to preci-
> sion and probing and competence. I had never seen such seri-
> ousness, profundity, and concentration in the interpretation of
> philosophic texts. ... Gradually the breadth of the revolution of
> thought which Heidegger was preparing dawned upon me and
> my generation. We saw with our own eyes that there had been
> no such phenomenon in the world since Hegel.[13]

What, then, was the "revolution in thought" that Heidegger
was preparing?

In 1927, Heidegger published his major work entitled *Being
and Time*. This book was an examination of "the question of
Being," which he took to be the deepest, the most fundamental
question of philosophy, the question preceding and underlying
all others. On its surface, it is hard to see how this question,

which would be of interest to no more than a handful of people, could give rise to problems of historical and political immediacy unknown since Hegel. Heidegger's claim is that the question of Being has been distorted ever since Plato attempted to locate the source of Being in the permanent, imperishable world of the Ideas over and beyond the finite, human world of becoming. It was Plato's attempt to provide a rational articulation to the question of Being that has led to a profound misunderstanding of the human condition. For Heidegger, the problem of an impending nihilism derives from a faulty attempt to grasp Being, which has disfigured the philosophical tradition from its beginning. Only a radical reconsideration of the question can save humankind from an impending moral and metaphysical collapse.

Being and Time proposes two apparently simple, but quite profound and radical ideas. In the first place, Being as understood by the Western philosophic tradition has been identified from the outset with a specific understanding of what it means "to be." The verb "to be," as the Greek philosophers perceived it, means "to be always." But for Heidegger it was precisely the search for a permanent, immutable core of Being that has blinded us to the true nature of the question. Being is not a substance or an essence, but is something closer to a problem or a question. It is something mutable and transitory: hence the title of the work *Being and Time*. The task is, then, to come to terms with the myriad ways in which Being reveals itself in time.

Second, Heidegger made clear that Being is not a thing like other things we happen to experience. We do not experience Being in the way that we come across houses and trees. Rather we are a part of Being and therefore our being, what he calls our "being-in-the-world" *(Dasein)*, necessarily makes up part of the investigation of what it means to be. Heidegger makes clear that it is not with human nature or self-consciousness that he is concerned but with Being as such. *Dasein* is rather the point of access or portal through which we encounter Being. Consequently we cannot understand Being as we would an object of scientific investigation, but must approach it as a form of existence, as "a way of life" as Wittgenstein would later put it, something in which we are already implicated. This is the fundamental insight of existentialism: the human subject cannot be divorced from knowledge; knowledge which forgets the "I" or the self is not genuine or authentic knowledge. At the core of this insight is something like the Socratic dictum that all knowledge is fundamentally self-knowledge.

So far, there is nothing especially ominous about any of this. Heidegger is still carrying out the program of Husserl, whose aim was to recover the ground or the fundamental presuppositions of scientific or rational inquiry in a preexisting "lifeworld" *(Lebenswelt)*. Like Husserl, Heidegger wanted to show how even our most abstract concepts and categories have as their precondition our being-in-the-world. But Heidegger went beyond Husserl in trying to show how being-in-the-world takes the form of a being-with-others, that is to say, it contains an ineradicably social component. We experience others as part of an "everyday" reality which includes received opinions and mundane material needs and concerns. From the outset, Heidegger's analytics of *Dasein* took the form of a phenomenology of everyday life. Rather than beginning with such abstractions as the natural man of the social contract tradition or the *ego cogitans* of Cartesianism, Heidegger sought to find a ground for human existence in the social and cultural situation in which we have been "thrown," as it were, by fate. The everyday world of fact and opinion would henceforth serve as the existential basis for ontology.

The critical function of *Being and Time* was only revealed by Heidegger's association of the everyday mode of being with the reign of inauthenticity. It is the very ordinariness or "readiness-to-hand" of things which points to the rule of what Nietzsche has called "the last man" or what Heidegger calls "the they" *(das Man)*.[14] To say that everyday life is inauthentic is to say that it is dominated by a kind of "idle talk" or chatter of a particularly ersatz kind. This kind of talk fundamentally obscures rather than reveals the problem of Being by concealing the groundlessness *(Abgrund)* at its core. The everyday is so unbearable precisely because it prohibits the asking of the most fundamental questions concerning *Dasein*.[15]

In *Being and Time,* Heidegger's response to the problem of the banality of the everyday mode of being is his call to live authentically. The call to the authentic life is interpreted by Heidegger as the call of "conscience."[16] It is the equivalent of Nietzsche's call to the superman to live freely and creatively. But Heidegger's call to the authentic life is not the same as the imperative of individuality. The conditions of *Dasein* are ineradicably collective. We cannot avoid this. Our task is to live authentically within a community or a people *(Volk)*. This is our fate and destiny.[17] But, one might ask, how is authenticity possible within society if society is the very root of the problem that authenticity seeks to overcome? While Heidegger never mentions Rousseau in any favorable light, we can see that the problem of *Being and Time* is very much the same as Rousseau's *Social Contract,* namely, how to find a kind of freedom within civil society when civil society is the very cause of our enslavement. The problem seems insuperable.

In *Being and Time,* Heidegger's answer to this problem remains abstract and unsatisfactory. His call to live authentically requires a serious confrontation with death and our own mortality. This confrontation is authentic when it is directed toward our own death, but inauthentic when it is directed against death in general. Instead of experiencing the possibility of death and hence coming to terms with our mortality, Heidegger maintains that we embark on ways of avoiding this confrontation. The entire edifice of modern science and technology, which plays the major role in Heidegger's later works, are all elaborate means of escaping the conditions of our mortality. Only by adopting an attitude of "resoluteness" in the face of death are we able to rise above the inauthenticity of day-to-day life.[18] It is this openness to the fragility of existence that puts us into the frame of mind better able to grasp the question of Being.

Heidegger's works throughout the 1930s and 1940s, especially *An Introduction to Metaphysics, The Question Concerning Technology,* and the *Letter on Humanism,* all develop the theme that it is the "forgetfulness" of Being that is the hallmark of an increasingly nihilistic modernity. Underlying the forgetfulness of Being is the peculiar conjunction of metaphysics and technology. Now, this is a surprising observation given that metaphysics and technology are commonly thought to be the virtual antitheses of one

another. But part of Heidegger's history of Being is to show
how the impulse toward technological control and domination
of the earth is deeply rooted in the Western metaphysical tradition. It is on this basis that he calls for a *Destruktion* of metaphysics.[19]

The origin of this metaphysical impulse, Heidegger, like
Nietzsche, traces back to Plato.[20] The original sin of Plato, which
has been compounded ever since, was the attempt to grasp or
lay hold of Being through reasoned speech and discourse. Plato,
Heidegger shows in his analysis of the "allegory" of the cave in
the *Republic*, went so far as to propose a new "doctrine of truth"
that sets the West on its course once and for all.[21] Truth, Heidegger contends, is our translation of the Greek noun *aletheia*,
which originally meant "unhiddenness" or "unconcealment."
Truth was always something that had to be "torn away," "ex-
torted," or even "stolen" from the Being that concealed it.
There was always an element of struggle and even violence in
Heidegger's account of the original process of "wresting" truth
away from hiddenness (represented by the cave in Plato's allegory).[22]

But within the same dialogue, Plato advances a new and
different conception of truth based upon the identification of
Being not with an original struggle but with *logos* and ultimately
with the *eidos*.[23] The basic feature of the Platonic *eidos*, and
especially with the Idea of the Good, is its transformation of the
older pre-Socratic conception of Being from something hidden
and obscure to something present and at hand. Plato and the
entire metaphysical tradition thus denied any essential mystery
to Being by trying to show that it is something susceptible to
rational description and explanation. The result of this identification of Being with *eidos* is that truth came to be identified
with "correctness" or "agreement" between our mental concepts
and things of which they are ideas. It is this conception of truth
as correspondence that has come down to us through the Latin
veritas, to the Thomistic *adequatio*, and to Cartesian certainty
that has set the standard for all Western thinking.[24] This change
in the meaning of truth also set in motion a fatal "subjectivity"
which further identifies the Idea of the Good (previously a
purely functional concept) with the morally good and hence

with the theory of values. The long itinerary begun with Plato has culminated in the "unfettered" Platonism of Nietzsche for whom truth itself is nothing but a value.[25]

Plato had initiated a conception of Being that came to dominate the subsequent history or fate of the West. This metaphysical impulse to grasp and manipulate came to a peak in the modern Enlightenment established by such theorists as Descartes, Kant, and Hegel. What the Enlightenment added was an unprecedented emphasis on human subjectivity whether in the form of the Cartesian *cogito,* the Kantian "I think," the Hegelian *Geist,* or even the Nietzschean "will to power." Modern science and technology are simply the ultimate expression of this peculiar combination of aggression and subjectivity that marks off modernity from all previous epochs. Heidegger insists that the essence of technology is not itself anything technological. It is not the application of physical science to solve human problems, but rather the peculiar idea of research *(Forschung)* that has come to dominate thinking in both the natural and the human sciences.[26]

Modern scientific research consists in the first instance of the specification of a circumscribed object-domain that can be studied by experimental means. But what modern science means by experimentation is not simple observation, but "the laying down of a law," that is, representing the object as something inherently stable and reproducible under specified conditions.[27] This method of experimentation Heidegger calls by the term "enframing" *(Gestell)* which means a kind of "setting in place." The act of enframing is fundamental to Heidegger's conception of technology which views all beings—mortals, earth, sky, divinities—as so many objects to be manipulated and controlled for the sake of serving subjectively chosen ends and purposes. Technology culminates in the last instance in the service of domination and control.[28]

The corollary of this new idea of science is an increasing specialization or particularization of tasks. Specialization is not the result but the prerequisite for all research conceived as an essentially "ongoing" or "progressive" enterprise. But for science to be progressive, it must also be institutionalized in the modern research university. Here we reach the apotheosis of technology: the modern "research man" or *Fachmensch*. The older idea of the scholar who needs books and a library is here progressively replaced by the researcher who is "constantly on the move," who "negotiates at meetings and collects information at congresses" and who "contracts for commissions with publishers," who in turn decide what needs to be written. In a word: the modern university professor. Heidegger notes, almost as an afterthought, that the older tradition of scholarly erudition ("increasingly thin and empty") will continue "to persist for some time in a few places," but is being progressively consigned to extinction by men of a "different stamp."[29]

The development of Western metaphysics comes to a head in the thought of Nietzsche. Nietzsche was in many ways a prototype for Heidegger. Neitzsche's beliefs that "God is dead" and that we must prepare ourselves for the coming of the superman seem to anticipate Heidegger's views on the "darkening of the world" and living in anticipation of new divinities. One could say, in a sense, of Heidegger what Nietzsche said of his Zarathustra, namely, that he is "the most pious of all those, who do not believe in God."[30] But for Heidegger, Nietzsche did not so much solve the problem of nihilism as deepen it. For Heidegger, Nietzsche's philosophy is nothing less than a comprehensive meditation on Being as the will to power. The eternally recurrent will to power is merely Nietzsche's answer to the age-old metaphysical problem "what is Being?" or, put another way, is the culmination of metaphysics understood as subjectivity. The will to power completes the Enlightenment's project of subordinating both man and nature to the imperatives of control. This represents the completion of "the struggle for the domination of the earth" which Nietzsche wrote will be waged in the name of "fundamental philosophical doctrines."[31] But just what are these doctrines that will determine the struggle for domination? And in the service of which ideologies did Nietzsche pretend to speak?

It is only now that the history of metaphysics has run its course that we can begin to call for its destruction. "The darkening of the world" and "the destruction of the earth" are Heidegger's metaphors for the growing alienation and forgetfulness of Being that is the characteristic feature of modernity in all of its manifestations. From this point of view, he wrote in the *Introduction to Metaphysics* that Europe remained situated between American democracy and Russian communism. Both of these were for Heidegger simply expressions of the age of technology. "Metaphysically speaking," he wrote, "Russia and America are the same, the same dreary technological frenzy, the same unrestricted organization of the average man."[32] The danger is that Germany, "the most metaphysical of nations," is at the same time subject to "the severest" historical "pressures."[33] Heidegger saw in both democracy and communism similar forms of conformism, levelling, and brutalization. It was against this conception of Germany as stuck between these gigantic "pincers" that Heidegger opted for Nazism, which he believed would offer a new assessment of what he called "the encounter between global technology and modern man."[34]

The task that Heidegger attributed to Hitler's Reich was nothing short of the recovery of some authentic mode of Being from the spiritual impoverishment and emptiness of the urban workaday world. In the *Rektoratsrede* he spoke of the destiny of Germany as a "spiritual" nation.[35] Here, for the first time, he began to speak of the great poets, lawgivers, and artists as the true founders of nations. Each nation or *Volk* has its own unique fate or destiny imprinted upon it by its founders. To live authentically meant to accept one's subordination to the work of a creative founder or leader. Further, Heidegger emphasized the violent and war-like character of founding a people. It consists of a struggle *(Kampf)* between man and Being. The leader is described as the one who must have "the strength to be able to walk alone."[36] Heidegger concluded the *Rektoratsrede* with a quotation taken from the sixth book of Plato's *Republic,* which he translated to read "all that is great stands in a storm."[37] In the context of the politics of the 1930s, no one could possibly have misunderstood to what storm Heidegger was alluding.

Heidegger's politics during the 1930s were prompted neither by opportunism nor naiveté but by his understanding of Germany's historical "situation."[38] This situation as described in the *Introduction to Metaphysics* is one of the "enfeeblement" and "emasculation" of the spirit created by the collapse of German idealism.[39] Faith in science or the "historical process" or divinity or even reason had given way to a resolve to act. Karl Löwith has described Heidegger's resolve as follows:

> When in 1933 in Germany the decisive "instant" had come Heidegger took a resolute stand within the world-historical situation by charging himself very emphatically with the "leadership" of Freiburg University. This political commitment . . . was not—as naive people thought—a deviation from the main path of his philosophy, but a consequence of his concept of historical existence which only recognizes truths that are relative to the actual and proper.[40]

Löwith attributes Heidegger's reprehensible politics to a "radical temporalization" of truth, to his affirmation of the Nietzschean thesis that if there is no truth then "everything is permitted." But there were many historicists and relativists who were not Nazis, much less committed and articulate ones. Heidegger's politics were the result of a combination of his radical historicism coupled with a belief that the destiny of Germany was to rescue the West from the wasteland of a nihilistic modernity. Heidegger's thought may not have compelled surrender to Hitler, but it did nothing to prevent that surrender.[41]

Heidegger's politics were premised on the belief that there was a kind of natural, primordial affinity between the Germans and the ancient Greeks. The ancient, or at least the prephilosophic, Greeks held the same position of honor for him as the archaic Homeric nobility held for Nietzsche. Just as Nietzsche depended upon Homer and the tragedians for his view of a master morality, so did Heidegger look to Heraclitus and the other pre-Socratics for the original dispensation of Being. For the pre-Socratics, Being was primarily a struggle or *agon* in which the polis was the greatest achievement. The ancient polis was not for Heidegger the foundation of democracy and democratic institutions as it has been portrayed by generations of conventional scholarship. Rather, Heidegger treats the polis as the creation of great "poets, thinkers, and statesmen" who use their power both to create and impose a "destiny" on a people.[42] Heidegger seems to take pleasure, even delight, in his description of the violence that inevitably attends all political foundings. The use of great power *(Gewalt)* is not just an accidental quality but an essential feature of historical *Dasein*.[43] We are the "strangest of all creatures" *(deinotaton)* precisely because of our ability to use power to establish new beginnings. It is always the beginnings that are "strangest and mightiest," with decay and decadence setting in later on.[44]

In this context Heidegger cites Heraclitus's famous statement to the effect that war *(polemos)* is the father of all things.[45] Heidegger translates the Greek *polemos* by the German *Auseinandersetzung* or a "setting apart."[46] This setting apart does not signify war or conflict in the ordinary sense, but a separation of Being into the high and the low. Archaic Being appears, then, not as a mere collection or "heaping up," but as a hierarchy where "rank and domination are implicit" and where "what has higher rank is stronger."[47] The polis was originally a site not only between men struggling for glory or fame *(kleos)*, but between men and gods. As such, the polis was not only a setting apart but a setting of limits.[48] One was always aware of its extreme fragility. The polis was a home *(Heimat)* or dwelling place *(offene-Statte)* in which man could establish himself. The kind of home or public space provided by the polis was virtually the opposite of the large, impersonal, bureaucratically organized states of modernity.

For Heidegger, it was the unique destiny of the German people to recover something like the sense of public space that constituted the Greek polis. No reader (or hearer) of the *Rektoratsrede* could fail to note how the three forms of service to the German Reich are modeled after the three classes of the Platonic *Republic*.[49] Typically, Heidegger thought of this destiny as shaped by the poets and philosophers, especially Hölderlin, who sought to inspirit his contemporaries by announcing the coming of new divinities. The work of the true poets and artists was never simply aesthetic beautification, but the opening up of a world or space in which new possibilities could emerge. It is only through "great poetry" that a people enter into history. Poetry is the original language, the *Ursprache,* of a people by means of which they establish themselves as a community or *Volk*.[50]

What Homer and Sophocles were to the Greeks, so in Heidegger's opinion is Hölderlin to the Germans. Hölderlin was not just any poet, but one who was uniquely attuned to the

German soul and as such "the poet who points toward the
future, who expects a god."[51] Hölderlin, the contemporary of
Hegel and Schelling, was deeply troubled by what he perceived
to be the end of the Greco-Christian era and the consequent
disenchantment of the world. For Hölderlin, it was the gods
who had deserted the world ("Aber freund! wir kommen zu spat"),
and left it in a state of spiritual destitution. What is worse is not
only that the gods have fled but that modern men are scarcely
aware of the loss.[52] This state of destitution is not, however, the
same as a condition of despair. A state of destitution may pose
grave dangers, but also great possibilities for redemption. The
flight of the old gods may portend new ones if one responds
properly. The task of the poet, then, who lives in an age of
destitution is to awaken the sense of possibility that attends the
flight of the gods. Heidegger enjoyed quoting the following
lines from Hölderlin's Patmos: "But where danger is, grows the
saving power also" ("Wo aber Gefahr ist, wächst Das Rettende
auch").[53] Not only was Heidegger's appeal to the redemptive
powers of danger highly irresponsible given the context of the
times, it could not but appeal to the most dangerous ambitions
of dangerously ambitious men.

It remained to the German people as a spiritual nation, or at
least to its poets and philosophers, to prepare the way for new
divinities and a new aesthetic. Following Hölderlin, Heidegger
recommended adopting an attitude of holy mourning for the
lost gods. Only by becoming aware of what has been lost can the
"saving power" be received. But this power is a profoundly
political or collective force, not a theological or individual one.
Its aim is to rescue the "homeland" or "fatherland" from the
grip of technological nihilism. After the war, Heidegger denied
that he used these ideologically loaded terms in a political sense.
In calling on his "countrymen" to find their homeland, he
claimed not to be invoking the "egoism" of any particular nation. Rather, the homeland in question was "a belongingness to
the destiny of the West." The German's true homeland was a
historical "nearness to Being."[54]

It may well have been his disappointment with the Nazi experiment that led Heidegger to withdraw from public life and retire

to a cottage in the Black Forest.[55] From here he described his work as "intimately rooted" in the conditions of peasant life. He increasingly saw in urban life the combination of loneliness, alienation, and anomie that arises from the peculiar conditions of modernity. Only that which is "rooted in a tradition" or has a "home" contains the possibility of greatness.[56] His celebration of the land and the soil, the earth and its destiny, was the logical conclusion of his critique of metaphysics.

Heidegger's later thoughts turned on his studies of language and an attempt to establish a poetic, non-metaphysical definition of Being for a new age. The watchword of his last writings was *Gelassenheit* sometimes translated as "letting be."[57] Rather than adopting an attitude of sternness or resoluteness as he had in *Being and Time*, Heidegger emphasizes *Gelassenheit* or simply letting things be. Only a refusal to interfere, an attitude of Zen-like acceptance, can offset the metaphysical-technological mode of Being that Heidegger sought to transcend. This "turn" in Heidegger's thought is often taken to represent an unstated repudiation of his Nazi past. His rejection of human action seemed complete when he told an interviewer for the magazine *Der Spiegel* that "only a god can save us."[58] In the context, it was clear that he meant not some personal deity but rather a new and mysterious revelation of Being that we can do nothing to bring about but must be prepared to await.

Heidegger's last works, with their poetic evocation of Being, are often believed to represent a new mode or phase in the history of Being. This phase has lately been called the "post-modern" or "post-metaphysical" in order to designate a new dispensation. Heidegger did not, of course, use these terms but spoke more cryptically about the "overcoming" or "getting over" *(verwinden)* of metaphysics. He called for a new kind of thinking that would not be stuck on the older representational picture of thought. This overcoming of metaphysics is more than a mere change of attitude.[59] Metaphysics, Heidegger believes, is not something we can simply put aside like an article of clothing. Rather it is something that needs to be thought through from its roots. By an act of "recollection" *(Andenken)* Heidegger hoped that we could free ourselves from the grip of metaphysics and so open up "an other thinking" *(ein anderes Denken)*.[60]

We live today in the age of completed metaphysics which has brought with it "the collapse of the world" and "the desolation of the earth."[61] Heidegger traces this process back to Hegel's metaphysics of spirit as will after which "everything is merely a counter movement," and more importantly to Nietzsche's doctrine of the will to power which announces the closure of the age.[62] With the completion of metaphysics as will to power, philosophy as such has disappeared, replaced by technology as the highest form of rational consciousness. Under the rule of technology, Being has been reduced to the status of labor and the products of labor power as so much raw material to be consumed in the endless, repetitive cycle of production and consumption. It is the interpretation of Being as will to power that is at once "the fate of the West" and the cause of the Western dominance over the rest of the globe.[63]

Heidegger gives this diagnosis of the end of philosophy an unconditionally political interpretation. The struggle for power is said to be not only universal but undecidable because there is fundamentally nothing to decide.[64] The two world wars (which Heidegger always refers to in quotation marks) and now the cold war are nothing but the political expression of the global power struggle. It is of no use venting anger, frustration, or moral outrage at putative leaders *(Führer)* or leadership *(Führung)* because such persons and offices are merely functions of the age of planetary domination.[65] In such a world, the differences between a Churchill and a Hitler, to say nothing of pre- and post-war Germany, are reduced to nil.[66] Heidegger even suggests that new developments in the biological sciences and genetics are preparing the ground for a new type of humanity, a race of test-tube bred *homunculi* arising out of "the emptiness of the abandonment of Being." Under these circumstances, however, no action is enough to change anything. It is sufficient to wait like a nomad living "invisibly and outside the desert of the desolated earth" for a new post-technological order to reveal itself.[67]

Heidegger was naturally opaque when it came to saying what this new thinking would look like. As in any new dispensation, it is sometimes easier to state what it is against than what it is for. The new poetics of *Gelassenheit* would oppose the earlier technological urge to dominate and control reality. A new attitude of attentiveness or openness would replace the metaphysical search for permanent and stable foundations for Being. It is in this context that he began to speak of language as the "house of Being."[68] Language is not an instrument by which we achieve pragmatically chosen goals. It is not something we use to picture or map onto the world. Rather language is something lived. Only by becoming almost endlessly attentive to the rhythms and cadences of language can we free ourselves from the older metaphysics of *Gestell* and the "world picture."

The result of Heidegger's later thought was not to repudiate Nazism as his more pious defenders have wished. His poetics of *Gelassenheit* did not result in a more democratic humanitarianism. Rather, Nazism itself became, along with Americanism and communism, one more form of the modern age. Nazism became normalized—another way of being "forgetful" of Being but no worse than any other. The problem with Nazism was not its inhumanity, Heidegger reported. Rather it suffered from an *excess* of humanism. By humanism he meant here just another form of subjectivism and assertive self-imposition. All of the "isms" and ideologies of the modern age, from Marxism to democracy to nationalism, were forms of Western humanism with their willful attempts to dominate the globe. The result of these efforts to assert mastery was to render modern man absolutely "homeless."[69]

Heidegger did not shrink from the implications of his "antihumanism." In what is perhaps the most odious statement ever uttered by a thinker of the first order, Heidegger wrote in 1949:

Agriculture is now a mechanized food industry. As for its essence, it is the same thing as the manufacture of corpses in the gas chambers and the death camps, the same thing as the blockades and reduction of countries to famine, the same thing as the manufacture of hydrogen bombs.[70]

Heidegger's efforts to define the essence of technology led in the end to an almost inhuman indifference to the uses to which technology is put. To say that the production of food to feed the starving is "the same thing" as the production of Zyklon B for Auschwitz is to exhibit neither naiveté or cynicism, but grows logically out of Heidegger's understanding of the Holocaust as a purely technical problem. Heidegger was never at a loss to complain about the despoilation of the forests and rivers of his beloved Schwarzwald, but could not find so much as a word of regret for the true victims of National Socialism.

The paradox of Heidegger's later work is that he wrote not to demean humanity but to elevate it. In the *Letter on Humanism,* he took special exception to the Aristotelian definition of man as the rational animal not because Aristotle thought that we were rational, but because he thought that we were animals.[71] It is our "openness" to or "nearness" to Being, he now asserted, that defined our species. Our species, uniquely capable of receptivity and reflection, seeks to impose itself on the world through thought and action. Through a combination of subjectivity and aggressiveness we lose touch with those experiences that could serve to remind us of our situation and its limits. We are to become not the "lord of beings" but the "shepherd of Being."[72]

Yet at the same time that he called us to a new, higher humanism, elevated beyond a mean-spirited calculating rationality, Heidegger was able to turn a blind eye to the very real moral and political differences of the world around him. At issue is the very abstractness of Heidegger's articulation of Being. The extreme artificiality and unnaturalness of regarding human beings under the anonymous rubric of historical *Dasein* could not but anesthetize him to the problems of actual persons. It is worth recalling here Hans Jonas's remark that apart from the "blasphemous ring" of Heidegger's use of religious imagery, "it is hard to hear man hailed as the shepherd of Being when he has just so dismally failed to be his brother's keeper."[73] It was precisely his attitude of responsibility for Being, not for beings, that could account for his submission to, even his acceptance of, the verdict of "the least wise and least moderate part of his nation while it was in its least wise and least moderate mood."[74] Heidegger's Nazism was not the result of thoughtlessness as is sometimes alleged; it was the result of his deepest thoughts.

The lessons of Heidegger for the problem of theory and

practice are both profound and chastening. His teachings are profound in that they have awakened a much-heightened sensitivity to the perceived failures of modern society, especially its faith in the munificence of technology to cure all of our ills. As chastened post-moderns we are no longer prone to accord a simple belief in the benefits of science that earlier generations apparently took for granted. If anything, we are more inclined to see the ominous side of the technological society. No one who has lived through the century of global war, the Holocaust, and the nuclear threat, all of which were made possible by developments in science and technology, can simply entertain an optimistic picture of modernity. Add to this the problems of global warming brought about through the burning of fossil fuel, acid rain, to say nothing of experiments in the fields of cybernetics and genetic engineering, and we are apt to see in the liberated powers of technology a new kind of Frankenstein's monster.

At the same time that his teachings have alerted us to the ominous side of the Enlightenment and its technological vision of society, Heidegger's poetic conception of Being led him to acquiesce in and even welcome the greatest monstrosities of this and perhaps any age. His wholesale critique of modernity as the culmination of metaphysics created its own peculiar kind of forgetfulness, the forgetfulness of politics and the preeminence of political philosophy. Unlike Plato, for whom politics was never removed from any of his dialogues, Heidegger wrote a history of Being in which politics and ethics played at most a secondary or tertiary part. If Aristotle was right, and I believe he was, when he said that man is the political animal, the *zoon politikon,* then we must conclude that Martin Heidegger must have been either a beast or a god.

NOTES

1. See Victor Farias, *Heidegger and Nazism,* trans. Paul Burrell and Gabriel R. Ricci (Philadelphia: Temple University Press, 1989). A critical appraisal of the malestrom produced by the book is provided by Thomas Sheehan, "Heidegger and the Nazis," *New York Review of Books*

(June 16, 1988), 38–47; see also his "A Normal Nazi," *New York Review of Books* (January 14, 1993), 30–35; for a somewhat more defensive reaction see Hans-Georg Gadamer, "Superficiality and Ignorance: On Victor Farias's Publication," *Martin Heidegger and National Socialism: Questions and Answers*, ed. Gunther Neske and Emil Kettering (New York: Paragon, 1990), 141–44.

2. Martin Heidegger, "The Self-Assertion of the German University," trans. Karsten Harries, *Review of Metaphysics* 38 (1985): 467–80.

3. Heidegger, "Self-Assertion," 475–76.

4. Martin Heidegger, *An Introduction to Metaphysics*, trans. Ralph Mannheim (New Haven: Yale University Press, 1975), 199.

5. Among the works that have emphasized the political core of Heidegger's works are Alexander Schwann, *Politische Philosophie im Denken Heideggers* (Koln/Opladen: Westdeutscher, 1965); Karsten Harries, "Heidegger as a Political Thinker," *Review of Metaphysics* 29 (1976): 642–69; Mark Blitz, *Heidegger's "Being and Time" and the Possibility of Political Philosophy* (Ithaca: Cornell University Press, 1981); Luc Ferry and Alain Renaut, *Heidegger and Modernity*, trans. Philip Franklin (Chicago: University of Chicago Press, 1990); Philippe Lacoue-Labarthe, *Heidegger, Art, and Politics*, trans. Chris Turner (Oxford: Basil Blackwell, 1990); Richard Wolin, *The Politics of Being: The Political Thought of Martin Heidegger* (New York: Columbia University Press, 1990).

6. See Hannah Arendt, "Martin Heidegger at Eighty," *Heidegger and Modern Philosophy*, ed. Michael Murray (New Haven: Yale University Press, 1978), esp. 301–3, where she attributes this "episode" of "ten short hectic months" to Heidegger's relative youth as well as to "the attraction to the tyrannical" that can be "demonstrated theoretically in many of the great thinkers." Arendt makes this preposterous statement on the basis of Plato's association with Dionysius, the tyrant of Syracuse, as if there can be any comparison between a minor Sicilian satrap and Hitler's demonic evil! For the classic study of the relation between philosophy and tyranny, see Xenophon's *Hiero*.

7. Hugo Ott, *Martin Heidegger: Unterwegs zu seiner Biographie* (Frankfurt: Campus Verlag, 1988). Much of the evidence on which Ott's study is based has been collected by Guido Schneeberger, *Nachlese zu Heidegger: Dokumente zu seinem Leben und Denken* (Bern: 1962) and Jean-Michel Palmier, *Les ecrits politiques de Heidegger* (Paris: L'Herne, 1968).

8. See Karl Löwith, "Last Meeting with Heidegger," *Martin Heidegger and National Socialism*, 157–59.

9. See Reiner Schurmann, *Heidegger on Being and Acting: From Principles to Anarchy*, trans. Christine-Marie Gros (Bloomington: Indi-

ana University Press, 1987); see also Fred Dallmayr, "Ontology of Freedom: Heidegger and Political Philosophy," *Political Theory* 12 (1984): 204–34; and Stephen White, *Political Theory and Postmodernism* (Cambridge: Cambridge University Press, 1991), 42–53.

10. For Schmitt's views see his *Political Theology: Four Chapters on the Concept of Sovereignty,* trans. George Schwab (Cambridge: MIT Press, 1988), 31–35, 48–49.

11. For an excellent discussion of Heidegger's diverse influences, see Michael E. Zimmerman, *Heidegger's Confrontation with Modernity: Technology, Politics, Art* (Bloomington: Indiana University Press, 1990).

12. See Jeffrey Andrew Barash, "Martin Heidegger in the Perspective of the Twentieth Century: Reflections on the Heidegger *Gesamtausgabe," Journal of Modern History* 64 (1992): 52–78.

13. Leo Strauss, "An Introduction to Heideggerian Existentialism," *The Rebirth of Classical Political Rationalism,* ed. Thomas L. Pangle (Chicago: University of Chicago Press, 1989), 27–28.

14. Martin Heidegger, *Being and Time,* trans J. Macquarrie and E. Robinson (New York: Harper & Row, 1962), 126–29; (references will be to the German pagination included in the margins of the text).

15. Heidegger, *Being and Time,* 165, 167–70.

16. Heidegger, *Being and Time,* 289–97.

17. Heidegger, *Being and Time,* 384–85.

18. Heidegger, *Being and Time,* 298, 383; see also *Introduction to Metaphysics,* 21.

19. Heidegger, *Being and Time,* 19–27.

20. Martin Heidegger, "Plato's Doctrine of Truth," *Philosophy in the Twentieth Century,* ed. W. Barrett and H. D. Aiken, trans. John Barlow (New York: Random House, 1962), 251–70.

21. Heidegger, "Plato's Doctrine of Truth," 257, where he mentions the possibility of imposing a "violent reinterpretation" on the text.

22. Heidegger, "Plato's Doctrine of Truth," 260.

23. Heidegger, "Plato's Doctrine of Truth," 261.

24. Heidegger, "Plato's Doctrine of Truth," 260, 266–67.

25. Heidegger, "Plato's Doctrine of Truth," 263.

26. Martin Heidegger, "The Age of the World Picture," *The Question Concerning Technology and Other Essays,* trans. William Lovitt (New York: Harper & Row, 1977), 123.

27. Heidegger, "The Age of the World Picture," 121.

28. Heidegger, "The Age of the World Picture," 126–27; see also "The Question Concerning Technology," 23ff.

29. Heidegger, "The Age of the World Picture," 125.

30. Nietzsche, *Thus Spoke Zarathustra,* trans. Walter Kaufmann

(Harmondsworth: Penguin, 1978), Part IV, "Retired"; see also Heidegger's description of Nietzsche as "the last German philosopher" who was also a "passionate seeker of God" in "Self-Assertion," 474.

31. Martin Heidegger, "The Word of Nietzsche: 'God Is Dead,' " *The Question Concerning Technology*, 101.

32. Heidegger, *Introduction to Metaphysics*, 37.

33. Heidegger, *Introduction to Metaphysics*, 38.

34. Heidegger, *Introduction to Metaphysics*, 199.

35. Heidegger, "Self-Assertion," 470.

36. Heidegger, "Self-Assertion," 475.

37. Heidegger, "Self-Assertion," 480; see Plato, *Republic*, 497d. Bloom translates the passage as "all great things carry with them risk of a fall and, really as the saying goes, fine things are hard" while Grube renders it "all great things are risky and, as the saying goes, what is beautiful is difficult."

38. Heidegger, *Being and Time*, 310–16.

39. Heidegger, *Introduction to Metaphysics*, 45.

40. Karl Löwith, "M. Heidegger and F. Rosenzweig or Temporality and Eternity," *Philosophy and Phenomenological Research* 3 (1942–43): 75.

41. Emil Fackenheim, *Encounters Between Judaism and Modern Philosophy: A Preface to Future Jewish Thought* (New York: Schocken, 1980), 216.

42. Heidegger, *Introduction to Metaphysics*, 62.

43. Heidegger, *Introduction to Metaphysics*, 149–50.

44. Heidegger, *Introduction to Metaphysics*, 155.

45. The passage reads: "War is the father of all and king of all; and some he has shown as gods, others men; some he has made slaves, others free." C. H. Kahn, *The Art and Thought of Heraclitus* (Cambridge: Cambridge University Press, 1979), frag. 83, p. 67; the translation is from H. Diels, *Die Fragmente der Vorsokriter* (Berlin, 1951), 53.

46. Heidegger, *Introduction to Metaphysics*, 113–14.

47. Heidegger, *Introduction to Metaphysics*, 133.

48. Heidegger, *Introduction to Metaphysics*, 144.

49. Heidegger, "Self-Assertion," 476–77. Heidegger speaks here of the three estates *(Stände)* composing the Reich as consisting of Labor Service *(Arbeitsdienst)*, Armed Service, *(Wehrdienst)*, and Knowledge Service *(Wissensdienst)*.

50. Heidegger, *Introduction to Metaphysics*, 165, 171–72; see also "Hölderlin and the Essence of Poetry," *Existence and Being*, trans. W. Brock (Chicago: Regnery, 1949), 283–84.

51. Martin Heidegger, " 'Only a God Can Save Us': The *Spiegel* Interview (1966)," trans. William J. Richardson, in *Heidegger: The Man*

and the Thinker, ed. Thomas Sheehan (New York: Precedent, 1981), 62.

52. Martin Heidegger, "What Are Poets For?" *Poetry, Language, Thought,* ed. Albert Hofstadter (New York: Harper & Row, 1971), 96.

53. Heidegger, "The Question Concerning Technology," 28.

54. Martin Heidegger, "Letter on Humanism," *Basic Writings,* ed. David Krell (New York: Harper & Row, 1977), 218.

55. See Martin Heidegger, "Why Do I Stay in the Provinces?" trans. Thomas Sheehan in *Heidegger: The Man and the Thinker,* 27–29.

56. Heidegger, "Only a God Can Save Us," 57.

57. Martin Heidegger, "Memorial Address," *Discourse on Thinking,* trans. John Anderson and E. Hans Freund (New York: Harper & Row, 1966), 43–57.

58. Heidegger, "Only a God Can Save Us, 57.

59. Martin Heidegger, "Uberwindung der Metaphysik," *Vortrage und Aufsätze* (Pfullingen: Neske, 1954), 63.

60. Martin Heidegger, "The Thing," *Poetry, Language, Thought,* 181.

61. Heidegger, "Uberwindung der Metaphysik," 64.

62. Heidegger, "Uberwindung der Metaphysik," 68, 73.

63. Heidegger, "Uberwindung der Metaphysik," 69.

64. Heidegger, "Uberwindung der Metaphysik," 82.

65. Heidegger, "Uberwindung der Metaphysik," 85.

66. Cf. Martin Heidegger, *What Is Called Thinking,* trans. Glenn Gray (New York: Harper & Row, 1968), 66–67: "What did the Second World War really decide? (We shall not mention here its fearful consequences for my country, cut in two.) This world war has decided nothing—if we use 'decision' in so high and wide a sense that it concerns solely man's essential fate on this earth."

67. Heidegger, "Uberwindung der Metaphysik," 89–90.

68. Heidegger, "What are Poets For?" 132.

69. Heidegger, "Letter on Humanism," 218–19.

70. This occurs in Heidegger's unpublished lecture, *Die Gefahr (The Danger),* cited in Lacoue-Labarthe, *Heidegger, Art and Politics,* 34; see also Karsten Harries, "Introduction," *Martin Heidegger and National Socialism,* xxix–xxxi.

71. Heidegger, "Letter on Humanism," 202–3.

72. Heidegger, "Letter on Humanism," 221.

73. Hans Jonas, "Heidegger and Theology," *The Phenomenon of Life* (New York: Harper & Row, 1966), 258.

74. Leo Strauss, "What Is Political Philosophy?" *What Is Political Philosophy and Other Studies* (Glencoe: Free Press, 1959), 27.

16

A PERFORMER OF POLITICAL THOUGHT: VÁCLAV HAVEL ON FREEDOM AND RESPONSIBILITY

JEAN BETHKE ELSHTAIN

The problem of human identity remains at the center of my thinking about human affairs. . . . All my plays in fact are variations on this theme, the disintegration of man's oneness with himself and the loss of everything that gives human existence a meaningful order, continuity and its unique outline. . . . As you must have noticed from my letters, the importance of the notion of human responsibility has grown in my meditations. It has begun to appear, with increasing clarity, as that fundamental point from which all identity grows and by which it stands or falls; it is the foundation, the root, the center of gravity, the constructional principle or axis of identity. . . . It is the mortar binding it together, and when the mortar dries out, identity too begins irreversibly to crumble and fall apart.

—Václav Havel, *Letters to Olga*

Anyone who claims that I am a dreamer who expects to transform hell into heaven is wrong. I have few illusions, but I feel a responsibility to work towards the things I consider good and right. I don't know whether I'll be able to change certain things for the better, or not at all. Both outcomes are possible.

—Václav Havel, *Summer Meditations*

Theory and practice, or *theoria* and *praxis*, as they are sometimes couched, thus drawing attention to the classical lineage of both the categories and the vexations they deed us, form a central conundrum to many political theorists and philosophers. The distinction is, for many past and present, made exigent precisely because there is a gap between that which we can theorize and that which we can realize. Now, to some, this gap is part of the human condition. We always aspire to more than we can attain so it behooves us to keep our feet on the ground and not to engage in theoretical or wishful overreach. To others, this gap is, quite simply, unacceptable. They yearn for a more perfect order; a fullness of political being; an amplitude of justice or equality or wisdom; a state of unity and never-ending brotherhood and sisterhood, perhaps. For those who thus pine, the distinction between aspiration and "reality" may come to seem an unacceptable blot on the fortunes or misfortunes of humankind.

Many of our great movements of social and political yearning derive from one version of such recognitions. I think here of the anti-slavery movement, especially the slave's expressed desire for freedom, for that which is denied. But, alas, a good number of political and social catastrophes can be traced to this aspiration should it become a relentless drive to overturn any and all distinctions between that which is and that which, in theory, ought to be. In this latter case, our practices are always struggling to catch up to our theories and, in the process, much overturning and gnashing of teeth and shedding of blood may be inevitable. So one revolutionary story goes. This leads to my central concern, one that moves through this essay and helps to frame my interpretation of the work of Václav Havel. Havel, for me, represents an exemplary figure in part because he simply refuses to be drawn into the theory/practice dilemma as it is usually posed, thus opening up fresh ways of thinking; in part because he very delicately (for that is his way) summons up the best that is in us without stirring up the beasts that are always lurking at the same time.

Havel helps me to understand my own problem with the theory/practice problem, namely, that the issues at hand are too often so abstractly couched. It is difficult to get a handle on what, precisely, is at stake. I refer to the dilemma as it has been presented to me by political philosophers committed to the notion that the presumed divide or tension between theory and practice could be quite overcome in some future perfect world of transparent human relations and human communication. The theory/practice dilemma was such only because there were barriers in the way of instantiating in practice an abstract theoretical understanding. One variant on the Marxist project was particularly given to an odd combination of deep cynicism about the present, with its distorted relations, consciousness, and practices, by contrast to some future moment within an emancipated human community. In that future community, presumably, no theory/practice dilemma would persist because distinctions, boundaries, and tensions would have melted away and a "oneness"—that oceanic feeling Freud described and mocked so effectively—would have triumphed. The individual would be at one with himself or herself, the social order cured of its previous dissensions, conflicts, and divisions.

Dreams of this sort die hard. The notion of "positive transcendence" of estrangement will always beckon. Thus, one version of the theory/practice conundrum holds that the dilemma itself exists only because we live in a world of flawed and imperfect social forms. Once the universe is administered a stiff dose of the right medicine and cures itself, no dilemma—no distinction of this sort or of most other problematic sorts—will persist. This, of course, is a quite unbelievable political fantasy, believed in devoutly because it promises an overarching *Weltanschauung* of the sort described and decried by Freud, "an intellectual construction which solves all the problems of our existence on the basis of one overriding hypothesis which, accordingly, leaves no question unanswered and in which everything that interests us finds its fixed place."[1] Before practice can be perfect, or nearly so, one requires a theory that explains all, determines all, and can be enacted more or less in toto.

Now, one might have thought those those committed to ridding us of foundational superstition would resolve this dilemma, falsely couched within totalizing theories, by pointing out that the world is a dense and rather intractable place, that our practices can never be made perfect any more than our theories can explain all that wants explaining or help us to understand all that requires understanding. Not necessarily so. Take, for example, Richard Rorty's treatment of the theory/ practice vexation. For him, too, it simply ceases to be a question because one jettisons the "theory" end of the pole. However mistakenly cast this may be in Marxist and critical-theory formulations of the problem, eliminating the question altogether does not seem terribly helpful. But Rorty is deeply committed to insouciance. This is how it works. Rorty reassures us that things are pretty much moving along as they were meant to. The committed "contingentist" understands this; therefore, he also understands that even those who *claim* that their political actions and their very identities are imbricated with a set of deep theoretical or philosophical understandings are simply mistaken about their own project and the nature of its entanglement with such understandings.

Rortyanism requires that we all join the ranks of an army of contingent "we's." For Rorty contingency is what one is left with when one rejects the correspondence theory of truth and similarly eschews any strong convictions concerning the nature of reality. Rorty links his commitment to contingency to a rough-and-ready progressivist teleology (even though he cannot permit himself teleological arguments, he relies tactily on Whiggish history) when he claims, as but one example: "Europe gradually lost the habit of using certain words and gradually acquired the habit of using others."[2] Aside from the peculiarity of granting agency to a continent, what is at work here appears to be a conviction that although there is nothing intrinsic or essential about anything that has happened, or that led to the construction of "we liberal ironists," we are still in pretty good shape if we endorse a loose liberal utopia in which things pretty much continue to move along the way they have been moving because the contingencies seem to be on "our side." At least this is the way I interpret a statement such as: "A liberal society is one which is content to call 'true' whatever the upshot of such encounters turns out to be."[3] The encounters in question here are basic good guys versus bad guys stuff in which, over time, the good guys appear to be winning, more or less. Given the blithe certainty of Rorty's commitment to contingency with progress, it is, perhaps, unsurprising that he should claim that those who claim they require certain philosophical understandings or metaphysical commitments in order, in fact, to understand and to commit are making a big mistake. In a review of the work of Jan Patočka, Václav Havel's philosophical mentor and himself a signatory of Charter 77, Rorty allows for the possibility that we might find ourselves enthralled by—or in thrall to—an unconditional moral obligation grounded, he says, in groundless hope. In criticizing Patočka—and Havel—he endorses unconditional obligation but severs it from, indeed he mocks, the identity out of which such obligation grows, on the account of Patočka and, as we shall learn shortly, Havel as well.

But it is hard for Rorty to sustain this maneuver, even as verbal foreplay. He writes: "Non-metaphysicians cannot say that democratic institutions reflect a moral reality and that tyrannical regimes do not reflect one, that tyrannies get something *wrong* that democratic societies get *right*." But just one sentence further, Rorty claims: "Patočka's conscience led him to do the right thing."[4] How does Rorty know this? How can he claim that Patočka, a dissident in danger, stripped of the reasons he himself proffers for doing what he did, would have done what he did without those reasons and the beliefs to which they gave force and fervor? He can claim it, in part, because he endorses his own version of practice being unproblematic in relation to theory; indeed, what is problematic, on Rorty's view, is assuming there is any problem, or question, or deep dilemma at all.

I will argue or, perhaps more accurately, display the ways in which the thought of Václav Havel and his actions as a dissident/ President fall through the grid of Marxist and critical theory formulations of the theory/practice relation and, as well, offer a powerful alternative to anti-foundationalism, with its evasion or excision of the question. For Havel concerns himself not only with the immediate—the ways in which he enacts thought, his role as a performer of political thought—but the ways in which current enactors are, at one and the same time, re-enactors who must take responsibility for the past without repeating it. As he noted in his first speech as President of a (then united) Czechoslovakia, "It would be unreasonable to understand the sad legacy of the last forty years as something alien, which some distant relative bequeathed us. On the contrary, we have to accept this legacy as something we committed against ourselves. If we accept it as such, we will understand that it is up to us all, and up to us only, to do something about it."[5]

Let me begin by situating Václav Havel in relation to a number of current political possibilities and positions. It is, perhaps, Havel's misfortune to have become a hero.[6] The upshot is that various partisans representing entrenched positions of the sort Havel himself disdains now vie either to identify themselves with Havel or to insist that Havel "really" belongs to them— whether democratic socialist, or mainstream liberal, or more free-market capitalist. There are those who emphasize his skeptical ironic stance and see him as a leading exemplar of a modernist, perhaps even a post-modernist temperament. Others appropriate him to a distinctly religious sensibility. Such moves to secure Havel, to pin him down, are rather beside the point. With Hannah Arendt, indeed in identical words, Havel declares that he is going to say what he has to say, do what he has to do, think in an unfettered way save insofar as all serious thought takes place against a "horizon of Being," without regard for labels, without checking in first with the guardians of political correctness (whether of the left or the right) to be sure he hasn't crossed some line or other.

Consider the following exchange between Hannah Arendt and Hans Morgenthau:

HANS MORGENTHAU: What are you? Are you a conservative? Are you a liberal? Where is your position within contemporary possibilities?

ARENDT: I don't know. I really don't know and I've never known. And I suppose I never had any such position. You know the left think that I am conservative, and the conservatives sometimes think I am left or I am a maverick or God knows what. And I must say I couldn't care less. I don't think that the real questions of this century will get any kind of illumination by this kind of thing.[7]

Now Havel from a little manifesto entitled, "What I Believe":

I refuse to classify myself as left or right. I stand between these two political and ideological front-lines, independent of them. Some of my opinions may seem left-wing, no doubt, and some right-wing, and I can even imagine that a single opinion may seem left-wing to some and right-wing to others—and to tell you the truth, I couldn't care less.[8]

It is precisely this refreshing refusal to be captured by one determined side or another that helps to account for the freshness of Havel's "take" on theory and practice. Mind you, he doesn't discuss action in relation to thought in precisely those categories, understanding, surely, that this might commit him to a lot of other things from which he seeks to be free. Suffice it to say that Havel defies easy definition. Here one begins. But to end on this irenic note would be a serious cop-out. What makes Havel an exemplary performer of political thought is the way he works the boundaries of various commitments and modes of thought and inquiry; the care he takes to locate himself, and the politics of his own society and of our time more generally, in a permanent *agon*, a never-ending contestation between tradition and transformation.

In a discussion in Prague, on September 25, 1992, Havel responded to questions about politics and "public space" by reiterating his longstanding view that politics is a sphere of concrete responsibility, just as the theater is a concrete institution in which characters enact positions. Real life, he continued, is bound to be richer than any politics. There is always a dramatic reduction from life to politics and one must exercise freedom within finiteness. One can never know enough to make an absolutely sure, certain, clean-cut decision about much of anything. One must try to pretend that behavior is decent "after all," acting always in a mode of "as if" in order to get things to proceed decently. Asked to comment explicity on a theory/practice question, Havel simply avoided the dilemma as presented. He was enjoined to explain how he fit into the distinction to be marked between an ethics of intention and an ethics of consequence. Given that Havel avoids both pure intentionality and pure consequentialism, I (for one) anticipated that his response might be to work the theoretical turf between these alternatives, or to explain the way he puts intention and consequence together in a fruitful mix. But instead he told a story. Imagine, he suggested, two scenes: the politician with the expert, on the one hand, and the politician with the ordinary citizen, on the other. A decent politician can always find an expert to inform him of certain things or to do certain things. Far more important is the relation of the politician to the ordinary citizen, for politics is a special kind of vocation and one drawn to this vocation should be more urgently committed to the citizen, with his or her complex but non-expert understandings. This way of doing things makes people nervous because we hanker after experts to solve problems. But the search for solutions in this way invites ideology and ideology is absolutely the worst way to hold things together. Inventing ideologies and utopias is easy, too easy, but we must follow a more complicated course, he suggested.

What, then, is this more complicated course and how does it help us to think in supple ways about how political thought may be performed in a manner that keeps ideas alive and practice robust? What follows is a general discussion of the contours of Havel's reflections on responsibility, reflections that put on display his resolute commitment to a worldview that rejects latter-day Protagorean efforts to make man the measure of all things. For Havel, free responsibility is an outgrowth of a commitment to live "in truth" and that commitment, in turn, is inescapably shaped by a loss of metaphysical certainties coupled with an equally sure and certain insistence on the need for a "higher horizon," for a transcendental or suprapersonal moral authority which alone can check the human will to power, an anthropocentric arrogance that threatens the human "home."[9]

Because Havel is mostly talked about and treated as a trendy playwright-president who would as soon entertain the Rolling Stones as heads of state, it seems best to proceed chronologically in order to unpack the rhythmic continuities in his thought. As a thinker, to press a metaphor familiar to students of political thought, for all his foxiness, there is a rather stubborn hedgehog at work and it is the fusion of solidity of being—living in truth—with irony that makes for Havel's uniqueness and, as well, ideally suits him as a guide through the miasma of the *fin de siècle*.

Havel is deeply indebted, in a rough-and-ready way although more systematically than he sometimes seems to allow, both to the phenomenological tradition of Husserl and Heidegger as "translated" by the great Czech philosopher, Jan Patočka, mentioned above in my criticism of Rortyian anti-foundationalism, and to Masarykian humanism. Shaped by the overlapping of many movements and traditions, Havel places himself under no obligation to systematize or, for that matter, to synthesize. He is not only temperamentally unsuited to the logic-chopper's or Hegelian "over-comers" task, he is opposed on principle to both sorts of efforts—the former because it issues into a penury and niggardliness of thought; the latter because it promotes ideology whose dead-hand soon closes over "life itself." Havel notes the "intellectual and spiritual" dimensions of his own cultural identity as a complex but very specific amalgam of many currents, many forces:

> We live in the very centre of Central Europe, in a place that from the beginning of time has been the main European crossroads of every possible interest, invasion, and influence of a political, military, ethnic, religious, or cultural nature. The intellectual and spiritual currents of east and west, north and south, Catholic and Protestant, enlightened and romantic—the political movements of conservative and progressive, liberal and socialist, imperialist and national liberalist—all of these overlapped here, and bubbled away in one vast cauldron, combining to form our national and cultural consciousness, our traditions, the social models of our behavior, which have been passed down from generation to generation. . . . We are like a sponge that has gradually absorbed and digested all kinds of intellectual and cultural impulses and initiatives.[10]

Departing from Masaryk's "positivist belief in progress," Havel found a philosophical home inside the general themes offered by Patočka, a philosopher nearly unknown outside Czechoslovakia.[11] For Patočka, philosophy begins once life is no longer something that can be taken for granted. The alternative to a world of certain meaning is not subjectivism, however, but another sort of engagement with the world, specifically with the *life-world* rooted in a distinctly premodern sensibility but which the modern sensibility must knowingly affirm and grant as "that which is"—something objective and tangible—in order to get out of a perverse preoccupation with self-absorbed wishes, preferences and feelings.

The contrast points for Patočka's (and Havel's) thought, then, are a mechanistic and austere rationalism, on the one hand, and a perfervid, labile romanticism, on the other. A central preoccupation in a world which ceases to "respect any so-called higher metaphysical values—the Absolute, something higher than themselves, something mysterious"—necessarily becomes the self—human identity—and, with it, the nature of human burdens and responsibilities appropriate to this self. There are philosophers who hold the everyday in contempt as womanish stuff, a potion that dilutes the bracing tonic quaffed by real thinkers. Not so Patočka and Havel. Both begin with philosophy "from the bottom," and from a "humbly respected boundary of the natural world." Both view the self as one who, while passing away, has an identity and a unique and independent purpose. We become acquainted with others through acts of responsible surrender to that which is required of us rather than supererogation or arrogation. One begins by taking the natural world for granted as the horizon of doing and knowing—a horizon which is always there and against which we define our own being.

Freedom in this scheme of things is not the working out of a foreordained teleology of self-realization; rather, freedom comes from embracing that which it is given one to do; the "secret of man," writes Havel, "is the secret of his responsibility." This responsibility consists, in part, in a knowing rejection of God-likeness and mastery. For when man takes on this hubristic role, he becomes the sole source of meaning in a world rendered dead and meaningless. Man exceeds his strength and he becomes despairing, a destructive Titan ruining himself and others.[12] We are not perched on top of the earth as sovereigns; rather, we are invited into companionship with the earth as the torn and divided beings we are. Even our duty is not one. Havel is so committed to the need to strip our practices of theoretical hubris, he insisted that the draft of the constitution for the new Czech Republic refer to man as part of the universe rather than as "the master of everything."

The fusion of freedom and responsibility worked out in Patočka's phenomenology yields a distinct but definite *political* conclusion: democracy is the political form that permits and requires human freedom as responsibility, not as an act of self-overcoming, nor pure reason, but in service to the notion that there are things worth suffering for. Patočka, it should be noted, remained a theist throughout his life: without God the world, he insisted, is quite literally unthinkable. For this reason the atheist is more likely to be dominated in a rather uninteresting way by a particular construction of theism than is the phenomenologist who articulates explicitly the horizon of his or her thought. Although Havel evokes God, especially in his later works, he is reticent about the status of his own relationship to theism and considers that belief in a "personal God" is not the pressing philosophic question. What gives urgency to this matter for Havel is the fact that once the supra-human is repudiated or forgotten and man crowns himself lord and master of all he surveys, the world loses its human dimensions. If this be theism, he might say, then make the most of it.

Tracking the question of responsibility in Havel's most famous political essays as well as his *Letters to Olga*, the casual or careless reader might be tempted to jettison the philosophical frame within which Havel nests his own understanding of responsibility as unnecessarily cumbersome, a clumsy and even redundant accessory to an otherwise very straightforward insistence upon accountability. But this would be a mistake. On this score Havel is quite insistent. Humans confront nothing less than a general crisis that manifests itself in many ways and this crisis is, at base, spiritual. Something is "profoundly wrong," for the horizon of thought itself is increasingly beclouded, even despoiled; the order of nature (yes, nature) is ruptured and the result is estrangement, demoralization, and indifference. We face a crisis of human identity and this crisis *must* be understood—can only be understood—when projected against a shrinking screen emblematic of a declining human awareness of "the absolute." Human reason has wrenched itself free from human *Being* and the results are both tawdry and tragic.

The argument continues in this vein: the world is possible only because we are grounded and once this world of "personal responsibility" with its characteristic virtues and marks of decency (justice, honor, friendship, fidelity) is ruptured or emptied, what rushes in to take its place is politics as a superannuated "rational technology of power" whose exemplar is the manager, the *apparatchik*. Humans play god and the wreckage intensifies. Man finds himself "in the rut of totalitarian thought, where he is not his own and where he surrenders his own reason and conscience."[13] Man lives within a lie; he gives himself over to the social auto-totality and he or she who does so surrenders identity and responsibility falters.

Responsibility within Havel's philosophical thematic flows from the aims of life "in its essence" which are plurality, diversity, and independent self-constitution as against the conformity, uniformity, and stultifying discipline of the social auto-totality, which not only abandons reality and assaults life but corrodes the "very notion of identity itself." To live within the truth is to give voice to a self which has embraced responsibility for the here and now. "That means that responsibility is ours, that we must accept it and grasp it *here, now,* in this place in time and space where the Lord has set us down, and that we cannot lie our way out of it by moving somewhere else, whether it be to an Indian ashram or to a parallel *polis.*"[14] The only "solution" to the crisis Havel sketches is to deepen human responsibility in and through hope for the moral reconstitution of society. And this reconstitution can only come about through a radical revision of the relationship of human beings to the human order: trust, openness, solidarity—if these three do not abide; if we cannot rehabilitate such values, our rootedness in the life-world, which alone gives rise to openness and dynamism and plurality, is "forgotten" and, along with it, responsibility falls into forgetfulness, down something on the level of consciousness akin to the "memory hole" in Orwell's 1984.

In *Letters to Olga,* Havel is insistent that his evocation of responsibility not be conflated with conforming to convention, or following the rules. If anything, responsibility, rooted and concretely construed, imposes far heavier burdens of freedom on one living in truth than rote, rule-governed behavior allows. Responsibility—acceptance of the risks of free action—forms the very basis of one's identity; any mode of thought that reduces human responsibility to the extent it does shrinks the horizon of human possibility. This responsible self must act in a kind of twilight, never knowing for certain what the outcome of his or her deeds may be. Responsibility is not only vouching for oneself but taking on the task of neighborliness.

A crisis in responsibility (the "intrinsic responsibility that man has to and for the world") is a crisis in human identity and human integrity.[15] To assume "full responsibility" is not to lapse into dour moralism, nor to universalize a kind of giddy and boundless compassion, but to take up the very specific and concrete burdens of one's own time and place. Havel himself sums this up nicely in Letters 142 and 143 of *Letters to Olga:* "The crisis of today's world, obviously, is a crisis of human responsibility (both responsibility for oneself and responsibility 'toward' something else) and thus it is a crisis of human identity as well."[16] Also:

> Love, charity, sympathy, tolerance, understanding, self-control, solidarity, friendship, feelings of belonging, the acceptance of concrete responsibility for those close to one—these are, I think, expressions of that new (or more precisely, continually renewed and betrayed by all of human history) 'interexistentiality' that alone can breathe new meaning into the social formations and collectivities that, together, shape the fate of the world.[17]

Let me now focus on a central fault-line in Havel's work, namely, his lively acceptance of paradox coupled with his rejection of fixed categories. Such a philosophic stance and existential temperament is most often associated with a repudiation of foundationalism or theism in our epoch. Not so in Havel's case. Stubbornly (here the hedgehog), he reiterates time and time again his conviction that rootedness alone gives birth to an authentic paradoxical outlook, an awareness of irony that cuts to the bone rather than appearing as froth on the latest wave to hit the shore. Unembarrassedly, Havel speaks of his "mission," the need to "bear witness" to the "terrors" of his time and to "speak the truth." He rejects words that obscure rather than illuminate (like "socialism") and with this goes an "antipathy to overly fixed categories, empty ideological phrases and incantations that petrify thought in a hermetic structure of static concepts."[18] He would, I believe, argue that this very particular and pointed blend of belief in the need for an "absolute horizon" for thought and action alone offers a certain block against the speciousness of ideology with its illusory identities and excusatory functions, hence against the deadliness of that terrible and seductive (and ultimately false) hope embodied in the word "utopia."

Utopianism—the vision of a "radiant tomorrow"—yields inevitably to an impersonal "juggernaut of power," hence to that ethical crisis which marks late modernity and requires an ethical-political reconstitution grounded in authentic hope—the humble and simple hope for trust, openness, and solidarity. On this score Havel has been consistent and insistent for nearly three decades—from his earliest "dissident" writings to his most recent presidential "meditations." With Simone Weil, Albert Camus, Hannah Arendt, George Orwell, Czeslaw Milosz, and other independent thinkers of this century (their numbers, alas, are not legion), Havel scores utopianism as a

> typically intellectual phenomenon—the greatest revolutionaries were all intellectuals. It is an arrogant attempt by human reason to plan life. But it is not possible to force life to conform to some abstract blueprint. Life is something unfathomable, ever-changing, mysterious, and every attempt to confine it within an artificial, abstract structure inevitably ends up homogenizing, regimenting, standardizing and destroying life, as well as curtailing everything that projects beyond, overflows or falls outside the abstract project. What is a concentration camp, after all, but an attempt by utopians to dispose of those elements which don't fit in?[19]

In response to those who parry by suggesting that a life without utopias would be horrible and unthinkable, would reduce life (as one of Havel's interlocutors put it) to "hopelessness, despair, and resignation to the daily corruption and absurdity," Havel replies by contrasting "openness towards mysteriously changing and always rather elusive and never quite attainable ideals such as truth and morality, and, on the other hand, an unequivocal identification with a detailed plan for implementing those ideals which in the end becomes self-justifying."[20] Hope is not the same as joy in the certainty that things are going well, or the willingness to invest in enterprises that are obviously headed for success, but, rather, an ability to work for something because it is good, not just because it stands a chance to succeed. Hope is definitely not the same as optimism. The over-intellectualizing ideologue and revolutionary forgets this in his zeal to get everything right and in order.

The theme of *trahison des clercs* is nothing new. What adds freshness and piquancy to Havel's project is that he has personally paid the price for his resistance to the seduction of ideology and that he does so, not in the name of a restorationist ideal, but in the name of an elemental, forward-pressing, yet limited ideal of free responsibility. Havel's "higher horizon" opens up rather than forecloses on genuine political possibility. In Havel's world, individual responsibility deepens and expands to the extent that utopianism—giving oneself over to a *Weltanschauung*—is eschewed.

Havel often muses on (and is bemused by) the "genuinely human." For our very humanness to come into sharp focus our worlds must be shaped and formed against a horizon rather than sunk in an immanent sea. That is, the human dimension cannot be derived from a flatness of being, a world cut and dried to our own measure, but stands out and takes shape from externality. This externality should not be construed as absolutely Other, as utterly transcendent—and here things get tricky—but should and must be *recognized* as absolute and supra-personal. Identity and responsibility are shaped, molded, and hammered out of the material of a world understood against the frame of a horizon of Being. This prevents or serves to guard against a blurred, all-purpose, and limitless collapse into universal empathy which promotes, finally, a vapid because unbounded pseudo-responsibility for everything everywhere.[21] In order for our lives lived among others on the horizontal plane to bear fruit, we must resist fusion with the auto-totality which is nothing more nor less than the socio-political expression of a world without a supra-personal horizon of Being against which to measure itself.

To those who argue, as Rorty does, for example, that Havel and his mentor, Patočka, really do not require what they themselves claim they require—a transcendental horizon or grounding for thought, action, and responsibility—Havel might insist that Rorty and many contemporary anti-foundationalists in fact rely on what Hannah Arendt called *bannisters* for their thought. That is, for all their anti-foundationalism they remain wedded to a teleology of progress, a nearly unbounded faith in the possibility of enlightenment in that glorious epiphany once the debris and clutter of metaphysical thought is swept away once and for all (hence the "more liberal" a policy or thought or whim can be said to be "the better"). This attitude often gets coupled to an utter insouciance concerning power. The tacit bannister to which such thinkers cling remains intact but it is a stairway not to heaven but to yet another utopian hell.[22] With Arendt, Havel is utterly resistant to the alchemy of "the dialectic" which transforms concrete evils into abstract goods. There is a beyond and that is why the here and now, this moment as a concrete slice of all moments, takes on such shimmering vitality and importance.

Havel's response to those who claim his own thought is murky and unrealistic and will not survive a move into the realm of practical politics is complex, amounting to something akin to an invitation for them to help him take stock in order that his own words not become empty cliches. The process of enacting thought in a situation of murky uncertainty—for society is a very "mysterious animal with many hidden faces and potentialities"—can never yield transparent translations from the "mysterious" to the pragmatically clear. No one knows the full potentiality of any given moment, for good or for evil. Hence the importance of the "purely moral act that has no hope of any immediate and visible political effect" for such an act can "gradually and indirectly, over time, gain in political significance."[23] One must be patient and not so excessively result-oriented that the humanly possible work begins to look tawdry and unworthy. Havel tells one interlocutor that he tries to "live in the spirit of Christian morality," not as a doctrinalist but as a practitioner of hope who attempts to see things "from below" in a tough-minded, not sentimental way. His unabashed embrace of life is precisely an embrace of a post-Babelian world in which there are wondrous varieties of human "homes," identities, languages, particular possibilities, but there is as well a trans-particular world framing our fragile globe united perhaps only in its travail. Real hope is not hope for some "happy ending" or for glorious heroes to save the day but hope that human beings, in taking responsibility for a state of affairs (in the broadest sense), might "see it as their own project and their own home, as something they need not fear, as something they can—without shame—love, because they have built it for themselves." [24] Havel shares the basic gospel hope that all might have life and might have it more abundantly.

For Havel, hope, responsibility, freedom, and irony are all of a piece and to lop one bit off in order to better serve our purposes will not do. What makes Havel such a fascinating performer of political thought is that he provokes the complacent, mocks the smug, tweaks the arrogant, and suffers without excusing the weak. In his rejection of the petrified politics deeded us by the legacy of the French Revolution and a century of total wars, Havel helps us to move into a future dis-illusioned, hence paradoxically free.

I think he would agree that a central task of political philosophy for our time lies in recognizing what has happened for what it is. What has happened for what it is in Europe, at this point, is the definitive collapse of an attempt to rebuild human society on some overarching ideal or Weltanschauung. What has been undermined is the comforting myth that we have transparent and direct instruction and relations. Europe, Havel noted in Prague, has entered the long tunnel at the end of the light. The problems which lie before it could not be more exigent and will not be dealt with in a kind of lightning flash. One must continue to perform political thought, not knowing how the draw ends nor, with any finality, who—or what—is its author.

The last words shall be his:

Genuine politics, politics worthy of the name, and in any case the only politics that I am willing to devote myself to, is simply serving those close to oneself: serving the community, and serving those who come after us. Its deepest roots are moral because it is a responsibility, expressed through action, to and for the whole, a responsibility that is what it is—a "higher" responsibility, which grows out of a conscious or subconscious certainty that our death ends nothing, because everything is forever being recorded and evaluated somewhere else, somewhere "above us," in what I have called "the memory of Being," an integral aspect of the secret order of the cosmos, of nature, and of life, which believers call God and to whose judgment everything is liable. Genuine conscience and genuine responsibility are always, in the end, explicable only as an expression of the silent assumption that we are being observed "from above," and that "up there" everything is visible, nothing is forgotten, and therefore earthly time has no power to wipe away the pangs brought on by earthly failure: our spirit knows that it is not the only one that knows of these failures.

If there is to be a minimum chance of success, there is only one way to strive for decency, reason, responsibility, sincerity, civility, and tolerance: and that is decently, reasonably, responsibly, sincerely, civilly, and tolerantly.[25]

NOTES

1. Sigmund Freud, "The Question of a *Weltanschauung*," *New Introductory Lectures, Standard Edition* 22, (London: Hogarth Press, 1964), 158.

2. Richard Rorty, *Contingency, Irony, and Solidarity* (Cambridge: Cambridge University Press, 1989), 6. My general argument is that Rortyanism is all contingency, finally, as authentic irony is dependent upon deeper reflections and recognitions than Rorty permits himself, even as solidarity demands a much "thicker" account of the self. Portions of this paragraph and one or two others are drawn from my essay, "Don't Be Cruel: Reflections on Rortyian Liberalism," in Daniel W. Conway and John E. Seery, eds., *The Politics of Irony* (New York: St. Martin's Press, 1992), 199–218.

3. Ibid., 52.

4. Richard Rorty, "The Seer of Prague," *New Republic* (July 1, 1991): 37.

5. Václav Havel, "The Art of the Impossible," text of the first speech as President of Czechoslovakia, *The Spectator* (January 27, 1990): 12.

6. I draw liberally upon my essay, "A Man for This Season," *Perspectives on Political Science* 21, no. 14 (Fall 1992): 207–11. for my analysis of Havel's political thought.

7. See Melvyn A. Hill, *Hannah Arendt: The Recovery of the Public World* (New York: St. Martin's Press, 1979), 333–34.

8. Václav Havel, *Summer Meditations* (New York: Knopf, 1992), 60.

9. What follows relies on my reading of Havel's works in English. I will provide notes only for longer quotations. The works I will draw upon include Jan Vladislav, *Václav Havel or Living in Truth* (London: Faber and Faber, 1987); Václav Havel, et al., *The Power of the Powerless: Citizens against the State in Central-Eastern Europe* (Armonk, N.Y.: M. E. Sharpe, 1985); Václav Havel, *Letters to Olga* (New York: Henry Holt, 1989); Václav Havel, *Disturbing the Peace* (New York: Knopf, 1990); Václav Havel, *Open Letters: Selected Writings, 1965–1990* (New York: Knopf, 1991); and Havel, *Summer Meditations.*

10. Havel, *Summer Meditations*, 125–26.

11. Patočka's works, or selections from them, have only recently appeared in English. See Erazim Kohan, ed., *Jan Patočka: Philosophy and Selected Writings* (Chicago: University of Chicago Press, 1989).

12. This is the theme of Patočka's essay, "Titanism," written in 1936, and it echoes persistently throughout Havel's work. See 139–45 of the Patočka collection.

13. Havel, "Politics and Conscience," in *Living in Truth*, 151.

14. Havel, "The Power of the Powerless," *Living in Truth*, 104.

15. See *Letters to Olga*, 266–68.

16. *Letters to Olga*, 365.

17. *Letters to Olga*, 371.

18. *Disturbing the Peace*, 9.

19. Havel, in *TLS* interview, 82.

20. Ibid.

21. Havel's pointedly ironic rejoinders to Western peace activists is a prime example of his rejection of an immanentist politics of empathy. See "An Anatomy of Reticence" in *Living in Truth*.

22. See Rorty's review of Patočka's work in *The New Republic*, as noted above, in which he claims Patočka was mistaken about the need to ground his political commitments in certain ethico-philosophical claims.

23. Comments from *Disturbing the Peace*, 109, 114–15.

24. *Summer Meditations*, 128.

25. Václav Havel, "Paradise Lost," *New York Review of Books* (April 9, 1992): 6, 7.

INDEX

483